Praise for Essential Windows Communication Foundation

"Resnick, Crane, and Bowen have surveyed the essence of Microsoft's Web services platform. Whether this is the first time or the fifty-first time you're using WCF, you'll learn something new by reading this book."

—Nicholas Allen, Program Manager, Web Services, Microsoft

"As developers, we are constantly called upon to be 'instant experts' in many areas. When the time comes for you to begin working with distributed systems development and messaging in the new Microsoft .NET 3.x world, you find yourself confronted by the new 800-pound gorilla called Windows Communication Foundation (WCF). This is the book you want sitting on your desk when that day comes."

—Ron Landers, Senior Technical Consultant, IT Professionals, Inc.

"Designing and writing distributed applications was one of the most complex and frustrating challenges facing .NET developers and architects. What technologies do you pick? There were so many choices and so little coding time. Windows Communication Foundation (WCF) solves this problem as the single unified platform to build distributed applications for .NET. Like any distributed system, WCF has a lot of choices and possibilities. This book provides an easy-to-digest approach that answers the spectrum of choices with real-world explanations and examples. Starting with the basics of WCF and building from there, this book answers the how you can use WCF today. It's a must-read for application developers and architects building any type of distributed application."

—Thom Robbins, Director of .NET Platform Product Management, Microsoft

"Essential Windows Communication Foundation (WCF) is a truly comprehensive work that presents the technology in a clear, easy to read, yet comprehensive manner. The book will be an invaluable asset for both the advanced reader and newcomer to WCF."

—Willy-Peter Schaub, Technology Specialist,
Barone, Budge, and Dominick Ltd., Microsoft MVP

"It's clear the authors drew on years of distributed applications development to distill and present the essence of WCF. The result is a book full of practical information designed to save you time and guide you on your WCF project. The chapter on diagnostics alone will save you hours of troubleshooting and frustration. Highly recommended."

—Yasser Shohoud, Technical Director, Microsoft Technology Center, Dallas

Essential
Windows
Communication
Foundation

Microsoft .NET Development Series

John Montgomery, *Series Advisor*
Don Box, *Series Advisor*
Brad Abrams, *Series Advisor*

The Microsoft .NET Development Series is supported and developed by the leaders and experts of Microsoft development technologies including Microsoft architects. The books in this series provide a core resource of information and understanding every developer needs in order to write effective applications and managed code. Learn from the leaders how to maximize your use of the .NET Framework and its programming languages.

Titles in the Series

For more information go to www.informit.com/msdotnetseries/

Essential Windows Communication Foundation

For .NET Framework 3.5

- Steve Resnick
- Richard Crane
- Chris Bowen

Addison-Wesley

Upper Saddle River, NJ • Boston • Indianapolis • San Francisco
New York • Toronto • Montreal • London • Munich • Paris
Madrid • Cape Town • Sydney • Tokyo • Singapore • Mexico City

Library of Congress Cataloging-in-Publication Data:

Resnick, Steve.
  Essential Windows Communication Foundation (WCF) / Steve Resnick, Richard Crane, Chris Bowen.
    p. cm.
  Includes index.
  ISBN 0-321-44006-4 (pbk. : alk. paper) 1. Application software—Development. 2. Microsoft Windows (Computer file) 3. Web services. 4. Microsoft .NET. I. Crane, Richard. II. Bowen, Chris. III. Title.
  QA76.76.A65R46 2008
  005.2'768—dc22

                              2007049118

ISBN-13: 978-0-321-44006-8
ISBN-10: 0-321-44006-4
Text printed in the United States on recycled paper at Courier in Stoughton, Massachusetts.
Third printing, April 2009

Editor-in-Chief
Karen Gettman

Acquisitions Editor
Joan Murray

Development Editors
Sheri Cain
Chris Zahn

Managing Editor
Gina Kanouse

Project Editor
Betsy Harris

Copy Editor
Barbara Hacha

Indexer
Tim Wright

Proofreader
Paula Lowell

Technical Reviewers
Nicholas Allen
Jeff Barnes
Keith Brown
Tom Fuller
John Justice
Ron Landers
Steve Maine
Willy-Peter Schaub
Sowmy Srinivasan

Publishing Coordinator
Kim Boedigheimer

Cover Designer
Chuti Prasertsith

Compositor
Nonie Ratcliff

This Book Is Safari Enabled

The Safari® Enabled icon on the cover of your favorite technology book means the book is available through Safari Bookshelf. When you buy this book, you get free access to the online edition for 45 days.

Safari Bookshelf is an electronic reference library that lets you easily search thousands of technical books, find code samples, download chapters, and access technical information whenever and wherever you need it.

To gain 45-day Safari Enabled access to this book:

- Go to http://www.informit.com/onlineedition
- Complete the brief registration form
- Enter the coupon code 1VMP-W7PL-FRLY-LXLN-G4L1

If you have difficulty registering on Safari Bookshelf or accessing the online edition, please e-mail customerservice@safaribooksonline.com.

To my parents for pointing me in the right direction, to Zamaneh for making the journey so sweet, and to Noah and Hannah for showing me the future.
—Steve

Dedicated to my loving wife, Nicki, my son, Matthew, and my daughter, Charlotte. Thank you for your support and understanding. I love you all very much and look forward to spending more time together.
—Rich

Thank you to my wife, Jessica, and my daughters, Deborah and Rachel, for their love and understanding as I again devoted long nights and weekends to research and writing. We have a book we can be proud of, but now I'm going to enjoy catching up on that missed family time.
—Chris

Contents

Figures

Tables

Foreword

I'm WRITING THIS foreword in December of 2007, a little more than a year after the first release of Windows Communication Foundation hit the streets as part of .NET Framework 3.0 and less than a month after we shipped significant additions to the platform as part of .NET Framework 3.5. Saying there's a lot to absorb in those two releases is something of an understatement.

One of the goals of WCF was to unify the programming experience for building all types of distributed applications on the Microsoft platform. We wanted a core set of concepts that were simple and approachable, yet expressive enough to model the underlying semantics of all the technologies we intended to replace. The Microsoft stacks that came before us (ASMX, Remoting, COM+, MSMQ, and WSE) had strong benefits as well as significant limitations; our mission was to leverage ideas that had worked well in the past and learn from those that didn't. If we succeeded, developers would be able to write many different types of distributed applications without having to learn many different (and often wildly discontinuous) programming models.

To make the vision of a unified developer experience successful in the real world, we needed a highly flexible runtime architecture that matched the richness of the programming model. Key areas of variability had to be identified and isolated into generalized extensibility mechanisms to avoid unnecessarily restricting the capabilities of our new platform. Our goal with the runtime was to make sure that, if our default behavior didn't meet the needs of a particular application or we lacked a feature required by a specific scenario, there would be a natural point in the runtime into which an external developer could plug some customization to address the issue.

The most exciting part about WCF for me is the amazing breadth of scenarios to which this technology can be applied. Nothing demonstrates that more concretely than the feature set we delivered in .NET 3.5. This release had two parallel thrusts covering very different types of distributed application scenarios. One thrust was about integrating WCF with the power of Windows Workflow Foundation to provide a substrate for long-running, declarative, connected business processes. The other thrust was about extending the reach of WCF to address the needs of today's evolving Web. Both of these scenarios impose unique requirements on the runtime and programming model, and the fact that we were able to address these requirements via extensions to WCF *without requiring significant changes to the existing implementation* is a strong indicator that the WCF architecture will be able to address the evolving needs of distributed applications for a long time to come.

Now that we're a year out from shipping our first bits, it's exciting to see real customers make big bets on our platform. It's more exciting to hear about the gains they see in the areas of developer productivity, performance, and interoperability as a result of betting on WCF. We judge the success of our platform first and foremost by the success of our customers, and by that metric WCF will be a very successful platform indeed.

Really, this is all just a long-winded way of saying that the time you invest in learning WCF is well spent. To that end, you're very lucky to be holding this book in your hands right now. Rich, Chris, and Steve have done a fantastic job distilling the broad story of WCF down to the essential elements required to be productive on our platform. The authors' unique combination of technical acumen, field experience, and close relationship with the product team has yielded a book that will undoubtedly hold a distinguished place on every WCF developer's bookshelf. I'm incredibly happy to have these guys telling the technical story of our product. By the end of this book, I'm sure you'll feel the same way.

Steve Maine

Seattle, Washington

December 2007

Preface

WINDOWS COMMUNICATION FOUNDATION (WCF) is the unified programming model for writing distributed applications on the Microsoft platform. It subsumes the prior technologies of ASMX, .NET Remoting, DCOM, and MSMQ and provides an extensible API to meet a wide variety of distributed computing requirements. Prior to WCF, you needed to master each of those technologies to select the right approach for a particular distributed application requirement. WCF simplifies this considerably by providing a unified approach.

XML Web Services is the most common technique for distributed computing in modern applications. They're used to expose technical and business functions on private or public networks. Sometimes they use the SOAP specification, sometimes they don't. They typically transmit information as text documents containing angle brackets, but not always. They generally use HTTP for the transport, but again, not always. WCF is a framework for working with XML Web Services and is compatible with most technology stacks.

Rich, Chris, and I have each developed code with .NET from the beginning (circa 1999). We work at Microsoft in the field, helping customers use WCF to solve real-world problems. Our customers range from large multi-national corporations to ISVs to Web startups. Each has different challenges, needs, and priorities that we individually address. We show them what's possible, recommend what works well, and steer clear of what doesn't. We have experience building distributed applications and leverage that experience in teaching others about WCF.

Our goal for this book is to present WCF in a way that can immediately be put to use by software developers. We cover the material in enough detail that you know how and why to use different features. We go a bit further in most cases, describing some of the subtleties in the framework, but not so far as to document the API.

The Blogosphere is rich with WCF details. Much of it comes from the .NET product team and much of it comes from other developers learning it along the way. We made extensive use of blogs as source material. This book brings order to that repository by organizing it in a way that can be easily consumed from your desk, sofa, or wherever you do your best reading.

Who Should Read This Book?

We wrote this book for software developers who want to build distributed applications on the .NET platform. As fellow developers, we know the importance of solid advice and clear examples on how to use new technology. We've trolled the Blogosphere, scoured internal Microsoft e-mail aliases, and wrote plenty of code to provide you with the best examples for doing the things you need to do.

Architects who need to understand WCF will also benefit from this book. The chapters covering basics, bindings, channels, behaviors, hosting, workflow, and security describe important aspects of designing and implementing services with WCF. Reading the two- to three-page introductions in each of these chapters may be the best way to get the 50,000-foot view of the technology.

Our goal in writing this book is to shorten your learning curve for WCF. We describe and demonstrate how to do the common tasks, addressing the basics as well as advanced topics. Throughout the book, we approach topics as a series of problems to be solved. Rather than documenting the API, we describe how to use WCF to accomplish your goals.

Prerequisites for this book are modest. If you're interested in WCF, you probably already have grounding in .NET. You're probably competent in C# or Visual Basic, or at least you were at one point. And, of course, you probably know your way around Visual Studio. So we're assuming that you can write decent .NET code and are motivated to make the best use of your time in becoming proficient in WCF.

Installation Requirements

WCF is a key component of the Microsoft .NET Framework 3.x. WCF was first released with .NET 3.0 and has been enhanced in .NET 3.5. The delta between the two releases is modest: enhancements for non-SOAP Web services, integration between WCF and WF, and a healthy service pack. This book covers .NET 3.5. Unless there's a reason to use an older release, this is the clear recommendation.

.NET is packaged in two forms: the redistributable runtime libraries and the software development kit (SDK). The runtime libraries are meant for target machines—those machines that are not for development. This includes testing, staging, and production environments. The SDK is meant for your development machines. The SDK contains code samples, documentation, and tools that are useful for development. Each of these .NET packages, the runtime and SDK versions, can be downloaded from Microsoft's MSDN site at http://msdn2.microsoft.com/en-us/netframework/default.aspx. The .NET 3.5 SDK also ships with Visual Studio 2008.

The Microsoft .NET Framework 3.5 can be installed on Windows XP SP2, Windows Vista, Windows Server 2003, and Windows Server 2008.

Organization

We don't expect you to read the book cover to cover. If you're new to WCF, you may want to read and try the samples in Chapter 1, "Basics," first. Following that, each subsequent chapter covers a major feature set of WCF. We include a few introductory pages in each chapter to describe the motivation and some design goals, and then we cover subtopics within the chapter.

Chapter 1, "Basics," is where we cover the basics of building and consuming WCF services. We discuss and demonstrate how to implement different types of interfaces and why you may choose each. By the end of this chapter, you'll be able to produce and consume services using WCF.

Chapter 2, "Contracts," covers the three primary types of contacts in WCF: service contracts, data contracts, and message contracts. Each of these enables you to define complex structures and interfaces in code. Data contracts map .NET types to XML, service contracts expose service interface endpoints in WSDL that can be consumed in a cross-platform manner, and message contracts enable developers to work directly on the XML in a message, rather than working with .NET types. For each of these contracts, WCF tools generate and export standards-based WSDL to the outside world.

Chapter 3, "Channels," covers channels and channel stacks. The channel model architecture is the foundation on which the WCF communication framework is built. The channel architecture allows for the sending and receiving of messages between clients and services. Channel stacks can be built to exactly match your needs.

Chapter 4, "Bindings," describes how to configure the communication stack to use exactly the protocols you need. For instance, if you're communicating within an enterprise and won't be crossing firewalls, and you need the fastest performance, a binding named `netTcpBinding` will give you best results. If you're looking to communicate with every last Web client out there, then HTTP and text encoded XML is necessary, so `basicHttpBinding` is the way to go. A binding is synonymous with a preconfigured channel stack.

Chapter 5, "Behaviors," covers service behaviors. In WCF, behaviors are the mechanism for affecting service operation outside of the actual message processing. Everything that is done after a message is received but before it is sent to the service operation code is the domain of behaviors. In WCF, this is where concurrency and instance management is handled, as well as transactional support. This chapter also demonstrates how to build custom behaviors for additional service control.

Chapter 6, "Serialization and Encoding," describes the process by which data is serialized from a .NET Type (class) to an XML Infoset and the way that XML Infoset is represented on the wire. We typically think of XML as a text document with angle brackets around field names and values, but the XML Infoset is a more basic data structure. This chapter discusses ways of converting that structure into a format that can be exchanged over a network.

Chapter 7, "Hosting," describes the various options in hosting a WCF service. The most common environment, IIS, is described, but it is by far **not** the only option. WCF services can be hosted in Managed .NET applications, Windows Activation Services, or any other .NET program. This chapter discusses the options and techniques for hosting.

Chapter 8, "Security," is a large chapter and covers the multitude of security options. Different authentication schemes are discussed and demonstrated. Transport- and message-level security are compared, with examples of each. Intranet and Internet scenarios are also described.

Chapter 9, "Diagnostics," describes how to use the built-in trace facilities in .NET to capture WCF events. Trace Listeners are described, along with examples that show how to configure the settings for different events. The Trace Viewer, a powerful tool that is shipped with WCF, is also described, which enables you to trace activities across service call boundaries.

Chapter 10, "Exception Handling," offers practical guidance on handling exceptions within WCF. SOAP faults are described using fault contracts, and examples demonstrate how to throw and catch them to minimize errors.

Chapter 11, "Workflow Services," covers the integration points between WCF and Windows Workflow Foundation (WF) introduced in Visual Studio 2008 and .NET 3.5. We describe how to call WCF services from WF and how to expose WF workflows in WCF.

Chapter 12, "Peer Networking," shows how to build client-to-client applications that leverage a network mesh to enable clients to find each other. We cover mesh addressing and techniques for establishing point-to-point connections after the client addressing is resolved.

Chapter 13, "Programmable Web," covers how to use WCF for non-SOAP Web Services. Examples are shown with Asynchronous JavaScript and XML (AJAX) and JSON for simpler, JavaScript-friendly data formats. The hosting classes specific to non-SOAP protocols are described. Like WCF-WF integration, this is new with .NET 3.5.

Finally, the appendix, "Advanced Topics," covers advanced topics that we didn't fit into other chapters. Rather than burying them somewhere they don't belong, we include them separately.

Because of the broad nature of the WCF subject, not all topics are covered in equal depth. This book's goal is to help developers be super productive when working with WCF. If we do our job, readers will use this book as they learn the technology. This book does not attempt to document WCF—that's what the good tech writers at Microsoft have done with the help files and MSDN. But a combination of that documentation and the good guidance found in these pages should enable developers to quickly and productively build robust applications with WCF.

> ■ **NOTE**   Code Continuation Arrows
>
> When a line of code is too long to fit on one line of text, we have wrapped it to the next line. When this happens, the continuation is preceded with a code-continuation arrow (➡).

Acknowledgments

IT TOOK THE efforts of many people to deliver this book. We started this more than two years ago as "Indigo" entered its first public beta. Between then and now, we built our samples, tested and revised them with each update, and did it one last time with .NET 3.5 and Visual Studio 2008. In addition to coding, we wrote the book that you're now holding in your hands. But that's the fun part in working with such rapidly changing technology.

This book could not have been possible without great support from the WCF product team and from other really smart people at Microsoft. Each contributed by reviewing our words and code and setting us straight when we veered off course. We'd like to thank the following people for their time, thoughts, and patience: Wenlong Dong, Bill Evjen, Steve Maine, Doug Purdy, Ravi Rao, Yasser Shohoud, and David Stampfli.

We'd also like to thank the technical reviewers, who read, commented, argued, and ultimately made this a much better book. We've been fortunate to have some of the top WCF experts on our side. So to our reviewers, please accept this note of gratitude for your help: Nicholas Allen, Jeff Barnes, Ron Landers, Sowmy Srinivasan, Tom Fuller, and Willy-Peter Schaub. We'd like to offer a special thanks to John Justice, who helped navigate the product team to find our reviewers. Also special thanks to Thom Robbins, who taught us how to write in plain English.

XXXIV ■ **Acknowledgments**

We also must thank Liam Spaeth and the whole Microsoft Technology Center team for supporting our effort. Ideas came from the worldwide MTC team as a whole and from colleagues and customers at the Boston MTC.

In addition to the Microsoft crowd, we also owe gratitude to Keith Brown and Matt Milner at PluralSight for their thorough review of the security and workflow material. These two topics are deep enough and new enough that we greatly needed and benefited from their expertise.

And finally, the good folks at Addison-Wesley really pulled this together. We might know how to code and how to write, but they know how to make a book. So, thank you to Joan Murray, Betsy Harris, and team.

About the Authors

Steve Resnick has worked at Microsoft since the mid-1990s, spanning architect, developer, and evangelist roles in the field. He specializes in Internet technologies, architecting and designing high-volume, high-value Web applications. Steve is the National Technology Director for the Microsoft Technology Centers in the United States, where he sets strategy and direction so that his team can solve the toughest customer challenges. He has worked with .NET since the beginning and is an expert in Web services, BizTalk, transaction processing, and related technologies. He holds a M.S. and B.S. in Computer Science from Boston University and University of Delaware, respectively.

Rich Crane is a Technical Architect at the Microsoft Technology Center in Waltham, Massachusetts. A software architect and engineer with more than 18 years of experience, Rich has spent the last six years helping customers architect and build solutions on the Microsoft platform. He has worked with numerous Microsoft products and technologies and is an expert in BizTalk, SQL Server, SharePoint, Compute Cluster Server, and of course Visual Studio and the .NET Framework. He has spoken at conferences and community events such as TechEd and Code Camp. He graduated Summa Cum Laude from Drexel University with a B.S. degree in Electrical and Computer Engineering.

Chris Bowen is Microsoft's Developer Evangelist for the northeastern United States, specializing in development tools, platforms, and architectural best practices. A software architect and engineer with 15 years of experience, Chris joined Microsoft after holding senior positions at companies such as Monster.com, VistaPrint, Staples, and IDX Systems, and consulting on Web presence and e-commerce projects with others. He is coauthor of *Professional Visual Studio 2005 Team System* (2006, WROX) and holds an M.S. in Computer Science and a B.S. in Management Information Systems, both from Worcester Polytechnic Institute.

1

Basics

WINDOWS COMMUNICATION FOUNDATION (WCF) is all about services. It's about creating, hosting, consuming and securing them. It's about standards and interoperability. It's about developer productivity. In short, it's all about putting distributed computing within reach of professional software developers.

In this chapter, we will cover the basic concepts you'll need to understand to work with WCF services. We'll focus on the most commonly used features. By following the text and examples, you will be able to create and consume services locally and across the network.

Why WCF Matters

Before going too far with the *how* of services, it's important to understand the *why*. So, why is WCF important? Simple—because services are the core of the global distributed network, and WCF is the easiest way to produce and consume services on the Microsoft platform. By leveraging WCF, developers can focus on their applications rather than on communication protocols. It's a classic case of technology encapsulation and tooling. Developers are more productive if their tools encapsulate (but not hide) technical chores wherever possible. WCF, combined with Visual Studio 2008, does just this.

Modern application architecture takes devices, client software, and services into account. There is no doubt that the model of the circa 1995 Web site (host an application on a Web server and deliver the UI via HTML to any browser) will endure, but new models that combine local software with Web services will also become common. Examples are the iPod, XBOX 360, RSS, AJAX, Microsoft Office, and SharePoint and 3D immersive environments, where they each combine locally installed software and Web services.

For consumer applications, the prevalent Web service interface circa 2008 is Representational Entity State Transfer (REST). This combines HTTP and a good URI scheme for addressing XML-based data. Data manipulation using REST typically mirrors the Create Read Update Delete (CRUD) pattern, and simplicity is the hallmark of the REST protocol.

For business applications, the prevalent Web service interface circa 2008 is Simple Object Access Protocol (SOAP). This provides a more robust model for exchanging complex data. SOAP messages contain an envelope and body so they can be encrypted and securely routed around the Internet. If the message is part of a logical session or transaction, semantics are placed in the envelope and propagate along with the message. If the information must be secured, the body of the message can be encrypted, with security information placed in the envelope. SOAP messages are strongly typed, which makes them developer friendly. Like REST, SOAP messages circa 2008 are primarily transmitted over HTTP and encoded as text.

WCF is agnostic to protocol and message format. Chapter 2 of this book, "Contracts," describes services using SOAP message formats. Chapter 13, "Programmable Web," describes the same using REST protocols. Although some subtle but important distinctions exist between the two, you'll see far more similarities than differences in the programming model covered in the remainder of the book.

Regardless of the wire protocol used, writing solid code requires solid software engineering practices. Developers writing the code for business transactions in a service, or compelling user experiences in a client, typically prefer not to work directly with XML. Why not? Because decades of language research and compiler design have produced much better tools. Working with objects, classes, and components produces more robust code than laborious string manipulation in XML.

Developers building .NET applications use Visual Studio. WCF and Visual Studio provide the tooling for implementing services. WCF has a built-in model for hosting, so services can reside within IIS or in Managed Services on Windows. It provides a rich threading and throttling model where instancing is controlled with minimal effort. Whether defining a singleton or a multithreaded service to handle simultaneous requests, the programming model remains constant, and the developer is insulated (but not obfuscated) from the details.

WCF supports various message exchange patterns, such as request-response, one-way, and duplex. Peer networking is also supported by leveraging mesh networks and addressing so that clients can find and communicate with each other without a central control mechanism.

In summary, WCF matters because the modern applications are all about services, and that's what WCF is all about.

Introduction

As a comprehensive system for working with services, WCF comes with a set of terms that you need to be familiar with to be productive. In most cases, these terms don't necessarily represent new concepts, but they provide a consistent taxonomy that we can use to discuss the new technology.

At its core, a service is a set of *endpoints* that provide useful capabilities to clients. An endpoint is simply a resource on the network to which messages can be sent. Clients access these capabilities by sending messages to the endpoints, formatted according to the contract agreed on by both the client and the service. Services listen for messages on the address specified by the endpoint and expect the message to arrive in a particular format. Figure 1.1 shows the basic relationship between client and service.

FIGURE 1.1 Communication between client and service

For the client to communicate meaningful information to the service, it needs to know the ABCs: the address, the binding, and the contract.

- **"A" is for address, the *where*.** It defines where on the network messages should be sent so that the endpoint receives them. This is the location to which messages must be sent by the client. For HTTP, the address would look like http://myserver/myservice/; for TCP, it would look like net.tcp://myserver:8080/myservice.

- **"B" is for binding, the *how*.** The binding defines the *channel* used to communicate with an endpoint. Channels are the conduit through which all messages pass within a WCF application. A channel is composed of a series of *binding elements*. The lowest level binding element is the transport, which delivers messages over the network. The built-in transports include HTTP, TCP, Named Pipes, PerChannel, and MSMQ. Above this are binding elements that specify security and transactions. Fortunately, WCF ships with system-provided bindings that have the channels stacked and configured correctly to save you the time of figuring it out yourself. The basicHttpBinding facilitates communication with most Web services built prior to 2007. It corresponds to WS-I BP 1.1 and is included for its widespread interoperability. The wsHttpBinding implements the common WS-* protocols to enable secure, reliable, and transacted messaging.

- **"C" is for contract, the *what*.** It defines the capability, or feature set, offered by the endpoint. The contract defines the operations that an endpoint exposes and the message formats that the operations require. Contract operations map to class methods that implement the endpoint, including the signature of parameters passed in and out of the methods.

As shown in Figure 1.2, multiple endpoints compose a WCF service, where each endpoint is defined by an address, binding, and contract. Because message flow is typically bidirectional, clients also implicitly host endpoints.

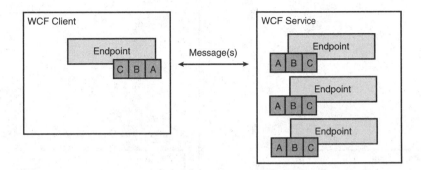

FIGURE 1.2 Communication between client and service endpoints

A service endpoint cannot respond to messages until the service is hosted in a running operating system process. The host can be any process, such as an unattended server process, a Web server or even a client application running full screen on a desktop or minimized in the Windows tray. Services have behaviors that control their concurrency, throttling, transactions, security, and other system semantics. Behaviors may be implemented using .NET attributes, by manipulating the WCF runtime, or through configuration. Behaviors, in conjunction with a flexible hosting model, greatly reduce the complexity of writing multithreaded code.

As shown in Figure 1.3, a main program can instantiate a `ServiceHost` class to create the endpoints of the service.

For discoverability, a service may include an infrastructure endpoint called the Metadata Exchange (MEX) endpoint. This endpoint is accessible by clients to obtain the ABCs of the service and returns Web Service Description Language (WSDL). The MEX endpoint is called when you click Add Service Reference in Visual Studio 2008 or when you use the `svcutil.exe` utility at design time. After the WSDL is obtained, two artifacts are generated: a proxy class in the language of the project and an `app.config` file. The proxy class mirrors the signature of the endpoint operations so that client code can simply "call" an endpoint. The proxy interface doesn't have to be identical to the service signature, but the proxy needs to ensure that the message transmitted to the service is precisely what is described by the service contract. The app.config file contains the binding specifics.

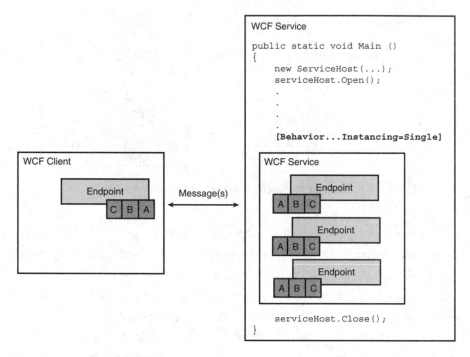

FIGURE 1.3 Hosting a service

Implementing a WCF Service

This section describes how to implement a simple service with WCF. By simple, we'll assume HTTP as the wire protocol, and we'll assume a text-based representation of an XML document on the wire. For security, we'll assume it's handled somehow in the application. We'll assume a synchronous request-reply conversation and that our service supports just one operation, which takes a string as input and returns a double as output. In later chapters, we'll vary all these assumptions, but for now, we'll exclude unnecessary complexity.

Just the ABCs

To define a service endpoint, remember the ABCs: address, binding, and contract. In Listings 1.1 to 1.3, the following are described:

- **"A" is for address, the *where*.** This service listens for incoming requests at http://localhost:8000/EssentialWCF.
- **"B" is for binding, the *how*.** This example uses `basicHttpBinding`, which directs WCF to implement WS-I Basic Profile 1.1, the common protocols of Web service communication.
- **"C" is for contract, the *what*.** This is the syntactic description of what operations the service responds to and what message formats it expects in and out. In this example, the contract is defined by the `StockService` class.

In this section we will implement the service twice. First we'll demonstrate the solution completely in code, where the ABCs are defined directly in the source code. This will remove external dependencies. Then we'll demonstrate the solution again using configuration files. This will result in less code but will increase the service complexity because of dependencies between code and configuration. In reality, you'll probably take the latter approach because the increased complexity is richly rewarded with flexibility. The flexibility derives from exposing some features in configuration, where system administrators can modify them, while exposing other features in code, where only developers can make changes.

Writing a WCF Service Entirely in Code

At a super-high level, writing a WCF service is similar to writing any other service, regardless of internals. You first write some code that implements a capability or feature; then you host that code in an operating system process, and that process listens for requests and responds. WCF formalizes these steps a bit and makes it easy for the developer to do the right thing at each juncture. For instance, using the system-supplied bindings and encoders, WCF services will communicate though standards-based SOAP messages. By default, threading, concurrency, and instancing are well implemented and have predicable behavior.

To implement a WCF service, you implement a .NET class and then decorate the class with `System.ServiceModel` attributes. The `System.ServiceModel` namespace is installed with .NET 3.0 and contains most of the WCF implementation. When the code compiles, the CLR interprets those attributes, replacing them with runtime code. Attributes are nothing new to .NET; they've been around since .NET 1.0. WCF, like ASMX in .NET 1.0 and 1.1 and 2.0, uses attributes to make you more productive when writing services.

Listing 1.1 shows the complete code for a WCF service that is hosted in a console application. In this example, we do the following.

- **Define the contract.** Write a .NET class that does something useful and decorate it with WCF attributes. The `[ServiceContract]` attribute marks a class as a contract. Expressed in standards-based WSDL, the `[ServiceContract]` defines a `PortType`. The `[OperationContract]` attribute defines methods that can be invoked on the class through the service interface. It also defines the messages that are passed to and from those class methods. Expressed in WSDL, the `[Operation Contract]` defines Operations and Messages. Listings 1.1 to 1.3 use a class named `StockService` that has a single method, `GetPrice`.

> ■ **NOTE**
>
> The samples in this book use very simplistic interfaces, often accepting and returning a single string or number. In practice, your service operations will likely accept and return complex types. Communicating over a wire should be more "chunky" than "chatty," minimizing network traffic and response latency. This requires passing more information with each call, requiring complex types for input and return values.

- **Define an endpoint.** Within the endpoint definition, we'll specify an address, binding, and contract by using the `AddServiceEndpoint` method on the `ServiceHost` class. The address is blank, which indicates that the address of the endpoint is the same as the base address or the service. The binding is basicHttpBinding, which is WS-I BP 1.1 compliant and interoperable with most systems that implement XML Web Services. WS-I, or Web Services Interop, is a collaborative effort among major system vendors including Microsoft, IBM, BEA, Oracle, and others to determine and publicize compliance levels. WS-I doesn't define standards; it provides guidance and tools for determining whether software complies with existing standards, such as HTTP and XML.

- **Host the service in a process so it is listening for incoming requests.** Listings 1.1 to 1.3 host the service in a console application by using the ServiceHost class. The service listens at http://localhost:8000/EssentialWCF.

LISTING 1.1 **Service Implemented Entirely in Code**

```
using System;
using System.ServiceModel;

namespace EssentialWCF
{
    [ServiceContract]
    public interface IStockService
    {
        [OperationContract]
        double GetPrice(string ticker);
    }

    public class StockService : IStockService
    {
        public double GetPrice(string ticker)
        {
            return 94.85;
        }
    }

    public class service
    {
        public static void Main()
        {
            ServiceHost serviceHost = new
                    ServiceHost(typeof(StockService),
```

LISTING 1.1 continued

```
                            new Uri("http://localhost:8000/EssentialWCF"));

        serviceHost.AddServiceEndpoint(
                typeof(IStockService),
                new BasicHttpBinding(),
                "");
        serviceHost.Open();

        Console.WriteLine("Press <ENTER> to terminate.\n\n");
        Console.ReadLine();

        serviceHost.Close();
        }
    }
}
```

Writing a Service with Code and Configuration Files

WCF provides rich support for defining service attributes in configuration files. You still need to code the feature or algorithm you're exposing in the service, but endpoint addressing, bindings, and behaviors can be moved from the code into configuration files.

Defining endpoints and behaviors in configuration files makes for a much more flexible solution when compared with defining this in code. For example, suppose that an endpoint was implemented to communicate with clients via HTTP. In Listing 1.1, this is implemented by specifying BasicHttpBinding in the call to AddServiceEndpoint. But suppose that you'd like to change the binding to WSHttpBinding, which delivers better security by implementing message-level in addition to transport-level security. In that case, you'd need to change and recompile the code. By moving the binding selection from code to configuration, this change can be made without a recompile. Or, if you'd like to expose the contract over both protocols, you can define two endpoints: one for basic HTTP and the other that uses WS-Security without changing code. This makes the code more manageable.

Listing 1.2 shows the complete code for a WCF service that is hosted in a console application. This code requires a configuration file that defines behavior and endpoint information. In this example, we do the following.

- **Define the contract.** Write a .NET class that does something useful and decorate it with WCF attributes. There is no difference in a service definition, whether it is exposed in code or configuration. Listing 1.2 uses a class named StockService that is identical to Listing 1.1.

- **Host the service in an operating system process so it can be accessed by a client on the network.** This is done by creating a ServiceHost object defined in System.ServiceModel namespace and calling its Open method, as it was in Listing 1.1.

- **Define a configuration file that specifies the base address for a service and the ABCs of the service endpoint.** Note that the code in Listing 1.2 does not reference the configuration file. When the ServiceHost.Open method is called, WCF looks in the application's configuration file (app.config or web.config) for the <servicemodel> to apply the configuration data.

LISTING 1.2 Service Implemented in Code and Configuration Files

```
using System;
using System.ServiceModel;
namespace EssentialWCF
{
    [ServiceContract]
    public interface IStockService
    {
        [OperationContract]
        double GetPrice(string ticker);
    }

    public class StockService : IStockService
    {
        public double GetPrice(string ticker)
        {
            return 94.85;
        }
    }

    public class service
    {
        public static void Main()
        {
            ServiceHost serviceHost = new
                        ServiceHost(typeof(StockService));
```

LISTING 1.2 continued

```
                serviceHost.Open();

                Console.WriteLine("Press <ENTER> to terminate.\n\n");
                Console.ReadLine();

                serviceHost.Close();
            }
        }
    }
```

Listing 1.3 shows the complete configuration file that works with the code in Listing 1.1. In the ServiceModel section, define the endpoint. For each endpoint, define the address, binding, and contract. The address is blank, which indicates that the endpoint address is the same as the base address for the service. If there is more than one endpoint, each endpoint must have a unique address. The binding in this case is basicHttpBinding and the contract name is the class name defined in the source code, EssentialWCF.StockService.

LISTING 1.3 Configuration for a Service Implemented in Code and Configuration Files

```xml
<?xml version="1.0" encoding="utf-8" ?>
<configuration>
  <system.serviceModel>

    <services>
      <service name="EssentialWCF.StockService">
        <host>
          <baseAddresses>
            <add baseAddress="http://localhost:8000/EssentialWCF"/>
          </baseAddresses>
        </host>
        <endpoint address=""
                  binding="basicHttpBinding"
                  contract="EssentialWCF.IStockService" />
      </service>
    </services>
  </system.serviceModel>
</configuration>
```

More on Configuration Files

The service configuration file, web.config or app.config depending on how the service is hosted, must contain a <system.serviceModel> node. Under this node, services, bindings, behaviors, clients, diagnostics, extensions, hosting environment, and COM+ interop settings can be specified. At a minimum, there must be a `<services>` node that contains endpoints and at least one non-infrastructure `<endpoint>` node under that. Within that, the ABCs are defined for each endpoint.

The `address` attribute defines the URI to which clients will send messages to the endpoint. For instance, if a service is using the `basicHttpBinding`, a binding based on the HTTP protocol, the URI will look like *http://www. myserver.com:8080/MyService/*. If an address specified is an absolute address (that is, not blank and not just a path), this address overrides the base address specified by the host when creating the service. When the service is started by a host, WCF starts the listener, which listens on this address for incoming requests. In the case of IIS hosting, the listener is likely already started, so WCF registers with it so that requests for that URI are directed to the WCF service.

The `binding` attribute defines the communications details needed to connect to the service. It defines the entire channel stack, which at a minimum includes the network adapter channel. It could also include encryption, compression, and other channels. Many system-provided bindings ship with WCF, such as `BasicHttpBinding`, which is compatible with ASMX, `WSHttpBinding`, which implements more advanced Web services that require message-level security, transactions, and other advanced features, and `NetTcpBinding`, which implements a secure fast wire format similar to .NET Remoting and DCOM.

The `contract` attribute references the type defined by the service endpoint. WCF inspects the type and exposes that as metadata at the MEX endpoint, if a MEX endpoint is present in the service. WCF finds the type information by looking first in the \bin folder and then in the Global Assembly Cache (GAC) for the machine. If it can't find the type information, the service will return error information to Add Service Reference or `svcutil.exe` when those tools request the WSDL. If the MEX endpoint does not exist, the service will function fine, but clients will not be able to inspect its ABCs.

More on Service Hosting

WCF enables you to host services in any operating system process. In the majority of situations, IIS is the right hosting environment to achieve great performance, manageability, and security. If you already have IIS running in your environment, you already have security practices in place. Sophisticated IT shops often define explicit policies and procedures for security and have automated tools for verifying compliance. Smaller shops often use the implicit security built in to IIS and Windows 2003. In either case, existing security practices would be applied to IIS-hosted WCF services.

But there are also reasons to not use IIS for hosting. You may not want to use HTTP as the protocol. You may want explicit control of the startup and shutdown events. Or you may want to provide a custom administration interface rather than using the IIS tools. If you don't want to use IIS for hosting, this is no problem. WCF makes *self-hosting* very easy and flexible. Self-hosting is the term used to describe a hosting method where the developer instantiates the service host, rather than relying on IIS or Windows Process Activation Services (WAS).

The simplest way of hosting a service is to write a console application, as shown in Listing 1.1. This isn't too useful in production because having command windows on a server isn't a great practice, but for getting started, it eliminates all dependencies on IIS infrastructure. The main program creates a new instance of `ServiceHost`, which, as the name implies, will host the service. The program calls the `Open` method on the `ServiceHost` and then continues about its business. In this case, there's nothing to do except wait for someone to press Enter, at which point the application calls the `Close` method on the ServiceHost.

After `Open` is called, the `ServiceHost` listens on the addresses specified by the endpoints. When messages arrive, the `ServiceHost` does a few things. First, based on the channel stack defined by the binding, it applies any decryption, decompression, and security rules. Second, based on the contract, it deserializes the incoming message into .NET types, creates a new object, and then invokes the proper operation on the object.

Exposing the Metadata Exchange (MEX) Endpoint

Metadata in WCF refers to the information that describes precisely how to communicate with a service. Clients can request metadata from a running service to learn about their endpoints and the message formats that they require. At design time, clients send a request message defined by the WS-MetadataExchange standard and receive WSDL in return. The WSDL can be used by the client to define a proxy class and configuration file that will later be used at runtime to communicate with the service. Figure 1.4 shows this interaction.

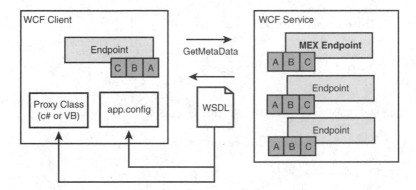

FIGURE 1.4 Obtaining metadata through MEX endpoint

By default, WCF services do not expose a MEX endpoint. This means that nobody can query the service to find out how to communicate with it. Without knowing the address, binding, and contract, it's very difficult to communicate with the service, unless the service is listed in a registry. Fortunately, WCF makes it easy to expose a MEX endpoint so that clients can communicate properly with services. The MEX endpoint can be exposed in code or in configuration.

Listing 1.4 shows the code necessary to expose a MEX endpoint in a service. This expands on the example in Listing 1.1 in a few ways. First, a behavior is added to the service that directs WCF to include the MEX contract, `IMetadataExchange` in the service. Second, an endpoint is added to the service, where the contract is `IMetadataExchange`, the transport is HTTP, and the address is "mex". Because the address is specified as a relative address, the base address of the service is used as the prefix, so the full address is http://localhost:8000/EssentialWCF/mex. Note that the behavior is also modified to enable HTTP GET. This is not required but allows users to access the MEX endpoint via a browser.

LISTING 1.4 Service Exposing MEX Endpoint in Code

```
using System;
using System.ServiceModel;
using System.ServiceModel.Description;

namespace EssentialWCF
{
    [ServiceContract]
    public interface IStockService
    {
        [OperationContract]
        double GetPrice(string ticker);
    }

    public class StockService : IStockService
    {
        public double GetPrice(string ticker)
        {
            return 94.85;
        }
    }

    public class service
    {
        public static void Main()
        {
            ServiceHost serviceHost = new
                    ServiceHost(typeof(StockService),
                    new Uri("http://localhost:8000/EssentialWCF"));

            serviceHost.AddServiceEndpoint(
                    typeof(IStockService),
                    new BasicHttpBinding(),
                    "");

            ServiceMetadataBehavior behavior = new
                    ServiceMetadataBehavior();
            behavior.HttpGetEnabled = true;
            serviceHost.Description.Behaviors.Add(behavior);

            serviceHost.AddServiceEndpoint(
                    typeof(IMetadataExchange),
                    MetadataExchangeBindings.CreateMexHttpBinding(),
                    "mex");

            serviceHost.Open();

            Console.WriteLine("Press <ENTER> to terminate.\n\n");
            Console.ReadLine();
```

```
                serviceHost.Close();
            }
        }
    }
}
```

If you choose to specify endpoints in configuration files rather than code, you need to expose the MEX endpoint in the configuration file. Listing 1.5 shows how the configuration file in Listing 1.3 is modified to expose the MEX endpoint. A MEX endpoint is added to the service and a Service-Behavior is added so that the MEX endpoint can be accessed via HTTP.

LISTING 1.5 Service Exposing MEX Endpoint in Configuration

```xml
<?xml version="1.0" encoding="utf-8" ?>
<configuration>

  <system.serviceModel>

    <services>
      <service name="EssentialWCF.StockService"
               behaviorConfiguration="myServiceBehavior">
        <host>
          <baseAddresses>
            <add baseAddress="http://localhost:8000/EssentialWCF"/>
          </baseAddresses>
        </host>
        <endpoint address=""
                  binding="basicHttpBinding"
                  contract="EssentialWCF.IStockService" />
        <endpoint address="mex"
                  binding="mexHttpBinding"
                  contract="IMetadataExchange" />
      </service>
    </services>

    <behaviors>
      <serviceBehaviors>
        <behavior name="myServiceBehavior">
          <serviceMetadata httpGetEnabled="True"/>
        </behavior>
      </serviceBehaviors>
    </behaviors>

  </system.serviceModel>
</configuration>
```

Implementing a Client for a WCF Service

WCF provides a rich API for clients to use when communicating with a service. The API, implemented by System.ServiceModel, takes care of serializing types to XML and sending a message from the client to the service. You can either program directly to that API, or you can use tools to generate a proxy class and configuration file. In this section, we will first demonstrate how to call a service directly in code, and then we'll do the same using tools. The former approach involves less code and externalizes the configuration data. The latter approach has fewer dependencies and gives more fine-grained control over invocation. There are situations when each solution is the best alternative.

Writing a WCF Client Entirely in Code

Just as a service endpoint must define the ABCs of WCF to expose its capabilities on the network, a client must know the ABCs to access those capabilities. Therefore, when writing the code to access services endpoints, the ABCs are coded into the client application.

The *endpoint* address is simple—it's a network address to which messages are sent. Its format is defined by the transport protocol being used in the binding. The endpoint *binding* defines the exact communication mechanism though which the endpoint is exposed. WCF ships with a set of preconfigured bindings, such as netTcpBinding, wsHttpBinding, and basicHttpBinding. The *contract* defines the precise XML format that the service understands. It's typically expressed using [ServiceContract] and [DataContract] notation in class and/or interface definition in code, and WCF serializes the class structure to XML for transmission over the wire.

Listing 1.6 shows code to invoke a service operation. This code embodies the ABCs of the service endpoint so that it can access its capabilities.

First, the client defines the interface it wants to call. This interface definition is shared between the client and service. Syntactically, the C# definition is very different from XML or WSDL, but semantically it's the same. That is, it precisely describes how to access the service capabilities, including the name of the operation and its parameters. Then the client creates a ChannelFactory class to create a channel, passing in the ABCs. In this case, the address is an address hosted by an IIS server, the binding is BasicHttpBinding, and the contract is the IStockService interface. Finally, the client creates the channel to establish communication with the service and "calls a method" on the service.

LISTING 1.6 WCF Client Entirely in Code

```
using System;
using System.ServiceModel;

namespace Client
{
    [ServiceContract]
    public interface IStockService
    {
        [OperationContract]
        double GetPrice(string ticker);
    }
    class Client
    {
        static void Main(string[] args)
        {

            ChannelFactory<IStockService> myChannelFactory =
            new ChannelFactory<IStockService>(
                    new BasicHttpBinding(),
                    new EndpointAddress
                      ("http://localhost:8000/EssentialWCF"));

            IStockService wcfClient = myChannelFactory.CreateChannel();

            double p = wcfClient.GetPrice("msft");
            Console.WriteLine("Price:{0}",p);


        }
    }
}
```

Writing a Client with Code and Configuration

Back in 2001, Visual Studio introduced Add Web Reference, which in just three words reduced a major undertaking in distributed computing to a right-click. This was a good thing, because it delivered an entry point to scalable, standards-based distributed computing to most professional developers. But in making distributed computing so accessible, it hid many of the important complexities. Visual Studio 2008 continues to support Add Web Reference for compatibility with ASMX and other Web services, but also introduces Add Service Reference (ASR) to support WCF. Because WCF is protocol independent and supports a variety of serialization, encoding, and security mechanisms, ASR offers great flexibility in providing support for manageability, performance, and security.

The ASR feature of Visual Studio is used to obtain metadata from a WCF service and generate a proxy class and configuration file, as shown in Figure 1.4. Behind the scenes, ASR calls `svcutil.exe`, which invokes a service's MEX endpoint to query for its interfaces and to generate a proxy class and configuration file. The proxy class enables the client to access the service operations as if they were methods of a local class. The proxy class uses WCF classes to build and interpret SOAP messages according to the contract defined by the service endpoint. The configuration file stores the ABCs of the service.

There are two steps to writing a client that invokes a service: first, generate a configuration file and the proxy class, and second, write code that uses the proxy class to invoke the service. To use ASR within Visual Studio 2008, right-click the Service References node within the Solution Explorer and then select Add Service Reference from the context menu. This will launch a dialog box shown in Figure 1.5.

This dialog calls the svcutil utility to create a source code file that implements the proxy class in the language of the project. It also creates an `app.config` file with a `<system.serviceModel>` node that stores the address, binding, and contract information necessary to call the endpoints.

As an alternative to using ASR, you can also use the `svcutil.exe` utility directly. This utility, found in the C:\Program Files\Microsoft SDKs\ Windows\v6.0\Bin folder, takes many switches, and help is available by using the –h switch from the command line. The utility accepts metadata as input and can produce various forms of output. The metadata can come from the DLL that implements the class, from a WSDL file, or from the WSDL returned by a WS-Metadata call to a running service. Listing 1.7 shows how to use `svcutil.exe` to generate metadata from the service defined in Listings 1.4 and 1.5.

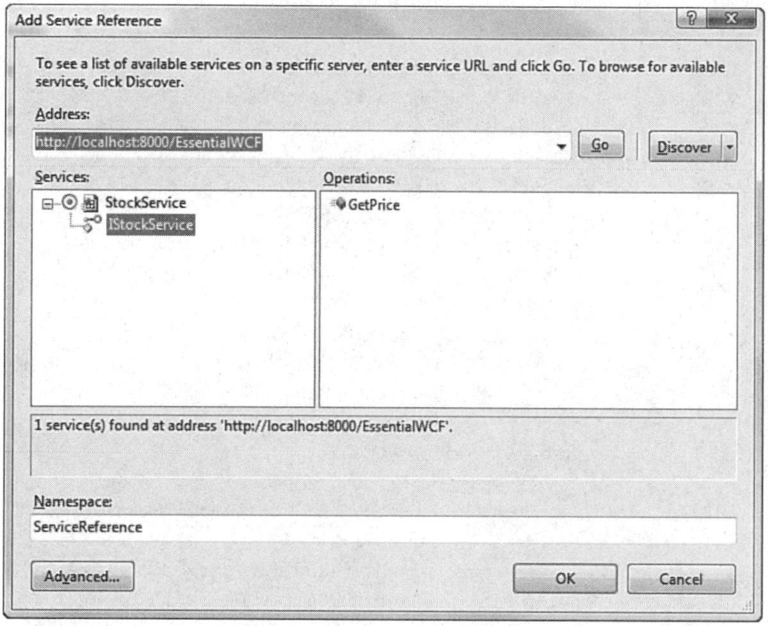

FIGURE 1.5 Visual Studio generating client proxy class and configuration file

LISTING 1.7 `svcutil.exe` Generating Client Proxy Class and Configuration File

```
svcutil http://localhost:8000/EssentialWCF/mex/
        -config:app.config
        -out:generatedProxy.cs
```

Regardless of which technique is used to generate the proxy and configuration file, `svcutil.exe` produces the same result. Listing 1.8 shows the configuration file. Note that the client-side configuration file is quite a bit more verbose than the services from which it was generated (refer to Listing 1.3). This gives the client the flexibility to override specific attributes, such as timeouts, buffers, and client-supplied security credentials.

LISTING 1.8 `app.config` Generated from `svcutil.exe`

```
<?xml version="1.0" encoding="utf-8"?>
<configuration>
    <system.serviceModel>
        <bindings>
            <basicHttpBinding>
                <binding name="BasicHttpBinding_StockService"
```

LISTING 1.8 continued

```
                        closeTimeout="00:01:00" openTimeout="00:01:00"
                        receiveTimeout="00:10:00" sendTimeout="00:01:00"
                        allowCookies="false" bypassProxyOnLocal="false"
                        hostNameComparisonMode="StrongWildcard"
                        maxBufferSize="65536" maxBufferPoolSize="524288"
                        maxReceivedMessageSize="65536"
                        messageEncoding="Text" textEncoding="utf-8"
                        transferMode="Buffered" useDefaultWebProxy="true">
                        <readerQuotas maxDepth="32"
                                      maxStringContentLength="8192"
                                      maxArrayLength="16384"
                                      maxBytesPerRead="4096"
                                      maxNameTableCharCount="16384" />
                    <security mode="None">
                        <transport clientCredentialType="None"
                                   proxyCredentialType="None"
                                   realm="" />
                        <message clientCredentialType="UserName"
                                 algorithmSuite="Default" />
                    </security>
                </binding>
            </basicHttpBinding>
        </bindings>
        <client>
            <endpoint address="http://localhost:8000/EssentialWCF"
                binding="basicHttpBinding"
                bindingConfiguration="BasicHttpBinding_StockService"
                contract="StockService"
                name="BasicHttpBinding_StockService" />
        </client>
    </system.serviceModel>
</configuration>
```

After the configuration file and proxy class are generated, invoking a request-response service operation is quite simple. The name of the proxy class is the name of the ServiceContract appended with "Client." The name of proxy class for the service defined in Listings 1.4 and 1.5 is StockServiceClient. The client code creates an instance of the proxy class and then calls a method on that class. Listing 1.9 shows the code.

LISTING 1.9 Client Code for Invoking a Service Operation

```
using System;
using System.ServiceModel;

namespace EssentialWCF
```

```
{
    class Client
    {
        static void Main(string[] args)
        {
            StockServiceClient proxy = new StockServiceClient();
            double p = proxy.GetPrice("msft");
            Console.WriteLine("Price:{0}", p);
            proxy.Close();
        }
    }
}
```

Hosting a Service in IIS

A WCF service can be hosted by any managed process running in the operating system. The service itself typically doesn't know or care about how it is hosted, although there are plenty of APIs through which it can find out. It can be hosted in an unattended Windows Service that starts when the machine is booted and shuts down only when the machine does so, or even in a client-side application minimized in the Windows system tray. The most common usage, however, is to host a WCF service in IIS.

Discussion

IIS is well suited for hosting services. It's built in to Windows and there is a significant knowledge base published about managing, securing, and developing applications. IIS is scalable, reliable, and can be made quite secure so it provides an excellent base for hosting services. ASMX, based on IIS, was the most widely adopted mechanism for publishing Web services before WCF, and WCF builds on that legacy. ASMX is replaced by WCF in .NET 3.5 as the recommended way to publish Web services in IIS.

Again, remember the ABCs of WCF: address, binding, and contract. When hosting in IIS, the address of a service is defined by the virtual directory that contains the service files. The binding will always use the HTTP/S protocol because that's what IIS understands, so basicHttpBinding and wsHttpBinding are available. These are just two of the system-defined bindings that can be used; any binding that leverages the HTTP protocol is valid for IIS hosting. The contract, the SOAP definition of the service endpoints, is not constrained by the fact that IIS is hosting the service, so no special contract rules apply for IIS hosting.

Like ASMX, metadata, in the form of WSDL, can be obtained from an IIS-hosted service by addressing the service with WSDL as a parameter (http://localhost/myservice.svc?wsdl). When IIS receives this request, it calls the MEX endpoint of the service and returns the result as WSDL. Unlike ASMX, however, the MEX endpoint is not exposed by default, so it will not respond to metadata requests from Visual Studio 2008 Add Service Reference or svcutil.exe. You must explicitly enable the MEX endpoint in code (shown in code Listing 1.4) or configuration (shown in Listing 1.5).

Hosting a Service in IIS in Three Steps

There are three steps in hosting a service in IIS:

- Create a virtual application in IIS to store the service.
- Create a SVC file to define the service implementation.
- Augment the web.config file to include a <system.serviceModel> section.

Define an IIS Virtual Application

A virtual application in IIS associates an application pool and a virtual directory. For WCF, the application pool creates the ServiceHost and the virtual directory stores of the service files (SVC, config, .dll).

Create an SVC File

The SVC file references the service implementation. The SVC file can be created using any text editor or Visual Studio. In most cases, the implementation class will reside in a DLL and will be referenced by the SVC file. The DLL must reside in the /bin folder in the virtual directory or stored in the GAC. Listing 1.10 shows an SVC file that references a compiled .NET class.

LISTING 1.10 SVC File Referencing a Compiled Service

```
<%@ServiceHost Service="EssentialWCF.StockService" %>
```

Alternatively, the SVC file can contain the actual implementation. In that case, the SVC file will be longer, but there will be fewer external dependencies. Because the source code is resident on the IIS server that is hosting the service, the source code can be modified by an operations or support team without access to a development environment for compiling a DLL. This has obvious risks and benefits. Risks include loss of control over intellectual property and change management, because the code is visible and updatable on every Web server. Also, performance will suffer with this method. Benefits include code transparency and break-fixes, because customers know exactly what the code does and how to change it if necessary. Listing 1.11 shows an SVC file that contains a service implementation. This code will be compiled on its first invocation.

LISTING 1.11 SVC File Containing Inline Implementation

```csharp
<%@ServiceHost Language=c# Service="EssentialWCF.StockService" %>

using System;
using System.ServiceModel;

namespace EssentialWCF
{
    [ServiceContract]
    public interface IStockService
    {
        [OperationContract]
        double GetPrice(string ticker);
    }

    public class StockService : IStockService
    {
        public double GetPrice(string ticker)
        {
            return 94.85;
        }
    }
}
```

Implement `<System.serviceModel>` in `web.config`

Because IIS is hosting the service, the service endpoint definitions must be specified in configuration rather than code. The configuration information is stored in `web.config`, under the `<system.serviceModel>` node. As with other hosting models, the endpoint must define the ABCs: address, binding, and contract. Listing 1.12 shows a `web.config` file that hosts a service within IIS. Note that the `<system.serviceModel>` node is identical to Listing 1.5.

The address of the service is defined by the address of the virtual directory in which the SVC file resides. If there's just one endpoint defined in the service, then the endpoint address can be blank, which implies that the endpoint address is the same as the service address. If there are multiple endpoints defined in a service, then each endpoint can have a relative address.

The binding must use a channel stack that uses HTTP as the transport. Two transports that are built in to WCF are `basicHttpBinding` and `wsHttpBinding`. Custom bindings, those that compose a channel stack differently than the built-in implementations are also supported, so long as they use http as their transport. Custom bindings are covered in detail in Chapters 3 and 4.

The endpoint contract defines the class implemented by the service. The runtime code must be accessible to the service, either in the /bin directory, in the GAC, or inline in the SVC file.

LISTING 1.12 `web.config` Defining a Service

```
<?xml version="1.0" encoding="utf-8" ?>
<configuration>

  <system.serviceModel>
    <services>
      <service name="EssentialWCF.StockService"
               behaviorConfiguration="MEXServiceTypeBehavior" >
        <endpoint address=""
                  binding="basicHttpBinding"
                  contract="EssentialWCF.IStockService " />
        <endpoint address="mex"
                  binding="mexHttpBinding"
                  contract="IMetadataExchange" />
      </service>
    </services>

    <behaviors>
      <serviceBehaviors>
        <behavior name="MEXServiceTypeBehavior" >
          <serviceMetadata httpGetEnabled="true" />
```

```
        </behavior>
      </serviceBehaviors>
    </behaviors>
  </system.serviceModel>

</configuration>
```

Implementing a WCF Client for an ASMX Service

WCF clients can call any standards-based service regardless of the target hosting environment. Web services built on the .NET 1.1 Framework (ASMX) are fully compatible. The standard defined by WS-I Basic Profile 1.1 ensures they are callable from WCF clients.

Tools Support

Just like calling a WCF service, you can use Add Service Reference (ASR) or Svcutil.exe to create the proxy class and configuration file to invoke ASMX service operations. After these artifacts are created, the client can communicate with ASMX Web services by instantiating the proxy and calling its methods. Alternatively, you can use the Add Web Reference (AWR) or wsdl.exe to generate the proxy class and configuration file. Again, after the artifacts are created, the client calls methods on the proxy to communicate with the service.

For new client applications calling existing ASMX Web services, it's best to use ASR or svcutil.exe. For existing applications that already have proxies generated by AWR/wsdl.exe, it's best to continue to use AWR/wsdl.exe. This way, the client doesn't have two types of proxies and configuration files in use to communicate with the ASMX services. If the client is enhanced to call new WCF services that use the basicHttpBinding, you can still use AWR/wsdl.exe to generate new proxies for the WCF services.

TABLE 1.1 Options for Generating Proxy Class and Configuration File

	ASMX Service	WCF Service
Modifying existing client that already references ASMX services	Add Web Reference or `wsdl.exe`	Add Web Reference or `wsdl.exe`
Developing new clients for ASMX services	Add Service Reference or `svcutil.exe`	Add Service Reference or `svcutil.exe`

Regardless of whether you use `svcutil.exe` or `wsdl.exe` to generate the proxy class, the client code uses that proxy to access the remote service. In addition, entries are made in the `app.config` for the client program to support the proxy class.

Generating Client Proxy Class and Configuration Files

If you are modifying an existing client that already had ASMX proxies, you should use Add Web Reference. Listing 1.13 shows the client code that uses a proxy generated by Add Web Reference to call a service operation.

LISTING 1.13 Client Code Using Add Web Reference Proxy to Access an ASMX Service

```
using System;
namespace Client
{
    class Program
    {
        static void Main(string[] args)
        {
            ASMXReference.StockService proxy =
                            new ASMXReference. StockService ())
            double p = proxy.GetPrice("msft");
            Console.WriteLine("Price:{0}", p);
            proxy.Close();
        }
    }
}
```

Listing 1.14 shows a configuration file that was generated by Visual Studio from Add Web Reference. Notice that the only attribute stored in the `app.config` is the address of the service. This is in stark contrast to the detail described in the `app.config` generated by Add Service Reference shown in Listing 1.16. The additional configuration specified by Add Service Reference enables developers or administrators to change parameters, such as timeouts, without changing code.

LISTING 1.14 `app.config` Generated by Add Web Reference for an ASMX Service

```
<?xml version="1.0" encoding="utf-8" ?>
<configuration>
    <configSections>
        <sectionGroup name="applicationSettings"
          type="System.Configuration.ApplicationSettingsGroup,
          System, Version=1.0.0.0, Culture=neutral,
          PublicKeyToken=b77a5c561934e089" >
            <section name="Client.Properties.Settings"
                     type="System.Configuration.ClientSettingsSection,
                     System, Version=1.0.0.0, Culture=neutral,
                     PublicKeyToken=b77a5c561934e089"
                     requirePermission="false" />
        </sectionGroup>
    </configSections>
    <applicationSettings>
        <Client.Properties.Settings>
            <setting name="Client_ASMXReference_StockService"
                     serializeAs="String">
                <value>http://localhost/asmx/service.asmx</value>
            </setting>
        </Client.Properties.Settings>
    </applicationSettings>
</configuration>
```

If you are creating a new client that doesn't already have ASMX proxies, you should use Add Service Reference so that you start the new project with new proxies. Listing 1.15 shows the client code that uses a proxy generated by Add Service Reference with an ASMX service. Note that the endpoint name, `StockServiceSoap`, must be specified when the proxy is created. This is because Add Service Reference adds two endpoints into the `app.config` file: one that uses `basicHttpBinding` and one that uses a custom binding compliant with SOAP 1.1.

LISTING 1.15 Client Code Using Add Service Reference Proxy to Access ASMX

```
using System;
namespace Client
{
```

LISTING 1.15 continued

```
    class Program
    {
        static void Main(string[] args)
        {
            using (WCFReference.StockServiceSoapClient proxy =
                new client.WCFReference.StockServiceSoapClient
                    ("StockServiceSoap"))
            {
                double p = proxy.GetPrice("msft");
                Console.WriteLine("Price:{0}", p);
            }
        }
    }
}
```

Listing 1.16 shows a configuration file that was generated by Visual Studio from Add Service Reference to an ASMX service. Notice the full detail of binding and endpoint information that was derived from the ASMX service and stored in the app.config. Also notice that two endpoints are defined. The first endpoint, StockServiceSoap, uses the basicHttpBinding, which complies with the WS-I Basic Profile 1.1 standard. The second endpoint, StockServiceSoap12, uses a custom binding that communicates using a later SOAP protocol. Because ASMX is WS-I Basic Profile 1.1 compliant, the 1.1 endpoint is used.

LISTING 1.16 app.config Generated by Add Service Reference for an ASMX Service

```
    <?xml version="1.0" encoding="utf-8" ?>
    <configuration>
        <system.serviceModel>
            <bindings>
                <basicHttpBinding>
                    <binding name="StockServiceSoap" closeTimeout="00:01:00"
                      openTimeout="00:01:00" receiveTimeout="00:10:00"
                      sendTimeout="00:01:00" allowCookies="false"
                      bypassProxyOnLocal="false"
                      hostNameComparisonMode="StrongWildcard"
                      maxBufferSize="65536" maxBufferPoolSize="524288"
                      maxReceivedMessageSize="65536"
                      messageEncoding="Text" textEncoding="utf-8"
                      transferMode="Buffered"
                      useDefaultWebProxy="true">
                        <readerQuotas maxDepth="32"
                          maxStringContentLength="8192" maxArrayLength="16384"
                          maxBytesPerRead="4096"
```

```
                            maxNameTableCharCount="16384" />
                    <security mode="None">
                        <transport clientCredentialType="None"
                                   proxyCredentialType="None"
                                   realm="" />
                        <message clientCredentialType="UserName"
                                 algorithmSuite="Default" />
                    </security>
                </binding>
            </basicHttpBinding>
            <customBinding>
                <binding name="StockServiceSoap12">
                    <textMessageEncoding maxReadPoolSize="64"
                        maxWritePoolSize="16"
                        messageVersion="Soap12" writeEncoding="utf-8">
                        <readerQuotas maxDepth="32"
                            maxStringContentLength="8192"
                            maxArrayLength="16384"
                            maxBytesPerRead="4096"
                            maxNameTableCharCount="16384" />
                    </textMessageEncoding>
                    <httpTransport manualAddressing="false"
                        maxBufferPoolSize="524288"
                        maxReceivedMessageSize="65536"
                        allowCookies="false"
                        authenticationScheme="Anonymous"
                        bypassProxyOnLocal="false"
                        hostNameComparisonMode="StrongWildcard"
                        keepAliveEnabled="true" maxBufferSize="65536"
                        proxyAuthenticationScheme="Anonymous"
                        realm="" transferMode="Buffered"
                        unsafeConnectionNtlmAuthentication="false"
                        useDefaultWebProxy="true" />
                </binding>
            </customBinding>
        </bindings>
        <client>
            <endpoint address="http://localhost/asmx/service.asmx"
                    binding="basicHttpBinding"
                    bindingConfiguration="StockServiceSoap"
                    contract="Client.WCFReference.StockServiceSoap"
                    name="StockServiceSoap" />
            <endpoint address="http://localhost/asmx/service.asmx"
                    binding="customBinding"
                    bindingConfiguration="StockServiceSoap12"
                    contract="Client.WCFReference.StockServiceSoap"
                    name="StockServiceSoap12" />
        </client>
    </system.serviceModel>
</configuration>
```

SUMMARY

In this chapter, we covered the basics of WCF, neatly described as the ABCs. A service is composed of endpoints, and each endpoint has the ABCs: address, binding, and contract. Services also have behaviors that describe their operating semantics, such as threading and concurrency, but that will be covered in later chapters.

Services can be hosted in any operating system process, from a console application running on a Windows desktop to an IIS server in a server farm. We showed an example of hosting in each. IIS is the most common mechanism for hosting WCF services. When .NET 3.5 is installed on an IIS server, requests for SVC resources are dispatched to WCF. The SVC file contains a reference to the service implementation. The implementation is either in a DLL in the /bin of the IIS virtual directory hosting the SVC file, in a DLL loaded into the global assembly cache (GAC) of the server, or it can be inline in source code in the SVC file.

Clients communicate with services exclusively through messages. For developer productivity, Visual Studio provides tools for building client-side proxy classes to represent server operations. Client applications use the proxy classes to communicate with the service. Inside the proxy class, WCF serializes the parameters as XML and sends the XML message to the proper service endpoint address. Configuration needed by the client proxy is stored in an `app.config` file on the client. The proxy and configuration files are generated by `svcutil.exe` or by using Add Service Reference from within the Visual Studio environment. Although the tools can greatly improve productivity, there are cases when you'd rather code directly to the WCF API. This is entirely possible.

ASMX services are compatible with the WS-I Basic Profile 1.1 specification. The `basicHttpBinding` WCF binding is also compatible with that specification, so using this binding, WCF clients can access ASMX services.

Using the information in this chapter, you should be able to define, expose, and consume WCF services.

2

Contracts

IN THE WORLD OF atoms and money, a *contract* is a binding agreement between two or more parties that specifies the supply of goods or services for a known price. In the world of bits and services, a contract has a similar function: It's an agreement between two or more parties that specifies the messages that can be exchanged and the terms and conditions of those messages.

A contract is a description of the messages that are passed to and from service endpoints. Each endpoint is defined by the ABCs: an addressable location on the network where messages are sent, a binding that describes how messages are sent, and a contract that describes the message formats.

Remember that a service is really a collection of endpoints, and the endpoints implement the specific algorithms in code. They can implement high-level business functions, such as entering orders into a fulfillment system, or they can be more fine-grained, such as looking up a customer's address. High-level functions typically require complex data structures, whereas targeted functions often work in more basic data types. In either case, an endpoint must specify the operations it implements and the data formats it expects. Together, these specifications make up the contract.

There are three types of contracts in WCF:

- **Service contracts.** Service contracts describe the functional operations implemented by the service. A service contract maps the class methods of a .NET type to WSDL services, port types, and operations. Operation contracts within service contracts describe the service operations, which are the methods that implement functions of the service.

- **Data contracts.** Data contracts describe data structures that are used by the service to communicate with clients. A data contract maps CLR types to XML Schema Definitions (XSD) and defines how they are serialized and deserialized. Data contracts describe all the data that is sent to or from service operations.

- **Message contracts.** Message contracts map CLR types to SOAP messages and describe the format of the SOAP messages and affect the WSDL and XSD definitions of those messages. Message contracts provide precise control over the SOAP headers and bodies.

To make contracts interoperable with the widest range of systems, they are expressed in Web Service Description Language (WSDL). So, before going too much further in discussing contracts, a short review of WSDL is helpful. According to the W3C, the standards body through which industry vendors (Microsoft, IBM, and so on) defined the WSDL specification

> WSDL is an XML format for describing network services as a set of endpoints operating on messages containing either document-oriented or procedure-oriented information. The operations and messages are described abstractly, and then bound to a concrete network protocol and message format to define an endpoint. Related concrete endpoints are combined into abstract endpoints (services). WSDL is extensible to allow description of endpoints and their messages regardless of what message formats or network protocols are used to communicate[;] however, the only bindings described in this document describe how to use WSDL in conjunction with SOAP 1.1, HTTP GET/POST, and MIME.

The full specification, available at www.w3.org/TR/wsdl, describes the key concepts and supporting details so that vendors such as Microsoft can build tools to produce and consume WSDL. The major elements of WSDL are described in Table 2.1, paraphrased and expanded from the public specification.

TABLE 2.1 WSDL Elements

WSDL Element	Description
Type	Data type definitions used to describe the messages exchanged. These are typically expressed in XML Schema Definition.
Message	Represents an abstract definition of the data being transmitted. A message consists of logical parts, each of which is associated with a definition within some type system. A message is similar to a formal parameter in a function call or a method parameter in an interface and is used to define the signature of operations.
Operation	A name and description of an action supported by the service. The operations expose the capability or functionality of a service endpoint.
PortType	A named set of abstract operations and the abstract messages involved. A service endpoint implements a PortType, which groups related operations.
Binding	Defines the message format and protocol details for operations and messages defined by a particular PortType.
Port	Defines an individual endpoint by specifying a single address for a binding.
Service	Defines a set of related ports.

Because contracts are described in WSDL and XSD but code typically works with CLR types, there needs to be a mapping between the two systems. WCF facilitates that mapping in a three-stage process. First, when writing service code, you decorate the class with the WCF-defined attributes [ServiceContract], [OperationContract], [FaultContract],

[MessageContract], and [DataContract]. Then, when writing the client code, you query the service to learn the contract details and to generate a proxy class that exposes a service interface, which can be called from the code. This is done using Visual Studio or svcutil.exe, which invokes a metadata infrastructure endpoint on the service to generate WSDL from the attributed code. Finally, at runtime when a client calls a method on a service interface, WCF serializes the CLR types and method calls into XML and sends the message over the wire according to the binding and encoding scheme agreed upon in the WSDL.

Four constructs are in play here; two on the .NET side and two on the XML side. On the .NET side, a *CLR type* defines the structure of data or capabilities, but not until an *object* of that type is instantiated can it do anything. On the XML side, an *XSD* defines the structure of data, but not until an *XML Instance* is created does an actual message exist.

So to properly understand how WCF works, you need to understand both the code and WSDL artifacts. Fortunately, WCF ships with two essential tools for mapping between the two. The first tool, SvcUtil.exe, can be explicitly called from the command line or implicitly called when you use Add Service Reference from Visual Studio. This tool, with its many switches, produces WSDL and generates proxy classes that facilitate mapping between .NET types and XSD, and .NET class methods and WSDL operations. The second tool, Service Trace Viewer, or SvcTraceViewer.exe, is a graphical tool that reads and interprets diagnostics log files written by WCF. Using this tool, we can see the message formats received and sent by endpoints and trace the message flow. This tool is described in detail in Chapter 9, "Diagnostics."

In this chapter we will describe how to use four of the five contract types. We'll start by looking at service contracts that expose the endpoints and operation contracts that define the methods. Then we'll examine data contracts that describe the data passed in and out of the endpoints. Finally, we'll cover message contracts that provide more control over SOAP messages. We'll discuss fault contracts later in the book, in Chapter 10, "Exception Handling."

Service Contracts

A service contract describes the interface to operations implemented by a service endpoint. Service contracts reference message formats and describe how they are exchanged. Message formats are further described by data contracts and message contracts. This section covers the message exchange patterns that service contracts implement.

Service contracts are used by WCF at design time and runtime. At design time, they identify classes in code that should be exposed as endpoints in WSDL. A class marked with [ServiceContract] and its methods marked with [OperationContract] are exposed in WSDL so that they can be accessed by clients. The class is identified as wsdl:service and the operations are identified as wsdl:operation. At runtime, when the WCF dispatcher receives a message, it looks at the wsdl:operation name to determine which class method marked with [OperationContract] should receive the deserialized message. Figure 2.1 depicts the high-level translation of code to WSDL.

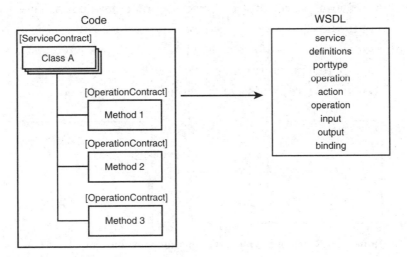

FIGURE 2.1 High-level translation of code artifacts to WSDL

Figure 2.2 shows the same translation depicted in Figure 2.1, but shows also the syntax of the C# and WSDL elements for clarity.

Compiled Code   WSDL

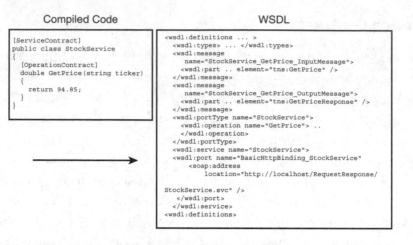

```
[ServiceContract]
public class StockService
{
  [OperationContract]
  double GetPrice(string ticker)
  {
    return 94.85;
  }
}
```

```
<wsdl:definitions ... >
  <wsdl:types> ... </wsdl:types>
  <wsdl:message
    name="StockService_GetPrice_InputMessage">
    <wsdl:part .. element="tns:GetPrice" />
  </wsdl:message>
  <wsdl:message
    name="StockService_GetPrice_OutputMessage">
    <wsdl:part .. element="tns:GetPriceResponse" />
  </wsdl:message>
  <wsdl:portType name="StockService">
    <wsdl:operation name="GetPrice"> ..
    </wsdl:operation>
  </wsdl:portType>
  <wsdl:service name="StockService">
  <wsdl:port name="BasicHttpBinding_StockService">
    <soap:address
      location="http://localhost/RequestResponse/

StockService.svc" />
  </wsdl:port>
  </wsdl:service>
<wsdl:definitions>
```

FIGURE 2.2 High-level translation of code syntax to WSDL

Synchronous Request-Response Operations

The synchronous request-response message exchange is the most common pattern for service operations. This pattern is familiar to anyone who has programmed in a procedural or object-oriented language. The request-response pattern is the prototypical local procedure call and is also quite common for remote procedure calls. Figure 2.3 shows a request-response interaction, where a proxy running within a client sends a request to a service and the service responds synchronously back to the client.

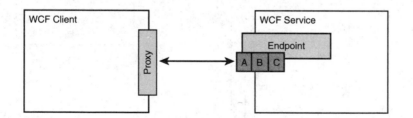

FIGURE 2.3 Synchronous request-response communication

WCF makes request-response communication between client and service very easy. At design time, you use Add Service Reference or svcutil.exe to call the service's Metadata Exchange (MEX) endpoint and generate a client-side proxy that mimics the signature of the service operations. This allows the client code to call methods on the proxy as local function calls. The proxy serializes the method name and parameters into a SOAP message, sends the SOAP message to the service, listens for a message to be sent back from the service, and then creates a .NET type representing the message response from the service.

Listing 2.1 shows a service contract definition. One service contract and one operation contract are defined in the code. The operation contract represents a method that can be called by a client or, more accurately, a message that can be sent by the client and understood by the service. Note that the contract is defined on the interface, not the class definition.

LISTING 2.1 Request-Response Service

```
using System;
using System.ServiceModel;

namespace EssentialWCF
{
    [ServiceContract]
    public interface IStockService
    {
        [OperationContract]
        double GetPrice(string ticker);
    }

    public class StockService : IStockService
    {
        public double GetPrice(string ticker)
        {
            return 94.85;
        }
    }
}
```

Listing 2.2 shows the client code, using a proxy generated by Add Service Reference that calls the service in Listing 2.1. This is similar to the code shown in Listing 1.2.

LISTING 2.2 Request-Response Client

```
using System;
using System.ServiceModel;

namespace Client
{
    class client
```

LISTING 2.2 continued

```
        {
            static void Main(string[] args)
            {
                localhost.StockServiceClient proxy =
                            new localhost.StockServiceClient();
                double price = proxy.GetPrice("msft");
                Console.WriteLine("msft:{0}", price);
                proxy.Close();
            }
        }
    }
```

Listing 2.3 shows the SOAP message that is sent from the client to the service endpoint. There are a few points worth noting:

- The namespace of the SOAP message is http://tempuri.org/, which is the default unless overridden in the [ServiceContract] attribute. If the service is going to be exposed outside an application or outside a relatively small organization, you should override the default because the namespace construct is designed to uniquely identify your service and eliminate ambiguity as multiple services are combined.

- The method name in the class definition in Listing 1.1, GetPrice is used to form the wsa:Action in the SOAP header. The full action value is a combination of the contract namespace, the contract name (interface name or the class name, if no explicit service interface is used), the operation name, and an additional string (Response) if the message is a correlated response.

- The SOAP body is controlled by the signature of the method and the qualifiers specified with the [OperationContract] and [DataContract] attributes.

- The SOAP header includes the address to which the message is sent. In this case, it's the SVC file hosted on the IIS machine.

LISTING 2.3 SOAP Message Sent in Request-Response Pattern

```
<s:Envelope xmlns:s="http://schemas.xmlsoap.org/soap/envelope/">
<s:Header>
  <To s:mustUnderstand="1"
    xmlns="http://schemas.microsoft.com/ws/2005/05/addressing/none">
    http://localhost/RequestResponseService/StockService.svc
  </To>
    <Action s:mustUnderstand="1"
      xmlns="http://schemas.microsoft.com/ws/2005/05/addressing/none">
      http://tempuri.org/StockService/GetPrice
    </Action>
  </s:Header>
  <s:Body>
    <GetPrice xmlns="http://tempuri.org/">
      <ticker>msft</ticker>
    </GetPrice>
  </s:Body>
</s:Envelope>
```

Asynchronous Request-Response Operations

Good design minimizes situations in which the user must wait for one task to complete before initiating the next task. For instance, when an e-mail client is downloading new messages, you can still read or delete messages already downloaded. Or while a Web browser is downloading images referenced on a Web page, you can still scroll the page or navigate elsewhere. This form of multitasking within the client program is accomplished through an asynchronous design pattern.

In WCF, request-response service operations cause the client to block while the service operation is executing. One level deeper, the proxy code generated by svcutil.exe uses a blocking call to the WCF channel stack responsible for communicating with the service. This forces the client application to block for the duration of the service call. If a service takes ten seconds to complete, the client application will freeze for the duration of the call waiting for the response.

Fortunately, you can use the asynchronous programming pattern in the .NET Framework to introduce asynchronous behavior on the client. This pattern, introduced in .NET 1.0, enables a caller of any synchronous

method to call it asynchronously. It accomplishes this by introducing the
IAsyncResult class and by creating two methods, Begin*OperationName* and
End*OperationName*. The client first calls Begin*OperationName* and then can
continue executing code on its current thread while the asynchronous operation executes a different thread. For each call to Begin*OperationName*, the
client later calls End*OperationName* to get the results of the operation. The
client passes a delegate to the Begin*OperationName,* which is called when
the asynchronous operation is called and can store state information from
the Begin*OperationName* call.

You can direct Add Service Reference to generate asynchronous
methods. This is done by clicking the Advanced button in the Add Service
Reference dialog box and selecting the Generate Asynchronous Operations
check box. The Service Reference Settings dialog is shown in Figure 2.4.
Alternatively, the SvcUtil utility with the /async switch uses this pattern to
create a Begin<operation> and End<operation> method for each service
operation, in addition to the synchronous method.

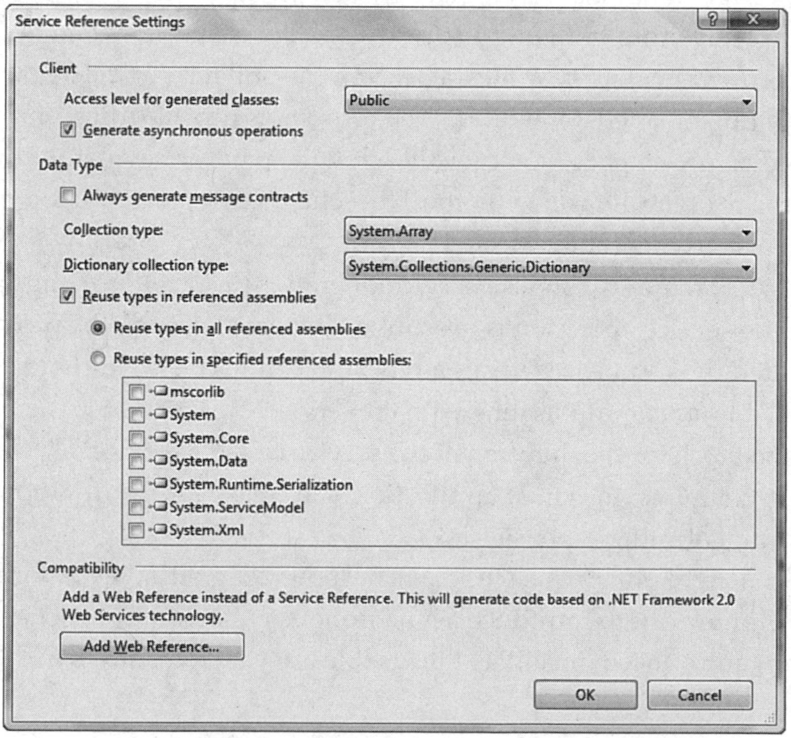

FIGURE 2.4 Specifying asynchronous methods in Add Service Reference

Figure 2.5 shows the .NET Framework asynchronous pattern in use with a proxy generated by SvcUtil. Note that the service doesn't know that the client is using asynchronous programming; the contract for the service just specifies request-response communication while the client implements the asynchronous pattern without participation from the service.

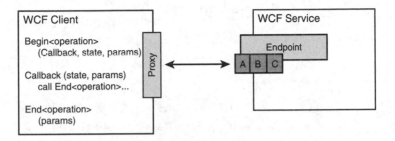

FIGURE 2.5 Asynchronous request-response communication

Listing 2.4 demonstrates using the BeginGetPrice and EndGetPrice along with the IAsyncResult to maintain status of the service operation. BeginGetPrice takes two parameters in addition to the string that is defined as input for the service operation. The first argument, the AsyncCallback routine, is a local method that accepts one parameter, AsyncResult. The second argument can be any object and is used to communicate state from the initiating routine to the AsyncCallback routine. It is passed as the AsyncResult.AsyncState property to AsyncCallback when the service operation completes. It's helpful to pass the proxy that initiated the service communication so EndGetPrice can be called from within the AsyncCallback to get the service operation response. The static variable, c, is used to prevent the client from exiting before the service completes, and the Interlocked class is used to ensure proper thread safety on multiprocessor machines.

LISTING 2.4 Request-Response Client Using .NET Async Pattern

```
using System;
using System.Threading;

namespace AW.EssentialWCF.Samples
{
  class Program
  {
    static int c = 0;
```

LISTING 2.4 continued

```
      static void Main(string[] args)
      {
        StockServiceClient proxy = new StockServiceClient();
        IAsyncResult arGetPrice;
        for (int i = 0; i < 10; i++)
        {
          arGetPrice = proxy.BeginGetPrice("msft",
                                          GetPriceCallback, proxy);
          Interlocked.Increment(ref c);
        }

        while (c > 0)
        {
          Thread.Sleep(1000);
          Console.WriteLine("Waiting... Calls outstanding:{0}", c);
        }
        proxy.Close();
        Console.WriteLine("Done!");
      }

      // Asynchronous callbacks for displaying results.
      static void GetPriceCallback(IAsyncResult ar)
      {
        double d = ((StockServiceClient)ar.AsyncState).EndGetPrice(ar);
        Interlocked.Decrement(ref c);
      }
    }
  }
```

One-Way Operations

The one-way message exchange pattern is useful when a client needs to send information to a service but doesn't receive a response. With this pattern, the client just needs acknowledgement of successful delivery; it does not need an actual response from the service. Sometimes the one-way pattern is erroneously called "fire-and-forget." In reality, it's "fire and acknowledge" because the caller receives an acknowledgement that the message was successfully committed to the communication channel.

WCF supports the one-way message exchange pattern at the service operation level. That is, service operations can be marked as one-way and the infrastructure will optimize for that case. When a client calls a one-way method on the service, or more accurately, when a client sends a message to a service endpoint whose operation is marked as one-way, control is returned to the caller before the service operation completes. One-way operations are specified on the [OperationContract] attribute by using the IsOneWay=true modifier. Listing 2.5 exposes a service contract with two service operations. The implementation of both is the same, but one is marked as a one-way operation. When a client application calls DoBigAnalysisFast, the client-side proxy call returns immediately and doesn't wait the ten seconds while the service is in the Thread.Sleep statement. When the client calls DoBigAnalysisSlow, the client-side proxy call blocks for ten seconds while the service executes the Thread.Sleep statement.

Note that as with other message patterns, the code does not know about the binding or communication protocol being used to deliver the message. Just because netTcpBinding supports bidirectional communication and basicHttpBinding supports request response, either could be used to support the one-way pattern.

LISTING 2.5 One-Way Operation Contract

```
[ServiceContract]
public interface IStockService
{
    [OperationContract(IsOneWay = true)]
    void DoBigAnalysisFast(string ticker);

    [OperationContract]
    void DoBigAnalysisSlow(string ticker);
}

public class StockService : IStockService
{
    public void DoBigAnalysisFast(string ticker)
    {
            Thread.Sleep(10000);
    }
    public void DoBigAnalysisSlow(string ticker)
    {
            Thread.Sleep(10000);
    }
}
```

Duplex Operations

Request-response communication is the most prevalent message-exchange pattern between a client and the service. Communication is initiated on the client, the client sends a request message to the service, and then the service sends a response message back to the client. If the response is expected quickly, this can be implemented synchronously, so the client application blocks waiting for the response. If a delay is expected between the request and the response, a request-response pattern can be implemented asynchronously on the client using standard .NET techniques. In that case, WCF returns control to the client application immediately after sending the request to the service. When the response is received from the service, a .NET callback routine is called to complete the WCF reply.

However, what if the service needs to initiate a message, such as a notification or an alert? What if the client and service need to correlate information at a level higher than the individual message, where numerous requests sent from the client are correlated to one response sent by the service? What if a request is expected to take ten minutes to complete?

WCF enables bidirectional communication through *duplex* service contracts. A duplex service contract implements the duplex message pattern, in which unsolicited messages can be sent in either direction after the communication channel is established. Operations over a duplex channel can be request-reply or one-way.

Because messages can flow in either direction, from client to service or service to client, both parties need an address, binding, and contract defining where, how, and what messages can be sent. To facilitate messages flowing back from the service to the client, WCF may create an additional channel. If the initial channel cannot support bidirectional communication, then WCF creates a second channel, using the same protocol as was specified by the service's endpoint, making the protocols symmetrical in both directions. This is illustrated in Figure 2.6.

Depending on the binding used when establishing the session from the client to the service, WCF will create one or two channels to implement the duplex message pattern. For protocols that support bidirectional communication, such as named pipes and TCP, only one channel is required. For those that don't support bidirectional communication, such as http, WCF creates an additional channel for communication from the service back to the client. Of the preconfigured WCF bindings, those with *dual* in the name (for example, *wsDualHttpBinding*) implement two channels. Custom bindings, which are combinations of channel elements that meet a specific need, can also implement this dual channel pattern by specifying *compositeDuplex* in the channel stack. Custom bindings are covered in detail in Chapter 4, "Bindings."

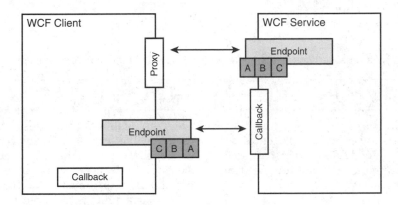

FIGURE 2.6 Duplex communication

When sending messages from the client to the service, the client uses the address specified in the service's endpoint. Conversely, when sending messages from the service back to the client over a composite duplex channel, the service must also know the client's endpoint address. The address of the client-hosted, WCF-generated endpoint is generated by the WCF channel. This address, which is the network location to which messages are sent from the service back to the client, can be overridden by setting the client-BaseAddress attribute of the compositeDuplex element of the binding.

Paired One-Way Versus Duplex Contracts

You can solve the problem of two-way messaging with two distinct message exchange patterns. You could either use a pair of one-way contracts or you could use a single duplex contract. With a pair of one-way contracts, both the client and service are independent WCF hosts. They each expose endpoints to which the other sends messages. Because they are full-fledged services, they can expose multiple endpoints, use multiple bindings, and version their contracts independently. With a duplex contract, the client does not explicitly become a WCF service and does have the complexity (and freedom) to choose bindings or expose other endpoints. Rather, the address, binding, and contract that defines the client-side endpoint are implemented by the channel factory when the duplex communication is initiated by the client.

A comparison of two one-way contracts versus a single duplex contract is shown in Table 2.2.

TABLE 2.2 Paired One-Way Versus Duplex Contracts for Bidirectional Communication

Paired One-Way Contracts	Duplex Contract
Contracts can be versioned independently. Because the client is a full-fledged service, it can expose and version contracts independent of the service	Client-side callback contract is determined by the service. If the service versions its contract, this might require a change on the client. This suggests that the only consumer of the client's callback capability is the service that defines it.
Each one-way contract defines its binding, so you can use a different protocol, encoding, or encryption in each direction.	The communication protocol will be the same in both directions because it is defined by the service's binding.

Implementing the Server Portion of a Duplex Service Contract

A duplex contract contains the interface specifications for both the service and the client endpoints. In this type of contract, portions of the service-side contract are implemented on the client.

Listing 2.6 defines a service contract for a service that provides stock price updates. It uses duplex communication so that a client can register for updates, and the service will periodically send updates to the client. The client initiates communication by calling the service's RegisterForUpdates operation. The service then creates a thread that will periodically send updates to that client by calling the client's PriceUpdate operation.

LISTING 2.6 Duplex Service Contract: Server-Side Implementation

```
[ServiceContract(CallbackContract = typeof(IClientCallback))]
public interface IServerStock
{
    [OperationContract (IsOneWay=true)]
    void RegisterForUpdates(string ticker);
}


public interface IClientCallback
{
    [OperationContract(IsOneWay = true)]
    void PriceUpdate(string ticker, double price);
}


public class ServerStock : IServerStock
{
    // This is NOT a good notification algorithm as it's creating
    // one thread per client.  It should be inverted so it's creating
    // one thread per ticker instead.
    public void RegisterForUpdates(string ticker)
    {
        Update bgWorker = new Update();
        bgWorker.callback =
            OperationContext.Current.
                            GetCallbackChannel<IClientCallback>();
        Thread t = new
            Thread(new ThreadStart(bgWorker.SendUpdateToClient));
        t.IsBackground = true;
        t.Start();
    }
}


public class Update
{
    public IClientCallback callback = null;
    public void SendUpdateToClient()
    {
        Random p = new Random();
        for (int i=0;i<10;i++)
        {
            Thread.Sleep(5000); // updates occurs somewhere
            try
            {
                callback.PriceUpdate("msft", 100.00+p.NextDouble());
            }
```

LISTING 2.6 continued

```
            catch (Exception ex)
            {
                Console.WriteLine("Error sending cache to client: {0}",
                                 ex.Message);
            }
        }
    }
}
```

And for completeness, the associated configuration file is shown in Listing 2.7. Note the dual binding that is used.

LISTING 2.7 Duplex Service Contract: Server-Side Configuration

```xml
<?xml version="1.0" encoding="utf-8" ?>
<configuration>
  <system.serviceModel>
    <services>
      <service behaviorConfiguration="MEXServiceTypeBehavior"
               name="EssentialWCF.StockService">
        <endpoint address="" binding="wsDualHttpBinding"
               contract="EssentialWCF.IStockService" />
        <endpoint address="mex" binding="mexHttpBinding"
               contract="IMetadataExchange" />
      </service>
    </services>
    <behaviors>
      <serviceBehaviors>
        <behavior name="MEXServiceTypeBehavior" >
          <serviceMetadata httpGetEnabled="true" />
        </behavior>
      </serviceBehaviors>
    </behaviors>
  </system.serviceModel>
</configuration>
```

One problem with the code in Listing 2.6 is that it creates one thread per client. For this scenario, there's an unpredictable number of clients (could be millions), but there's a finite number of stock tickers (thousands). Therefore, it would be better to create a thread per stock ticker rather than per client.

Listing 2.8 shows an alternative algorithm. In this example, a hashtable is maintained to track the stock tickers for which clients requested updates. Update class is stored in the hashtable and each Update class runs on its own thread. The list of client callbacks is stored in thread local storage in the Update class, so the Update class can notify all clients about a particular stock ticker. Notice that a lock is placed when accessing the client list collection, both from the RegisterForUpates method of the main StockService class and in the Update class itself. This is necessary so the collection isn't updated by the StockService class as it's being iterated by the Update class.

LISTING 2.8 Duplex Service Contract: Server-Side Implementation
(Better Thread Utilization)

```
public class StockService : IStockService
{
    public class Worker
    {
        public string ticker;
        public Update workerProcess;
    }
    public static Hashtable workers = new Hashtable();

    public void RegisterForUpdates(string ticker)
    {
        Worker w = null;

        // if needed, create a new worker, add it to the hashtable
        // and start it on a new thread
        if (!workers.ContainsKey(ticker))
        {
            w = new Worker();
            w.ticker = ticker;
            w.workerProcess = new Update();
            w.workerProcess.ticker = ticker;
            workers[ticker] = w;

            Thread t = new Thread(new
                        ThreadStart(w.workerProcess.SendUpdateToClient));
            t.IsBackground = true;
            t.Start();
        }

        // get the worker for this ticker and
        // add the client proxy to its list of callbacks
        w = (Worker)workers[ticker];
        IClientCallback c =
                    OperationContext.Current.
                        GetCallbackChannel<IClientCallback>();
        lock (w.workerProcess.callbacks)
```

LISTING 2.8 continued

```
                        w.workerProcess.callbacks.Add(c);
        }
    }

    public class Update
    {
        public string ticker;
        public List<IClientCallback> callbacks =
                                new List<IClientCallback>();
        public void SendUpdateToClient()
        {
            Random w = new Random();
            Random p = new Random();
            while(true)
            {
              Thread.Sleep(w.Next(5000)); // assume updates from somewhere
              lock (callbacks)
                    foreach (IClientCallback c in callbacks)
                    try
                    {
                        c.PriceUpdate(ticker, 100.00+p.NextDouble()*10);
                    }
                    catch (Exception ex)
                    {
                        Console.WriteLine("Error sending cache to client: {0}",
                                        ex.Message);
                    }
            }
        }
    }
}
```

With either the thread-per-client implementation shown in Listing 2.7 or the thread-per-ticker implementation shown in Listing 2.8, there are still reliability questions. For instance, if service cannot call the client callback operation, it logs a message to the console, but it never retries. Should the service retry, and if so, how often, and when should it stop? Or, if there is a scheduled window during which the client knows it won't be available to receive updates, where can the updates be queued so that they are delivered at a later time? These are important issues that are resolved by using a message broker such as Microsoft BizTalk Server or similar product. Message brokers typically have durable storage (database, file system, or message queue) at the heart of the system and include robust configuration tools for specifying transports and retry protocols. But they also bear overhead in terms of performance, complexity, and cost, so the solution will vary depending on requirements.

Implementing the Client Portion of a Duplex Contract

To participate in a duplex message exchange pattern, the client must implement the ABCs of WCF—it must define an address on the client where the service sends messages, a binding that directs how the service sends messages to the client, and a contract that defines exactly what the messages look like. Fortunately, this is largely taken care of when you generate a client-side proxy and by the channel infrastructure at runtime.

To generate the client-side proxy, use can use svcutil.exe or Add Service Reference. The proxy defines an interface with the same name as the service, with Callback appended to the end. If the service contract interface is IStockService, the client interface is IStockServiceCallback. The client must implement a class derived from this interface.

At runtime, just like the service, the client is accessed strictly through the endpoint definition and by sending messages to it. The major difference between the service-side endpoint and the client-side endpoint is that the client-side endpoint is created dynamically by WCF. There is no configuration file or explicit ServiceHost call in the client code. Again, WCF takes care of this, so the client just needs to implement a class derived from the generated interface.

Listing 2.9 shows a client that calls the RegisterForUpdates method of the StockService service to request periodic updates. It also implements a callback interface, PriceUpdate, as required by the service, with stock price updates. Notice that an InstanceContext object is instantiated and used to create the proxy. The InstanceContext object stores context information for a service, such as references to incoming and outgoing channels created on the client's behalf.

LISTING 2.9 Duplex Service Contract Implemented in a Client

```
using System;
using System.ServiceModel;

namespace Client
{
```

LISTING 2.9 continued

```
public class CallbackHandler : IServerStockCallback
{
    static InstanceContext site =
                    new InstanceContext(new CallbackHandler());
    static ServerStockClient proxy = new ServerStockClient (site);

    public void PriceUpdate(string ticker, double price)
    {
        Console.WriteLine("Received alert at : {0}. {1}:{2}",
                            System.DateTime.Now, ticker, price);
    }

    class Program
    {
        static void Main(string[] args)
        {
            proxy.RegisterForUpdates("MSFT");

            Console.WriteLine("Press Enter or any key to exit");
            Console.ReadLine();
        }
    }
}
```

Multiple Contracts and Endpoints in a Service

A service is defined as a collection of endpoints. Each endpoint has an address, binding, and contract. The contract is what exposes the endpoint capabilities. The address is simply where those application (or service) capabilities live on the network, and the binding is how to access them.

There is a one:many relationship between endpoints and contracts. An endpoint can have only one contract, but a contract can be referenced by many endpoints. And although an endpoint can specify only one contract, interface aggregation enables a single contract to expose multiple interfaces. In addition, multiple endpoints with the same binding but different contracts can be located at the same address, giving the illusion that a single endpoint implements both contracts.

By exposing a contract through multiple endpoints in a service, you can make it available through multiple bindings. You can define one endpoint that exposes a contract using the WS-I Basic Profile binding for maximum reach while exposing it through another endpoint that uses TCP protocol and binary encoding for much faster performance. By aggregating multiple interfaces into one, you can provide consolidated access to capabilities initially codified into separate interfaces in a single service.

Listing 2.10 shows two service contracts, IGoodStockService and IGreatStockService, that are aggregated into a third service contract, IStockServices. The methods defined in those interfaces are implemented in the aggregate. Although the service interfaces can be inherited, the [ServiceContract] attribute must be defined to expose each interface.

LISTING 2.10 Exposing Multiple Contracts in an Endpoint

```
namespace EssentialWCF
{
    [ServiceContract]
    public interface IGoodStockService
    {
        [OperationContract]
        double GetStockPrice(string ticker);
    }
    [ServiceContract]
    public interface IGreatStockService
    {
        [OperationContract]
        double GetStockPriceFast(string ticker);
    }

    [ServiceContract]
    public interface IAllStockServices :
                    IGoodStockService, IGreatStockService { };

    public class AllStockServices : IAllStockServices
    {
        public double GetStockPrice(string ticker)
        {
            Thread.Sleep(5000);
            return 94.85;
        }
        public double GetStockPriceFast(string ticker)
        {
            return 94.85;
        }
    }
}
```

Listing 2.11 shows a configuration file that exposes multiple endpoints for the three contracts. There is one endpoint for the IGoodStockService contract, two endpoints for the IGreatStockService contract, and one endpoint for the IAllStockServices contract.

Because there are multiple endpoints using the binding that shares an addressing scheme, a different address must be specified for each endpoint. Relative addresses are used, so the full address of each endpoint is the services-based address plus the relative qualifier.

LISTING 2.11 Exposing Multiple Endpoints in a Service

```xml
<?xml version="1.0" encoding="utf-8" ?>
<configuration>

  <system.serviceModel>

    <services>
      <service name="EssentialWCF.StockServices"
                    behaviorConfiguration="mexServiceBehavior">
        <host>
          <baseAddresses>
            <add baseAddress="http://localhost:8000/EssentialWCF/"/>
          </baseAddresses>
        </host>
        <endpoint name="GoodStockService"
                  binding="basicHttpBinding"
                  contract="EssentialWCF.IGoodStockService" />
        <endpoint name="BetterStockService"
                  address="better"
                  binding="basicHttpBinding"
                  contract="EssentialWCF.IGreatStockService" />
        <endpoint name="BestStockService"
                  address="best"
                  binding="wsHttpBinding"
                  contract="EssentialWCF.IGreatStockService" />
        <endpoint name="AllStockServices"
                  address="all"
                  binding="wsHttpBinding"
                  contract="EssentialWCF.IAllStockServices" />
        <endpoint address="mex"
                  binding="mexHttpBinding"
                  contract="IMetadataExchange" />
      </service>
    </services>
```

```
    <behaviors>
      <serviceBehaviors>
        <behavior name="mexServiceBehavior">
          <serviceMetadata httpGetEnabled="True"/>
        </behavior>
      </serviceBehaviors>
    </behaviors>

  </system.serviceModel>
</configuration>
```

Because the IGreatStockService contract is exposed at multiple endpoints, client applications must reference the endpoint by name when creating a proxy instance to that contract. If the endpoint name wasn't specified, WCF would throw an error because it couldn't know which endpoint to use. Listing 2.12 shows the use of the GreatStockServiceClient proxy two times: first to access the BetterStockService using basicHttpBinding and second to access BestStockService using wsHttpBinding.

LISTING 2.12 Specifying Endpoints by Name When Multiples Are Defined

```
using (localhost.GreatStockServiceClient proxy = new
        Client.localhost.GreatStockServiceClient
                                 ("BetterStockService"))
{
    Console.WriteLine(proxy.GetStockPriceFast("MSFT"));
}
using (localhost.GreatStockServiceClient proxy = new
        Client.localhost.GreatStockServiceClient
                                 ("BestStockService"))
{
    Console.WriteLine(proxy.GetStockPriceFast("MSFT"));
}
```

Names of Operations, Types, Actions, and Namespaces in WSDL

WCF generates the externally exposed service artifacts based on the internally named classes and attributes defined in the source code of the service. These artifacts are exposed through the MEX endpoint of the service and typically consumed as WSDL by a client at design time. On the client side, the WSDL is then used to write code that builds the proper message format through which it communicates with the service. So the names you choose for classes, methods, and parameters can potentially have a life far beyond the service boundary.

However, it's generally bad form to expose internal names and details externally at the service interface. For instance, you may have an allocation algorithm called BurgerMaster that you'd like to expose externally as an operation called Resources. Or there may be coding standards in place that dictate how you should name interfaces. Fortunately, you can control all names exposed from the service by modifying the [ServiceContract], [OperationContract], and [ServiceBehavior] attributes. Table 2.3 lists how to control the WSDL terms with WCF attributes in code.

TABLE 2.3 WCF Attributes That Override Default WSDL Names

WSDL Term	WCF Attribute
targetNamespace	Defaults to http://tempuri.org. Can be changed by using [ServiceBehavior] attribute in code.
wsdl:service and wsdl:definitions	[ServiceBehavior(Name="myServiceName")]
wsdl:porttype	[ServiceContract(Name="myContractName")]
wsdl:operation and soap:operation	[OperationContract(Name="myOperationName")]
xs:element	[MessageParameter(Name = "myParamName")]
wsdl:input and wsdl:output	[OperationContract(Action=" myOperationAction", ReplyAction="myOperationReplyAction")]
wsdl:Binding	Use and Style attributes of [DataContract] and [ServiceContract]

The service defined in Listing 2.13 uses WCF attributes to override the default names generated by WCF.

LISTING 2.13 Service Definition Controlling WSDL Names

```
[ServiceBehavior (Namespace="http://MyService/")]
[ServiceContract
            (Name="MyServiceName",
             Namespace="http://ServiceNamespace")]
public class BurgerMaster
{
    [return: MessageParameter(Name = "myOutput")]
    [OperationContract
            (Name="OperationName",
             Action="OperationAction",
             ReplyAction="ReplyActionName")]

    public double GetStockPrice(string ticker)
    {
        return 100.00;
    }
}
```

The `svcutil.exe` utility with the `-t:metadata` switch can be used to generate WSDL from a service. Alternatively, if the service exposes a MEX endpoint over an http binding, the WSDL can be viewed by accessing the base address from Internet Explorer. The format of the WSDL will vary slightly whether you use `svcutil.exe` or Internet Explorer to view it, but the differences are insignificant and just relating to packaging. In either case, Listing 2.14 shows the WSDL associated with the code listed in Listing 2.13. The `wsdl:portType`, `wsdl:operation` and `wsdl:action` names are controlled by the code. Note that the `wsdl:portType` name is `MyServiceName` and not `BurgerMaster`, as the class is named in Listing 2.13.

LISTING 2.14 WSDL Listing by Controlling Names

```
<?xml version="1.0" encoding="utf-8"?>
<wsdl:definitions
  xmlns:soap="http://schemas.xmlsoap.org/wsdl/soap/"
  xmlns:xsd="http://www.w3.org/2001/XMLSchema"
  xmlns:tns="http://ServiceNamespace"
  targetNamespace="http://ServiceNamespace"
  .
  .
  .
```

LISTING 2.14 continued

```
      xmlns:wsdl="http://schemas.xmlsoap.org/wsdl/">
      <wsdl:types>
        <xsd:schema targetNamespace="http://ServiceNamespace/Imports">
          <xsd:import
              schemaLocation=
                      "http://localhost:8000/EssentialWCF/?xsd=xsd0"
              namespace="http://ServiceNamespace" />
          <xsd:import
              schemaLocation=
                      "http://localhost:8000/EssentialWCF/?xsd=xsd1"
               namespace="http://schemas.microsoft.com/
                               2003/10/Serialization/"/>
        </xsd:schema>
      </wsdl:types>

      <wsdl:message name="MyServiceName_OperationName_InputMessage">
        <wsdl:part name="parameters" element="tns:OperationName" />
      </wsdl:message>
      <wsdl:message name="MyServiceName_OperationName_OutputMessage">
        <wsdl:part name="parameters" element="tns:OperationNameResponse" />
      </wsdl:message>
      <wsdl:portType name="MyServiceName">
        <wsdl:operation name="OperationName">
          <wsdl:input wsaw:Action="OperationAction"
              message="tns:MyServiceName_OperationName_InputMessage" />
          <wsdl:output wsaw:Action="ReplyActionName"
              message="tns:MyServiceName_OperationName_OutputMessage" />
        </wsdl:operation>
      </wsdl:portType>
    </wsdl:definitions>
```

Data Contracts

Inside a service, functional application capabilities are implemented in code. Outside a service, functional capabilities are defined in WSDL. Inside a WCF service, application data is represented in simple and complex types while outside the service data is represented by XML Schema Definitions (XSD). WCF data contracts provide a mapping function between .NET CLR types that are defined in code and XML Schemas Definitions defined by the W3C organization (www.w3c.org/) that are used for communication outside the service.

Using WCF, developers spend more time with code and interface semantics and less time with XSD and WSDL syntax. That's not to say that XSD and WSDL syntax aren't important; they are crucial elements in building interoperable systems across heterogeneous platforms. But it turns out that compilers are good at translating data structures written in a .NET language into their XSD and WSDL representation required for cross-platform interoperability.

At design time, the [DataContract] attribute is used to indicate which classes should be represented as an XSD and included in the WSDL exposed by the service. The [DataMember] attribute further defines the XSD by indicating which class members should be included in the external representation. At runtime, the DataContractSerializer class serializes objects to XML using the rules described by the [DataContract] and [DataMember] attributes. Figure 2.7 shows the classes, which are native to a .NET implementation represented as XML Schema, which is interoperable with other systems.

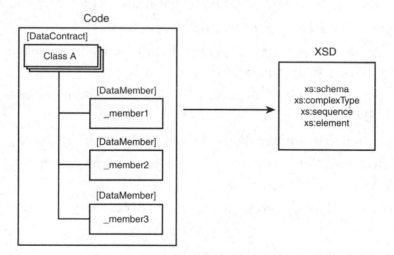

Figure 2.7 High-level translation of code artifacts to XSD

Figure 2.8 shows the same translation depicted in Figure 2.7, but shows also syntax of the C# and XSD elements for clarity.

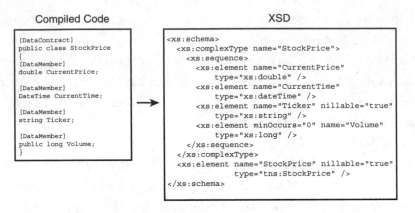

FIGURE 2.8 High-level translation of code syntax to XSD

The `DataContractSerializer` will serialize types and expose them in WSDL contracts if they meet any of the following conditions:

- Types marked with the `[DataContract]` and `[DataMember]` attributes
- Types attributed with `[CollectionDataContract]`
- Types derived from `IXmlSerializable`
- Types marked with `[Serializable]` attribute whose members are not marked with `[NonSerialized]`
- Types marked with `[Serializable]` attribute and implements `ISerializable`
- CLR built-in primitive types, such as int32 and string
- Bytes array, DateTime, TimeSpan, Guid, Uri, XmlQualifiedName, XmlElement, and XmlNode
- Arrays and collections such as `List<T>`, `Dictionary<K,V>` and `Hashtable`
- Enumerations

Defining XML Schema for a .NET Class

The `[DataContract]` attribute, defined in `System.Runtime.Serialization`, indicates that a class should be exposed as an XSD in the WSDL that represents the service. If a class doesn't have the `[DataContract]` attribute, it will not be present in the WSDL. By default, the name of the XML Schema is the same as the name of the class and the target namespace of the schema is `http://schemas.datacontract.org/2004/07/` concatenated with the .NET namespace of the class. Both of these can be overridden. You may want to override them to control the names exposed outside the service. For instance, an internal class name of `reqOrderIn` can be exposed as `Order` in the XSD. Listing 2.16 shows how to override the name and namespace of an XSD.

The `[DataMember]` attribute, also defined in `System.Runtime.Serialization`, identifies members of the .NET class marked with the `[DataContract]` attribute to include in the XML Schema. If a class member is not attributed with `[DataMember]`, it is not included in the XML Schema, even though it's a member of the class. By default, class members are not contained in the XML Schema Definition, which makes this strictly an opt-in model. The scoping of .NET class members, whether it's public or private, does not impact its inclusion in the XML Schema; that decision is strictly made based on the presence of the `[DataMember]` attribute.

Listing 2.15 demonstrates a class definition, `StockPrice`, with five public data members. Three of them, `ticker`, `theCurrentPrice`, and `theCurrentTime`, are required because they are marked with `isRequired=true`. A few additional features of `[DataMember]` are also shown:

- The names of class members are all prefixed with m_ in the code. The class member names are overridden so that m_ notation is not carried into the XSD defined in the service interface.

- The order of class members is specified in the `[DataMember]` attribute. If the order isn't specified, the elements would appear in alphabetical order in the XSD. Order is typically not important, but controlling it is necessary for interoperability. If you're sending messages to a service that expects elements ordered in a particular way, this attribute can control the order of the elements encoded in the text XML.

- The class members `m_CurrentPrice`, `m_CurentType` and `m_ticker` are marked as required, but `m_dailyVolume` and `m_dailyChange` are not. Nonrequired class members can be absent from XML instances and still are considered valid according to the XSD.

LISTING 2.15 Defining a Data Contract

```csharp
using System;
using System.ServiceModel;
using System.Runtime.Serialization;

namespace EssentialWCF
{
    [DataContract (Namespace="http://EssentialWCF",Name="StockPrice")]
    public class clsStockPrice
    {
        [DataMember (Name="CurrentPrice",Order=0,IsRequired=true)]
        public double theCurrentPriceNow;

        [DataMember(Name = "CurrentTime", Order=1, IsRequired = true)]
        public DateTime theCurrentTimeNow;

        [DataMember(Name = "Ticker", Order=2, IsRequired = true)]
        public string theTickerSymbol;

        [DataMember(Name = "DailyVolume", Order=3, IsRequired = false)]
        public long theDailyVolumeSoFar;

        [DataMember(Name = "DailyChange", Order=4, IsRequired = false)]
        public double theDailyChangeSoFar;
    }

    [ServiceContract]
    public class StockService
    {
        [OperationContract]
        private clsStockPrice GetPrice(string ticker)
        {
            clsStockPrice s = new clsStockPrice();
            s.theTickerSymbol = ticker;
            s.theCurrentPriceNow = 100.00;
            s.theCurrentTimeNow = System.DateTime.Now;
            s.theDailyVolumeSoFar = 450000;
            s.theDailyChangeSoFar = .012345;
            return s;
        }
    }
}
```

The svcutil.exe -t:metadata command generates the XSD using the [DataMember] elements defined by a class. Listing 2.16 shows the XSD generated by the code shown in Listing 2.15. Notice that the element names and order are defined according to the attributes in code. Also note that the non-required class members are indicated as minOccurs=0 in the XML Schema.

LISTING 2.16 Generated XSD Representing a Data Contract

```
<?xml version="1.0" encoding="utf-8"?>
<xs:schema xmlns:tns="http://EssentialWCF" elementFormDefault="qualified"
targetNamespace="http://EssentialWCF"
xmlns:xs="http://www.w3.org/2001/XMLSchema">
  <xs:complexType name="StockPrice">
    <xs:sequence>
      <xs:element name="CurrentPrice" type="xs:double" />
      <xs:element name="CurrentTime" type="xs:dateTime" />
      <xs:element name="Ticker" nillable="true" type="xs:string" />
      <xs:element minOccurs="0" name="DailyVolume" type="xs:long" />
      <xs:element minOccurs="0" name="DailyChange" type="xs:double" />
    </xs:sequence>
  </xs:complexType>
  <xs:element name="StockPrice" nillable="true" type="tns:StockPrice"/>
</xs:schema>
```

Defining Class Hierarchies

Complex types are typically implemented as classes in code. Complex classes are further defined through inheritance as a way of representing increasingly specific constructs. This way, a general type like 'price' can be subclassed to a more specific type like 'stock price' or 'house price'. WCF supports class hierarchies by representing them properly in WSDL, serializing and deserializing them between class structure and XML and by carrying the attributes of each class forward into the aggregate.

In Listing 2.17, the class Price is defined with three elements and a subclass, StockPrice, which inherits from Price. The namespace is provided with both classes so they can be resolved through fully qualified names in XML. Each element retains its namespace.

LISTING 2.17 Class Hierarchy Defined with Data Contract

```
[DataContract(Namespace = "http://EssentialWCF/Price/")]
public class Price
{
    [DataMember] public double CurrentPrice;
    [DataMember] public DateTime CurrentTime;
    [DataMember] public string Currency;
}

[DataContract(Namespace = "http://EssentialWCF/StockPrice")]
public class StockPrice : Price
{
```

LISTING 2.17 continued

```
        [DataMember] public string Ticker;
        [DataMember] public long DailyVolume;
        [DataMember] public double DailyChange;
    }
```

The two XML Schemas generated to support this hierarchy are shown in Listing 2.18. First, the `Price` XML Schema is shown. Then the `StockPrice` XML Schema is shown. Note that `StockPrice` imports the `Price` schema. Note that in the XSD, all elements are attributed with `minOccurs=0` because in the code, none were attributed with `[isRequired=true]`.

LISTING 2.18 Class Hierarchy Defined in XML Schemas

```
<?xml version="1.0" encoding="utf-8"?>
<xs:schema xmlns:tns="http://EssentialWCF/Price/"
                elementFormDefault="qualified"
                targetNamespace="http://EssentialWCF/Price/"
                xmlns:xs="http://www.w3.org/2001/XMLSchema">
  <xs:complexType name="Price">
    <xs:sequence>
      <xs:element minOccurs="0" name="Currency"
                    nillable="true" type="xs:string" />
      <xs:element minOccurs="0" name="CurrentPrice" type="xs:double" />
      <xs:element minOccurs="0" name="CurrentTime" type="xs:dateTime"/>
    </xs:sequence>
  </xs:complexType>
  <xs:element name="Price" nillable="true" type="tns:Price" />
</xs:schema>

<?xml version="1.0" encoding="utf-8"?>
<xs:schema xmlns:tns="http://EssentialWCF/StockPrice"
                elementFormDefault="qualified"
                targetNamespace="http://EssentialWCF/StockPrice"
                xmlns:xs="http://www.w3.org/2001/XMLSchema">
  <xs:import namespace="http://EssentialWCF/Price/" />
  <xs:complexType name="StockPrice">
    <xs:complexContent mixed="false">
      <xs:extension xmlns:q1="http://EssentialWCF/Price/"
                        base="q1:Price">
        <xs:sequence>
          <xs:element minOccurs="0" name="DailyChange"
                                    type="xs:double" />
          <xs:element minOccurs="0" name="DailyVolume"
                                    type="xs:long" />
          <xs:element minOccurs="0" name="Ticker"
                                    nillable="true" type="xs:string" />
```

```
          </xs:sequence>
        </xs:extension>
      </xs:complexContent>
    </xs:complexType>
    <xs:element name="StockPrice" nillable="true" type="tns:StockPrice"/>
  </xs:schema>
```

The SOAP body of a serialized `StockPrice` type is shown in Listing 2.19. Notice that the namespaces of `Price` and `StockPrice` are carried from the code in Listing 2.17 to the XML Schema in Listing 2.18 all the way through to the SOAP body.

LISTING 2.19 Class Hierarchy Serialized in SOAP body

```
<s:Body>
  <GetPriceResponse xmlns="http://EssentialWCF/FinanceService/">
    <GetPriceResult
            xmlns:a="http://EssentialWCF/StockPrice"
            xmlns:i="http://www.w3.org/2001/XMLSchema-instance">
      <Currency xmlns="http://EssentialWCF/Price/">Dollars</Currency>
      <CurrentPrice xmlns="http://EssentialWCF/Price/">
                  100</CurrentPrice>
      <CurrentTime xmlns="http://EssentialWCF/Price/">
                  2006-12-13T21:18:51.313-05:00</CurrentTime>
      <a:DailyChange>0.012345</a:DailyChange>
      <a:DailyVolume>450000</a:DailyVolume>
      <a:Ticker>msft</a:Ticker>
    </GetPriceResult>
  </GetPriceResponse>
</s:Body>
```

Exposing Additional Types in WSDL with KnownTypes

Data types are exposed in WSDL if they meet any of the conditions described earlier. There are additional cases, however, when you would also like to force a type to be included in the WSDL contract.

One example is class hierarchies. If a serialized derived class arrives at an endpoint that is expecting the serialized base class, WCF will not know how to deserialize the class because the derived class was not part of the contract. Another example is a `hashtable` class, which stores other classes as its element. The WSDL will define the `hashtable` class, but not the classes contained in the `hashtable`.

In these cases, you must tell WCF about the classes that should explicitly be included in the WSDL contract. This is done with KnownTypes. It can be done in four ways: by adding the KnownType attribute to a [DataContract], by the attribute in the [ServiceContract] or [OperationContract], by adding a reference to it and its assembly into the configuration, or by determining it when generating the WSDL.

Listing 2.20 shows a data contract that defines a base class, Price, and two classes derived from the base class, StockPrice and MetalPrice. Note the [KnownType] attribute on the data contract. This tells WCF to include the XSD representation of StockPrice and MetalPrice in the WSDL when exposing the contract. The listing also contains an implementation of the service. The GetPrice operation is polymorphic and returns either a StockPrice or MetalPrice type, depending on what was requested. The client code that calls GetPrice through the proxy must cast the result to the expected type to access the return value class.

LISTING 2.20 KnownType Defined in a Data Contract

```
using System;
using System.ServiceModel;
using System.Runtime.Serialization;

namespace EssentialWCF
{
    [DataContract(Namespace = "http://EssentialWCF/")]
    [KnownType(typeof(StockPrice))]
    [KnownType(typeof(MetalPrice))]
    public class Price
    {
        [DataMember] public double CurrentPrice;
        [DataMember] public DateTime CurrentTime;
        [DataMember] public string Currency;
    }

    [DataContract(Namespace = "http://EssentialWCF/")]
    public class StockPrice : Price
    {
        [DataMember] public string Ticker;
        [DataMember] public long DailyVolume;
    }
    [DataContract(Namespace = "http://EssentialWCF/")]
    public class MetalPrice : Price
    {
        [DataMember] public string Metal;
```

```
        [DataMember] public string Quality;
    }


[ServiceBehavior (Namespace="http://EssentialWCF/FinanceService/")]
[ServiceContract (Namespace="http://EssentialWCF/FinanceService/")]
public class StockService
{
    [OperationContract]
    private Price GetPrice(string id, string type)
    {
        if (type.Contains("Stock"))
        {
            StockPrice s = new StockPrice();
            s.Ticker = id;
            s.DailyVolume = 45000000;
            s.CurrentPrice = 94.15;
            s.CurrentTime = System.DateTime.Now;
            s.Currency = "USD";
            return s;
        }
        if (type.Contains("Metal"))
        {
            MetalPrice g = new MetalPrice();
            g.Metal = id;
            g.Quality = "0.999";
            g.CurrentPrice = 785.00;
            g.CurrentTime = System.DateTime.Now;
            g.Currency = "USD";
            return g;
        }
        return new Price();
    }
}
}
```

Alternatively, you can define the KnownType at the OperationContract level with the [ServiceKnownType] attribute. When KnownTypes are defined at the Operation level, the derived types can be used only in the operation that defines the known types. In other words, not all operations in a service can use the derived types. Listing 2.21 shows a snippet of code that uses a [ServiceKnownType] attribute. In this example, a client can call GetPrice and when the message is returned from the service, the deserializer will create a StockPrice or MetalPrice object. But the client can pass only a Price object, not a StockPrice or MetalPrice, when calling SetPrice, because the serializer will not know how to represent those derived types in XML.

LISTING 2.21 KnownType Defined in an Operation Contract

```
        .
        .
        .

    [ServiceBehavior (Namespace="http://EssentialWCF/FinanceService/")]
    [ServiceContract (Namespace="http://EssentialWCF/FinanceService/")]
    public class StockService
    {
        [ServiceKnownType(typeof(StockPrice))]
        [ServiceKnownType(typeof(MetalPrice))]
        [OperationContract]
        private Price GetPrice(string id, string type)
        {
            .
            .
            .
        }
        [OperationContract]
        Void SetPrice(Price p)
        {
            .
            .
            .
        }
```

The disadvantage of defining known types in code, whether at the data contract or service contract level, is that you need to know the universe of derived types at compile time. If a new type is added, you need to recompile the code. This can be resolved with two methods.

First, you can move the known type reference from code to configuration and include known type information in the system.runtime.serialization section of the service configuration file. Respecting the class hierarchy, you need to add a reference to the base class and then add knownType references to the derived classes. This is shown in Listing 2.22, where EssentialWCF.Price is the base class and EssentialWCF.StockPrice and EssentialWCF.MetalPrice are the derived classes. StockService is the DLL hosting these types.

LISTING 2.22 KnownType Defined in Configuration

```
<system.runtime.serialization>
  <dataContractSerializer>
    <declaredTypes>
      <add type="EssentialWCF.Price, StockService,
                 Version-1.0.0.0, Culture=neutral,
                 PublicKeyToken=null">
        <knownType type="EssentialWCF.StockPrice, StockService,
                 Version=1.0.0.0, Culture=neutral,
                 PublicKeyToken=null"/>
        <knownType type="EssentialWCF.MetalPrice, StockService,
                 Version=1.0.0.0, Culture=neutral,
                 PublicKeyToken=null"/>
      </add>
    </declaredTypes>
  </dataContractSerializer>
</system.runtime.serialization>
```

The most general solution for specifying the derived types in the contract is to generate it at runtime. This can be done thanks to some hooks exposed in WCF. The constructor of both the [KnownType] attribute and [ServiceKnownType] attribute accepts a string parameter. This string is a method name that is called at serialization or deserialization time to return a list of known types. If you use a metadata repository, you could look up type information from the repository or database and expose the types at runtime. Listing 2.23 shows a simpler implementation, where the type names are hardcoded in the GetKnownTypes method rather than being pulled from an external repository.

LISTING 2.23 KnownType Defined in Code at Runtime

```
[DataContract(Namespace = "http://EssentialWCF/")]
[KnownType("GetKnownTypes")]
public class Price
{
    [DataMember] public double CurrentPrice;
    [DataMember] public DateTime CurrentTime;
    [DataMember] public string Currency;
    static Type[] GetKnownTypes()
    {
        return new Type[] { typeof(StockPrice),
                            typeof(MetalPrice) };
    }
}
```

LISTING 2.23 continued

```
[DataContract(Namespace = "http://EssentialWCF/")]
public class StockPrice : Price
{
    [DataMember] public string Ticker;
    [DataMember] public long DailyVolume;
}
[DataContract(Namespace = "http://EssentialWCF/")]
public class MetalPrice : Price
{
    [DataMember] public string Metal;
    [DataMember] public string Quality;
}
```

Versioning Data Contracts

Change is inevitable. Businesses change, technologies change, laws change, and so do software contracts. In the face of software changes, a solid versioning strategy is essential. Care must be taken up front to plan for inevitable changes and to preserve backward compatibility with existing clients.

The most common need for data contract versioning is when members are added to an existing data contract. By following the nonbreaking changes described in this section, you can freely do this without breaking existing clients. But if you need to break backward compatibility with existing clients, you must version the entire data contract by changing its name or namespace.

A little caution is in order with respect to nonbreaking changes. Nonbreaking, from WCF's standpoint, could quite possibly break compatibility with other systems. For instance, if communicating with a system that requires strict schema validation, that system may reject messages if it receives XML instances with unexpected elements. The term "nonbreaking" change in this chapter refers to changes that can be made without impacting WCF to WCF communication.

Nonbreaking Changes

Two types of changes will not break compatibility with existing clients:

- Adding new nonrequired data members
- Removing existing nonrequired data members

In both of these cases, it's possible to create an old type from a new message by simply ignoring the new or missing nonrequired data members. Conversely, it's also possible to create a new message from the old type. The DataContractSerializer will do this automatically at runtime.

Breaking Changes

Although you can change certain attributes in a data contract that preserve backward compatibility, many item changes will break existing clients. If you make any of these changes to a data contract defined, existing clients will no longer function properly:

- Change the name or namespace of a data contract.
- Rename an existing data member that was previously required.
- Add a new data member with a name that has been used previously.
- Change the data type of an existing data member.
- Add new members with `IsRequired=true` on `DataMemberAttribute`.
- Remove existing members with `IsRequired=true` on `DataMemberAttribute`.

Listing 2.24 shows two data contract definitions: The first is defined in a V1 service, the second in the V2 version of that service. Notice that between V1 and V2, the data member `Currency` is removed and `DailyVolume` is added. This change is nonbreaking.

LISTING 2.24 Nonbreaking Change to a Data Contract—Adding and Removing Data
Members

```
[DataContract (Namespace="http://EssentialWCF")]
public class StockPrice //V1
{
    [DataMember] public double CurrentPrice;
    [DataMember] public DateTime CurrentTime;
    [DataMember] public string Ticker;
    [DataMember] public string Currency;
}

[DataContract (Namespace="http://EssentialWCF")]
public class StockPrice //V2
{
    [DataMember] public double CurrentPrice;
    [DataMember] public DateTime CurrentTime;
    [DataMember] public string Ticker;
    [DataMember] public int DailyVolume;
}
```

For existing clients to properly pass around data after new members are
added, the original data contract must support extensibility. That is, the original contract must support serialization of unknown future data. This enables
round tripping, where a client can pass V2 data to a V1 service and have the V1
service return V1 data back to the client with the V2 elements still intact. WCF
implements extensibility by default in the proxy code generated by
svcutil.exe. If you do not want to support this capability, it can be disabled
by specifying <dataContractSerializer   ignoreExtensionDataObject=
"true"/> in the ServiceBehavior section of the service configuration file.

Listing 2.25 shows client code that calls GetPrice to obtain a StockPrice
object and then passes that object to StoreStockPrice. Assume that the
proxy for the StockService was generated using svcutil.exe pointing to
the V1 service, and then the service was upgraded to V2 from Listing 2.24.
When the client runs against the V2 service, GetPrice will return XML with
the DailyVolume member added and the Currency member missing. The
data contract deserializer, who knows about V1 StockPrice object, will
place that DailyVolume member in the ExtensionData field of the object
and will not complain about the missing Currency member. The client code
will receive the expected StockPrice object, only to find it with Currency
initialized to its default value and the overall object being a bit "heavier."

This is because extra extension data (`DailyVolume`) is available in the class. This way, the service is passing valid V2 data and the client is consuming a valid V1 representation of that data.

LISTING 2.25 Calling a V2 Service with a V1 Contract

```
localhost.StockServiceClient proxy=new localhost.StockServiceClient())
localhost.StockPrice s = proxy.GetPrice("msft");
proxy.StoreStockPrice(s);
```

Data Contract Equivalence

If you're using WCF to expose a service and using `svcutil.exe` to build a proxy for accessing the service, you typically don't need to be concerned about the wire representation of the messages passed between client and service. Data contracts direct WCF to serialize a .NET type into an XML Infoset and to deserialize an XML Infoset back into a .NET type. The XML Infoset might be encoded as text or binary on the wire according to the binding used for communication, but again, the .NET code is unaware of the encoding. This way, you work with .NET types in code but an encoded representation of the standards-based XML Infoset is transmitted on the wire.

There are cases, however, where you may work with different types in the client versus in the service. This could occur if the client and service are developed by different organizations, or if only one side of the communication is using WCF. In fact, if you're not using `svcutil.exe` or Add Service Reference to generate the proxy on the client, there's a good chance that member names on the client will be different from member names on the service. But by controlling those names with the [`DataMember`] attribute, you can make them appear the same in the XML representation. As long as both the client and service work with an equivalent XML representation, it's okay for WCF to deserialize the XML Infoset into different .NET types. If two classes serialize into the same XML schema, the data contracts representing those classes are said to be equivalent. For data contracts to be equivalent, they must have the same namespace and name and members. The data members must be of the same type and appear in the same order within the XML. In summary, they must be indistinguishable on the wire.

Listing 2.26 shows two equivalent data contracts. The first contract is exposed by the service; the second class is described by the client. The two are equivalent and generate identical XML Schema Definitions. In the service, by default, WCF will order the XML elements alphabetically so the second schema forces the order to be alphabetical. Because of the Name="StockPriceSvc" and Name="Currency" attributes placed on the DataContract and DataMember respectively, the XSD generated in the second contract is identical to the first.

LISTING 2.26 Equivalent Data Contracts

```
[DataContract(Namespace = http://EssentialWCF)]
public partial class StockPriceSvc
{
    [DataMember] public double CurrentPrice;
    [DataMember] public DateTime CurrentTime;
    [DataMember] public string Ticker;
    [DataMember] public string Currency;
}


[DataContract(Namespace = http://EssentialWCF, Name="StockPriceSvc")]
public partial class StockPrice
{
    [DataMember(Order=4)] public string Ticker;
    [DataMember(Order=2)] public double CurrentPrice;
    [DataMember(Order=3)] public DateTime CurrentTime;
    [DataMember(Order=1, Name="Currency")] public string Money;
}
```

Working with Collections

Collections are very convenient data constructs in .NET that combine the benefits of dynamic memory allocation, enumeration, and list navigation. Although useful, there is no XSD or WDSL standard equivalent of a collection. Therefore, to serialize a collection into XML, WCF treats them as arrays. In fact, the wire-level serialization of a collection is identical to that of an array. In addition to collections (types that implement ICollection<T>), this is also true for types that implement the IEnumerable<T> or IList<T>.

Listing 2.27 shows a service contract and operation that uses a collection. The collection is decorated with the [CollectionDataContract] attribute, which is a special WCF attribute specifically provided for this purpose. This

attribute directs WCF to serialize any type that supports IEnumerable and
implements an Add method into an array. The StockPriceCollection class
inherits from the List generic, which implements the base ICollection
interface to enable serialization.

LISTING 2.27 Exposing a Collection from a Service

```
using System;
using System.ServiceModel;
using System.Runtime.Serialization;
using System.Collections.Generic;

namespace EssentialWCF
{
    [DataContract(Namespace = "http://EssentialWCF")]
    public class StockPrice
    {
        [DataMember] public double CurrentPrice;
        [DataMember] public DateTime CurrentTime;
        [DataMember] public string Ticker;
    }

    [CollectionDataContract]
    public class StockPriceCollection : List<StockPrice>
    {
    }

    [ServiceContract]
    public class StockService
    {
        [OperationContract]
        private StockPriceCollection
                    GetPricesAsCollection(string[] tickers)
        {
            StockPriceCollection list = new StockPriceCollection();
            for (int i = 0; i < tickers.GetUpperBound(0) + 1; i++)
            {
                StockPrice p = new StockPrice();
                p.Ticker = tickers[i];
                p.CurrentPrice = 94.85;
                p.CurrentTime = System.DateTime.Now;
                list.Add(p);
            }
            return list;
        }
    }
}
```

Message Contracts

Message contracts describe the structure of SOAP messages sent to and from a service and enable you to inspect and control most of the details in the SOAP header and body. Whereas data contracts enable interoperability through the XML Schema Definition (XSD) standard, message contracts enable you to interoperate with any system that communicates through SOAP.

Using message contracts gives you complete control over the SOAP message sent to and from a service by providing access to the SOAP headers and bodies directly. This allows use of simple or complex types to define the exact content of the SOAP parts. Just as you can switch from the `DataContractSerializer` to `XmlSerializer` when you need complete control over the data serialization, you can switch from `DataContracts` to `MessageContracts` when you need complete control over the SOAP message.

Passing information in SOAP headers is useful if you want to communicate information "out of band" from the operation signature. For instance, session or correlation information can be passed in headers, rather than adding additional parameters to operations or adding this information as fields in the data itself. Another example is security, where you may want to implement a custom security protocol (bypassing WS-Security) and pass credentials or tokens in custom SOAP headers. A third example, again with security, is signing and encrypting SOAP headers, where you may want to sign and/or encrypt some or all header information. All these cases can be handled with message contracts. The downside with this technique is that the client and service must manually add and retrieve the information from the SOAP header, rather than having the serialization classes associated with data and operation contracts do it for you.

The `[MessageContract]` attribute defines the structure of SOAP messages. There aren't many modifiers to this attribute because its purpose is to define the boundary of the message, not the content itself. The only modifiers relate to how multiple bodies are wrapped into a single SOAP message, specifying whether to wrap at all and, if so, specifying the name and namespace of the wrapper.

Typed messages use [MessageHeader] and [MessageBodyMember] attributes to describe the structure of the SOAP header and body. The client and the service can then reference this data using serialized types. Additional information can be associated with headers, such as name and namespace, whether the message can be relayed, and who is the final actor or recipient of the message. Additional information can also be associated with the body, such as name and namespace. If multiple bodies are used, the MessageContract can define the order of those parts. Both the header and body can have simple or complex type definitions.

Untyped messages do not use any attributes to describe their contents. It's left entirely up to the runtime code to make sense of the contents. This is very useful for working directly with the InfoSet of the XML message, in which case you'd want WCF to stay out of the way as you code directly to the Document Object Model. Service operations that work with untyped messages accept and return message types, which implement the XML Infoset.

Typed Messages

Listing 2.28 shows a typed message contract, StockPrice. The header contains a simple type, DateTime, and the body contains a complex type, PriceDetails. The PriceDetails class must be serializable, either by using a [DataContract] attribute or, as shown here, with the [Serializable] attribute. This example has just one header and one body, but there can be numerous headers and bodies specified.

You may want to specify numerous headers or bodies if they are to be consumed by different layers of software on the client. For instance, one layer may want correlation information in the SOAP header to associate a response with a request, whereas another layer may want to identity information so it can route the message appropriately. In this case, two headers have two purposes, so there's no reason to combine them into one structure.

Note that the service operation receives and sends message types. When using message contract, both input and output parameters must be messages and marked with the [MessageContract] attribute. More specifically, operations must contain exactly one input parameter and must return exactly one result, both of which are messages, because the request and response messages sent to and from the operation will map directly their SOAP representation. In addition, message-based programming and parameter-based programming cannot be mixed, so you cannot specify a DataContract as an input argument to an operation and have it return a MessageContract, or specify a MessageContract as the input argument to an operation and have it return a DataContract. You can mix typed and untyped messages, but not MessageContracts and DataContracts. Mixing message and data contracts will cause a runtime error when you generate WSDL from the service.

To generate client-side proxy code that represents the typed message in the [MessageContract], you need to check the Always Generate Message Contracts option in the Advanced dialog box of Add Service Reference, as shown in Figure 2.9.

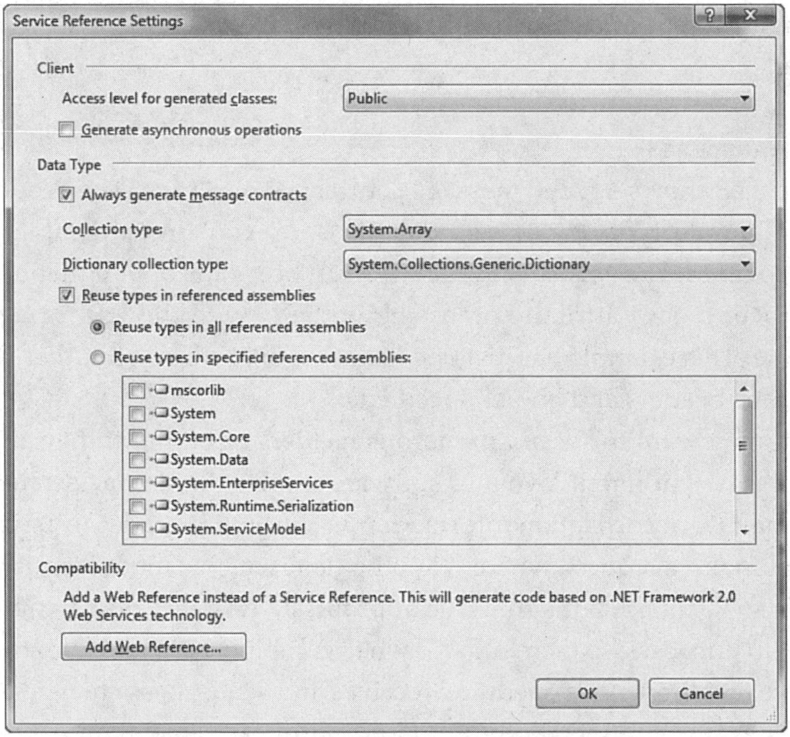

FIGURE 2.9 Specifying message contracts in Add Service Reference

Alternatively, you can use the /messageContract , or /mc, switch on svcutil.exe. This causes svcutil.exe to generate the proxy with public methods accepting the typed message so clients can call method-oriented methods. If you use svcutil.exe without the /mc switch, or if you use Add Service Reference without checking the Always Generate Message Contracts, the proxy will be generated with public methods accepting parameters and will internally call the message-based operation. In either case, the same XML messages are sent on the wire.

LISTING 2.28 Defining a Typed Message Contract

```
namespace EssentialWCF
{
    [Serializable]
    public class PriceDetails
    {
        public string Ticker;
        public double Amount;
    }
    [MessageContract]
    public class StockPrice
    {
        [MessageHeader]
        public DateTime CurrentTime;
        [MessageBodyMember]
        public PriceDetails Price;
    }

    [MessageContract]
    public class StockPriceReq
    {
        [MessageBodyMember] public string Ticker;
    }

    [ServiceContract]
    public interface IStockService
    {
        [OperationContract]
        StockPrice GetPrice(StockPriceReq req);
    }

    public class StockService : IStockService
    {
```

LISTING 2.28 continued

```
        public StockPrice GetPrice(StockPriceReq req)
        {
            StockPrice resp = new StockPrice();
            resp.Price = new PriceDetails();
            resp.Price.Ticker = req.Ticker;
            resp.Price.Amount = 94.85;
            return resp;
        }
    }
}
```

Listing 2.29 shows the XML that's passed on the wire when the SOAP message is returned from the service back to the client. Note that the [MessageHeader] element, CurrentTime, is in the SOAP header and the [MessageBodyMember] element, Price, is in the SOAP body.

LISTING 2.29 SOAP Response Generated Using a Typed Message Contract

```
<s:Envelope xmlns:s="http://schemas.xmlsoap.org/soap/envelope/">
  <s:Header>
    <h:CurrentTime xmlns:h="http://tempuri.org/">
              2006-12-18T10:31:55.0584-05:00
    </h:CurrentTime>
  </s:Header>
  <s:Body>
    <StockPrice xmlns="http://tempuri.org/">
      <Price
        xmlns:a="http://schemas.datacontract.org/2004/07/EssentialWCF"
        xmlns:i="http://www.w3.org/2001/XMLSchema-instance">
        <a:Amount>94.85</a:Amount>
        <a:Ticker>MSFT</a:Ticker>
      </Price>
    </StockPrice>
  </s:Body>
</s:Envelope>
```

Untyped Messages

In some scenarios, you may not know the structure of messages passed between a client and service at design time. For instance, intelligence might be built in to the messages themselves, such as routing and service operations that are determined at runtime. Or a layer of software (or hardware) might be between the client and service that manipulates SOAP messages and requires special data formats. For these cases, untyped operation contracts can be very useful.

Untyped operation contracts enable the client and service to pass virtually any content in the SOAP body, as long as the content can be encoded by the binding stack being used for communication. The contents of the message are effectively opaque to the WSDL because there is no XSD to define the data. The client and service work with the Message class, which is defined in System.ServiceModel.Channels, to create, read, and write messages.

Listing 2.30 shows an operation contract that uses the message type as input and output. Notice that the GetBody method of the message is a generic method that deserializes the message body into a type. This method uses an XMLReader to read the <body> element of the SOAP message. Because it uses an XML Reader, the <body> can be read only once; if you want to read it more than once, you should use the CreateBufferedCopy method of the message. The SOAP action on the reply is the request action with "Response" concatenated to the end. This can be overridden by a (ReplyAction=) in the [OperationContract] attribute.

The Message class has numerous methods for creating, reading, and writing the message contents. The client is responsible for creating a message before sending it to the service and the service is responsible for creating a message to send back. Before sending the message, the contents must be placed in the body. This can be done with CreateMessage, WriteMessage, or WriteBody methods.

LISTING 2.30 Defining and Implementing Untyped Message Contract

```
[ServiceContract (Namespace="http://EssentialWCF")]
public class StockService
{
    [OperationContract]
    private Message GetPrice(Message req)
    {
        string ticker = req.GetBody<String>();
        Message resp = Message.CreateMessage(
                    req.Version,
                    req.Headers.Action + "Response",
                    ticker + "|" + "94.85");
        return resp;
    }
}
```

The client code is similar to the service code, using `CreateMessage` to create the message with the proper version to match the binding and then using `GetBody` to read the result that comes back from the service. Note that the `CreateMessage` method used takes three parameters: the version, the action, and the string message. When creating the message, the version of the message must be compatible with the binding used to communicate with the service, as defined by the MessageVersion property in the channel. The action, in this case `http://EssentialWCF/StockService/GetPrice`, is used by SOAP and the WCF infrastructure to route the message to the proper operation in the service. Listing 2.31 shows client code that initiates communications with the service listed in Listing 2.30.

LISTING 2.31 Client Initiating Communication Using an Untyped Message Contract

```
using (localhost.StockServiceClient proxy =
        new localhost.StockServiceClient())
{
    new OperationContextScope(proxy.InnerChannel);
    Message msgReq = Message.CreateMessage(
        OperationContext.Current.OutgoingMessageHeaders.
                                                MessageVersion,
        "http:// EssentialWCF /StockService/GetPrice",
        "msft");
    Message msgResp = proxy.GetPrice(msgReq);
    Console.WriteLine("Returned {0} ", msgResp.GetBody<string>());
}
```

Listing 2.32 shows the SOAP message transmitted back from the service to the client in response to the request in Listing 2.31. Notice that the action in the SOAP header has "Response" concatenated to the end, and that the body of the SOAP message is a string with no XML formatting.

LISTING 2.32 SOAP Response Generated Using an Untyped Message Contract

```
<s:Envelope xmlns:s="http://schemas.xmlsoap.org/soap/envelope/">
  <s:Header>
    <Action s:mustUnderstand="1"
      xmlns="http://schemas.microsoft.com/ws/2005/05/addressing/none">
        http://EssentialWCF/StockService/GetPriceResponse
    </Action>
  </s:Header>
  <s:Body>
    <string xmlns=
```

```
                       "http://schemas.microsoft.com/2003/10/Serialization/">
        msft|94.85
      </string>
    </s:Body>
  </s:Envelope>
```

Using SOAP Headers with Untyped Messages

Whether you're working with typed or untyped messages, you may want to pass information in the SOAP header in addition to the SOAP body. A common need is to pass session or context information along with a message. So, rather than creating additional wrapper messages, the SOAP header is a convenient and well-understood mechanism of passing that information.

If you're using typed messages, WCF explicitly supports this through the [MessageHeader] attribute as demonstrated in Listing 2.28. If using an untyped message, however, you need to explicitly add an untyped message header.

Listing 2.33 shows a service contract that implements an untyped message operation and reads data from the message header. Note how the message header data, timeZone, is accessible with one line of code.

LISTING 2.33 Service Accessing Message Headers with an Untyped Message Contract

```
[ServiceContract]
public class StockService
{
    [OperationContract]
    private Message GetPrice(Message req)
    {
        string timeZone =
                OperationContext.Current.IncomingMessageHeaders.
                    GetHeader<String>
                            ("TimeZone", "http://EssentialWCF/");

        string ticker = req.GetBody<String>();
        Message resp = Message.CreateMessage(
                req.Version,
                req.Headers.Action + "Response",
                timeZone + "|" + ticker + "|" + "94.85");
        return resp;
    }
}
```

Listing 2.34 demonstrates how a client can add a SOAP header to an untyped message being sent to a service. First a message is created with CreateMessage and data is placed in that message with the constructor. Then a typed MessageHeader is created; in this case it's a string, and the data is placed in the header with the constructor. Next, an untyped MessageHeader is created from the typed one, and then finally, that untyped MessageHeader is added to the message being sent to the service.

LISTING 2.34 Client Inserting Message Headers into an Untyped Message

```
static void Main(string[] args)
{
    using (localhost.StockServiceClient proxy
            = new localhost.StockServiceClient())
    {
        new OperationContextScope(proxy.InnerChannel);
        Message msgReq =
                    Message.CreateMessage
                        (OperationContext.Current.
                         OutgoingMessageHeaders.MessageVersion,
                         "http://tempuri.org/StockService/GetPrice",
                         "msft");
        MessageHeader<String> msgHeader = new
                    MessageHeader<string>("GMT-05:00");
        MessageHeader untypedHeader =
                    msgHeader.GetUntypedHeader("TimeZone",
                                "http://EssentialWCF/");
        msgReq.Headers.Add(untypedHeader);
        Message msgResp = proxy.GetPrice(msgReq);
    }
}
```

Listing 2.35 shows the SOAP message generated from the client-side code. Notice the TimeZone element that is inserted into the message header in the proper namespace.

LISTING 2.35 Client Inserting Message Headers into an Untyped Message

```
<s:Envelope xmlns:s="http://schemas.xmlsoap.org/soap/envelope/">
  <s:Header>
    <TimeZone xmlns="http://EssentialWCF/">GMT-05:00</TimeZone>
    <To s:mustUnderstand="1"
        xmlns="http://schemas.microsoft.com/ws/2005/05/addressing/none">
        http://localhost/UntypedMessageHeader/StockService.svc
```

```
          </To>
          <Action s:mustUnderstand="1"
             xmlns="http://schemas.microsoft.com/ws/2005/05/addressing/none">
             http://tempuri.org/StockService/GetPrice
          </Action>
        </s:Header>
        <s:Body>
          <string
             xmlns="http://schemas.microsoft.com/2003/10/Serialization/">
            msft
          </string>
        </s:Body>
      </s:Envelope>
```

SUMMARY

This chapter covers quite a bit of ground with contracts, which are the basis for interoperability. Contracts precisely describe the messages that a service understands.

WCF heavily leverages SOAP for contract definitions. Specifically, it uses WDSL for describing service endpoints and XSD for describing data. The service operations defined in WSDL are used to route incoming messages to the correct .NET class at runtime. Similarly, the XML documents defined by XSD contracts are deserialized into .NET types and passed to the service operations at runtime. Together, the WSDL and XSD definitions provide a standards-based representation of the .NET types used within a service implementation.

Three types of contracts were defined in detail:

- **Service contracts.** Service contracts describe the functional operations implemented by the service.
- **Data contracts.** Data contracts describe the data structures through which the service communicates. A data contract serializes CLR types to XML and is strictly opt-in with their data members.
- **Message contracts.** Message contracts work with typed and untyped data and provide precise control over the SOAP headers and bodies.

Service Contracts

Service contracts define service operations—the methods that the service class interface exposes. They provide the formal WSDL interface to a service. Service contracts are defined with the [ServiceContract] and [OperationContract] attributes. Operation names are derived from the class and method names but can be overridden when defining these attributes. Service contracts support three message exchange patterns: request-response, one-way, and duplex.

Request-response operation contracts are blocking calls on the client, where the client waits for the service operation to complete before regaining execution control. Therefore, they should be used only for relatively fast service calls where the user is willing to wait for the response. In the client, the .NET asynchronous pattern can be applied to the request-response message exchange pattern to prevent the client from blocking while a long-running service request is executing.

One-way operation contracts are, as the name implies, one way; they do not return a result to the client. Service operations must have a return type of void and are marked by [IsOneWay=true] on the [OperationContract] attribute. One-way contracts can be implemented over any transport, including MSMQ.

Duplex operation contracts provide the greatest flexibility and performance because they decouple the request and response execution from the client and service. After the duplex channel is established between the client and service, either the client or service can initiate a message. This pattern is well suited for client notification.

Data Contracts

Data contracts define the application data interface to services. Classes marked with [DataContract] and [DataMember] attributes are included in the XML Schema Definitions in the part of WSDL representing the service contract. Other data types can also be exposed in WSDL, such as base types and those marked with [Serializable]. Because [DataContract] has serialization rules designed for interoperability, it is the preferred serialization mechanism for WCF.

Class members are included in a data contract with the [DataMember] attribute. This is strictly an opt-in model so only members with this attribute are included in the contract. This also makes [DataContract] a more suitable serialization mechanism than [Serializable] because the latter can cause internal structures to be exposed outside of the service.

Class hierarchies are supported and their namespaces are carried through the hierarchy. To support polymorphism and collections that contain objects, WCF enables a service to publish the list of known types. Data contracts are also designed for versioning. When new members are added to a contract, existing clients will continue to work, providing certain rules are followed.

Message Contracts

Message contracts are operation contracts that enable access to SOAP headers and bodies. Messages can be typed with [DataContract] or [Serializable], or they can simply be of the type Message. Typed messages are defined with [MessageHeader] and [MessageBody] attributes. Message data can be undefined at design time, enabling the greatest flexibility. Untyped messages also have access to the SOAP headers and body.

3
Channels

A CHANNEL IS THE CONDUIT through which all messages pass to and from WCF applications. It is responsible for preparing and delivering messages in a consistent way. Channels are defined for transports, protocols, and message interception. Channels are layered together to create a channel stack. A channel stack is a layered communication stack that processes messages. For example, a channel stack could be constructed using a TCP transport channel and a transaction protocol channel. Such a channel stack would allow sending and receiving messages across a network using the TCP protocol and transactions to flow from client to server.

The goal of a channel stack is to transform a message into a wire format compatible with the sender and receiver and to transport the message. There are two types of channels that are used to do this: *transport channels* and *protocol channels*. Transport channels always sit at the bottom of the channel stack and are responsible for transporting messages using a transport protocol. WCF provides a number of transport protocols, including HTTP, TCP, MSMQ, peer-to-peer, and named pipes. Protocol channels reside on top of transports or other protocol channels. Because protocol channels reside on top of other channels, they are often referred to as *layered channels*. Protocol channels are responsible for implementing wire-level protocols by transforming and modifying messages. WCF provides many types of protocol channels. Examples include protocol channels that implement support for security, transactions, and reliable messaging.

> **■ TIP   Transport Channels**
>
> WCF provides several transport channels, including HTTP, TCP, MSMQ, peer-to-peer, and named pipes. Other transports are available in sample code or through third parties for a wide range of transports, including SMTP, FTP, UDP, WebSphere MQ, and SQL Service Broker. Many of these transports can be found on the http://wcf.netfx3.com Web site. The UDP transport channel can be found in the Windows SDK. The transport channel for WebSphere MQ can be found on IBM's alphaWorks Web site.

For communication to occur, clients and servers each need to instantiate a channel stack that is compatible with others. Between .NET applications, this is typically done by using the same channel stack on the client and the server. In general, this means that their capabilities must match. We use *bindings* to simplify the creation of channel stacks. A binding captures the configuration of the channel stack and knows how to create that channel stack at runtime. Bindings are built from a collection of *binding elements*, which typically represent channels in the channel stack. Bindings and binding elements will be discussed in detail in Chapter 4, "Bindings."

The WCF channel architecture provides enormous flexibility by allowing the communication to be abstracted away from the application. This enables developers to build services that can be exposed over multiple communication mechanisms, which allows application services to change over time as the requirements change. For example, a WCF service exposed between two .NET applications can easily be exposed to a Java application without modifying the application. Support for additional features such as interoperability, durable messaging, and transactions can easily be added to WCF services as the requirements change. Prior Microsoft technologies (such as ASP.NET Web Services, .NET Remoting, Enterprise Services, or MSMQ) required you to rewrite portions of the application for each new form of communication. With WCF, you can now pick and choose the features you want without requiring a significant rewrite of the application.

The capability for WCF to offer such flexibility can be found in how WCF composes a channel stack using layering. Figure 3.1 shows how a message flows from a WCF client application through a client-side channel stack over a given transport to a server. The server's channel stack listens for messages and then dispatches them to the server application.

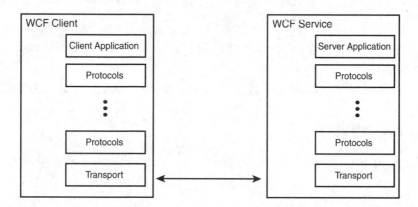

FIGURE 3.1 Channel stack

A channel stack is a series of channels that are configured using binding elements. A preconfigured channel stack is also called a binding. A binding is made up from a series of binding elements, just as a channel stack is made from a series of channels. At the top of the stack are the protocol channels. Protocol channels interact with a message and facilitate security, reliable messaging, transactions, and logging features. There can be any number of protocol channels in a channel stack, depending on the required features.

Transport channels are responsible for sending bytes over a transmission protocol such as TCP or HTTP. They are also responsible for using an *encoder* to convert messages into an array of bytes for transport. It is the job of an encoder to convert a message from its XML representation to an array of bytes. Encoders are exposed to the transport channel using binding elements. Transport channels look in the binding context for an implementation of a `MessageEncoder` class. If none are available, the transport channel can specify a default message encoder.

> ■ **TIP**   Channel Stacks Have a Transport and an Encoder
>
> Channel stacks have at least one transport and one encoder. Usually the transport will specify a default encoding to use. An example is the `tcpTransport` transport channel, which specifies the use of the `binaryMessageEncoding`. This is all that is needed to implement a channel stack in WCF. Protocol channels are optional when you are composing a channel stack.

Channel Shapes

WCF supports three distinct message-exchange patterns: one-way, duplex, and request-reply. To facilitate each of these patterns, WCF provides ten different interfaces called channel shapes. The five shapes are `IOutputChannel`, `IInputChannel`, `IDuplexChannel`, `IRequestChannel`, and `IReplyChannel`. Each of these shapes has an equivalent shape to support sessions. These include `IOutputSessionChannel`, `IInputSessionChannel`, `IDuplexSessionChannel`, `IRequestSessionChannel`, and `IReplySessionChannel`. These interfaces implement the different message-exchange patterns within a channel stack. In this section, we will look at each of the communication patterns and the various interfaces associated with them.

One-Way Communication Pattern

In the one-way communication pattern, messages are sent in only one direction, from the client to the server. One-way communication is common when the sender does not need an informational response back right away; the sender just needs an acknowledgement that the message was sent. After the message is sent, that is the end of the communication exchange. The two interfaces used to facilitate one-way communication are the `IOutputChannel` and the `IInputChannel` interface. Figure 3.2 shows how messages flow between a client and server for one-way communication.

In this pattern, the `IOutputChannel` interface is responsible for sending messages, and the `IInputChannel` is responsible for receiving messages. Listing 3.1 shows a client application that uses the `IOutputChannel` channel shape to send a message.

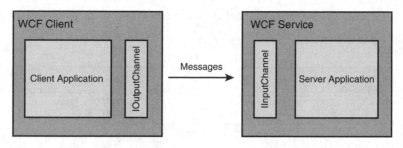

FIGURE 3.2 One-way communication

LISTING 3.1 `IOutputChannel` Example

```
using System;
using System.Collections.Generic;
using System.ServiceModel;
using System.ServiceModel.Channels;
using System.Text;

namespace EssentialWCF
{
    class Program
    {
        static void Main(string[] args)
        {
            BasicHttpBinding binding = new BasicHttpBinding();
            BindingParameterCollection parameters =
new BindingParameterCollection();

            Message m =
Message.CreateMessage(MessageVersion.Soap11, "urn:sendmessage");
            IChannelFactory<IOutputChannel> factory =
binding.BuildChannelFactory<IOutputChannel>(parameters);
            IOutputChannel channel = factory.CreateChannel(
new EndpointAddress("http://localhost/sendmessage/"));
            channel.Send(m);
            channel.Close();
            factory.Close();
        }
    }
}
```

Duplex Communication

Duplex communication uses two one-way channel shapes combined into a third interface called `IDuplexChannel,` as shown in Figure 3.3. The advantage of duplex communication over one-way or request-reply is that messages can be sent from either the client or the server.

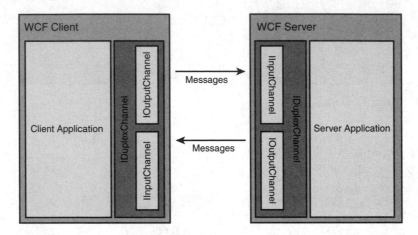

FIGURE 3.3 Duplex communication

An example of duplex communication is an event notification system. A server will send events to a client that receives events. The client provides an endpoint on which the server can send messages to the client. The server will then use this endpoint to send messages to the client. Listing 3.2 shows an example of a client that uses the IDuplexChannel channel shape.

LISTING 3.2 IDuplexChannel Example

```
using System;
using System.Collections.Generic;
using System.ServiceModel;
using System.ServiceModel.Channels;
using System.Text;

namespace EssentialWCF
{
    class Program
    {
        static void Main(string[] args)
        {
            NetTcpBinding binding = new NetTcpBinding();
            BindingParameterCollection parameters =
new BindingParameterCollection();

            Message m =
Message.CreateMessage(MessageVersion.Soap12WSAddressing10,
```

```
"urn:sendmessage");
            IChannelFactory<IDuplexChannel> factory =
binding.BuildChannelFactory<IDuplexChannel>(parameters);
            IDuplexChannel channel = factory.CreateChannel(
new EndpointAddress("net.tcp://localhost/sendmessage/"));
            channel.Send(m);
            channel.Close();
            factory.Close();
        }
    }
}
```

Request-Reply Communication

Request-reply communication is a special form of two-way communication where there is exactly one reply for each request, and it is always initiated by the client. After the client sends a request, it must wait for a response before it can send another request.

A common use of request-reply communication is an HTTP request from a browser. The browser makes an HTTP request to the server, such as GET or POST, the server processes that request, and then a reply is sent back. WCF handles request-reply communication using the IRequestChannel and IReplyChannel interfaces as shown in Figure 3.4.

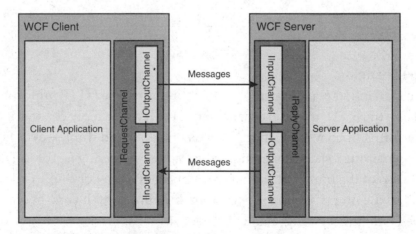

FIGURE 3.4 Request-reply communication

Listing 3.3 shows a client application that uses the IRequestChannel to send a message. Notice that the Request method returns the reply message as the return parameter.

LISTING 3.3 IRequestChannel Example

```csharp
using System;
using System.Collections.Generic;
using System.ServiceModel;
using System.ServiceModel.Channels;
using System.Text;

namespace EssentialWCF
{
    class Program
    {
        static void Main(string[] args)
        {
            BasicHttpBinding binding = new BasicHttpBinding();
            BindingParameterCollection parameters =
new BindingParameterCollection();

            Message request =
Message.CreateMessage(MessageVersion.Soap11, "urn:sendmessage");
            IChannelFactory<IRequestChannel> factory =
binding.BuildChannelFactory<IRequestChannel>(parameters);
            IRequestChannel channel = factory.CreateChannel(
new EndpointAddress("http://localhost/sendmessage/"));
            Message response = channel.Request(request);
            channel.Close();
            factory.Close();
        }
    }
}
```

Shape Changing

There is an inherent request-reply nature built in to the HTTP protocol, and therefore the HTTP transport channel uses the request-reply channel shape. Other forms of communication, such as one-way and duplex over HTTP, are done through shape changing. This is done by layering a protocol channel on top of the transport channel to support one-way or duplex communication. Listing 3.4 shows a custom binding that layers a one-way shape-changing binding element, OneWayBindingElement, on top of an HTTP transport. We will see more advanced examples of shape changing using the CompositeDuplexBindingElement binding element in Chapter 12, "Peer Networking."

LISTING 3.4 `OneWayBindingElement` Example

```
using System;
using System.Collections.Generic;
using System.ServiceModel;
using System.ServiceModel.Channels;
using System.Text;

namespace EssentialWCF
{
    class Program
    {
        static void Main(string[] args)
        {
            CustomBinding binding = new CustomBinding(
                    new OneWayBindingElement(),
                    new TextMessageEncodingBindingElement(),
                    new HttpTransportBindingElement());
        }
    }
}
```

Operation Contract and Channel Shapes

Channels use channel shapes to implement the various types of message exchange patterns that they support. For example, a transport channel based on TCP would implement the `IInputChannel` and `IOutputChannel` because these transports are inherently one-way. Other transports based on other protocols such as TCP may implement multiple channel shapes. Developers do not work with channel shapes directly. Instead, WCF chooses the channel shape based on the `OperationContract` of a service. Table 3.1 lists the various attributes that you can set on an `OperationContract` and the resulting channel shape. Notice that most channel shapes have a sessionless (default) and session-aware variant. Session-aware channels pass an identifier from the client to the server. This can be used to maintain state between client and server. This is similar to how ASP.NET does state management. There is no state-management feature built in to WCF, but you can use sessions with instancing to be able to manage state. Instance management is described in Chapter 5, "Behaviors."

TABLE 3.1 Channel Shapes Based on `OperationContract` Attributes

OneWay	Request/ Reply	Session	Callback	Channel Shape
Any	Any	No	Yes	`IDuplexChannel`
Any	Any	No	Yes	`IDuplexSessionChannel`
Any	Any	Yes	Yes	`IDuplexSessionChannel`
Yes	Yes	No	No	`IDuplexChannel`
Yes	Yes	No	No	`IRequestChannel`
Yes	Yes	No	No	`IDuplexSessionChannel`
Yes	Yes	Yes	No	`IDuplexSessionChannel`
Yes	Yes	Yes	No	`IRequestSessionChannel`
Yes	No	No	No	`IOutputChannel`
Yes	No	No	No	`IDuplexChannel`
Yes	No	No	No	`IDuplexSessionChannel`
Yes	No	No	No	`IRequestChannel`
Yes	No	Yes	No	`IOutputSessionChannel`
Yes	No	Yes	No	`IDuplexSessionChannel`
Yes	No	Yes	No	`IRequestSessionChannel`
No	Yes	No	No	`IRequestChannel`
No	Yes	No	No	`IDuplexChannel`
No	Yes	No	No	`IDuplexSessionChannel`
No	Yes	Yes	No	`IRequestSessionChannel`
No	Yes	Yes	No	`IDuplexSessionChannel`

Not all channels implement each of these interfaces. If the underlying channel does not support a particular channel shape, WCF will try to adapt an existing channel shape to suit its needs. For example, if a channel does not implement the IInputChannel and IOutputChannel interfaces for one-way communication, WCF will try to use either the IDuplexChannel or the IRequestChannel/IReplyChannel instead.

Channel Listeners

Channel listeners form the basis for server-side communication within WCF. They are responsible for listening for incoming messages, creating channel stacks, and providing a reference to the top of the stack to applications. They receive messages from either the transport channel or the channel below in the channel stack. Most developers will not work with channel listeners directly. They will use the ServiceHost class to host services, which uses a channel listener to listen for messages. See Chapter 7, "Hosting," for more details about the ServiceHost class. Listing 3.5 shows a channel listener being created to receive a message. The BuildChannelListener method of the binding builds a channel listener based on the channel shape specified. In this case we are using the BasicHttpBinding and the IReplyChannel shapes.

LISTING 3.5 Using a Channel Listener

```
using System;
using System.Collections.Generic;
using System.Text;
using System.ServiceModel;
using System.ServiceModel.Channels;

namespace EssentialWCF
{
    class Program
    {
        static void Main(string[] args)
        {
            BasicHttpBinding binding = new
BasicHttpBinding(BasicHttpSecurityMode.None);

            Uri address = new Uri("http://localhost/request");
            BindingParameterCollection bpc = new
BindingParameterCollection();

            Console.WriteLine("Starting service...");
```

LISTING 3.5 continued

```
                IChannelListener<IReplyChannel> listener =
    binding.BuildChannelListener<IReplyChannel>(address, bpc);
                listener.Open();
                IReplyChannel channel = listener.AcceptChannel();
                channel.Open();
                Console.WriteLine("Service started!");

                Console.WriteLine("Waiting for request...");
                RequestContext request = channel.ReceiveRequest();
                Message message = request.RequestMessage;
                string data = message.GetBody<string>();
                Message replymessage =
    Message.CreateMessage(message.Version,
                        "http://localhost/reply",
                        data);
                request.Reply(replymessage);
                Console.WriteLine("Service stopped!");

                message.Close();
                request.Close();
                channel.Close();
                listener.Close();

                Console.ReadLine();
            }
        }
    }
```

Channel Factories

A channel factory creates a channel for sending messages and maintains ownership of the channels it creates. Most developers will never use a channel factory directly. Instead, they will use a class derived from ClientBase<>, which is typically generated from svcutil.exe or Add Service Reference in Visual Studio. However, it is important to understand channel factories because they form the basis for client-side communication within WCF.

> **■ TIP   Channel Factories Own Their Channels**
>
> One important distinction between channel listeners and factories is
> that channel factories are responsible for closing down all associated
> channels; channel listeners are not. This distinction was made so that
> channel listeners could be shut down independent of their channels.

Listing 3.6 shows the use of a channel factory to call a service. This is the
client to the server in Listing 3. The code uses the `CreateChannel` method of
the binding to create a new channel.

LISTING 3.6 Using Channel Factories

```
using System;
using System.Collections.Generic;
using System.Text;
using System.ServiceModel;
using System.ServiceModel.Channels;

namespace EssentialWCF
{
    class Program
    {
        static void Main(string[] args)
        {
            BasicHttpBinding binding = new
BasicHttpBinding(BasicHttpSecurityMode.None);

            IChannelFactory<IRequestChannel> factory =
                binding.BuildChannelFactory<IRequestChannel>(
                        new BindingParameterCollection());
            factory.Open();
            IRequestChannel channel = factory.CreateChannel(
                new EndpointAddress("http://localhost/request"));
            channel.Open();

            Message requestmessage = Message.CreateMessage(
                MessageVersion.Soap11,
                "http://contoso.com/reply",
                "This is the body data");
```

LISTING 3.6 continued

```
        Console.WriteLine("Sending message...");
        Message replymessage = channel.Request(requestmessage);
        string data = replymessage.GetBody<string>();
        Console.WriteLine("Reply received!");
        requestmessage.Close();
        replymessage.Close();
        channel.Close();
        factory.Close();

        Console.ReadLine();
    }
  }
 }
```

ChannelFactory<>

Two classes refer to channel factories within WCF: ChannelFactory and
ChannelFactory<>. They might seem similar, but they are actually separate
classes that do different things. The ChannelFactory<> class is used in
advanced situations where multiple clients need to be created. Essentially
it works with a given ChannelFactory, but it does not have any responsi-
bilities for creating a channel stack. The ChannelFactory<> class is used by
defining the class with a specific ServiceContract type. Listing 3.7 shows
an example of using the ChannelFactory<> class to call a service that implements the IStockQuoteService interface.

■ TIP   Using Statement and ChannelFactory<>

Be careful when implementing the using statement to close the
ChannelFactory. Listing 3.7 shows a best practice of having a
try..catch around the service call so that any errors from the service
are known. If we didn't have this try..catch, any exceptions would
bubble up through the using. At that point the channel factory would
throw an exception because it is closed. This would mask the previous
error raised from the service call. We use two try..catch blocks so that
we can catch any errors from the service calls.

LISTING 3.7 Using ChannelFactory<>

```csharp
using System;
using System.Collections.Generic;
using System.Text;
using System.ServiceModel;
using System.ServiceModel.Channels;

namespace EssentialWCF
{
    class Program
    {
        static void Main(string[] args)
        {
            try
            {
                using (ChannelFactory<IStockQuoteService> cf =
new ChannelFactory<IStockQuoteService>())
                {
                    IStockQuoteService service = cf.CreateChannel();

                    try
                    {
                        double value = service.GetQuote("MSFT");
                    }
                    catch (Exception ex)
                    {
                        // check exception from call to GetQuote
                        Console.WriteLine(ex.ToString());
                    }
                }
            }
            catch (Exception ex)
            {
                // check exception for creating channel
                Console.WriteLine(ex.ToString());
            }
            Console.ReadLine();
        }
    }
}
```

ICommunicationObject

The ICommunicationObject interface (see Listing 3.8) is the basis of all communication objects (channels, channel factories, channel listeners, and so on) within WCF. Developers who are planning to build custom channels or work with channels directly need to know this interface. Communication objects within WCF need to implement a specific state machine. The state machine represents the state that all communication objects go through. This approach is similar to what other communication objects (for example, sockets) go through. The purpose of the ICommunicationObject interface (and its associated methods, states, and events) is to implement that state machine. This allows WCF to treat all communication objects the same and abstracts away their underlying implementations.

LISTING 3.8 ICommunicationObject Interface

```
public interface ICommunicationObject
{
    // Events
    event EventHandler Closed;
    event EventHandler Closing;
    event EventHandler Faulted;
    event EventHandler Opened;
    event EventHandler Opening;

    // Methods
    void Abort();
    IAsyncResult BeginClose(AsyncCallback callback, object state);
    IAsyncResult BeginClose(TimeSpan timeout,
AsyncCallback callback, object state);
    IAsyncResult BeginOpen(AsyncCallback callback, object state);
    IAsyncResult BeginOpen(TimeSpan timeout,
AsyncCallback callback, object state);
    void Close();
    void Close(TimeSpan timeout);
    void EndClose(IAsyncResult result);
    void EndOpen(IAsyncResult result);
    void Open();
    void Open(TimeSpan timeout);

    // Properties
    CommunicationState State { get; }
}
```

Listing 3.9 shows the states provided by the CommunicationState enumeration.

LISTING 3.9 CommunicationState Enumeration

```
public enum CommunicationState
{
    Created,
    Opening,
    Opened,
    Closing,
    Closed,
    Faulted
}
```

The CommunicationState enumeration lists six states that communication objects go through. The initial state for all communication objects is Created. This is the state that communication objects are in when they are instantiated. The final state for all communication objects is Closed. Along the way, methods are called on the ICommunicationObject interface that transitions the communication object from one state to the next. For example, the Open() method is called to transition a communication object from the Created state to the Opened state. Figure 3.5 shows a state diagram showing the states and state transitions that a communication object goes through.

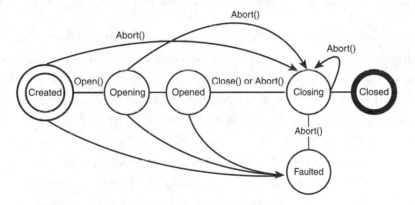

FIGURE 3.5 ICommunicationObject state diagram

One example of a communication object is the ClientBase<> class, which is the base implementation for clients generated from Add Service Reference from Visual Studio or svcutil.exe.

> **■ NOTE**   Cannot Reuse Clients
>
> There is no going back after a communication object has transitioned from the Opened state to either the Closing or Faulted state. This means that the communication state cannot go back to the Opened state without first re-creating the communication object. Therefore, clients need to be re-created after they are closed (that is, when they are in the Closed state).

Five events (Opening, Opened, Closing, Closed, and Faulted) are supported by the ICommunicationObject interface. These events are used to notify code of state transitions.

> **■ TIP**   Client Notifications
>
> It is common for applications to maintain a reference to a client proxy. In these situations it is important to use the state transitions events to be notified when the client proxy enters the Faulted state (and eventually the Closed state) so that communication between client and server can be maintained.

The ICommunicationObject interface is typically used by casting an existing communication object to the interface to gain access to the methods and events that the ICommunicationObject exposes. However, at other times you want to create a new communication object that extends the capabilities of WCF. In this situation, WCF has provided an abstract base class called CommunicationObject, which provides an implementation of the ICommunicationObject interface and the associated state machine. Listing 3.10 shows a StockQuoteServiceClient that was generated from svcutil.exe. This client inherits from the ClientBase<> class. The code shows the client being cast to an ICommunicationObject interface so that we can receive communication events.

LISTING 3.10 ICommunicationObject Example

```
using System;
using System.Collections.Generic;
using System.Net;
```

```csharp
using System.Text;
using System.ServiceModel;
using System.ServiceModel.Channels;

namespace EssentialWCF
{
    class Program
    {
        static void Main(string[] args)
        {
            string symbol = "MSFT";
            double value;

            StockQuoteServiceClient client =
new StockQuoteServiceClient());
            ICommunicationObject commObj =
(ICommunicationObject)client;

            commObj.Closed +=
new EventHandler(Closed);
            commObj.Faulted +=
new EventHandler(Faulted);
            value = client.GetQuote(symbol);

            Console.WriteLine("{0} @ ${1}", symbol, value);
            Console.ReadLine();
        }

        static void Closed(object sender, EventArgs e)
        {
            // Handle Closed Event
        }

        static void Faulted(object sender, EventArgs e)
        {
            // Handle Faulted Event
        }
    }
}
```

SUMMARY

A channel stack is a layered communication stack that is made up of one or more channels that process messages. Channels are either protocol or transport channels. Transport channels sit at the bottom of the channel stack and are responsible for transmitting messages over a transport mechanism (for example, HTTP, TCP, MSMQ). Protocol channels (a.k.a. layered channels) implement protocols (security, reliable messaging, transactions, and so on) by transforming and modifying messages.

Channel factories and listeners form the basis for sending and receiving messages. They are responsible for creating channel stacks and exposing the channel stack to applications.

WCF does a good job of abstracting away the details of the channel model from developers. Most developers will use a class derived from the `ClientBase<>` to send messages and the `ServiceHost` class to host services. These classes are built on top of the channel model architecture.

The channel model architecture forms the basis for all communication within WCF. After developers know about concepts within the channel model architecture, such as channel stacks, channels, channel factories, and channel listeners, they can use this knowledge to extend or customize communication within WCF.

■ 4 ■
Bindings

A S COVERED IN CHAPTER 3, "CHANNELS," a channel stack is a layered communication stack that is made up of one or more channels
that process messages. *Bindings* are preconfigured channel stacks. They represent wire-level agreements between a client and a server. Each binding
specifies the transport, encoding, and protocols involved in the communication. WCF encapsulates the configuration for the various communication
scenarios using bindings. The most common communication scenarios,
such as Web services, REST/POX services, and queue-based applications,
are provided out of the box. For example, the basicHttpBinding binding
is meant to work with services based on ASP.NET Web Services or WS-I
Basic Profile 1.1 compliant services. The ws2007HttpBinding and
wsHttpBinding bindings are similar to the basicHttpBinding binding, but
they support more features, such as reliable messaging and transactions,
and use newer standards such as WS-Addressing. The ws2007HttpBinding
binding ships with .NET 3.5 and is based on newer standards than the
wsHttpBinding binding. Table 4.1 lists the 12 bindings used for communication and a description of the use of each binding.

TABLE 4.1   WCF Communication Bindings in .NET Framework 3.5

Binding Name	Description	.NET Framework
basicHttpBinding	Binding for WS-I Basic Profile 1.1 Web Services including ASMX Web Services.	3.0/3.5
wsHttpBinding	Binding for advanced WS-* based Web Services such as WS-Security, WS-Transactions, and the like.	3.0/3.5
wsDualHttpBinding	Binding to support bidirectional communication using duplex contracts.	3.0/3.5
webHttpBinding	Binding that supports REST/POX-based services using XML and JSON serialization.	3.0/3.5
netTcpBinding	Binding for communication between two .NET-based systems.	3.0/3.5
netNamedPipeBinding	Binding for on-machine communication between one or more .NET-based systems.	3.0/3.5
netMsmqBinding	Binding for asynchronous communication using Microsoft Message Queue (MSMQ).	3.0/3.5
netPeerTcpBinding	Binding for building peer-to-peer networking applications.	3.0/3.5
msmqIntegrationBinding	Binding for sending and receiving messages to applications through the use of queues using MSMQ.	3.0/3.5
wsFederationHttpBinding	Binding for advanced WS-* based Web services using federated identity.	3.0/3.5
ws2007HttpBinding	Binding derived from the wsHttpBinding with additional support for the latest WS-* specifications based on standards available in 2007.	3.5

Binding Name	Description	.NET Framework
ws2007FederationHttpBinding	Binding derived from the wsFederationHttpBinding with additional support for the latest WS-* specifications based on standards available in 2007.	3.5

The bindings listed in Table 4.1 can be specified in either code or configuration. Listing 4.1 shows the basicHttpBinding binding specified in configuration. Using configuration allows developers the flexibility to change or modify the binding later on without recompiling the application.

LISTING 4.1 Using a Binding in Configuration

```
<?xml version="1.0" encoding="utf-8" ?>
<configuration>
  <system.serviceModel>
    <client>
      <endpoint address="http://localhost/helloworld"
                binding="basicHttpBinding"
                contract="EssentialWCF.HelloWorld">
      </endpoint>
    </client>
  </system.serviceModel>
</configuration>
```

The BasicHttpBinding binding class is shown in Listing 4.2. Using code allows a developer to use a specific binding without the possibility of its changing later on.

LISTING 4.2 Using a Binding in Code

```
using System;
using System.Collections.Generic;
using System.Net;
using System.Text;
using System.ServiceModel;
using System.ServiceModel.Channels;

namespace EssentialWCF
{
    class Program
    {
```

LISTING 4.2 continued

```
        static void Main(string[] args)
        {
            BasicHttpBinding binding = new BasicHttpBinding();

            using (HelloWorldClient client =
new HelloWorldClient(Binding,
"http://localhost/helloworld"))
                client.SayHello("Rich");

            Console.ReadLine();
        }
    }
}
```

Bindings compose a channel stack through a collection of *binding elements*. Binding elements represent a channel object in the channel stack. Each binding, such as the basicHttpBinding binding, is composed of several binding elements. You can examine this through code by instantiating the binding and enumerating over the binding element collection. This is shown in Listing 4.3.

LISTING 4.3 Examining BindingElementCollection

```
using System;
using System.Collections.Generic;
using System.Text;
using System.ServiceModel;
using System.ServiceModel.Channels;

namespace EssentialWCF
{
    class Program
    {
        static void Main(string[] args)
        {
            OutputBindingElements(new WSHttpBinding());
            OutputBindingElements(new NetTcpBinding());
            OutputBindingElements(new NetNamedPipeBinding());
            OutputBindingElements(new BasicHttpBinding());

            Console.ReadLine();
        }

        static void OutputBindingElements(Binding binding)
        {
```

```
        Console.WriteLine(" Binding : {0}", binding.GetType().Name);

        BindingElementCollection elements =
binding.CreateBindingElements();

        foreach (BindingElement element in elements)
            Console.WriteLine(" {0}", element.GetType().FullName);

        Console.WriteLine();
      }
    }
  }
```

Figure 4.1 shows the output for the code in Listing 4.3 using four of the out-of-the-box bindings: WSHttpBinding, NetTcpBinding, NetNamed-PipeBinding, and the BasicHttpBinding binding. We will look at the WSHttpBinding binding so we can understand the binding elements used to construct the binding.

The default configuration for the WSHttpBinding is made up of four binding elements: HttpTransportBindingElement, TextMessageEncoding-BindingElement, SymmetricSecurityBindingElement, and Transaction-FlowBindingElement. These binding elements allow for communication over the HTTP protocol, text-based message encoding, security, and transaction support, respectively. Note that the list of binding elements is based on the default configuration. The binding may add or remove binding elements depending on how you configure the binding.

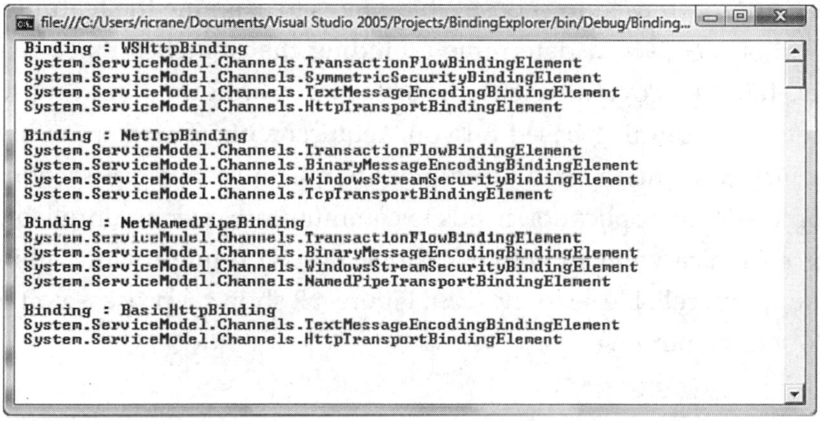

FIGURE 4.1 Binding Explorer

Note how each binding is composed of one or more binding elements and that some of those binding elements are common across bindings. For example, both the WSHttpBinding and the BasicHttpBinding use the HttpTransportBindingElement. These two bindings use the same transport mechanism but differ in the functionality and capabilities they support. We will discuss the difference between these bindings in this chapter.

The remainder of this chapter focuses on Web services, cross-machine, local-machine, and queue-based communication. These are the forms of communication that developers should know to get started with WCF. There are other forms of communication based on REST/POX, peer networking, and federated security that are discussed in more detail in Chapter 13, "Programmable Web," Chapter 12, "Peer Networking," and Chapter 8, "Security," respectively.

Choosing an Appropriate Binding

There are nine preconfigured bindings in WCF. Each of these provides the means for a particular distributed computing need. There are several factors that determine which binding to choose for a specific application, including security, interoperability, reliability, performance, and transaction requirements. Table 4.2 compares the nine preconfigured bindings by showing the common features they support. This table can be used to select a best binding for a particular need.

The approach used to choose a binding is to examine the features your application needs and determine a binding that matches those requirements. Table 4.2 compares features of each preconfigured binding so you can select the binding based on your requirements. There are many features, including interoperability, durability, reliability, and transactions. For example, if your application needs to communicate over an unreliable network, such as a wireless network connection, you might want a binding that supports reliable sessions (RS). Figure 4.2 shows a process you might use to select a binding.

TABLE 4.2 Supported Features of Each Binding

Binding Name	Communication			Performance	Reliable Sessions	Durable Reliable Messaging	WS-*Transactions	WS-* Interoperability	Message-Level Security	Transport-Level Security
	Duplex	One-way	Request/Reply							
basicHttpBinding		X	X	Good				X	X	X
wsHttpBinding		X	X	Good	RS*		X	X	X	X
wsDualHttpBinding	X	X	X	Good	RS*		X	X	X	X
netTcpBinding	X	X	X	Better	RS*		X		X	X
netNamedPipeBinding	X	X	X	Best			X			X
netMsmqBinding		X		Better		X			X	X
netPeerTcpBinding	X	X		Good						X
msmqIntegrationBinding		X		Better		X				X
wsFederationHttpBinding		X	X	Good	RS*		X	X	X	X
ws2007HttpBinding		X	X	Good	RS*			X	X	X
ws2007FederationHttpBinding		X	X	Good	RS*			X	X	X

* RS = WCF Reliable Sessions is an implementation of SOAP reliable messaging defined by the WS-Reliable Messaging (WS-RM) standard.

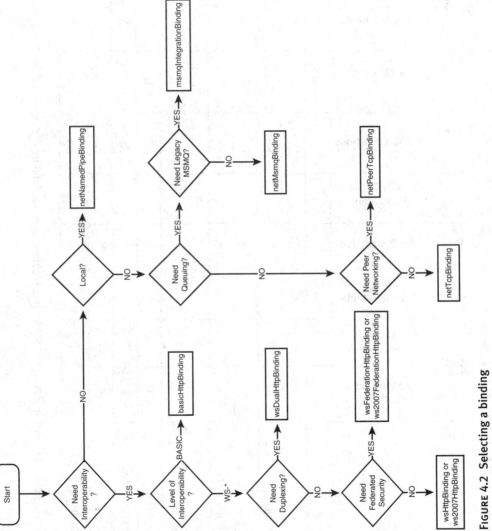

FIGURE 4.2 Selecting a binding

You need to consider many features when selecting a binding. Table 4.2 cannot list them all; therefore, you may need to do further investigation to select an appropriate binding.

Each of the bindings supports a particular communication scenario, such as cross-machine, on-machine, and interoperable communication using Web services. We will examine these scenarios along with the bindings associated with each. There are other scenarios, such as federated security and peer communication. These topics deserve deeper discussion and will be discussed in detail in Chapter 8, "Security," and Chapter 12, "Peer Networking," respectively.

Sample Application

We will now examine each of the preconfigured bindings available in WCF. To demonstrate each binding we will use a sample application based on stock quotes. The sample asks for quotes based on a ticker symbol and returns the stock price. The intent is to expose and consume the same service over different bindings and take note of any changes in code or configuration. Listing 4.4 shows the stock quote service.

LISTING 4.4 **StockQuoteService Service**

```
using System;
using System.Collections.Generic;
using System.Text;
using System.ServiceModel;
using System.Runtime.Serialization;

namespace EssentialWCF
{
    [ServiceContract]
    public interface IStockQuoteService
    {
        [OperationContract]
        double GetQuote(string symbol);
    }

    public class StockQuoteService : IStockQuoteService
    {
        public double GetQuote(string symbol)
        {
            double value;

            if (symbol == "MSFT")
```

LISTING 4.4 continued

```
                value = 31.15;
        else if (symbol == "YHOO")
                value = 28.10;
        else if (symbol == "GOOG")
                value = 450.75;
        else
                value = double.NaN;

        return value;
    }
  }
}
```

Listing 4.5 shows the client proxy that was generated using Add Service Reference from Visual Studio. We hand-edited the proxy to remove any comments and added using statements for commonly used namespaces for formatting purposes. Other than these minor edits, this is the same client code you should expect if you generate your proxies through Add Service Reference or svcutil.exe. Our intent is to use the same client code with the different bindings and take note of any changes in code or configuration.

LISTING 4.5 StockQuoteService Client Proxy

```
using System.CodeDom.Compiler;
using System.Diagnostics;
using System.ServiceModel;
using System.ServiceModel.Channels;

namespace EssentialWCF
{

    [GeneratedCodeAttribute("System.ServiceModel", "3.0.0.0")]
    [ServiceContractAttribute(
      ConfigurationName="IStockQuoteDuplexService",
      CallbackContract=typeof(IStockQuoteDuplexServiceCallback),
      SessionMode=SessionMode.Required)]
    public interface IStockQuoteDuplexService
    {

        [OperationContractAttribute(IsOneWay=true,
            Action="http://tempuri.org/IStockQuoteDuplexService/
            ➥SendQuoteRequest")]
        void SendQuoteRequest(string symbol);
    }
```

```csharp
[GeneratedCodeAttribute("System.ServiceModel", "3.0.0.0")]
public interface IStockQuoteDuplexServiceCallback
{

    [OperationContractAttribute(IsOneWay=true,
        Action="http://tempuri.org/IStockQuoteDuplexService/
        ➥SendQuoteResponse")]
    void SendQuoteResponse(string symbol, double price);
}

[GeneratedCodeAttribute("System.ServiceModel", "3.0.0.0")]
public interface IStockQuoteDuplexServiceChannel :
  IStockQuoteDuplexService, IClientChannel
{
}

[DebuggerStepThroughAttribute()]
[GeneratedCodeAttribute("System.ServiceModel", "3.0.0.0")]
public partial class StockQuoteDuplexServiceClient :
  DuplexClientBase<IStockQuoteDuplexService>,
  IStockQuoteDuplexService
{

    public StockQuoteDuplexServiceClient(
        InstanceContext callbackInstance)
        : base(callbackInstance)
    {
    }

    public StockQuoteDuplexServiceClient(
        InstanceContext callbackInstance,
        string endpointConfigurationName)
        : base(callbackInstance,
                endpointConfigurationName)
    {
    }

    public StockQuoteDuplexServiceClient(
        InstanceContext callbackInstance,
        string endpointConfigurationName,
        string remoteAddress)
        : base(callbackInstance,
        endpointConfigurationName,
                remoteAddress)
    {
    }

    public StockQuoteDuplexServiceClient(
        InstanceContext callbackInstance,
        string endpointConfigurationName,
```

LISTING 4.5 continued

```
            EndpointAddress remoteAddress)
          : base(callbackInstance,
                endpointConfigurationName,
                remoteAddress)
        {
        }

        public StockQuoteDuplexServiceClient(InstanceContext
callbackInstance, Binding binding, EndpointAddress remoteAddress)
            :
                base(callbackInstance, binding, remoteAddress)
        {
        }

        public void SendQuoteRequest(string symbol)
        {
            base.Channel.SendQuoteRequest(symbol);
        }
    }
}
```

This sample application is hosting the service using self-hosting. Listing 4.6 shows the code to self-host the StockQuoteService. See Chapter 7, "Hosting," for more information on self-hosting.

LISTING 4.6 StockQuoteService ServiceHost

```
using System;
using System.Collections.Generic;
using System.Configuration;
using System.Text;
using System.ServiceModel;

namespace EssentialWCF
{
    internal class MyServiceHost
    {
        internal static ServiceHost myServiceHost = null;

        internal static void StartService()
        {
            myServiceHost =
    new ServiceHost(typeof(EssentialWCF.StockQuoteService));
            myServiceHost.Open();
        }

        internal static void StopService()
```

```
        {
            if (myServiceHost.State != CommunicationState.Closed)
                myServiceHost.Close();
        }
    }
}
```

Cross-Machine Communication Between .NET Applications

This section describes the bindings used for cross-machine communication between .NET applications. We will demonstrate how to customize each binding through configuration and code. Each binding will be reviewed in the context of a typical scenario.

> **▪ TIP Bindings That Start with "net" Should Be Used with .NET Applications**
>
> WCF prefixes all bindings that are meant to be used between .NET applications with the "net" prefix. The binding name prefix is one indicator that you should use when selecting a particular binding to use. This means that these bindings have specific features that are available only to .NET applications. Conversely, all bindings that begin with the "ws" prefix are meant for interoperability with non-.NET applications using Web services.

netTcpBinding

The netTcpBinding binding is designed to support communication between .NET applications that are deployed on separate machines across a network, including communication across intranets and the Internet. We refer to this type of communication as *cross-machine communication*. In this situation there is no need for interoperability because both applications are built on .NET. This gives us a great deal of flexibility when communicating across the network. Because no interoperability requirement exists, communication can be optimized for the best performance.

The netTcpBinding binding uses binary encoding and the TCP protocol to achieve the best performance across the network. The general guideline is to use the `netTcpBinding` binding for cross-machine communication between .NET applications. This is not a hard-and-fast rule, but it covers most situations. An example of when the `netTcpBinding` binding is not appropriate is when a firewall separates the two .NET applications. Often the only way you can communicate across a firewall is to use HTTP. In this situation, you will need to use a binding that supports the HTTP protocol used by `basicHttpBinding` binding rather than `netTcpBinding` binding.

The following code shows the addressing format on the `netTcpBinding` binding:

```
net.tcp://{hostname}[:port]/{service location}
```

The default port for the TCP transport is 808. This is the case for any binding based on the `TcpTransportBindingElement` binding element, including the `netTcpBinding` binding.

Table 4.3 lists the binding properties that are configurable on the `netTcpBinding` binding. All of them are important to know, depending on the situation. For example, the default for the `netTcpBinding` binding is to turn off port sharing. This has an impact on your application if you plan to host multiple services over the same port. See the "Sharing Ports Between Services" section in the appendix, "Advanced Topics," for more information on port sharing. Another important property of the `netTcpBinding` is the `maxConnections` property. The `maxConnections` property limits the number of connections to an endpoint. The default value is 10. This needs to be increased in order to maximize throughput.

TABLE 4.3 `netTcpBinding` Binding Properties

Attribute Name	Description	Default
`closeTimeout`	The maximum time to wait for the connection to be closed.	00:01:00
`hostNameComparisonMode`	Specifies the method for hostname comparison when parsing URIs.	StrongWildCard

Attribute Name	Description	Default
listenBacklog	The maximum number of channels waiting to service a request. Any connections greater than this amount are queued.	10
maxBufferPoolSize	Maximum size of any buffer pools used by the transport.	524,888
maxBufferSize	Maximum number of bytes used to buffer incoming messages in memory.	65,536
maxConnections	The maximum number of outbound or inbound connections. Outbound and inbound connections are counted separately.	10
maxReceivedMessageSize	The maximum size of an incoming message.	65,536
name	The name of the binding.	n/a
openTimeout	The maximum time to wait for an open connection operation to complete.	00:01:00
portSharingEnabled	Enable port sharing for the service listener.	false
readerQuotas	Specify the complexity of messages that can be processed (for example, size).	n/a
receiveTimeout	The maximum time to wait for a receive operation to complete.	00:01:00
reliableSession	Specify whether the binding supports exactly once delivery assurances using WS-Reliable Messaging.	n/a
security	Specifies the security settings of the binding.	n/a
sendTimeout	The maximum time to wait for a send operation to complete.	00:01:00
transactionFlow	Enable transactions to flow from the client to the server.	false
transactionProtocol	The type of transactions supported—either OleTransactions or WSAtomic-Transactions.	Ole Trans-actions

n/a—means that the setting is a child element that requires multiple properties to be set or does not apply unless another property is set.

The following configuration information is meant to be used with the sample application shown in Listings 4.2 through 4.4. The configuration information shown in Listing 4.7 exposes the StockQuoteService service using the netTcpBinding binding.

LISTING 4.7 netTcpBinding Host CONFIGURATION

```xml
<?xml version="1.0" encoding="utf-8" ?>
<configuration>
  <system.serviceModel>
    <services>
      <service name="EssentialWCF.StockQuoteService">
        <host>
          <baseAddresses>
            <add baseAddress="net.tcp://localhost/stockquoteservice" />
          </baseAddresses>
        </host>
        <endpoint address=""
                  contract="EssentialWCF.IStockQuoteService"
                  binding="netTcpBinding" />
      </service>
    </services>
  </system.serviceModel>
</configuration>
```

Listing 4.8 shows the client configuration to consume the service using the netTcpBinding binding shown in Listing 4.7.

LISTING 4.8 netTcpBinding Client Configuration

```xml
<?xml version="1.0" encoding="utf-8" ?>
<configuration>
  <system.serviceModel>
    <client>
      <endpoint address="net.tcp://localhost/stockquoteservice"
                binding="netTcpBinding"
                contract="EssentialWCF.IStockQuoteService">
      </endpoint>
    </client>
  </system.serviceModel>
</configuration>
```

Local Machine Communication Between .NET Applications

Interprocess, or cross-process, communication refers to communication between two separate processes running on the same machine. Intraprocess, or in-process, communication refers to communication between two software components running within one process. Together these types of communication make up what we refer to as *local-machine* communication (a.k.a. *on-machine* communication)

Application domains (a.k.a. app-domains) are a mechanism in .NET for further partitioning a Windows process to support multiple .NET applications by isolating them along security and activation boundaries. This means that app-domains are another communication boundary that can be crossed by .NET applications. Because of this we define two additional terms: inter-appdomain and intra-appdomain.

- **inter-appdomain or cross-appdomain**. Communication that occurs between two .NET applications that run in separate app-domains within the same Windows process. This could also be communication within a single .NET application that is designed to run within multiple app-domains.

- **intra-appdomain or in-appdomain**. Communication that occurs within a single .NET application that runs in a single application domain. For our discussion, think of an app-domain as being one or more .NET processes that run within a Windows process.

WCF does not make a distinction between interprocess, intraprocess, inter-appdomain and intra-appdomain communication. Instead, WCF offers a single on-machine transport channel based on *named pipes*. Named pipes are a standard means of interprocess communications (IPC) on Windows as well as UNIX environments. The WCF team considered an in-process binding but decided that it was not necessary for most situations. Do not concern yourself over this decision. There is no loss in functionality. The only difference between a named pipe and a true in-process binding is performance.

The performance of the named pipes binding is good enough for most in-process communication situations. If you find that a single on-machine transport is not sufficient, you have the capability of creating a custom binding that uses a custom transport channel. See the "Creating a Custom Binding" section later in this chapter for more information on creating a custom binding.

netNamedPipeBinding

WCF supports interprocess and intraprocess communication scenarios with the netNamedPipeBinding binding. The netNamedPipeBinding binding leverages a named pipes transport. This is a great binding to use for doing interprocess communication (IPC) because it provides a significant performance increase over the other standard bindings available in WCF. See the "Comparing Binding Performance and Scalability" section later in this chapter for a quick comparison of the performance.

> ■ **TIP** **WCF Restricts the netNamedPipeBinding Binding to Local Machine Communication!**
>
> Although it is possible to use named pipes to communicate across a network, WCF restricts the use to local machine communication. This means that the netNamedPipeBinding binding (and any other binding based on the namedPipeTransport binding element) can be used to ensure that your service is not available across a network. This is accomplished using two mechanisms. First, the Network Security Identifier (SID: S-1-5-2) is denied access to the named pipe. Second, the name of the named pipe is randomly generated and stored in shared memory so only clients running on the same machine can access it.

An address using the netNamedPipeBinding binding is formatted as follows:

```
net.pipe://localhost/{service location}
```

Table 4.4 shows the binding properties that are configurable on the netNamedPipeBinding binding. An important property of the netNamedPipeBinding is the maxConnections property. The maxConnections property limits the number of connections to an endpoint. The default value is 10. This needs to be increased in order to maximize throughput.

TABLE 4.4 netNamedPipeBinding Binding Properties

Attribute Name	Description	Default
closeTimeout	The maximum time to wait for the connection to be closed.	00:01:00
hostNameComparisonMode	Specifies the method for hostname comparison when parsing URIs.	StrongWildCard
maxBufferPoolSize	Maximum size of any buffer pools used by the transport.	524,888
maxBufferSize	Maximum number of bytes used to buffer incoming messages in memory.	65,536
maxConnections	The maximum number of outbound or inbound connections. Outbound and inbound connections are counted separately.	10
maxReceivedMessageSize	The maximum size of an incoming message.	65,536
name	The name of the binding.	
openTimeout	The maximum time to wait for an open connection operation to complete.	00:01:00
readerQuotas	Specify the complexity of messages that can be processed (for example, size).	n/a
receiveTimeout	The maximum time to wait for a receive operation to complete.	00:01:00

continues

ute Name	Description	Default
security	Specifies the security settings of the binding.	n/a
sendTimeout	The maximum time to wait for a send operation to complete.	00:01:00
transactionFlow	Enable transactions to flow from the client to the server.	false
transactionProtocol	The type of transactions supported either OleTransactions or WSAtomicTransactions.	OleTransactions

n/a—means that the setting is a child element that requires multiple properties to be set or does not apply unless another property is set.

The following configuration information is meant to be used with the sample application shown in Listings 4.2 through 4.4. The configuration information shown in Listing 4.9 exposes the StockQuoteService service using the netNamedPipeBinding binding.

LISTING 4.9 netNamedPipeBinding Host Configuration

```xml
<?xml version="1.0" encoding="utf-8" ?>
<configuration>
  <system.serviceModel>
    <services>
      <service name="EssentialWCF.StockQuoteService">
        <host>
          <baseAddresses>
            <add baseAddress="net.pipe://localhost/stockquoteservice" />
          </baseAddresses>
        </host>
        <endpoint address=""
                  contract="EssentialWCF.IStockQuoteService"
                  binding="netNamedPipeBinding" />
      </service>
    </services>
  </system.serviceModel>
</configuration>
```

Listing 4.10 shows the client configuration to consume the service using the netNamedPipeBinding binding shown in Listing 4.9.

LISTING 4.10 netNamedPipeBinding Client Configuration

```xml
<?xml version="1.0" encoding="utf-8" ?>
<configuration>
  <system.serviceModel>
    <client>
      <endpoint address="net.pipe://localhost/stockquoteservice"
                binding="netNamedPipeBinding"
                contract="EssentialWCF.IStockQuoteService">
      </endpoint>
    </client>
  </system.serviceModel>
</configuration>
```

Communication Using Basic Web Services

Web services are the foundation for interoperable communication among heterogeneous systems. For example, services built on Java-based platforms such as IBM Websphere or BEA WebLogic must communicate seamlessly with clients and services built on .NET. And services built on .NET must communicate seamlessly with clients or services built on Java-based platforms. Prior to WCF, ASP.NET Web Services (ASMX) and Web Service Enhancements (WSE) provided this capability on the .NET platform. With .NET 3.0, WCF is a direct replacement for these technologies and provides a single unified framework for building Web services. WCF includes several bindings for exposing interoperable Web services, including basicHttpBinding, wsHttpBinding, wsDualHttpBinding, and wsFederationHttpBinding bindings.

In this section, we examine the basicHttpBinding binding, which offers support for Web services based on the WS-I Basic Profile 1.1. As of 2007, the WS-I Basic Profile 1.1 covers the most widely deployed set of Web service protocols and is the Web service technology that most developers are familiar with. Other bindings based on Web services are discussed in the "Communication Using Advanced Web Services" section later in this chapter and are also discussed in Chapter 8 of this book.

basicHttpBinding

The `basicHttpBinding` binding offers support for Web service communication based on the WS-I Basic Profile 1.1 (WS-BP 1.1) specification. This includes standards such as SOAP 1.1, WSDL 1.1, and Message Security 1.0 (including X.509 and UserName Tokens Profile v1.0). The WS-BP 1.1 specification has been around since 2004. Although the `basicHttpBinding` binding offers interoperability across heterogeneous systems, it does not offer support for the latest Web service standards such as transactions and reliable messaging. The `basicHttpBinding` binding is meant to be used with applications that use Web services based on the WS-BP 1.1 specification, such as ASP.NET ASMX Web Services.

> **■ NOTE   Create Services Based on the Latest Standards**
>
> The `basicHttpBinding` binding is meant to work with legacy Web services based on prior technologies such as ASP.NET. This means that the `basicHttpBinding` binding is configured by default to use older standards such as SOAP 1.1. The `basicHttpBinding` binding is also the only binding that is not secure by default. If you need to create new Web services, we recommend using the `ws2007HttpBinding` binding because it is configured to use newer standards and is secure by default.

The following code shows the addressing formats for the `basicHttpBinding` binding:

```
http://{hostname}[:port]/{service location}
https://{hostname}[:port]/{service location}
```

The default port is port 80 for http and port 443 for https. This is the case for any binding based on the `HttpTransportBindingElement` binding element, including the `basicHttpBinding` binding. The most common way to secure the `basicHttpBinding` binding is to use https, which uses SSL/TLS encryption.

Table 4.5 lists the binding properties that are configurable on the `basicHttpBinding` binding.

TABLE 4.5 `basicHttpBinding` Binding Properties

Attribute Name	Description	Default
bypassProxyOnLocal	Bypass the proxy settings for local endpoints.	false
closeTimeout	The maximum time to wait for the connection to be closed.	00:01:00
hostNameComparisonMode	Specifies the method for hostname comparison when parsing URIs.	StrongWildCard
maxBufferPoolSize	Maximum size of any buffer pools used by the transport.	524,888
maxBufferSize	Maximum number of bytes used to buffer incoming messages in memory.	65,536
maxReceivedMessageSize	The maximum size of an incoming message.	65,536
messageEncoding	The type of encoding used to encode messages.	Text
name	The name of the binding.	
openTimeout	The maximum time to wait for an open connection operation to complete.	00:01:00
proxyAddress	Specify a specific Web proxy to use. `useDefaultWebProxy` must be false for this setting to apply.	n/a
readerQuotas	Specify the complexity of messages that can be processed (for example, size).	n/a
receiveTimeout	The maximum time to wait for a receive operation to complete.	00:01:00

continues

TABLE 4.5 continued

Attribute Name	Description	Default
security	Specifies the security settings of the binding.	n/a
sendTimeout	The maximum time to wait for a send operation to complete.	00:01:00
textEncoding	The method of character encoding used to encode messages. messageEncoding must be set to Text for this setting to apply.	utf-8
transferMode	Determines how messages are sent across the network. Messages can either be buffered or streamed.	Buffered
useDefaultWebProxy	Use the default Web proxy specified by the operating system.	true

The following configuration information is meant to be used with the sample application shown in Listings 4.2 through 4.4. The configuration information shown in Listing 4.11 exposes the StockQuoteService service using the basicHttpBinding binding.

LISTING 4.11 basicHttpBinding Host Configuration

```xml
<?xml version="1.0" encoding="utf-8" ?>
<configuration>
  <system.serviceModel>
    <services>
      <service name="EssentialWCF.StockQuoteService">
        <host>
          <baseAddresses>
            <add baseAddress="http://localhost/stockquoteservice" />
          </baseAddresses>
        </host>
        <endpoint address=""
                  contract="EssentialWCF.IStockQuoteService"
                  binding="basicHttpBinding" />
      </service>
    </services>
  </system.serviceModel>
</configuration>
```

Listing 4.12 shows the client configuration to consume the service using the `basicHttpBinding` binding shown in Listing 4.11.

LISTING 4.12 `basicHttpBinding` Client Configuration

```
<?xml version="1.0" encoding="utf-8" ?>
<configuration>
  <system.serviceModel>
    <client>
      <endpoint address="http://localhost/stockquoteservice"
                binding="basicHttpBinding"
                contract="EssentialWCF.IStockQuoteService">
      </endpoint>
    </client>
  </system.serviceModel>

</configuration>
```

Communication Using Advanced Web Services

As mentioned previously, Web services are the foundation for interoperable communication among heterogeneous systems. Advanced Web services are those Web services exposed using the WS-* specifications (pronounced *ws-star*). WCF has support for the WS-* specifications including security, reliable messaging, and transactions. The list of supported specifications is shown in Table 4.6. Support for these features is available in the `wsHttpBinding`, `wsDualHttpBinding`, and `wsFederationHttpBinding` bindings.

> ■ **NOTE**   Bindings That Start with "ws" Should Be Used for Interoperability Using Web Services.
>
> Windows Communication Foundation prefixes all bindings that are meant for interoperability using Web services begin with the "ws" prefix. Conversely, all bindings that begin with the "net" prefix should be used only between .NET applications.

TABLE 4.6 WS-* Specifications Supported by the wsHttpBinding Binding

Standard	Description
SOAP 1.2	Lightweight protocol for exchange of information in a decentralized, distributed environment
WS-Addressing 2005/08	Transport-neutral mechanisms to address Web services and messages
WSS Message Security 1.0	Specification for securing Web services using a variety of mechanisms such as PKI, Kerberos, and SSL
WSS Message Security UsernameToken Profile 1.1	Support for security tokens based on a username and optionally a password (or password equivalent such as a shared secret)
WSS SOAP Message Security X509 Token Profile 1.1	Support for tokens based on X.509 certificates
WS-SecureConversation	Extensions to WS-Security to provide a secure context for multiple message exchanges
WS-Trust	Extensions to WS-Security to request and issue tokens and to manage trust relationships
WS-SecurityPolicy	Policy assertions for WS-Security, WS-SecureConversation, and WS-Trust, which are expressed using WS-Policy
WS-ReliableMessaging	A protocol for guaranteeing messages are delivered, properly ordered, and received without duplication
WS-Coordination	A framework for providing protocols that coordinate the actions of distributed applications
WS-Atomic Transactions	A protocol that coordinates the actions of distributed applications based on the atomic transactions
WS-Addressing	A transport-neutral mechanism for addressing Web services

wsHttpBinding

Support for WS-* is included throughout the WCF framework. The `wsHttp-Binding` binding is an example of this support. This binding provides interoperable communication across heterogeneous platforms as well as advanced infrastructure level protocols, such as security, reliable messaging, and transactions. The `wsHttpBinding` binding is the default binding in .NET Framework 3.0 whenever you need interoperable communication based on Web services.

The following code shows the addressing formats for the `wsHttpBinding` binding:

```
http://{hostname}:{port}/{service location}
https://{hostname}:{port}/{service location}
```

The default port is port 80 for http and port 443 for https. This is the case for any binding based on the `HttpTransportBindingElement` binding element, including the `wsHttpBinding` binding.

Table 4.7 shows the binding properties that are configurable on the `wsHttpBinding` binding.

TABLE 4.7 `wsHttpBinding` Binding Properties

Attribute Name	Description	Default
bypassProxyOnLocal	Bypass the proxy settings for local endpoints.	false
closeTimeout	The maximum time to wait for the connection to be closed.	00:01:00
hostNameComparisonMode	Specifies the method for hostname comparison when parsing URIs.	StrongWildCard
maxBufferPoolSize	Maximum size of any buffer pools used by the transport.	524,888
maxReceivedMessageSize	The maximum size of an incoming message.	65,536

continues

TABLE 4.7 continued

Attribute Name	Description	Default
messageEncoding	The type of encoding used to encode messages.	Text
name	The name of the binding.	
openTimeout	The maximum time to wait for an open connection operation to complete.	00:01:00
proxyAddress	Specify a specific Web proxy to use. useDefaultWebProxy must be false for this setting to apply.	n/a
readerQuotas	Specify the complexity of messages that can be processed (for example, size).	n/a
receiveTimeout	The maximum time to wait for a receive operation to complete.	00:01:00
reliableSession	Specify whether the binding supports exactly once delivery assurances using WS-Reliable Messaging.	n/a
security	Specifies the security settings of the binding.	n/a
sendTimeout	The maximum time to wait for a send operation to complete.	00:01:00
textEncoding	Determines how messages are sent across the network. Messages can either be buffered or streamed.	utf-8
transactionFlow	Enable transactions to flow from the client to the server.	false
useDefaultWebProxy	Use the default Web proxy specified by the operating system.	true

The following configuration information is meant to be used with the sample application shown in Listings 4.2 through 4.4. The configuration information shown in Listing 4.13 exposes the StockQuoteService service using the wsHttpBinding binding.

LISTING 4.13 wsHttpBinding Host Configuration

```xml
<?xml version="1.0" encoding="utf-8" ?>
<configuration>
  <system.serviceModel>
    <services>
      <service name="EssentialWCF.StockQuoteService">
        <host>
          <baseAddresses>
            <add baseAddress="http://localhost/stockquoteservice" />
          </baseAddresses>
        </host>
        <endpoint address=""
                  contract="EssentialWCF.IStockQuoteService"
                  binding="wsHttpBinding" />
      </service>
    </services>
  </system.serviceModel>
</configuration>
```

Listing 4.14 shows the client configuration to consume the service using the wsHttpBinding binding shown in Listing 4.13.

LISTING 4.14 wsHttpBinding Client Configuration

```xml
<?xml version="1.0" encoding="utf-8" ?>
<configuration>
  <system.serviceModel>
    <client>
      <endpoint address="http://localhost/stockquoteservice"
                binding="wsHttpBinding"
                contract="EssentialWCF.IStockQuoteService">
      </endpoint>
    </client>
  </system.serviceModel>
</configuration>
```

ws2007HttpBinding

.NET Framework 3.5 introduces a new binding for Web service interoperability called the ws2007HttpBinding binding. This binding is similar to the wsHttpBinding binding except that it supports the latest WS-* standards available for messaging, security, reliable messaging, and transactions. Table 4.8 lists the new WS-* standards that are supported by the ws2007HttpBinding binding.

TABLE 4.8 WS-* Specifications Supported by the ws2007HttpBinding Binding

Standard	Description
WS-SecureConversation v1.3	Extensions to WS-Security to provide a secure context for multiple message exchanges
WS-Trust v1.3	Extensions to WS-Security to request and issue tokens and to manage trust relationships
WS-SecurityPolicy v1.2	Policy assertions for WS-Security, WS-Secure-Conversation, and WS-Trust, which are expressed using WS-Policy
Web Services Reliable Messaging v1.1	A protocol for guaranteeing messages are delivered, properly ordered, and received without duplication
Web Services Atomic Transaction v1.1	A protocol that coordinates the actions of distributed applications based on the atomic transactions
Web Services Coordination v1.1	A framework for providing protocols that coordinate the actions of distributed applications

The following code shows the addressing formats for the ws2007Http-Binding binding:

```
http://{hostname}:{port}/{service location}
https://{hostname}:{port}/{service location}
```

The default port is port 80 for http and port 443 for https. This is the case for any binding based on the `HttpTransportBindingElement` binding element, including the `wsHttpBinding` binding.

Table 4.9 shows the binding properties that are configurable on the `wsHttpBinding` binding.

TABLE 4.9 `ws2007HttpBinding` Binding Properties

Attribute Name	Description	Default
bypassProxyOnLocal	Bypass the proxy settings for local endpoints.	false
closeTimeout	The maximum time to wait for the connection to be closed.	00:01:00
hostNameComparisonMode	Specifies the method for hostname comparison when parsing URIs.	StrongWildCard
maxBufferPoolSize	Maximum size of any buffer pools used by the transport.	524,888
maxReceivedMessageSize	The maximum size of an incoming message.	65,536
messageEncoding	The type of encoding used to encode messages.	Text
name	The name of the binding.	
openTimeout	The maximum time to wait for an open connection operation to complete.	00:01:00
proxyAddress	Specify a specific Web proxy to use. useDefaultWebProxy must be false for this setting to apply.	n/a
readerQuotas	Specify the complexity of messages that can be processed (for example, size).	n/a

continues

TABLE 4.9 continued

Attribute Name	Description	Default
receiveTimeout	The maximum time to wait for a receive operation to complete.	00:01:00
reliableSession	Specify whether the binding supports exactly once delivery assurances using WS-Reliable Messaging.	n/a
security	Specifies the security settings of the binding.	n/a
sendTimeout	The maximum time to wait for a send operation to complete.	00:01:00
textEncoding	Determines how messages are sent across the network. Messages can either be buffered or streamed.	utf-8
transactionFlow	Enable transactions to flow from the client to the server.	false
useDefaultWebProxy	Use the default Web proxy specified by the operating system.	true

n/a—means that the setting is a child element that requires multiple properties to be set or does not apply unless another property is set.

The following configuration information is meant to be used with the sample application shown in Listings 4.2 through 4.4. The configuration information shown in Listing 4.15 exposes the StockQuoteService service using the ws2007HttpBinding binding.

LISTING 4.15 ws2007HttpBinding Host Configuration

```
<?xml version="1.0" encoding="utf-8" ?>
<configuration>
  <system.serviceModel>
    <services>
      <service name="EssentialWCF.StockQuoteService">
        <host>
          <baseAddresses>
            <add baseAddress="http://localhost/stockquoteservice" />
```

```
            </baseAddresses>
        </host>
        <endpoint address=""
                  contract="EssentialWCF.IStockQuoteService"
                  binding="ws2007HttpBinding" />
      </service>
    </services>
  </system.serviceModel>
</configuration>
```

Listing 4.16 shows the client configuration to consume the service using the `ws2007HttpBinding` binding shown in Listing 4.15.

LISTING 4.16 `ws2007HttpBinding` Client Configuration

```
<?xml version="1.0" encoding="utf-8" ?>
<configuration>
  <system.serviceModel>
    <client>
      <endpoint address="http://localhost/stockquoteservice"
                binding="ws2007HttpBinding"
                contract="EssentialWCF.IStockQuoteService">
      </endpoint>
    </client>
  </system.serviceModel>
</configuration>
```

wsDualHttpBinding

The `wsDualHttpBinding` binding is similar to the `wsHttpBinding` binding, with additional support for duplex communication and lack of support for transport-level security. Duplex communication is accomplished through two shape-changing binding elements: the `OneWayBindingElement` and `CompositeDuplexBindingElement` binding elements. The `CompositeDuplexBindingElement` binding element layers a duplex communication channel on top of two one-way channels. The `wsDualHttpBinding` binding uses the `HttpTransportBindingElement` binding element. This transport supports only the request-reply message exchange pattern. The `OneWayBindingElement` binding element allows the `HttpTransportBindingElement` binding element to be used with the `CompositeDuplexBindingElement` binding element.

The wsDualHttpBinding binding does not support transport-level security. This means that SSL/TLS encryption is not possible using the wsDualHttpBinding binding.

The following code shows the addressing formats for the wsDualHttp-Binding binding.

```
http://{hostname}:{port}/{service location}
```

The default port is port 80 for http. This is the case for any binding based on the HttpTransportBindingElement binding element, including the wsDualHttpBinding binding.

Table 4.10 lists the binding properties that are configurable on the wsDualHttpBinding binding.

TABLE 4.10 wsDualHttpBinding Binding Properties

Attribute Name	Description	Default
bypassProxyOnLocal	Bypass the proxy settings for local endpoints.	false
closeTimeout	The maximum time to wait for the connection to be closed.	00:01:00
hostNameComparisonMode	Specifies the method for hostname comparison when parsing URIs.	StrongWildCard
maxBufferPoolSize	Maximum size of any buffer pools used by the transport.	524,888
maxReceivedMessageSize	The maximum size of an incoming message.	65,536
messageEncoding	The type of encoding used to encode messages.	Text
name	The name of the binding.	
openTimeout	The maximum time to wait for an open connection operation to complete.	00:01:00

Attribute Name	Description	Default
proxyAddress	Specify a specific Web proxy to use. `useDefaultWebProxy` must be false for this setting to apply.	n/a
readerQuotas	Specify the complexity of messages that can be processed (for example, size).	n/a
receiveTimeout	The maximum time to wait for a receive operation to complete.	00:01:00
reliableSession	Specify whether the binding supports exactly once delivery assurances using WS-Reliable Messaging.	n/a
security	Specifies the security settings of the binding.	n/a
sendTimeout	The maximum time to wait for a send operation to complete.	00:01:00
textEncoding	Determines how messages are sent across the network. Messages can either be buffered or streamed.	utf-8
transactionFlow	Enable transactions to flow from the client to the server.	false
useDefaultWebProxy	Use the default Web proxy specified by the operating system.	true

We have modified the `StockQuoteService` application for the `wsDualHttp-Binding` binding to support duplex communication. Listing 4.17 shows the `StockQuoteDuplexService` implementation. The service supports the duplex message exchange pattern using the `IStockQuoteCallback` contract, which is the callback contract specified for the `IStockQuoteDuplexService` contract.

LISTING 4.17 IStockQuoteDuplexService, IStockQuoteCallback, and
StockQuoteDuplexService

```csharp
using System;
using System.Collections.Generic;
using System.ServiceModel;
using System.Text;

namespace EssentialWCF
{
    [ServiceContract(CallbackContract = typeof(IStockQuoteCallback),
                     SessionMode = SessionMode.Required)]
    public interface IStockQuoteDuplexService
    {
        [OperationContract(IsOneWay = true)]
        void SendQuoteRequest(string symbol);
    }

    public interface IStockQuoteCallback
    {
        [OperationContract(IsOneWay = true)]
        void SendQuoteResponse(string symbol, double price);
    }

    [ServiceBehavior(InstanceContextMode =
InstanceContextMode.PerSession)]
    public class StockQuoteDuplexService : IStockQuoteDuplexService
    {
        public void SendQuoteRequest(string symbol)
        {
            double value;

            if (symbol == "MSFT")
                value = 31.15;
            else if (symbol == "YHOO")
                value = 28.10;
            else if (symbol == "GOOG")
                value = 450.75;
            else
                value = double.NaN;

            OperationContext ctx = OperationContext.Current;
            IStockQuoteCallback callback =
ctx.GetCallbackChannel<IStockQuoteCallback>();
            callback.SendQuoteResponse(symbol, value);
        }
    }
}
```

We must change the self-hosting code for our example because we changed the implementation that we are using to one that supports duplex messaging. Listing 4.18 shows the hosting code for the StockQuoteDuplexService service.

LISTING 4.18 StockQuoteDuplexService ServiceHost Service

```
using System;
using System.Collections.Generic;
using System.Configuration;
using System.Text;
using System.ServiceModel;

namespace EssentialWCF
{
    internal class MyServiceHost
    {
        internal static ServiceHost myServiceHost = null;

        internal static void StartService()
        {
            myServiceHost =
new ServiceHost(typeof(EssentialWCF.StockQuoteDuplexService));
            myServiceHost.Open();
        }

        internal static void StopService()
        {
            if (myServiceHost.State != CommunicationState.Closed)
                myServiceHost.Close();
        }
    }
}
```

The configuration information shown in Listing 4.19 exposes the StockQuoteDuplexService service using the wsDualHttpBinding binding.

LISTING 4.19 wsDualHttpBinding Host Configuration

```
<?xml version="1.0" encoding="utf-8" ?>
<configuration>
  <system.serviceModel>
    <services>
      <service name="EssentialWCF.StockQuoteDuplexService">
        <host>
          <baseAddresses>
            <add baseAddress="http://localhost/stockquoteservice" />
```

LISTING 4.19 continued

```
                </baseAddresses>
            </host>
            <endpoint address=""
                        binding="wsDualHttpBinding"
                        contract="EssentialWCF.IStockQuoteDuplexService">
            </endpoint>
          </service>
        </services>
      </system.serviceModel>
    </configuration>
```

The configuration information shown in Listing 4.20 is for the client to consume a service based on the IStockQuoteDuplexService contract using the wsDualHttpBinding binding. The clientBaseAddress specifies the endpoint on which the client will listen for callback messages.

LISTING 4.20 wsDualHttpBinding Client Configuration

```
<?xml version="1.0" encoding="utf-8" ?>
<configuration>
  <system.serviceModel>
    <client>
      <endpoint address="http://localhost/stockquoteservice"
                  binding="wsDualHttpBinding"
                  bindingConfiguration="SpecifyClientBaseAddress"
                  contract="IStockQuoteDuplexService">
      </endpoint>
    </client>
    <bindings>
      <wsDualHttpBinding>
        <binding name="SpecifyClientBaseAddress"
                  clientBaseAddress="http://localhost:8001/client/" />
      </wsDualHttpBinding>
    </bindings>
  </system.serviceModel>
</configuration>
```

The client application is shown in Listing 4.21. The client implements the IStockQuoteDuplexServiceCallback interface to receive callback messages from the service. The client application passes a reference to the IStockQuoteDuplexServiceCallback interface using the InstanceContext class. The InstanceContext class is passed to the constructor of the client proxy.

LISTING 4.21 wsDualHttpBinding Client Application

```csharp
using System;
using System.Collections.Generic;
using System.Net;
using System.Text;
using System.Threading;
using System.ServiceModel;
using System.ServiceModel.Channels;

namespace EssentialWCF
{
    public class Program : IStockQuoteDuplexServiceCallback
    {
        private static AutoResetEvent waitForResponse;

        static void Main(string[] args)
        {
            string symbol = "MSFT";

            waitForResponse = new AutoResetEvent(false);

            InstanceContext callbackInstance =
                new InstanceContext(new Program());
            using (StockQuoteDuplexServiceClient client =
                new StockQuoteDuplexServiceClient(callbackInstance))
            {
                client.SendQuoteRequest(symbol);
                waitForResponse.WaitOne();
            }

            Console.ReadLine();
        }

        #region IStockQuoteDuplexServiceCallback Members

        public void SendQuoteResponse(string symbol, double price)
        {
            Console.WriteLine("{0} @ ${1}", symbol, price);
            waitForResponse.Set();
        }

        #endregion
    }
}
```

Listing 4.22 shows the client proxy generated by svcutil.exe. The big difference between this client proxy and the previous implementation is

that the client derives from the DuplexClientBase class rather than the
ClientBase class. The DuplexClientBase class adds support for duplex
messaging.

LISTING 4.22 wsDualHttpBinding Client Proxy

```
using System.CodeDom.Compiler;
using System.Diagnostics;
using System.ServiceModel;
using System.ServiceModel.Channels;

namespace EssentialWCF
{

    [GeneratedCodeAttribute("System.ServiceModel", "3.0.0.0")]
    [ServiceContractAttribute(
        ConfigurationName = "IStockQuoteDuplexService",
        CallbackContract = typeof(IStockQuoteDuplexServiceCallback),
        SessionMode = SessionMode.Required)]
    public interface IStockQuoteDuplexService
    {

        [OperationContractAttribute(IsOneWay = true,
            Action="http://tempuri.org/IStockQuoteDuplexService/
➥SendQuoteRequest")]
        void SendQuoteRequest(string symbol);
    }

    [GeneratedCodeAttribute("System.ServiceModel", "3.0.0.0")]
    public interface IStockQuoteDuplexServiceCallback
    {

        [OperationContractAttribute(IsOneWay = true,
            Action="http://tempuri.org/IStockQuoteDuplexService/
➥SendQuoteResponse")]
        void SendQuoteResponse(string symbol, double price);
    }

    [GeneratedCodeAttribute("System.ServiceModel", "3.0.0.0")]
    public interface IStockQuoteDuplexServiceChannel :
        IStockQuoteDuplexService, IClientChannel
    {
    }

    [DebuggerStepThroughAttribute()]
    [GeneratedCodeAttribute("System.ServiceModel", "3.0.0.0")]
    public partial class StockQuoteDuplexServiceClient :
        DuplexClientBase<IStockQuoteDuplexService>,
```

```
        IStockQuoteDuplexService
    {

        public StockQuoteDuplexServiceClient(
                InstanceContext callbackInstance)
            : base(callbackInstance)
        {
        }

        public StockQuoteDuplexServiceClient(
                InstanceContext callbackInstance,
                string endpointConfigurationName)
            : base(callbackInstance, endpointConfigurationName)
        {
        }

        public StockQuoteDuplexServiceClient(
                InstanceContext callbackInstance,
                string endpointConfigurationName,
                string remoteAddress)
            : base(callbackInstance,
                endpointConfigurationName,
                remoteAddress)
        {
        }

        public StockQuoteDuplexServiceClient(
                InstanceContext callbackInstance,
                string endpointConfigurationName,
                EndpointAddress remoteAddress)
            : base(callbackInstance,
                endpointConfigurationName,
                remoteAddress)
        {
        }

        public StockQuoteDuplexServiceClient(
                InstanceContext callbackInstance,
                Binding binding,
                EndpointAddress remoteAddress)
            : base(callbackInstance, binding, remoteAddress)
        {
        }

        public void SendQuoteRequest(string symbol)
        {
            base.Channel.SendQuoteRequest(symbol);
        }
    }
}
```

Comparing Binding Performance and Scalability

Developers need to know about the performance and scalability characteristics of bindings. Performance and scalability are important when you are working with real-world applications where service-level agreements and user experience matters. Users will complain about an application that performs poorly. Applications that do not scale usually mean that business objectives are not being met.

We have provided a simple performance comparison of four bindings available in WCF. The operation under test is a simple operation that returns a 256-character string. Listing 4.23 shows the service being used to compare performance between each binding.

LISTING 4.23 Performance Test Service

```
public class PerformanceTestService : IPerformanceTestService
{
    private static string String256;

    static PerformanceTestService()
    {
        String256 = "".PadRight(256, 'X');
    }

    public string Get256Bytes()
    {
        return String256;
    }
}
```

The service was exposed over four different bindings: netNamedPipe Binding, netTcpBinding, wsHttpBinding, and basicHttpBinding. A test client called the Get256Bytes operation 50,000 times sequentially to compare the differences between the bindings. We then measured the average elapsed time, operations per second, and CPU time. All tests were performed on a single workstation running both server and client. This was done so that we could compare the performance of all the bindings. Figure 4.3 shows the average response time for each binding. You can use the response-time measurement to help examine user experience.

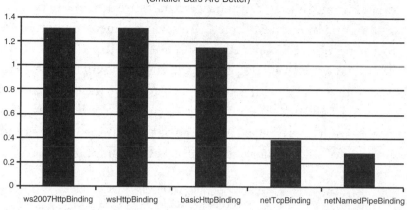

FIGURE 4.3 Average response time

Figure 4.4 shows the average number of operations per second for each binding. This measurement has an impact on the throughput. Only a single instance of the test client was used for these tests. Additional throughput could be achieved if multiple clients were used. Operations per second is one measurement we use to determine scalability.

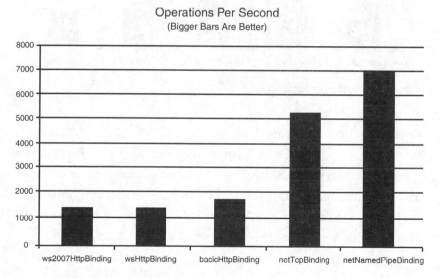

FIGURE 4.4 Operations per second

Scalability should also take into account hardware resources consumed for each operation. Figure 4.5 attempts to measure scalability by showing the cost of an operation in MCycles. MCycles is a measurement based on CPU processing power an operation uses. For the purposes of this test, we used a Dell 4700 with a 3.4GHz Pentium 4 processor, which equates to 3400 MCycles. Notice that the measurements for the `ws2007HttpBinding`, `wsHttpBinding`, and the `basicHttpBinding` bindings have significantly higher cost than the `netTcpBinding` or the `netNamedPipeBinding` bindings. This is because of the overhead needed for interoperability.

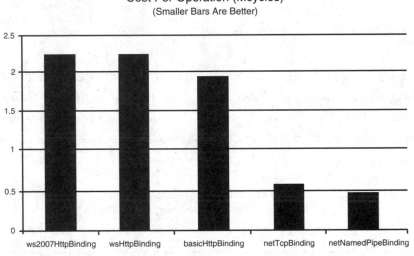

FIGURE 4.5 Cost per operation

The WCF team has released a whitepaper on the performance of WCF (available at http://msdn2.microsoft.com/en-us/library/bb310550.aspx). The paper goes into much more detail and considers security settings such as transport, message, and mixed mode, and compares previous technologies such as NET Remoting, Web Service Enhancements, ASP.NET Web Services, and Enterprise Services.

Communication Using Queued Services

Connected applications are applications that require both the client and the server to be running at the same time and reachable over a network.

Disconnected applications are ones in which the client can function without connectivity to the server, but not all features are available in that mode. Disconnected applications must cache data locally, must communicate in some asynchronous manner, and must persist any messages so they can be delivered when connectivity is reestablished.

Persisted queues are a common technique for building disconnected applications. Queues can be implemented in a file system as a series of folders and files, in a relational database as rows in a table, or using special purpose software. Regardless of the technique, queues offer many advantages, such as inherent asynchronous messaging and automatic load leveling. WCF offers the capability for communication through queues using Microsoft Message Queue (MSMQ). There are two bindings available to use with MSMQ: `netMsmqBinding` and `msmqIntegrationBinding`. The `netMsmqBinding` binding is used when you are developing a new application that wants to use WCF and MSMQ as a transport. The `msmqIntegrationBinding` binding is used for interoperability with an existing MSMQ application.

netMsmqBinding

MSMQ offers support for building distributed applications using queues. WCF supports communication through MSMQ queues as the underlying transport for the `netMsmqBinding` binding. The `netMsmqBinding` binding allows clients to post messages directly to a queue and services to read messages from a queue. There is no direct communication between the client and server; therefore, the communication is inherently disconnected. It also means that all communication must be one-way. Therefore, all operations must have the `IsOneWay=true` property set on the operation contract.

> ▪ **TIP** Creating Queues Dynamically
>
> It is common to automatically create MSMQ queues dynamically for use with the `netMsmqBinding` binding. This is especially true when building disconnected client applications where the queue resides on a user's desktop. This can be done using the `Create` static method of the `System.Messaging.MessageQueue` class.

The following code shows the addressing format for the netMsmq Binding:

```
net.msmq://{hostname}/[private/|[public/]]{queue name}
```

The default port for MSMQ is 1801 and is not configurable using the addressing scheme. Take note of the use of the words public and private in the address format. You can explicitly specify whether the queue name refers to either a private or public queue. If omitted, the queue name is assumed to refer to a public queue.

Table 4.11 shows the binding properties that are configurable on the netMsmqBinding binding.

TABLE 4.11 netMsmqBinding Binding Properties

Attribute Name	Description	Default
closeTimeout	The maximum time to wait for the connection to be closed.	00:01:00
customDeadLetterQueue	The location of the per-application dead letter queue. Dead letter refers to a message that has expired or failed delivery.	n/a
deadLetterQueue	The type of dead letter queue to use. The types are None, System, or Custom.	None
Durable	Specifies whether the queue is durable or volatile.	true
exactlyOnce	Specifies whether delivery supports exactly once delivery assurances.	true
maxBufferPoolSize	Maximum size of any buffer pools used by the transport.	524,888
maxReceivedMessageSize	The maximum size of an incoming message.	65,536
maxRetryCycles	The number of retries before a message is considered a poison message.	2

Attribute Name	Description	Default
queueTransferProtocol	Specifies the queued transport protocol. The types of queued transport protocols include Native, Srmp, and SrmpSecure. Native refers to the native MSMQ protocol, and Srmp refers to the Soap Reliable Messaging Protocol.	Native
name	The name of the binding.	n/a
openTimeout	The maximum time to wait for an open connection operation to complete.	00:01:00
readerQuotas	Specify the complexity of messages that can be processed (for example, size).	n/a
receiveErrorHandling	Specifies how poison messages are handled. Valid types include Drop, Fault, Move, and Reject.	Fault
receiveRetryCount	Maximum number of attempts to send a message before it enters the retry queue.	5
receiveTimeout	The maximum time to wait for a receive operation to complete.	00:10:00
retryCycleDelay	The type to wait between retry cycles.	00:10:00
Security	Specifies the security settings of the binding.	n/a
sendTimeout	The maximum time to wait for a send operation to complete.	00:01:00
timeToLive	The length of time that messages are valid before they are expired and put into the dead-letter queue.	1.00:00:00
useActiveDirectory	Specify whether the queued transport should resolve the computer name using Active Directory rather than DNS, NetBIOS, or IP.	false

continues

TABLE 4.11 continued

Attribute Name	Description	Default
useMsmqTracing	Specifies whether MSMQ tracing is enabled. Trace messages are sent to the report queue each time a message leaves or arrives in a queue.	false
useSourceJournal	Specifies whether a copy of each message should be sent to the journal queue.	false

The StockQuoteService sample application that we have been using in Listings 4.2 through 4.4 needs to be modified to work with the netMsmqBinding binding. The netMsmqBinding supports only one-way operations (see Table 4.2). Our original operation contract uses a request-reply message exchange pattern (see Listing 4.4). Rather than show a different example, we will modify the StockQuoteService example to show two-way communication over the netMsmqBinding binding.

We need to use two one-way operation contracts to maintain two-way communication between the server and the client. This means that we need to redefine our contracts to use the netMsmqBinding binding. Listing 4.24 shows the stock quote contracts written for use with the netMsmqBinding binding. First, notice that we separated out the request and response contracts into two separate service contracts: IStockQuoteRequest and IStockQuoteResponse. The operations on each contract are one-way. The IStockQuoteRequest contract will be used by the client to send a message to the server. The IStockQuoteResponse contract will be used by the server to send a message to the client. This means that both the client and the server will be hosting services to receive messages.

LISTING 4.24 IStockQuoteRequest, IStockQuoteResponse, and StockQuoteRequestService

```
using System;
using System.Collections.Generic;
using System.ServiceModel;
using System.ServiceModel.Channels;
using System.Text;
```

```csharp
using System.Transactions;

namespace EssentialWCF
{
    [ServiceContract]
    public interface IStockQuoteRequest
    {
        [OperationContract(IsOneWay = true)]
        void SendQuoteRequest(string symbol);
    }

    [ServiceContract]
    public interface IStockQuoteResponse
    {
        [OperationContract(IsOneWay = true)]
        void SendQuoteResponse(string symbol, double price);
    }

    public class StockQuoteRequestService : IStockQuoteRequest
    {
        public void SendQuoteRequest(string symbol)
        {
            double value;

            if (symbol == "MSFT")
                value = 31.15;
            else if (symbol == "YHOO")
                value = 28.10;
            else if (symbol == "GOOG")
                value = 450.75;
            else
                value = double.NaN;

            // Send response back to client over separate queue
            NetMsmqBinding msmqResponseBinding = new NetMsmqBinding();
            using (ChannelFactory<IStockQuoteResponse> cf =
➥new ChannelFactory<IStockQuoteResponse>("NetMsmqResponseClient"))
            {
                IStockQuoteResponse client = cf.CreateChannel();

                using (TransactionScope scope =
➥new TransactionScope(TransactionScopeOption.Required))
                {
                    client.SendQuoteResponse(symbol, value);
                    scope.Complete();
                }

                cf.Close();
            }
        }
    }
}
```

The next consideration for netMsmqBinding is the use of ServiceHost class. The previous examples were able to reuse the same ServiceHost code across different bindings. This was because the service contract could remain the same. This is not the case with the netMsmqBinding. The updated ServiceHost code to host the StockServiceRequestService service is showing in Listing 4.25. We have updated the code to dynamically create a MSMQ queue based on the queueName specified in configuration. This helps simplify configuration by allowing the application to be deployed without any additional configuration in MSMQ.

LISTING 4.25 StockQuoteRequestService ServiceHost Service

```
using System;
using System.Collections.Generic;
using System.Configuration;
using System.Messaging;
using System.Text;
using System.ServiceModel;

namespace EssentialWCF
{
    internal class MyServiceHost
    {
        internal static string queueName = null;
        internal static ServiceHost myServiceHost = null;

        internal static void StartService()
        {
            queueName = ConfigurationManager.AppSettings["queueName"];

            if (!MessageQueue.Exists(queueName))
                MessageQueue.Create(queueName, true);

            myServiceHost =
➥new ServiceHost(typeof(EssentialWCF.StockQuoteRequestService));

            myServiceHost.Open();
        }

        internal static void StopService()
        {
            if (myServiceHost.State != CommunicationState.Closed)
                myServiceHost.Close();
        }
    }
}
```

The configuration information shown in Listing 4.26 exposes the StockQuoteRequestService service using the netMsmqBinding binding. It also configures a client endpoint for the IStockQuoteResponse contract so that responses can be sent to the client.

LISTING 4.26 netMsmqBinding Host Configuration

```xml
<?xml version="1.0" encoding="utf-8" ?>
<configuration>
  <system.serviceModel>
    <client>
      <endpoint
        address="net.msmq://localhost/private/stockquoteresponse"
        contract="EssentialWCF.IStockQuoteResponse"
        binding="netMsmqBinding"
        bindingConfiguration="NoMsmqSecurity"
        name="NetMsmqResponseClient"
        />
    </client>
    <services>
      <service name="EssentialWCF.StockQuoteRequestService">
        <endpoint
          address="net.msmq://localhost/private/stockquoterequest"
          contract="EssentialWCF.IStockQuoteRequest"
          bindingConfiguration="NoMsmqSecurity"
          binding="netMsmqBinding"
          />
      </service>
    </services>
    <bindings>
      <netMsmqBinding>
        <binding name="NoMsmqSecurity">
          <security mode="None" />
        </binding>
      </netMsmqBinding>
    </bindings>
  </system.serviceModel>
  <appSettings>
    <add key="queueName" value=".\private$\stockquoterequest" />
  </appSettings>
</configuration>
```

The client application must host a service using the netMsmqBinding to receive responses and configure an endpoint to send requests to the server. Listing 4.27 shows the ServiceHost class that the client uses to host a service that implements the IStockQuoteResponse contract. We added code to dynamically create the queue on which the client is listening. Again, this helps simplify configuration by allowing the application to be deployed without any additional configuration in MSMQ.

LISTING 4.27 StockQuoteResponseService ServiceHost Client

```
using System;
using System.Collections.Generic;
using System.Configuration;
using System.Messaging;
using System.Text;
using System.ServiceModel;

namespace EssentialWCF
{
    internal class MyServiceHost
    {
        internal static ServiceHost myServiceHost = null;

        internal static void StartService()
        {
            string queueName =
              ConfigurationManager.AppSettings["queueName"];

            if (!MessageQueue.Exists(queueName))
                MessageQueue.Create(queueName, true);

            myServiceHost =
              new ServiceHost(typeof(EssentialWCF.Program));

            myServiceHost.Open();
        }

        internal static void StopService()
        {
            if (myServiceHost.State != CommunicationState.Closed)
                myServiceHost.Close();
        }
    }
}
```

Listing 4.28 shows the client implementation for the IStockQuoteResponse interface. The client implements this interface, which is then used by the server as a callback to send a response on. This is not using the duplex capabilities available within WCF. Instead, the callback is implemented using a separate one-way binding.

LISTING 4.28 **IStockQuoteResponse** Client

```csharp
using System;
using System.Collections.Generic;
using System.Messaging;
using System.ServiceModel;
using System.ServiceModel.Channels;
using System.Text;
using System.Threading;
using System.Transactions;

namespace EssentialWCF
{
    public class Program : IStockQuoteResponse
    {
        private static AutoResetEvent waitForResponse;

        static void Main(string[] args)
        {
            // Start response service host
            MyServiceHost.StartService();
            try
            {
                waitForResponse = new AutoResetEvent(false);

                // Send request to the server
                using (ChannelFactory<IStockQuoteRequest> cf =
➥new ChannelFactory<IStockQuoteRequest>("NetMsmqRequestClient"))
                {
                    IStockQuoteRequest client = cf.CreateChannel();

                    using (TransactionScope scope =
➥new TransactionScope(TransactionScopeOption.Required))
                    {
                        client.SendQuoteRequest("MSFT");
                        scope.Complete();
                    }

                    cf.Close();
                }

                waitForResponse.WaitOne();
            }
            finally
            {
                MyServiceHost.StopService();
            }

            Console.ReadLine();
```

LISTING 4.28 continued

```
        }

        #region IStockQuoteResponseService Members

        public void SendQuoteResponse(string symbol, double price)
        {
            Console.WriteLine("{0} @ ${1}", symbol, price);
            waitForResponse.Set();
        }

        #endregion
    }
}
```

The final piece to make the netMsmqBinding stock quote sample application work is the client configuration. Listing 4.29 shows the client configuration, which contains the information to host the IStockQuoteResponse service implementation, and the endpoint configuration to call the IStockQuoteRequest service.

LISTING 4.29 netMsmqBinding Client Configuration

```
<?xml version="1.0" encoding="utf-8" ?>
<configuration>
  <system.serviceModel>
    <client>
      <endpoint address="net.msmq://localhost/private/stockquoterequest"
                contract="EssentialWCF.IStockQuoteRequest"
                binding="netMsmqBinding"
                bindingConfiguration="NoMsmqSecurity"
                name="NetMsmqRequestClient"
                />
    </client>
    <services>
      <service name="EssentialWCF.Program">
        <endpoint
           address="net.msmq://localhost/private/stockquoteresponse"
           contract="EssentialWCF.IStockQuoteResponse"
           binding="netMsmqBinding"
           bindingConfiguration="NoMsmqSecurity"
           />
      </service>
```

```
        </services>
        <bindings>
          <netMsmqBinding>
            <binding name="NoMsmqSecurity">
              <security mode="None" />
            </binding>
          </netMsmqBinding>
        </bindings>
      </system.serviceModel>
      <appSettings>
        <add key="queueName" value=".\private$\stockquoteresponse" />
      </appSettings>
    </configuration>
```

msmqIntegrationBinding

The `msmqIntegrationBinding` binding is used to communicate between a
WCF application and an application that leverages MSMQ directly—for
example, using `System.Messaging`. This allows developers to leverage
WCF but still leverage their existing MSMQ applications. The `msmqInte-`
`grationBinding` binding allows for MSMQ messages to be mapped to WCF
messages. This is facilitated by wrapping MSMQ messages in the `MsmqMes-`
`sage` generic class. This class is located in the `System.ServiceModel.`
`MsmqIntegration` namespace. Instances can be sent or received using one-
way contracts.

The following code shows the addressing format for the `msmqIntegra-`
`tionBinding` binding:

```
msmq.formatname:{MSMQ format name}
```

The MSMQ address format does not require a port to be specified. However, MSMQ does require certain ports to be open, such as 1801. Table 4.12
shows the binding properties that are configurable on the `msmqIntegra-`
`tionBinding` binding.

TABLE 4.12 msmqIntegrationBinding Binding Properties

Attribute Name	Description	Default
closeTimeout	The maximum time to wait for the connection to be closed.	00:01:00
customDeadLetterQueue	The location of the per-application dead letter queue. Dead letter refers to a message that has expired or failed delivery.	n/a
deadLetterQueue	The type of dead letter queue to use. The types are None, System, or Custom.	None
Durable	Specifies whether the queue is durable or volatile.	true
exactlyOnce	Specifies whether delivery supports exactly once delivery assurances.	true
maxReceivedMessageSize	The maximum size of an incoming message.	65,536
maxRetryCycles	The number of retries before a message is considered a poison message.	2
nameName	The name of the binding.	n/a
openTimeout	The maximum time to wait for an open connection operation to complete.	00:01:00
readerQuotas	Specify the complexity of messages that can be processed (for example, size).	n/a
receiveErrorHandling	Specifies how poison messages are handled. Valid types include Drop, Fault, Move, and Reject.	Fault
receiveRetryCount	Maximum number of attempts to send a message before it enters the retry queue.	5

Attribute Name	Description	Default
receiveTimeout	The maximum time to wait for a receive operation to complete.	00:10:00
retryCycleDelay	The type to wait between retry cycles.	00:10:00
Security	Specifies the security settings of the binding.	n/a
sendTimeout	The maximum time to wait for a send operation to complete.	00:01:00
serializationFormat	Specifies the serialization for the message body. The available options include XML, Binary, ActiveX, ByteArray, and Stream.	Xml
timeToLive	The length of time that messages are valid before they are expired and put into the dead-letter queue.	1.00:00:00
useMsmqTracing	Specifies whether MSMQ tracing is enabled. Trace messages are sent to the report queue each time a message leaves or arrives in a queue.	false
useSourceJournal	Specifies whether a copy of each message should be sent to the journal queue.	false

Listing 4.30 shows the minimal configuration to expose a service using the msmqIntegrationBinding binding.

LISTING 4.30 msmqIntegrationBinding Host Configuration

```xml
<?xml version="1.0" encoding="utf-8" ?>
<configuration>
  <system.serviceModel>
    <services>
      <service name="EssentialWCF.StockQuoteRequestService">
        <endpoint binding="msmqIntegrationBinding"
                  contract="EssentialWCF.IStockQuoteRequest"
address="msmq.formatname:DIRECT=OS:.\private$\stockrequest" />
      </service>
```

LISTING 4.30 continued

```
        </services>
      </system.serviceModel>
    </configuration>
```

The minimal configuration to consume a service using the `msmqInte-grationBinding` binding is shown in Listing 4.31.

LISTING 4.31 `msmqIntegrationBinding` Client Configuration

```
<?xml version="1.0" encoding="utf-8" ?>
<configuration>
  <system.serviceModel>
    <services>
      <service name="EssentialWCF.HelloWorld">
        <endpoint binding="msmqIntegrationBinding"
                  contract="EssentialWCF.IStockQuoteRequestService"
address="msmq.formatname:DIRECT=OS:.\private$\stockquoterequest" />
      </service>
    </services>
  </system.serviceModel>
</configuration>
```

Creating a Custom Binding

There will be times when the preconfigured bindings do not meet the requirements of your service. Common scenarios include custom security and additional transports, which are not supported by WCF. One example is the lack of support for the UDP protocol within WCF. Support for the UDP protocol exists as a sample in the Windows SDK. For these situations WCF provides the capability to create custom bindings. Custom bindings can be created using either code or configuration. A custom binding is created in code using the `CustomBinding` class found in the `System.ServiceModel.Channels` namespace. This class exposes a collection of binding elements that you can add binding elements to. This allows you to compose a new binding based on a set of existing binding elements. Listing 4.32 shows a custom binding being created in code.

LISTING 4.32 Creating a Custom Binding in Code

```
CustomBinding customBinding = new CustomBinding();
customBinding.Elements.Add(new BinaryMessageEncodingBindingElement());
customBinding.Elements.Add(new UdpBindingElement());
```

A custom binding can be created in configuration using the customBinding element in configuration. Listing 4.33 shows a custom binding expressed in configuration. When using configuration, a custom binding must always use a named binding.

LISTING 4.33 Creating a Custom Binding in Configuration

```
<?xml version="1.0" encoding="utf-8" ?>
<configuration>
  <system.serviceModel>
    <bindings>
      <customBinding>
        <binding name="CustomBinding">
          <binaryMessageEncoding />
          <udpTransport />
        </binding>
      </customBinding>
    </bindings>
  </system.serviceModel>
</configuration>
```

Notice that the binding specifies a transport and an encoder. This is all that is needed to create a custom binding. The encoder can be optional if the transport specifies a default encoder. To change how a custom binding works is only a matter of a few lines of code or configuration. Be careful when using configuration, because it can be changed. Create your custom bindings in code if you do not plan to change the binding later on.

The following configuration information can be used with the sample application shown in Listings 4.2 through 4.4. The configuration information shown in Listing 4.34 exposes the StockQuoteService service using the customBinding binding. The binding exposes the service over the TCP transport with binary encoding. This custom binding is similar to the netTcpBinding binding but lacks any of the support for reliable messaging, transactions, and security.

LISTING 4.34 customBinding Host Configuration

```xml
<?xml version="1.0" encoding="utf-8" ?>
<configuration>
  <system.serviceModel>
    <services>
      <service name="EssentialWCF.StockQuoteService">
        <host>
          <baseAddresses>
            <add baseAddress="net.tcp://localhost/stockquoteservice" />
          </baseAddresses>
        </host>
        <endpoint address=""
                  contract="EssentialWCF.IStockQuoteService"
                  binding="customBinding"
                  bindingConfiguration="customBinding"/>
      </service>
    </services>
    <bindings>
      <customBinding>
        <binding name="customBinding">
          <binaryMessageEncoding />
          <tcpTransport />
        </binding>
      </customBinding>
    </bindings>
  </system.serviceModel>
</configuration>
```

Listing 4.35 shows the client configuration to consume the service using the customBinding binding shown in Listing 4.34.

LISTING 4.35 customBinding Client Configuration

```xml
<?xml version="1.0" encoding="utf-8" ?>
<configuration>
  <system.serviceModel>
    <client>
      <endpoint address="net.tcp://localhost/stockquoteservice"
                binding="customBinding"
                bindingConfiguration="customBinding"
                contract="EssentialWCF.IStockQuoteService">
      </endpoint>
    </client>
    <bindings>
      <customBinding>
        <binding name="customBinding">
          <binaryMessageEncoding />
          <tcpTransport />
```

```
        </binding>
      </customBinding>
    </bindings>
  </system.serviceModel>
 /configuration>
```

User-Defined Bindings

Bindings can be defined fully in code or configuration or they can be created by inheriting from the `Binding` class. This type of binding is called a user-defined binding. You still need to specify the binding elements that your binding supports.

The primary difference between a custom binding and a user-defined binding is that a user-defined binding is a specific instance of a class that performs all the steps needed to create your binding. This approach is preferred if you plan reuse the binding in a number of applications. If you choose this approach, the authors recommend that user-defined bindings support the capability to be created from configuration using a *binding extension*. A binding extension exposes a binding class through configuration. This is done by creating a new class that inherits from `BindingElementExtensionElement` found in the `System.ServiceModel.Configuration` namespace.

> ■ **TIP**   Provide a Binding Extension with Your Custom Binding
>
> Seriously consider exposing your custom bindings using a binding extension rather than using the `<customBinding>` configuration element. This will help avoid mistakes in configuration and avoid the associated problems.

Binding Elements

WCF provides numerous channels and encoders that are used in the pre-configured bindings. These channels provide bindings elements that can be used in custom bindings. This section provides a listing of the binding elements found within WCF and their uses.

Transports

The following is a list of transport channels and their associated binding classes, binding extensions, and their XML configuration element. Each of these represents a different transport channel that can be used in a custom binding. The transports available are TCP, HTTP, named pipes, HTTP with SSL/TLS encryption, MSMQ, and Peer Networking.

TCP Transport Channel	Transport channel based on the TCP protocol
Binding Class	`TcpTransportBindingElement`
Binding Extension	`TcpTransportElement`
Configuration Element	`<tcpTransport>`

Named Pipe Transport Channel	Transport channel based on the Named Pipe protocol
Binding Class	`NamedPipeBindingElement`
Binding Extension	`NamedPipeTransportElement`
Configuration Element	`<namedPipeTransport>`

HTTP Transport Channel	Transport channel based on the HTTP protocol
Binding Class	`HttpBindingElement`
Binding Extension	`HttpTransportElement`
Configuration Element	`<httpTransport>`

HTTPS Transport Channel	Transport channel based on the HTTP protocol
Binding Class	`HttpBindingElement`
Binding Extension	`HttpTransportElement`
Configuration Element	`<httpTransport>`

MSMQ Transport Channel	Transport channel based on the MSMQ protocol
Binding Class	MSMQTransportBindingElement
Binding Extension	MSMQTransportElement
Configuration Element	<msmqTransport>

MSMQ Integration Transport Channel	Transport channel based on the MSMQ protocol
Binding Class	MSMQIntegrationBindingElement
Binding Extension	MSMQIntegrationBindingElement
Configuration Element	<msmqIntegration>

Peer Transport Channel	Transport channel based on a Peer-to-Peer transport
Binding Class	PeerBindingElement
Binding Extension	PeerTransportElement
Configuration Element	<peerTransport>

The UDP transport channel is not included with .NET 3.5. It is provided as a sample in the Windows SDK. It is included here because it is a commonly requested transport for WCF.

UDP Transport Channel	Transport channel based on a UDP transport
Binding Class	UdpBindingElement
Binding Extension	UdpTransportElement
Configuration Element	<udpTransport>

Encoders

The following are a list of encoders that are included with WCF. They represent the manner in which a Message class is transformed into a byte stream by the transport channel. There are several types of message encoders, including Text, MTOM, Binary, and JSON encoders. Go to Chapter 6, "Serialization and Encoding," for more information about encoders.

Text Message Encoding	Supports text encoding of SOAP messages
Binding Class	TextMessageEncodingBindingElement
Binding Extension	TextMessageEncodingElement
Configuration Element	<textMessageEncoding>

Binary Message Encoding	Supports binary encoding of SOAP messages
Binding Class	BinaryMessageEncodingBindingElement
Binding Extension	BinaryMessageEncodingElement
Configuration Element	<binaryMessageEncoding>

MTOM Message Encoding	Supports MTOM encoding of SOAP messages
Binding Class	MTOMMessageEncodingBindingElement
Binding Extension	MTOMMessageEncodingElement
Configuration Element	<mtomMessageEncoding>

The JsonMessageEncoder and the WebMessageEncoder encoders are included with .NET 3.5, which is available with Visual Studio 2008. These encoders are implemented as behaviors; therefore, they are not included in this discussion. Refer to either Chapter 6 or Chapter 13 for more information on these encoders.

Security

The following is a list of security protocols that are used in WCF. Most of these are intended to be created using either the <security> configuration element or the SecurityBindingElement static methods. It is recommended that you create these binding elements using one of these methods because the `SecurityBindingElement` takes some of the guesswork out of configuring the binding elements by providing static methods that can be used to create the other security bindings.

Asymmetric Security	Channel security using asymmetric security
Binding Class	`AsymmetricSecurityBindingElement`
Binding Extension	`SecurityElement`
Configuration Element	`<security>`

Symmetric Security	Channel security using symmetric security
Binding Class	`SymmetricSecurityBindingElement`
Binding Extension	`SecurityElement`
Configuration Element	`<security>`

Transport Security	Support for mixed mode security
Binding Class	`TransportSecurityBindingElement`
Binding Extension	`SecurityElement`
Configuration Element	`<security>`

Transport Upgrades/Helpers

The following list of binding elements includes upgrades or helpers to transports. WCF allows bindings that use stream-oriented protocols such as TCP and named pipes to support stream-based transport upgrades. For example, the `SslStreamSecurityBindingElement` provides support for channel security using an SSL stream.

PNRP Peer Resolver	Peer name resolution using the PNRP protocol
Binding Class	PnrpPeerResolverBindingElement
Binding Extension	PnrpPeerResolverElement
Configuration Element	<pnrpPeerResolver>

SSL Stream Security	Channel security using an SSL stream
Binding Class	SslStreamSecurityBindingElement
Binding Extension	SslStreamSecurityElement
Configuration Element	<sslStreamSecurity>

Windows Stream Security	Used to specify Windows stream security settings
Binding Class	WindowsStreamSecurityBindingElement
Binding Extension	WindowsStreamSecurityElement
Configuration Element	<windowsStreamSecurity>

Shape Change

The following lists shape-changing binding elements that change the shape of the channel stack. Shape-changing channels change the message exchange pattern of the channel. See "Channel Shapes" in Chapter 3, "Channels," for more information on channel shapes and shape changing.

Composite Duplex Shape Change	Support for duplex communication over transports that don't support duplex communication
Binding Class	CompositeDuplexBindingElement
Binding Extension	CompositeDuplexElement
Configuration Element	<compositeDuplex>

One Way Shape Change	Support for one-way communication over a transport that does not support one-way communication
Binding Class	OneWayBindingElement
Binding Extension	OneWayElement
Configuration Element	<oneWay>

Other Protocols

The following is a list of binding elements that add support for various protocols such as transactions and reliability.

Reliable Sessions	Support for exactly once and ordered delivery of SOAP messages
Binding Class	ReliableSessionBindingElement
Binding Extension	ReliableSessionElement
Configuration Element	<reliableSession>

Transaction Flow	Support for flowing transactions from client to server
Binding Class	TransactionFlowBindingElement
Binding Extension	TransactionFlowElement
Configuration Element	<transactionFlow>

Exposing a Service Contract over Multiple Bindings

Earlier sections in this chapter demonstrated exposing services with the `netTcpBinding` and `wsHttpBinding` bindings. Each of these bindings is used to support specific communication scenarios. For example, the `netTcpBinding` binding is optimized for communication between .NET applications, the wsHttpBinding binding supports communication between different platforms using Web services, and the basicHttpBinding binding supports communication with Web services that don't support advanced protocols.

By using multiple endpoints within a service, you can configure a service to expose its capabilities through multiple bindings, as shown in the "Multiple Contracts and Endpoints in a Service" section of Chapter 2. This means that clients can connect to services using the most optimal binding supported. A common scenario is to expose a service to a .NET application using the netTcpBinding binding, expose the same service to a Java application using the wsHttpBinding binding, and expose the same service again using the basicHttpBinding binding for older clients.

WCF accomplishes this by abstracting away the underlying communication and lets the developer focus on building services. How they are exposed doesn't matter as long as the bindings support the features needed by the application. This means that a service can be exposed using different bindings.

■ **NOTE**   Use Multiple Bindings When Building Interoperable Services

The capability to expose a service using multiple bindings brings great flexibility. You can expose services using different bindings simultaneously. This allows a service to be exposed to both a WCF client and to a non-WCF client without losing performance because of interoperability. For example, you can use both the netTcpBinding and wsHttpBinding to expose a service. The netTcpBinding would be used for WCF clients and the wsHttpBinding would be used for non-WCF clients (such as Java). Just keep in mind that all the bindings used should support those features that your application requires. For example, you would not expose a service that requires transactions over a binding that does not support transactions.

Exposing a service to both a .NET and a Java application is just one example of using multiple bindings. Another example is to expose a service to a Web browser client and to a .NET Windows application. An example of exposing a service using multiple bindings is shown in Listing 4.36.

LISTING 4.36   Host Configuration Using Multiple Bindings

```xml
<?xml version="1.0" encoding="utf-8" ?>
<configuration>
  <system.serviceModel>
    <services>
      <service name="EssentialWCF.StockQuoteService">
        <endpoint binding="wsHttpBinding"
                  contract="EssentialWCF.IStockQuoteService"
                  address="http://localhost/wshttpendpoint" />
        <endpoint binding="netTcpBinding"
                  contract="EssentialWCF. IStockQuoteService"
                  address="net.tcp://localhost/nettcpendpoint" />
      </service>
    </services>
  </system.serviceModel>
</configuration>
```

SUMMARY

The channel architecture unifies a variety of distributed programming techniques into a single programming model. The architecture allows for services to be created independent of transports and encodings and therefore support numerous forms of communications. Bindings are preconfigured channel stacks that support particular types of communications. There are nine preconfigured bindings offered by WCF.

Here are some guiding principles for working channels and bindings within WCF:

- The netTcpBinding binding is used for cross-machine communication between .NET applications.
- The netNamedPipeBinding binding is used for all on-machine communication between .NET applications. This includes both interprocess and intraprocess (that is, inter-appdomain and intra-appdomain) communication.

- The `basicHttpBinding` binding supports legacy Web services based on the WS-I Basic Profile 1.1 standard. This binding is typically used to consume ASP.NET ASMX Web services. It can also be used to expose services to .NET 2.0 clients that do not need WS-* support.

- The `ws2007HttpBinding` and `wsHttpBinding` bindings are used to create Web services that support the WS-* specifications. The `ws2007HttpBinding` binding should be the default binding used to create Web services within WCF. It supports the latest WS-* standards for messaging, security, reliable messaging, and transactions.

- There are three additional bindings based on Web services: `wsDualHttpBinding`, `wsFederationHttpBinding`, and `ws2007FederationHttpBinding`. Use these if you need to support duplex messaging over HTTP or federated security, respectively. The `ws2007FederationHttpBinding` binding shipped with .NET 3.5 and has additional support for WSS SAML Token Profile 1.1.

- The `netMsmqBinding` binding is used to develop disconnected applications using Microsoft Message Queue (MSMQ).

- The `msmqIntegrationBinding` binding is used to integrate with existing applications built using MSMQ.

- The channel stack within WCF is composable and allows for the creation of custom bindings. Custom bindings can be used to support communication needs not supported by the preconfigured bindings.

- WCF supports exposing services over multiple bindings. This allows for optimal communication between a variety of different clients and the server.

- Use one of the preconfigured bindings if it meets your needs; otherwise, you can create a custom binding using the `CustomBinding` class.

∎ 5 ∎
Behaviors

B EHAVIORS ARE WCF CLASSES that affect runtime operation. Behaviors are invoked as the WCF runtime starts on the client and server and as messages flow between the two. Because behaviors run at these critical times, they are used to implement many built-in features in the WCF. They are also an important extensibility point for customizations.

For example, `ServiceHost` is responsible for defining the instancing and concurrency aspects of a server, in addition to dispatching messages to the proper operation. When a message is received by a service and dispatched to a certain method of a class, should `ServiceHost` create a new instance of that class for each request or should it reuse instances? And when `ServiceHost` calls the method on that class, should it enlist in a transaction? Both of these are specified in behaviors and used during initialization.

There are three primary types of behaviors. *Service behaviors* run at the service level and have access to all of the endpoints. They control items such as instancing and transactions. Service behaviors are also available for authorization and auditing. *Endpoint behaviors* are scoped to the service endpoint. These are well-suited for inspecting and taking actions on messages as they come in and out of service. *Operation behaviors* are scoped at the operation level and are well-positioned for manipulating serialization, transaction flow, and parameter handling for a service operation. In addition to these three, WCF also defines *callback behaviors*, which function similarly to service behaviors, but control the endpoints created on the client in duplex communication.

To understand how behaviors are used, it's helpful to consider how the runtime is initialized. This is done by the ChannelFactory on the client and by ServiceHost on the server. Both classes perform similar functions:

1. Accept a .NET type as input and read its attributed information.
2. Load configuration from app.config or web.config files. On the client, ChannelFactory is primarily looking at binding information; on the server, ServiceHost is primarily looking at contract and binding information.
3. Build the runtime environment structure, ServiceDescription.
4. Start communication. On the client, ChannelFactory uses the channel to connect to the service; on the server, ServiceHost opens the channel and listens for messages.

In step 1, behavior information is defined as attributes in code, as in [ServiceBehavior (TransactionTimeout="00:00:30")]. In step 2, behavior information is defined in configuration, as in <transactionTimeout= "00:00:30"> in an app.config file. During step 3, the ChannelFactory and ServiceHost classes build the WCF runtime and are responsible for inserting the behaviors found in steps 1 and 2 into the runtime. Also in step 3, behaviors can be manually added to the service model, as in Endpoint. Behaviors.Add(new MyBehavior()).

In addition to initialization, behaviors can also operate on data before it is transmitted or after it is received. On the client, behaviors can be used to perform three functions:

- **Parameter Inspection.** Inspect and/or change data in its .NET representation, before it has been converted to XML.
- **Message Formatting.** Inspect and/or change data during its conversion between .NET types to XML.
- **Message Inspection.** Inspect and/or change data in its XML representation, before it has been converted to .NET types.

On the server, behaviors can be used for two additional scenarios:

- **Operation Selection.** At the service level, inspect the incoming message and determine which operation should be called.
- **Operation Invocation.** At the operation level, invoke the class method.

Figure 5.1 depicts the flow of control among behavior elements that are invoked when messages are sent between the client and server. When application code on the client calls `GetPrices(...)`, the Parameter Inspector and Message Formatter are called and passed the parameters in their .NET format. Then, also on the client, the Message Inspector is called and passed the XML message. On the service, when the message arrives in the channel, the Message Inspector and Operation Selector are called and passed the incoming message to inspect and determine which operation should receive it. The Message Formatter is then called to format the message as a .NET type, and the Parameter Inspector is called and passed the message in its .NET representation. Finally, the Operation Invoker is called to invoke the method on the target class, doing any setup and teardown along the way.

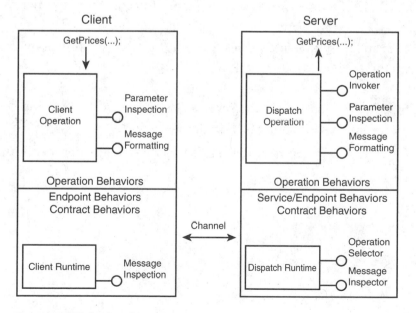

FIGURE 5.1 Behavior elements

As you can see in Figure 5.1, many interception points exist where behaviors can monitor and alter the flow of messages. They are also in the right position to affect overall performance of a service.

Concurrency and Instancing (Service Behavior)

Concurrency is a measure of how many tasks can be performed simultaneously and is measured in tasks (requests, jobs, transactions, and the like). *Execution time* is a measure of how long it takes a task to complete and is measured in time (milliseconds, seconds, and so on). *Throughput* is the measure of how many tasks are completed within a fixed time and is reported as tasks/time (requests/second, transactions/minute, and so on). Throughput is a function of concurrency and execution time.

There are two ways to increase throughput: either decrease execution time or increase concurrency. Decreasing the execution time for an individual task can be accomplished by either changing the task's internal algorithm or by adding additional hardware resources, so there's not much WCF can do about this. Concurrency can be increased by executing tasks in parallel. WCF has two behaviors available for controlling concurrency: `InstanceContextMode` and `ConcurrencyMode`.

The `InstanceContextMode` service behavior is used to control instancing and can be set to one of three values:

- **Single.** One instance of the service class handles all incoming requests. This implements a singleton.
- **PerCall.** One instance of the service class is created per incoming request.

- **PerSession.** One instance of the service class is created per client session. When using sessionless channels, all service calls behave as `PerCall`, even if the `InstanceContextMode` is set to `PerSession`.

The default setting, `InstanceContextMode.PerSession`, instructs WCF to create a new instance of the service class for each user (proxy, actually) while degrading to `PerCall` if a sessionless binding is used.

The `ConcurrencyMode` service behavior is used to control thread concurrency within a service instance. The default setting, `ConcurrencyMode.Single`, instructs WCF to execute only one thread at a time *per instance* of the service class. This behavior can be set to one of three values:

- **Single.** Only one thread at a time can access the service class. This is the safest setting because service operations do not need to worry about thread safety.
- **Reentrant.** Only one thread at a time can access the service class, but the thread can leave the class and come back later to continue.
- **Multiple.** Multiple threads may access the service class simultaneously. This setting requires the class to be built in a thread-safe manner.

Using these two settings, `InstanceContextMode` and `ConcurrencyMode`, together enables you to tailor the instancing and concurrency of a service to address specific performance needs.

TABLE 5.1 Combining InstanceContextMode and ConcurrencyMode

	InstanceContextMode Single	InstanceContextMode per Call	InstanceContextMode per Session (default)
ConcurrencyMode.Single (default)	Singleton—one instance is created and only one thread is created to process requests. While a request is being processed, all subsequent requests are queued and processed in FIFO (first in first out) order.	One instance is created per call. Concurrency mode doesn't matter because each instance will have its own thread of execution.	One instance is created per client session and only one thread is created to process requests for that session. If the client makes multiple asynchronous calls on a session, they are queued and processed in FIFO order.
ConcurrencyMode.Reentrant	Singleton—one instance is created and only one thread is created to process requests. While a request is being processed, all subsequent requests are queued and processed in FIFO order. The single thread can leave the method, do work on another thread, such as asynchronous coding or callbacks from another service, and come back later.	One instance is created per call. Concurrency mode doesn't matter because each instance will have its own thread of execution.	One instance is created per client session and only one thread is created to process requests for that session. If the client makes multiple asynchronous calls on a session, they are queued and processed in FIFO order. The single thread can leave the method, do other work, and come back later, as may be the case with server-side asynchronous coding.
ConcurrencyMode.Multiple	One instance is created but multiple threads can run in parallel through the instance. Class members must be protected with synchronization code because the same members can be modified by multiple threads.	One instance is created per call. Concurrency mode doesn't matter because each instance will have its own thread of execution.	One instance is created per client session but multiple threads can run in parallel through the instance. If the client makes multiple asynchronous calls on a session, they are processed in parallel. Class members must be protected with synchronization code because the same members can be modified by multiple threads.

Default Concurrency and Instancing with Sessionless Binding

Listing 5.1 shows a service that does not define any concurrency or instancing behavior, which directs WCF to use the default values, `ConcurrencyMode.Single` and `InstanceContextMode.PerSession`. When using these settings and a sessionless binding, such as `basicHttpBinding`, WCF creates a new instance of the service for each request it receives and executes the code on its own thread. It waits five seconds before returning.

LISTING 5.1 Service Using Default Concurrency and Instancing Behavior

```
[ServiceContract]
public interface IStockService
{
        [OperationContract]
        double GetPrice(string ticker);
}

public class StockService : IStockService
{
    StockService()
    {
        Console.WriteLine("{0}:
            Created new instance of StockService on thread",
            System.DateTime.Now);
    }
    public double GetPrice(string ticker)
    {
            Console.WriteLine("{0}: GetPrice called on thread {1}",
            System.DateTime.Now,
            Thread.CurrentThread.ManagedThreadId);
            Thread.Sleep(5000);
            return 94.85;
    }
}
```

Listing 5.2 shows client code that is calling the `GetPrice` method three times. It calls it three times asynchronously and then waits until all results have been returned before exiting.

LISTING 5.2 Asynchronous Client Calling a Service

```
class Program
{
    static int c = 0;
    static void Main(string[] args)
    {
        StockServiceClient proxy = new StockServiceClient();
        for (int i=0; i<3; i++)
        {
          Console.WriteLine("{0}: Calling GetPrice",
                              System.DateTime.Now);
          proxy.BeginGetPrice("MSFT", GetPriceCallback, proxy);
          Thread.Sleep(100); // for clarity in output messages
          Interlocked.Increment(ref c);
        }
        while (c > 0) // wait until all responses come back
        {
          Thread.Sleep(100);
        }
    }

    static void GetPriceCallback(IAsyncResult ar)
    {
        double price =
              ((StockServiceClient)ar.AsyncState).EndGetPrice(ar);
        Console.WriteLine("{0}: Price:{1}", System.DateTime.Now,
                            price);
        Interlocked.Decrement(ref c);
    }
}
```

Figure 5.2 shows the output from the client (left) and service (right). The client output shows that three requests are sent simultaneously and the results were returned five seconds later. The service output shows that a new instance of the service class was created for each client request and each request was processed on its own thread. Because basicHttpBinding doesn't support sessions, the PerSession default behaves as to PerCall in this example. The InstanceContextMode.PerSession behavior directed WCF to spin up a new instance per request, and the ConcurrencyMode.Single setting directed WCF to only allow one thread per instance.

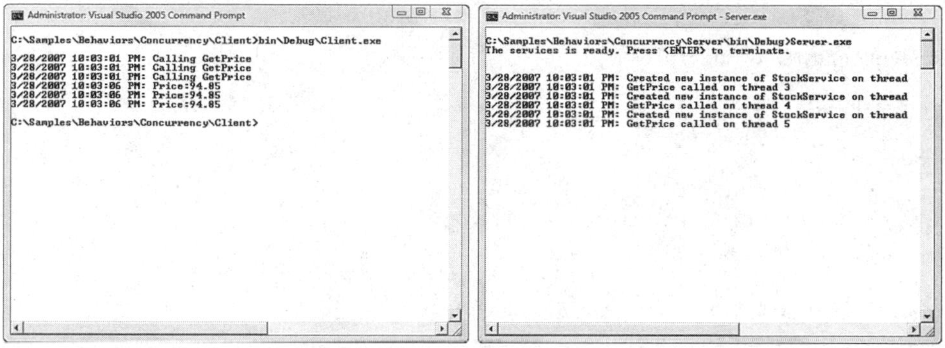

FIGURE 5.2 Output from default `InstanceContextMode` and `ConcurrencyMode` with sessionless binding

Multithreading a Single Instance

The default `InstanceContextMode` behavior setting directs WCF to create a new service instance for each request. In many cases, however, this is not the best approach. For instance, if a service has an expensive initialization routine (for example, a constructor that loads data from a database or builds a large in-memory structure), it may not be very efficient to create a new instance for each service request. To create a single service instance that is shared by concurrent threads, `InstanceContextMode.Single` should be used in conjunction with `ConcurrencyMode.Multiple`. The `InstanceContextMode.Single` setting indicates that only one instance should be created, whereas the `ConcurrencyMode.Multiple` setting directs WCF to execute that instance on multiple threads simultaneously. This can provide a significant scalability improvement, but the service code must handle synchronization to protect thread local storage.

Listing 5.3 shows the service code using `InstanceContextMode.Single` and `ConcurrencyMode.Multiple` behaviors. Note that the `ServiceBehavior` attribute is on the class, not the interface. This is because the `ServiceBehavior` attribute modifies the *behavior* of the service, not its contract.

LISTING 5.3 Service Using InstanceContextMode.Single and
ConcurrencyMode.Multiple

```
[ServiceContract]
public interface IStockService
{
        [OperationContract]
        double GetPrice(string ticker);
}

public class StockService : IStockService
{
    [ServiceBehavior(InstanceContextMode = InstanceContextMode.Single,
                ConcurrencyMode = ConcurrencyMode.Multiple)]
    StockService()
    {
        Console.WriteLine("{0}:
                Created new instance of StockService on thread",
                System.DateTime.Now);
    }
    public double GetPrice(string ticker)
    {
            Console.WriteLine("{0}: GetPrice called on thread {1}",
                System.DateTime.Now,
                Thread.CurrentThread.ManagedThreadId);
            Thread.Sleep(5000);
            return 94.85;
    }
}
```

Figure 5.3 shows the output from the client (left) and service (right). As
with the previous example, the client output shows that three requests are
sent simultaneously and the results were returned five seconds later. The
service output shows that only one instance of the service class was created,
but that client request was still processed on its own thread. The Instance-
ContextMode.Single setting directed WCF to spin up only one instance of
the service class, whereas the ConcurrencyMode.Multiple setting directed
WCF to allow multiple threads to execute that instance simultaneously.

Implementing a Singleton

There are cases in which there should be only one instance of a service, and
that instance should be single threaded. Tasks should be executed strictly in
a FIFO (first in first out) order with no parallelism. Although this greatly

reduces throughput, it facilitates scenarios in which state is shared across all callers where no adequate locking mechanism exists.

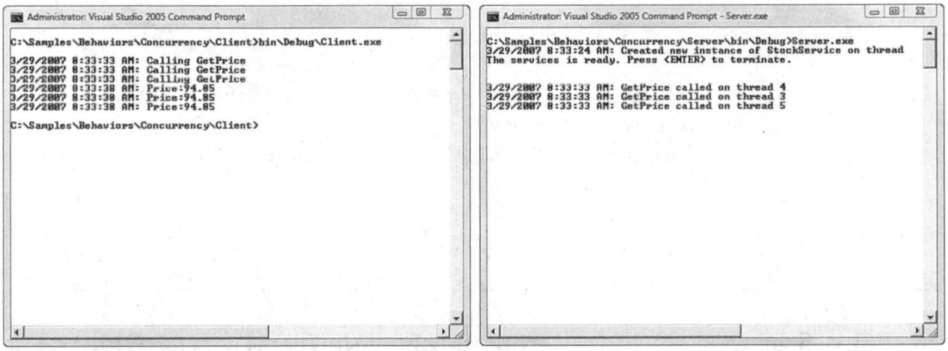

FIGURE 5.3 Output from `InstanceContextMode.Single` and `ConcurrencyMode.Multiple`

To create a single service instance that is single threaded, `InstanceContextMode.Single` should be used in conjunction with `ConcurrencyMode.Single`. The `InstanceContextMode.Single` setting indicates that only one instance should be created, whereas the `ConcurrencyMode.Single` setting directs WCF to execute that instance on only one thread at a time. These settings direct WCF to dispatch all requests in (FIFO) order.

Listing 5.4 shows the service code using `InstanceContextMode.Single` and `ConcurrencyMode.Single` behaviors.

LISTING 5.4 Implementing a Singleton

```
[ServiceContract]
public interface IStockService
{
        [OperationContract]
        double GetPrice(string ticker);
}

public class StockService : IStockService
{
    [ServiceBehavior(InstanceContextMode = InstanceContextMode.Single,
                    ConcurrencyMode = ConcurrencyMode.Single)]
    StockService()
    {
        Console.WriteLine("{0}:
```

LISTING 5.4 continued

```
                  Created new instance of StockService on thread",
                  System.DateTime.Now);
        }
        public double GetPrice(string ticker)
        {
                  Console.WriteLine("{0}: GetPrice called on thread {1}",
                      System.DateTime.Now,
                      Thread.CurrentThread.ManagedThreadId);
                  Thread.Sleep(5000);
                  return 94.85;
        }
    }
```

Figure 5.4 shows the output from the client (left) and service (right). The client sends three asynchronous requests, but note that the service processes only one request every five seconds. The service output shows that only one instance of the service class was created. It also shows that some requests reused a thread. The `InstanceContextMode.Single` setting directed WCF to spin up only one instance of the service class, whereas the `ConcurrencyMode.Single` setting directed WCF to allow only one thread at a time to execute that instance. Note that `ConcurrencyMode.Single` doesn't control how many threads are created in the service; it just specifies that only one should run through each instance.

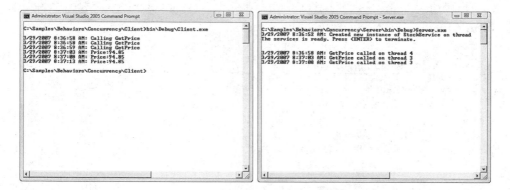

FIGURE 5.4 Output from singleton: `InstanceContextMode.Single` and `ConcurrencyMode.Single`

Session-Level Instances

Sessions are widely used for maintaining per-user state in distributed applications. On Web sites or in Web-based applications, it's common to store per-user state in sessions. In these cases, there's a 1:1 correspondence between users and sessions. WCF supports a similar concept with services. Using the `InstanceContextMode.PerSession` setting, WCF can be directed to create an instance of a service for each session.

> ■ **TIP**   **Instance Sessions Are Not the Same as Reliable Sessions**
>
> Per-session service instances should not be confused with another WCF feature, Reliable Sessions. That feature, which implements the WS-RM specification, is useful for ensuring reliable, in-order delivery of messages between endpoints over intermediaries. It has nothing to do with concurrency or object-creation behaviors.

To implement per-session service instances, two things must be done: enable sessions at the contract level and enable sessions at the service level.

At the contract level, sessions are enabled using the `SessionMode` behavior on the service contract. The value of the behavior can be `Allowed`, `NotAllowed`, or `Required`. Although sessions are specified at the contract level, they are actually implemented in the channel specified by the binding elements. Therefore, this contract behavior verifies that the contract and channel are compatible when the service first starts. For instance, if the channel requires sessions, but a binding is used that doesn't support sessions (such as `basicHttpBinding`), then session requirements of the contract cannot be met, so the contract behavior throws an exception when the service is started.

At the service level, sessions are enabled by setting the `InstanceContextMode` behavior property to `InstanceContextMode.PerSession`. This directs WCF to create an instance of the service class for each unique session that connects to the service. Other options for `InstanceContextMode` are `PerCall` or `Single`. `PerCall` creates a new service instance for each call and `Single` maintains just one instance for all callers.

Listing 5.5 shows the service code using InstanceContextMode. PerSession behavior. The InstanceContextMode behavior directs WCF to create a service instance per unique session. In addition to returning a stock price, the code also tracks how many times it was called. Because the InstanceContextMode is set to PerSession, the client sees the number of times that it called the service in the session, not the total number of times the service was called. If the InstanceContextMode is set to Single, the client would see the total number of calls in the service lifetime. If InstanceContextMode is set to PerCall, the client would always see one as the number of calls.

Note also that a lock is used to synchronize access to the n_calls variable in the class. This is necessary because ConcurrencyMode is set to Multiple and multiple threads will be executing within the session-scoped instance.

LISTING 5.5 PerSession Instancing

```
[DataContract]
class StockPrice
{
        [DataMember]
        public double price;
        [DataMember]
        public int calls;
}

[ServiceContract(SessionMode = SessionMode.Required)]
interface IStockService
{
        [OperationContract]
        StockPrice GetPrice(string ticker);
}

[ServiceBehavior(InstanceContextMode = InstanceContextMode.PerSession,
                    ConcurrencyMode = ConcurrencyMode.Multiple)]
class StockService : IStockService
{
        System.Object lockThis = new System.Object();
        private int n_Calls = 0;
        StockService()
        {
            Console.WriteLine("{0}: Created new instance of
```

```
                            StockService on thread",
            System.DateTime.Now);
    }
    public StockPrice GetPrice(string ticker)
    {
        StockPrice p = new StockPrice();
        Console.WriteLine("{0}: GetPrice called on thread {1}",
          System.DateTime.Now,
          Thread.CurrentThread.ManagedThreadId);
        p.price = 94.85;
        lock (lockThis)
        {
            p.calls = ++n_Calls;
        }
        Thread.Sleep(5000);
        return (p);
    }
}
```

Figure 5.5 shows the output from two clients (left) and the service (right). There are two windows on the left because two clients were run concurrently. Each client calls GetPrice synchronously three times. The service output shows that two instances of the service class were created—one per client session. Note that each sees the number of requests that they sent, not the total number processed by the service. This is because the counter, n_Calls, is stored in the service session instance so each has a counter initialized to 0. If the InstanceContextMode is changed to PerCall, each client output would see the call count remaining at one for successive calls. If the InstanceContextMode is changed to Single, the each client would see the call count increase from one to six for successive calls, accounting for both client calls.

Controlling the Number of Concurrent Instances

By default, WCF hosts will spin up as many instances as possible to process incoming requests. If the instancing and concurrency behavior of a service contract is not specified, WCF will create a service instance for each incoming request and will allocate threads as needed to respond to requests. Overall this is a good approach to performance and scalability because the server will scale with the capacity of the hardware.

FIGURE 5.5 Output from session-aware service

But there are cases when you may want to throttle this behavior. For this purpose, there are three settings to throttle the concurrency and instancing for a service. These are defined in the `serviceThrottling` element of the behavior section of the configuration file.

The `maxConcurrentInstances` behavior controls how many service instances can be created by a service. This setting is useful if `Concurrency-Mode` is `PerCall` or `PerSession`, because both of those settings direct WCF to create an instance on demand. By defining the maximum number of instances that WCF can create, you place an upper bound on the number of instances that will reside in memory. When the limit has been reached, no further instances will be created until other instances can be destroyed or reused.

Listing 5.6 shows a service that doesn't specify `ConcurrencyMode` and `InstancingMode`, which means the default values of `Single` and `PerSession` will be used, respectively. The service operation takes 20 seconds to complete.

LISTING 5.6 Service Using Default Concurrency and Instancing Behavior

```
[ServiceContract]
public interface IStockService
{
        [OperationContract]
        double GetPrice(string ticker);
}

public class StockService : IStockService
{
        StockService()
        {
            Console.WriteLine("{0}: Created new instance of
                                StockService",
                    System.DateTime.Now);
        }
        public double GetPrice(string ticker)
        {
            Console.WriteLine("{0}: GetPrice called on thread {1}",
                System.DateTime.Now,
                Thread.CurrentThread.ManagedThreadId);
            Thread.Sleep(20000);
            return 94.85;
        }
}
```

Listing 5.7 shows a client that calls the service ten times asynchronously.

LISTING 5.7 Client Calling a Service Ten Times Asynchronously

```
class Program
{
        static int c = 0;
        static void Main(string[] args)
        {
            Console.WriteLine();
            ServiceReference.StockServiceClient p = new
                    ServiceReference.StockServiceClient();
            for (int i = 0; i < 10; i++)
            {
                    Console.WriteLine("{0}: Calling GetPrice",
                            System.DateTime.Now);
                    p.BeginGetPrice("MSFT",
                            GetPriceCallback, p);
                    Interlocked.Increment(ref c);
            }
            while (c > 0) // wait until all responses come back
            {
                    Thread.Sleep(100);
```

LISTING 5.7 continued

```
            }
        }

        static void GetPriceCallback(IAsyncResult ar)
        {
            try
            {
                double price = ((ServiceReference.StockServiceClient)
                              ar.AsyncState).EndGetPrice(ar);
                Console.WriteLine("{0}: Price:{1}",
                                        System.DateTime.Now, price);
                ((ServiceReference.StockServiceClient)ar.AsyncState)
                    .Close();
                Interlocked.Decrement(ref c);
            }
            catch (Exception ex)
            {
                Console.WriteLine(ex.InnerException.Message);
            }
        }
    }
}
```

Listing 5.8 shows the app.config file for the service. The maxConcurrentInstances behavior is set to five, indicating that no more than five instances will be created in the service.

LISTING 5.8 Throttling Concurrency with maxConcurrentInstances

```xml
<?xml version="1.0" encoding="utf-8" ?>
<configuration>

  <system.serviceModel>

    <services>
      <service name="EssentialWCF.StockService"
            behaviorConfiguration="throttling">
        <host>
          <baseAddresses>
            <add baseAddress="http://localhost:8000/EssentialWCF"/>
          </baseAddresses>
        </host>
        <endpoint address=""
                binding="basicHttpBinding"
                contract="EssentialWCF.StockService" />
      </service>
    </services>
```

```xml
      <behaviors>
        <serviceBehaviors>
          <behavior name="throttling">
            <serviceThrottling maxConcurrentInstances="5"/>
          </behavior>
        </serviceBehaviors>
      </behaviors>


    </system.serviceModel>
  </configuration>
```

Figure 5.6 shows the output from the client (left) and service (right). In the client, note how ten calls are made immediately when the program starts, and then five results come back after 20 seconds while the remaining five results come back after another 20 seconds. In the service output, note how the first five instances are created immediately when requested by the client, but the next five instances are not created until after the first five are shut down.

FIGURE 5.6 Output controlling the number of concurrent instances

Controlling the Number of Concurrent Calls

When `InstancingMode` is specified as `Single`, WCF creates a single instance within the host, regardless of how many client requests are made. When `ConcurrencyMode` is specified as `Multiple`, WCF creates a thread per request (up to system limits) for parallel execution of the service methods. To throttle this, the `maxConcurrentCalls` behavior controls how many concurrent calls can be active.

Listing 5.9 shows a service with the behaviors for `InstanceContextMode.Single` and `ConcurrencyMode.Multiple`. The service operation takes 20 seconds to complete.

LISTING 5.9 Service Using `InstanceContextMode.Single` and `ConcurrencyMode.Multiple` Behavior

```
[ServiceContract]
public interface IStockService
{
        [OperationContract]
        double GetPrice(string ticker);
}

[ServiceBehavior(InstanceContextMode = InstanceContextMode.Single,
                 ConcurrencyMode = ConcurrencyMode.Multiple)]
public class StockService : IStockService
{
        StockService()
        {
            Console.WriteLine("{0}: Created new instance of
                                    StockService",
                    System.DateTime.Now);
        }
        public double GetPrice(string ticker)
        {
            Console.WriteLine("{0}: GetPrice called on thread {1}",
              System.DateTime.Now,
              Thread.CurrentThread.ManagedThreadId);
            Thread.Sleep(20000);
            return 94.85;
        }
}
```

Listing 5.10 shows the `app.config` file for the service. The `maxConcurrentCalls` behavior is set to five, indicating that no more than five calls can be currently active at the same time.

LISTING 5.10 Throttling Concurrency with `maxConcurrentCalls`

```
<?xml version="1.0" encoding="utf-8" ?>
<configuration>

  <system.serviceModel>

    <services>
      <service name="EssentialWCF.StockService"
```

```
                    behaviorConfiguration="throttling">
        <host>
          <baseAddresses>
            <add baseAddress="http://localhost:8000/EssentialWCF"/>
          </baseAddresses>
        </host>
        <endpoint address=""
                  binding="basicHttpBinding"
                  contract="EssentialWCF.StockService" />
      </service>
    </services>

    <behaviors>
      <serviceBehaviors>
        <behavior name="throttling">
          <serviceThrottling maxConcurrentCalls="5"/>
        </behavior>
      </serviceBehaviors>
    </behaviors>

  </system.serviceModel>
</configuration>
```

Figure 5.7 shows the output from the client in Listing 5.7 (left) and service
(right). In the client, note that ten calls are made immediately when the program starts. Of those ten requests, five results come back after 20 seconds
and the remaining five results come back after another 20 seconds. In the
service output, note that only one instance is ever created. Also note that
five calls to GetPrice start immediately after, each on its own thread. When
those five calls complete, the threads are reused and subsequent calls from
the client are handled.

Controlling the Number of Concurrent Sessions

When InstancingMode is specified as PerSession, WCF creates an instance
for each session that connects to the service. To control the number of sessions connected to a service, the maxConcurrentSessions behavior can be
used. When the maximum is reached, the next client that attempts to create a session will wait until another session is closed. This setting is useful
for limiting the number of users (or clients or servers) that can connect to
a service.

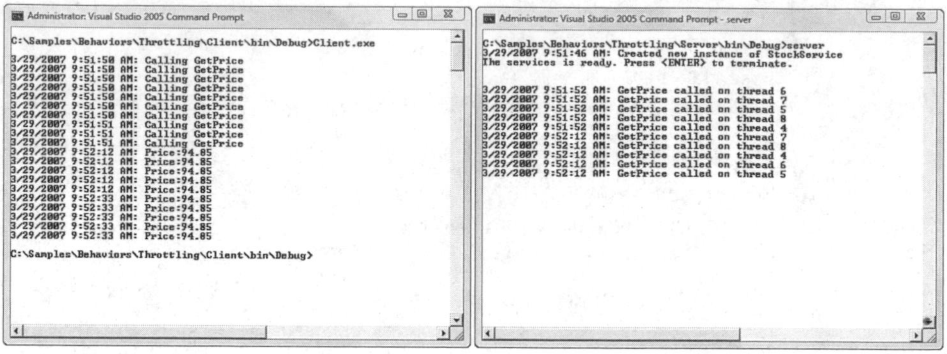

FIGURE 5.7 Output controlling the number of concurrent calls

Listing 5.11 shows a service with InstanceContextMode.PerSession and ConcurrencyMode.Multiple behaviors. The service operation takes 20 seconds to complete.

LISTING 5.11 Service Using InstanceContextMode.PerSession and ConcurrencyMode.Multiple Behavior

```
[ServiceContract(SessionMode = SessionMode.Required)]
public interface IStockService
{
        [OperationContract]
        double GetPrice(string ticker);
}


[ServiceBehavior(InstanceContextMode = InstanceContextMode.PerSession,
                ConcurrencyMode = ConcurrencyMode.Multiple)]
public class StockService : IStockService
{
        StockService()
        {
            Console.WriteLine("{0}: Created new instance:{1}",
                System.DateTime.Now,
                OperationContext.Current.SessionId);
        }
        public double GetPrice(string ticker)
        {
            Console.WriteLine("{0}: GetPrice called on thread {1}",
              System.DateTime.Now,
              Thread.CurrentThread.ManagedThreadId);
            Thread.Sleep(20000);
            return 94.85;
        }
}
```

Listing 5.12 shows the `app.config` file for the service. The `maxConcurrentSessions` behavior is set to 5, indicating that no more than five sessions can be created from clients to the service at the same time. Notice that `wsHttpBinding` is used rather than `basicHttpBinding` because the latter doesn't support sessions.

LISTING 5.12 Throttling Concurrency with `maxConcurrentSessions`

```
<?xml version="1.0" encoding="utf-8" ?>
<configuration>

  <system.serviceModel>

    <services>
      <service name="EssentialWCF.StockService"
               behaviorConfiguration="throttling">
        <host>
          <baseAddresses>
            <add baseAddress="http://localhost:8000/EssentialWCF"/>
          </baseAddresses>
        </host>
        <endpoint address=""
                  binding="wsHttpBinding"
                  contract="EssentialWCF.StockService" />
      </service>
    </services>

    <behaviors>
      <serviceBehaviors>
        <behavior name="throttling">
          <serviceThrottling maxConcurrentSessions="5"/>
        </behavior>
      </serviceBehaviors>
    </behaviors>

  </system.serviceModel>
</configuration>
```

Figure 5.8 shows the output from the client in Listing 5.7 (left) and service (right). In the client, ten calls are made immediately when the program starts. Of those ten requests, five results come back after 20 seconds and the remaining five results come back after another 20 seconds. In the service output, note that five sessions are created and five calls to `GetPrice` are started immediately after the client calls the service. After those five calls complete and the client closes the connection, subsequent sessions can be created.

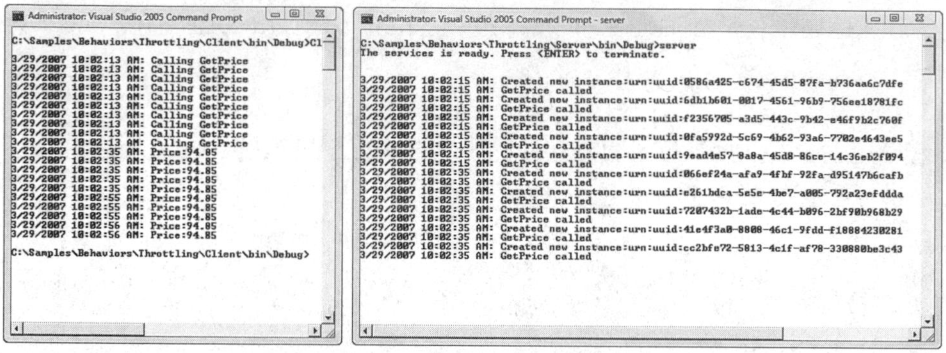

FIGURE 5.8 Output controlling the number of concurrent sessions

Exporting and Publishing Metadata (Service Behavior)

The ABCs of a service—its addresses, bindings, and contracts—are represented in metadata so that potential clients know where, how, and what to communicate. This information is collectively referred to as *service metadata*. The metadata service behavior is the first behavior that most developers encounter, because it's referenced in the configuration files generated by Visual Studio 2008 when you create WCF project. This behavior works in concert with a metadata endpoint to make metadata available to clients.

Two steps are necessary to make metadata useful for clients: export it in a format that they can read and publish it somewhere that they can find it. The default export format is WSDL, so as long as clients can read standards-based metadata format, they can understand how to communicate with the service. WCF publishes the metadata using the WS-MetadataExchange protocol over any supported transport, or it can publish the metadata in response to an HTTP GET. Both of these steps, the export and publishing the metadata, are implemented by the ServiceMetadataBehavior in a service.

Metadata is exposed from a service through a Metadata Exchange (MEX) endpoint. A MEX endpoint is like any other WCF endpoint: It has an address, a binding, and a contract. Like any other endpoint, a MEX endpoint can be added to a service either through configuration or through code.

A MEX endpoint should expose the `IMetadataExchange` interface as its contract. Defined in `System.ServiceModel.Description`, this interface provides methods that inspect a service and expose its metadata as WSDL. A number of system-supplied bindings are available for MEX endpoints, such as `mexHttpBinding`, `mexHttpsBinding`, `mexNamedPipeBinding` or `mexTcpBinding`. The address of a MEX endpoint can be either relative or absolute, following the normal addressing rules for endpoints.

Listing 5.13 shows a configuration file that defines and exposes metadata using the `serviceMetadata` behavior. The behavior is qualified with `httpGetEnabled="True"`, directing WCF to respond to HTTP GET requests on the endpoint in addition to WS-MEX requests.

The service contract includes an endpoint that exposes an `IMetadataExchange` interface. The endpoint uses relative addressing, using the HTTP transport, so the absolute address of the endpoint is http.//localhost:8000/EssentialWCF/mex. The endpoint uses `mexHttpBinding`, which creates a `wsHttpBinding` without security.

LISTING 5.13 Configuration for Enabling Metadata Publishing with **serviceMetadata**

```xml
<?xml version="1.0" encoding="utf-8" ?>
<configuration>

  <system.serviceModel>

    <services>
      <service name="EssentialWCF.StockService"
                  behaviorConfiguration="myBehavior">
        <host>
          <baseAddresses>
            <add baseAddress="http://localhost:8000/EssentialWCF"/>
          </baseAddresses>
        </host>
        <endpoint address=""
                  binding="basicHttpBinding"
                  contract="EssentialWCF.StockService" />
        <endpoint address="mex"
```

LISTING 5.13 continued

```
                        binding="mexHttpBinding"
                        contract="IMetadataExchange" />
        </service>
      </services>

      <behaviors>
        <serviceBehaviors>
          <behavior name=" myBehavior ">
            <serviceMetadata httpGetEnabled="True"/>
          </behavior>
        </serviceBehaviors>
      </behaviors>


    </system.serviceModel>
  </configuration>
```

Listing 5.14 shows a self-hosted service that exposes metadata. It is func-
tionally equivalent to the configuration in Listing 5.13.

LISTING 5.14 Self-Hosted Code for Enabling Metadata Publishing with
ServiceMetadataBehavior

```
[ServiceContract]
public interface IStockService
{
    [OperationContract]
    double GetPrice(string ticker);
}

public class StockService : IStockService
{
    public double GetPrice(string ticker)
    {
        return 94.85;
    }
}

public class service
{
  public static void Main()
  {
    ServiceHost serviceHost = new ServiceHost(typeof(StockService),
        new Uri("http://localhost:8000/EssentialWCF"));
    serviceHost.AddServiceEndpoint(
        typeof(IStockService),
```

```
        new BasicHttpBinding(),
        "");

    ServiceMetadataBehavior behavior = new ServiceMetadataBehavior();
    behavior.HttpGetEnabled = true;
    serviceHost.Description.Behaviors.Add(behavior);
    serviceHost.AddServiceEndpoint(
        typeof(IMetadataExchange),
        MetadataExchangeBindings.CreateMexHttpBinding(),
        "mex");

    serviceHost.Open();

    // The service can now be accessed.
    Console.WriteLine("Service is ready. <ENTER> to terminate.\n");
    Console.ReadLine();

    serviceHost.Close();
  }
}
```

Implementing Transactions (Operation Behavior)

There are two scenarios commonly referred to as *transactions*. *Multistep business processes* are long-running processes that typically span minutes, days, or months. They could involve multiple organizations and human-based workflow. *Short-running transactions* are business operations that typically complete in seconds and have few external dependencies. Although they both have well-defined interfaces and a deterministic workflow, they are fundamentally different animals. WCF supports short-running transactions. It does this by leveraging .NET and Windows infrastructure for transactions running in a Microsoft-only environment and by leveraging WS-* standards transactions that span platforms.

Multistep business processes typically combine both automated and manual workflow. They may take a few moments (for example, place an order) or a few months (for example, get a rebate). If a multistep process (for example, plan a business trip) fails part way through, earlier steps (for example, make a plane reservation) are undone by taking compensating steps (cancel the plane reservation). These transactions are best supported with a message broker or enterprise service bus such as BizTalk Server.

Short-running transactions encapsulate discrete business functions. They typically take seconds to complete. The business functions can be exposed at a high-level (for example, Open New Account) to aggregate or update information from multiple sources. The business functions can also be exposed at a lower level (Update Customer Address) to update just one data source. In either case, all data updates within the transaction must succeed or fail as an atomic unit to maintain integrity of the business function. If one component update fails within the transaction, the service must undo the updates that succeeded prior to the failure so that it leaves the data exactly as it was found before the operation began.

This behavior is commonly known as an ACID transaction. Much has been written on this topic, but in short ACID transactions are

- **Atomic.** All updates within the transaction are successful, or they're all rolled back. No partial updates are allowed. For instance, in a bank transfer, if the debit succeeds but the credit fails, the debit is rolled back so money isn't created or lost.
- **Consistent.** After the operation, all data is valid according to the business rules. For instance, in a bank transfer, the To and From accounts must be valid accounts or the transaction will abort.
- **Isolated.** While the operation is executing, no partial results are visible outside the transactions. For instance, as a bank transfer is being executed, other users will not see the balances part way through the transfer.
- **Durable.** After the transaction is committed, the data must be persisted in a way that can survive system failures.

Transactional Operations Within a Service

Transactional service operations succeed or fail as a unit. They are initiated by one party, which assumes that the result will be consistent, whether the operation succeeds or fails. Figure 5.9 depicts pseudo code of this behavior. The client opens a connection to the service and calls its `Transfer` method. `Transfer` executes a debit, a credit, and then marks the transaction complete. The client is uninvolved in the transactional semantics.

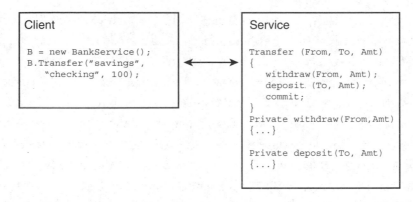

FIGURE 5.9 ACID transaction within an operation

To implement this behavior in WCF, the service operation must be marked as transactional using the [OperationBehavior(Transaction ScopeRequired=true)] attribute. This directs WCF to create a new transaction and enlist the execution thread on that transaction before dispatching control to the method. If the operation fails before it is complete, all partial updates to transactional resources within that transaction are rolled back.

If TransactionScopeRequired=false is specified, which is the default, the operation executes without a transaction. In that case, the operation will not support ACID properties. If the operation updates one table and then fails updating a second table, updates in the first table will be persisted and the ACID property is violated.

You can indicate that an operation is complete either implicitly or explicitly. By using the [OperationBehavior(TransactionAutoComplete =true)] behavior, the operation is implicitly considered complete if it doesn't throw an error. If it throws an error, it is considered incomplete and partial updates to transactional resources will be rolled back. Alternatively, you can use the [OperationBehavior(TransactionAutoComplete =false)] behavior and then explicitly call OperationContext.Current.SetTransactionComplete() before returning from the method. If you use the explicit method, you also need to use a session-based binding element in the communication channel, and you need to support sessions in the service contract with [ServiceContract(SessionMode=SessionMode.Allowed)].

Listing 5.15 shows a service, BankService, which exposes two service operations. The first service operation, GetBalance, is not transactional. It reads from the database and returns the result. The OperationBehavior TransactionScopeRequired=false is used to indicate that it does not require a transaction. The second operation, Transfer, is transactional and is marked as such with the operational behavior TransactionScopeRequired=true. It calls two internal methods, Withdraw and Deposit, and each updates the database through DBAccess. The Transfer operation implicitly marks the transaction as complete with the TransactionAutoComplete=true attribute. If neither Withdraw nor Deposit throws an error, the change from both are marked as complete.

The BankService service uses the internal class DBAccess for all database access. Note that its constructor opens a connection to the database. When DBAccess goes out of scope and there are no outstanding requests or transactions active, the garbage collector will close the connection. Aggressively attempting to close the connection in a destructor will cause an error because a transaction may still be active when the class goes out of scope.

LISTING 5.15 Transactional Operation

```
[ServiceContract]
public interface IBankService
{
    [OperationContract]
    double GetBalance(string AccountName);

    [OperationContract]
    void Transfer(string From, string To, double amount);
}

public class BankService : IBankService
{
    [OperationBehavior (TransactionScopeRequired=false)]
     public double GetBalance (string AccountName)
        {
            DBAccess dbAccess = new DBAccess();
            double amount = dbAccess.GetBalance(AccountName);
            dbAccess.Audit(AccountName, "Query", amount);
            return amount;
        }
```

```
[OperationBehavior(TransactionScopeRequired = true,
                TransactionAutoComplete = true)]
public void Transfer(string From, string To, double amount)
    {
        try
        {
            Withdraw(From, amount);
            Deposit(To, amount);
        }
        catch (Exception ex)
        {
            throw ex;
        }
    }

    private void Withdraw(string AccountName, double amount)
        {
            DBAccess dbAccess = new DBAccess();
            dbAccess.Withdraw(AccountName, amount);
            dbAccess.Audit(AccountName, "Withdraw", amount);
        }
    private void Deposit(string AccountName, double amount)
        {
            DBAccess dbAccess = new DBAccess();
            dbAccess.Deposit(AccountName, amount);
            dbAccess.Audit(AccountName, "Deposit", amount);
        }
    }


class DBAccess
{
        Private SqlConnection conn;
        public DBAccess()
        {
            string cs = ConfigurationManager.
                        ConnectionStrings["sampleDB"].ConnectionString;
            conn = new SqlConnection(cs);
            conn.Open();
        }

        public void Deposit(string AccountName, double amount)
        {
            string sql = string.Format("Deposit {0}, {1}, '{2}'",
                            AccountName, amount.ToString(),
                            System.DateTime.Now.ToString());
```

LISTING 5.15 continued

```
            SqlCommand cmd = new SqlCommand(sql, conn);
            cmd.ExecuteNonQuery();
        }
        public void Withdraw(string AccountName, double amount)
        {
            string sql = string.Format("Withdraw {0}, {1}, '{2}'",
                            AccountName, amount.ToString(),
                            System.DateTime.Now.ToString());
            SqlCommand cmd = new SqlCommand(sql, conn);
            cmd.ExecuteNonQuery();
        }
        public double GetBalance(string AccountName)
        {
            SqlCommand cmd = new SqlCommand("GetBalance " +
                            AccountName, conn);
            SqlDataReader reader = cmd.ExecuteReader();
            reader.Read();
            double amount = System.Convert.ToDouble
                            (reader["Balance"].ToString());
            reader.Close();
            return amount;
        }
        public void Audit(string AccountName, string Action,
                                            double amount)
        {
            Transaction txn = Transaction.Current;
            if (txn != null)
                Console.WriteLine("{0} | {1} Audit:{2}",
                    txn.TransactionInformation.DistributedIdentifier,
                    txn.TransactionInformation.LocalIdentifier,Action);
            else
                Console.WriteLine("<no transaction> Audit:{0}",
                            Action);
            string sql = string.Format("Audit {0}, {1}, {2}, '{3}'" ,
                            AccountName, Action, amount.ToString(),
                            System.DateTime.Now.ToString());
            SqlCommand cmd = new SqlCommand(sql, conn);
            cmd.ExecuteNonQuery();
        }


    }
```

The client code for this example is shown in Listing 5.16. The client is
unaware of the transaction on the service.

LISTING 5.16 Client Calling a Transactional Service

```
ServiceReference.BankServiceClient proxy = new
            ServiceReference.BankServiceClient();

Console.WriteLine("{0}: Before - savings:{1}, checking {2}",
                    System.DateTime.Now,
                    proxy.GetBalance("savings"),
                    proxy.GetBalance("checking"));

proxy.Transfer("savings", "checking", 100);

Console.WriteLine("{0}: After - savings:{1}, checking {2}",
                    System.DateTime.Now,
                    proxy.GetBalance("savings"),
                    proxy.GetBalance("checking"));
proxy.Close();
```

Because the two internal methods, Withdraw and Deposit, each create a new DBAccess class, they each open separate connections to the database. When Withdraw opens the first connection in the transaction, the transaction is part of a local transaction but not a distributed one. When it opens the second connection, the transaction is escalated to a distributed transaction so the work can be coordinated across both connections. The DBAccess.Audit method prints out the LocalIdentifier and the DistributedIdentier of the transaction, as shown in Figure 5.10. Notice that Withdraw executes without a distributed transaction, because it is the only connection open in the transaction at that time. But when the Deposit executes, it creates a distributed transaction since it is the second connection open with the transaction scope. Escalation happens automatically and has a dramatic negative effect on performance.

Listing 5.17 shows the optimized code, where the transfer operation opens a connection through DBAccess and passes that connection to both Withdraw and Deposit so that only one connection is used.

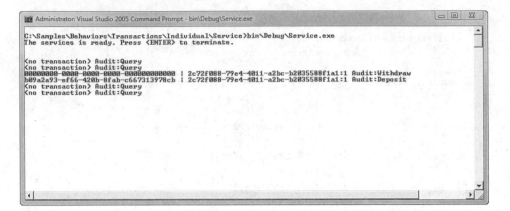

FIGURE 5.10 Output from transactional service showing local and distributed

transaction IDs

LISTING 5.17 Transactional Operation Optimized to Avoid Distributed Transactions

```
[OperationBehavior(TransactionScopeRequired = true,
                   TransactionAutoComplete = true)]
private void Transfer(string From, string To, double amount)
{
    DBAccess dbAccess = new DBAccess();
    Withdraw(From, amount, dbAccess);
    Deposit(To, amount, dbAccess);
}

private void Withdraw(string AccountName, double amount,
                                        DBAccess dbAccess)
{
    dbAccess.Withdraw(AccountName, amount);
    dbAccess.Audit(AccountName, "Withdraw", amount);
}
private void Deposit(string AccountName, double amount,
                                        DBAccess dbAccess)
{
    dbAccess.Deposit(AccountName, amount);
    dbAccess.Audit(AccountName, "Deposit", amount);
}
```

Figure 5.11 shows the output from the optimized service. Notice that the distributed transaction ID stays as all 0s, indicating that no distributed transaction is present.

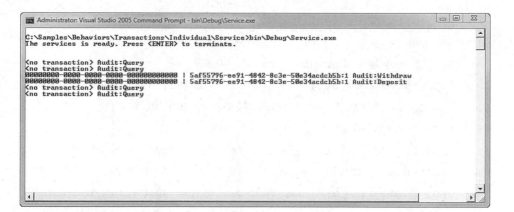

```
C:\Samples\Behaviors\Transactions\Individual\Service>bin\Debug\Service.exe
The services is ready. Press <ENTER> to terminate.

<no transaction> Audit:Query
<no transaction> Audit:Query
00000000-0000-0000-0000-000000000000 | 5af55796-ee91-4842-8c3e-50e34acdcb5b:1 Audit:Withdraw
00000000-0000-0000-0000-000000000000 | 5af55796-ee91-4842-8c3e-50e34acdcb5b:1 Audit:Deposit
<no transaction> Audit:Query
<no transaction> Audit:Query
```

FIGURE 5.11 Output from optimized transactional service

Flowing Transactions Across Operations

When working with distributed systems, transactions sometimes must span service boundaries. For instance, if one service managed customer information and another service managed orders, and a user wanted to place an order and ship the product to a new address, the system would need to invoke operations on each service. If the transaction completed, the user would expect that both systems were properly updated.

If infrastructure supports an atomic transactional protocol, the services can be composed into an aggregate transaction as just described. WS-AT (Web Service Atomic Transactions) provides the infrastructure for sharing information among participating services to implement the two-phase commit semantics necessary for ACID transactions. In WCF, flowing transactional information across service boundaries is referred to as *transaction flow*.

To flow transactional semantics across service boundaries, the following five steps must be taken:

- **(Service Contract) SessionMode.Required.** Service contracts must require sessions because this is how information will be shared between the coordinator (typically the client) and the participating services.

- **(Operation Behavior) TransactionScopeRequired=true.** Operation behavior must require a transaction scope. This will create a new transaction if one is not already present.

- **(Operation Contract) TransactionFlowOption.Allowed.** Operation contracts must allow transaction information to flow in the header of messages.

- **(Binding Definition) TransactionFlow=true.** The binding must enable transaction flow so that the channel can put transaction information into the SOAP header. Also note that the binding must support sessions because wsHttpBinding does but basicHttpBinding does not.

- **(Client) TransactionScope.** The party that initiates the transaction, typically the client, must use a transaction scope when calling the service operations. It must also call TransactionScope.Close() to commit the changes.

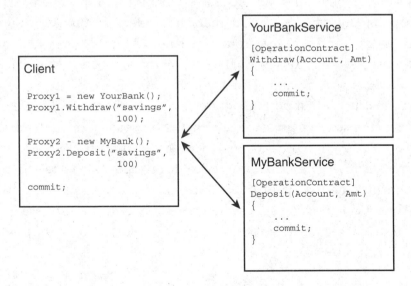

FIGURE 5.12 Transaction that spans service boundaries

The .NET 3.5 documentation on the TransactionScopeRequired attribute includes the following table to describe the relationship between these elements. It is repeated here for convenience.

TABLE 5.2 Interaction of `TransactionFlow` elements

`TransactionScopeRequired`	Binding Permits Transaction Flow	Caller Flows Transaction	Result
False	False	No	Method executes without a transaction.
True	False	No	Method creates and executes within a new transaction.
True or False	False	Yes	A SOAP fault is returned for the transaction header.
False	True	Yes	Method executes without a transaction.
True	True	Yes	Method executes under the flowed transaction.

Listing 5.18 demonstrates use of these elements. The code is similar to that shown in Listing 5.15, but while that code ensures transactional integrity of one service operation (`Transfer`), this code shows transactional integrity across services with the `TransactionFlowOption` attribute. Note a few points. First, the `ServiceContract` is marked as requiring sessions. To meet this requirement, a sessionful protocol, such as `wsHttpBinding` or `netTcpBinding`, must be used. Second, for illustrative purposes, the `TransactionAutoComplete` is set to false and the last line of the method is `SetTransactionComplete`. If execution doesn't reach `SetTransaction Complete`, the transaction will be automatically rolled back. Third, the `TransactionFlowOption.Allowed` is specified on each `OperationContract` to allow the transaction to span service calls.

LISTING 5.18 Flowing Transactional Context Across Boundaries

```
[ServiceContract(SessionMode=SessionMode.Required)]
public interface IBankService
{
    [OperationContract]
    double GetBalance(string AccountName);

    [OperationContract]
    void Transfer(string From, string To, double amount);
}

public class BankService : IBankService
{

[OperationBehavior(TransactionScopeRequired = false)]
public double GetBalance(string AccountName)
{
        DBAccess dbAccess = new DBAccess();
        double amount = dbAccess.GetBalance(AccountName);
        dbAccess.Audit(AccountName, "Query", amount);
        return amount;
}

[OperationBehavior(TransactionScopeRequired = true,
                    TransactionAutoComplete = true)]
public void Transfer(string From, string To, double amount)
    {
        try
        {
            Withdraw(From, amount);
            Deposit(To, amount);
        }
        catch (Exception ex)
        {
            throw ex;
        }
    }

[OperationBehavior(TransactionScopeRequired = true,
                    TransactionAutoComplete = false)]
[TransactionFlow(TransactionFlowOption.Allowed)]
private void Deposit(string AccountName, double amount)
    {
        DBAccess dbAccess = new DBAccess();
        dbAccess.Deposit(AccountName, amount);
        dbAccess.Audit(AccountName, "Deposit", amount);
        OperationContext.Current.SetTransactionComplete();
    }
```

```
[OperationBehavior(TransactionScopeRequired = true,
                          TransactionAutoComplete = false)]
[TransactionFlow(TransactionFlowOption.Allowed)]
private void Withdraw(string AccountName, double amount)
      {
            DBAccess dbAccess = new DBAccess();
            dbAccess.Withdraw(AccountName, amount);
            dbAccess.Audit(AccountName, "Withdraw", amount);
            OperationContext.Current.SetTransactionComplete();
      }
}
```

Listing 5.19 shows the configuration file. Notice that the binding is wsHttpBinding, which supports sessions. This is required because the code declares SessionMode.Required in the service contract. Also notice transactionFlow="true" is defined in the binding configuration section.

LISTING 5.19 Enabling Transactional Flow in Configuration

```
<?xml version="1.0" encoding="utf-8" ?>
<configuration>
  <system.serviceModel>
    <services>
      <service name="EssentialWCF.BankService">
        <host>
          <baseAddresses>
            <add baseAddress="http://localhost:8000/EssentialWCF"/>
          </baseAddresses>
        </host>
        <endpoint address=""
                  binding="wsHttpBinding"
                  bindingConfiguration="transactions"
                  contract="EssentialWCF.IBankService" />
      </service>
    </services>

    <bindings>
      <wsHttpBinding>
        <binding name="transactions"
            transactionFlow="true" >
        </binding>
      </wsHttpBinding>
    </bindings>
  </system.serviceModel>
</configuration>
```

Listing 5.20 shows client code that aggregates the work of the two services into a single transaction. Three proxies are created, two pointing to one service, the third pointing to another service. The two Query operations and the one Withdraw operation are called on proxy1, and then the Deposit operation is called on proxy2. If everything goes well within those service operations, they will each execute their SetTransactionComplete(). After both operations return, the client calls scope.Complete() to finish the transaction. Only if all parties in the transaction execute their SetTransactionComplete() method will the transaction be committed; if they do not, the entire transaction is rolled back. Finally, two more Query operations are called with proxy3 to verify that the changes persist past the transaction.

LISTING 5.20 Coordinating a Distributed Transaction from a Client

```
using (TransactionScope scope = new
                TransactionScope(TransactionScopeOption.RequiresNew))
{
    localhost1.BankServiceClient proxy1 = new
                        localhost1.BankServiceClient();
    localhost2.BankServiceClient proxy2 = new
                        localhost2.BankServiceClient();
    Console.WriteLine("{0}: Before - savings:{1}, checking {2}",
                        System.DateTime.Now,
                        proxy1.GetBalance("savings"),
                        proxy2.GetBalance("checking"));

    proxy1.Withdraw("savings", 100);
    proxy2.Deposit("checking", 100);
    scope.Complete();

    proxy1.Close();
    proxy2.Close();
}
localhost1.BankServiceClient proxy3 = new
                        localhost1.BankServiceClient();
Console.WriteLine("{0}: After - savings:{1}, checking {2}",
                        System.DateTime.Now,
                        Proxy3.GetBalance("savings"),
                        Proxy3.GetBalance("checking"));
```

Figure 5.13 shows output from a client and two services. The client is on the left and prints the balance from savings and checking before and after the transfer. The two services are on the right. The top service is accessed by Proxy1 and Proxy3; the bottom one is accessed by Proxy2. The top service executes two Query operations, a Withdraw operation and two more Query operations. The bottom service executes a Deposit operation. Note that the distributed transaction identifier is the same in both services, indicating that they are both part of the same transaction.

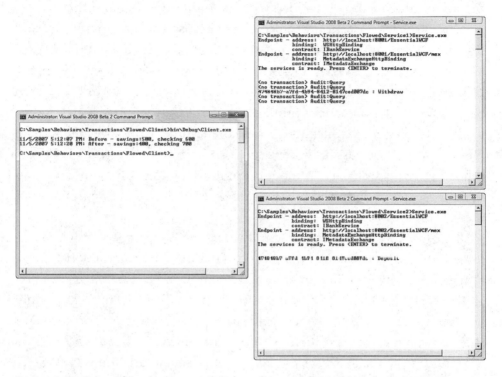

FIGURE 5.13 Output from two transactional services coordinated in a single transaction

Choosing a Transaction Protocol—OleTx or WS-AT

Transaction managers are responsible for coordinating work among multiple parties and committing work through *resource managers*. Resource managers are responsible for reliable, persistent storage. Depending on the resources used and the service or application boundaries crossed, WCF will use one of three transaction managers to implement transactions. The Lightweight Transaction Manager (LTM) is used for managing resources within one application domain. The Kernel Transaction Manager (KTM), available only on Vista and Windows Server 2008, is used for managing the transacted file system and transacted registry resources. The Distributed Transaction Coordinator (DTC) is used for managing transactions that cross application, process, or machine boundaries. The application does not control which transaction manager is used; WCF will choose the most appropriate one and escalate as needed without application intervention.

One of two transaction protocols may be used when communicating transition semantics across application, process, or machine boundaries. The OleTx protocol is a Windows-specific binary protocol. It is native to the DTC and is ideal for communication within an internal network. The Web Services Atomic Transactions protocol , or WS-AT, is a standards-based protocol that also spans application process or machine boundaries. But unlike OleTx, WS-AT is transport independent and can flow over TCP, HTTP, or other network protocols. Although applications don't have a choice in which resource manager to use, they do determine which transaction protocol to use.

It turns out that you can specify the transaction protocol only for certain bindings: those that support sessions (required by transactions), those that are two way (required by transaction flow), and those that are not tied to the WS-* stack (WS-* bindings always use WS-AT). This leaves only `netTcpBinding` and `netNamedPipeBinding`. The transaction protocol for these bindings can be specified in code or configuration. Listing 5.21 shows a configuration file that uses the TCP binding in conjunction with WS-AT that would enable transactions to flow between standards-based (WS-AT), fast (binary), secure (TCP) services over the Internet.

LISTING 5.21 Specifying WS-AT in a Binding

```
<bindings>
  <netTcpBinding>
    <binding name = "wsat"
       transactionFlow = "true"
       transactionProtocol = "WSAtomicTransactionOctober2004"
    />
  </netTcpBinding>
</bindings>
```

Transaction Service Behaviors

The two behaviors defined at the operation level, `TransactionScope Required` and `TransactionAutoComplete`, are described earlier in this section. At the service level, there are two additional behaviors to consider: `TransactionIsolationLevel` and `TransactionTimeout`.

The `TransactionIsolationLevel` attribute, as its name implies, affects the isolation level of the transaction. Isolation refers to the I in ACID and governs how isolated the transaction is from the environment around it. There are many isolation levels. *Serializable*, the default, provides the highest degree of isolation and prevents others from updating data until the transaction completes. For instance, if the transaction contains a `select count(*) from orders` statement, no other process can insert or delete any `orders` data until the transaction completes. *ReadUncommitted* provides the lowest level of isolation, enabling other processes to read and write data that a transaction updated before that transaction competes. In practice, it's best to leave the isolation level at its default, `Serializable`, and instead, avoid transactions that lock more data than necessary, as in the case of `select (*) from order`.

The transaction isolation level must be consistent between the `Trans-actionScope` defined by the client and the `TransactionIsolationLevel` defined by the service behavior. If neither is specified, the default, `Isola-tionLevel.Serializable`, is used. Listing 5.22 shows the client and service setting, each to `ReadUncommitted`.

The length of time that a transaction may run for can also be controlled. This can be set on the client or the service, each for different purpose. On the client, this may be done to limit the amount of time that a user-initiated transactional operation runs. On the server, it may be set by a system administrator to ensure that no one transaction can consume too many resources.

In Listing 5.22, `TransactionScopeOption.Timeout` is set to 30 seconds on the client, indicating that the user-initiated transaction should be aborted if it runs for more than 30 seconds. Also in Listing 5.22, the ServiceBehavior, `TransactionTimeout`, is set to 1 minute on the server, indicating that if any transaction runs for more than 1 minute, it will be automatically aborted.

LISTING 5.22 Setting the Transaction Isolation Level and Timeout

```
//
// Client code
//
TransactionOptions opt = new TransactionOptions();
opt.IsolationLevel = IsolationLevel.ReadUncommitted;
opt.Timeout = new System.TimeSpan(0, 0, 30);
using (TransactionScope scope = new
           TransactionScope (TransactionScopeOption.RequiresNew), opt))
{
    localhost.BankServiceClient proxy = new
               localhost.BankServiceClient();
    proxy.Transfer("savings", "checking", 100);
    scope.Complete();
    proxy.Close();
}


//
// Service Code
//
[ServiceContract(SessionMode=SessionMode.Required)]
[ServiceBehavior (TransactionIsolationLevel =
                            IsolationLevel.ReadUncommitted,
                 TransactionTimeout="00:01:00"))]
public class BankService
{
  [OperationContract]
  [OperationBehavior(TransactionScopeRequired = true,
                  TransactionAutoComplete = true)]
  [TransactionFlow(TransactionFlowOption.Allowed)]
   private void Transfer(string From, string To, double amount)
   {
    …
   }
}
```

Implementing Custom Behaviors

Custom behaviors enable you to insert code at crucial points as WCF builds
the runtime and the message processing pipeline. Behaviors can be added
in code, by manipulating the service description manually, with attributes
or with configuration. In all cases, the code can take ancillary actions, such
as looking up information in a directory or logging data for auditing
purposes.

Figure 5.14 shows the interfaces available for building custom behaviors on the client.

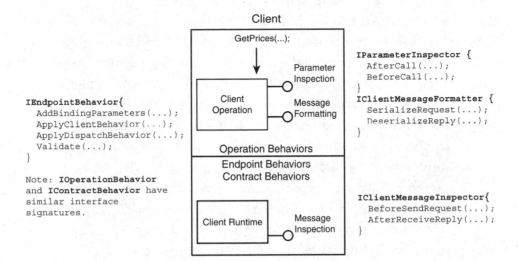

FIGURE 5.14 Interfaces for building custom behaviors on the client

Figure 5.15 shows the interfaces available for building and inserting custom behaviors on the server.

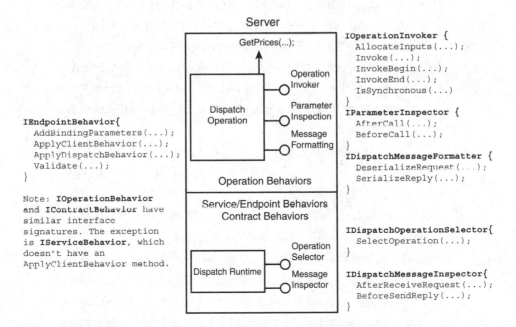

FIGURE 5.15 Interfaces for building custom behaviors on the server

Implementing custom behaviors requires three steps:

Step 1   Create a class that implements an `Inspector`, `Selector`, `Formatter`, or `Invoker` interface. This is typically where you'll do the business of the behavior. For instance, to log all incoming messages to a service (as is done for you when using `system.diagnostics` described in Chapter 9, "Diagnostics"), you can implement `IDispatchMessageInspector` and put code in the `AfterReceiveRequest` method. As another example, if you want code to run immediately before and after an operation call, you can implement `IOperationInvoker` and put code in the `Invoke` method. However, if your goal is to operate on the runtime (validate or manipulate the bindings of the channel stack), rather than operate on the message pipeline (inspect messages/parameters, or select/invoke operations), you can skip this step.

Step 2   Create a class that implements one of the behavior interfaces: `IServiceBehavior`, `IEndpointBehavior`, `IOperationBehavior`, or `IContractBehavior`. Using either the `ApplyClientBehavior` or `ApplyDispatchBehavior` method, add the class you created in the previous step to the list of behaviors. Again, if your goal is to operate on the runtime (validate or manipulate the bindings of the channel stack), rather than operate on the message pipeline (inspect messages/parameters, or select/invoke operations), you can just insert the logic into the `Validate` or `AddBindingParameter` methods of this class rather than applying a client or dispatch behavior to execute later.

Step 3   Configure the client or service to use the behavior. This can be accomplished with code, configuration, or attributes by using one of the following methods:

- Manipulate the `ServiceDescription` to add the behavior. If you're self-hosting a service, you can add the behavior class to the list of service behaviors (if you're adding an `IService Behavior`) or to the list of endpoint or contract behaviors on each endpoint (if you're adding an `IEndpointBehavior`, `IContractBehavior`, or `IOperationBehavior`). This is the most self-contained but least maintainable mechanism, because any behavior changes in the service will require a recompile.

- Use attributes to add the behavior into the client or server runtime. For this, you should implement the Attribute interface. This enables developers to use the attribute when defining the service, endpoint, or operations in their code.

- Use configuration to add a behavior into the client or server runtime. For this, you must do two additional steps. First, create a class that implements the `BehaviorExtensionElement` interface and defines the configuration data elements with the `[ConfigurationProperty]` attribute in that class. In that interface, you must also implement the `CreateBehavior` and `BehaviorType` methods to create and return your new `BehaviorExtension` class. Then, in the configuration file for the client or service that will use the behavior, you need to add a `<behaviorExtensions>` section where you reference the fully qualified type, and then use the behavior at the service or endpoint level.

After you complete these three steps, the behavior is ready to be used. It will automatically be called when the client or service is building its runtime and as each message is sent and received from the client or service. The rest of this section demonstrates specific behaviors.

Implementing a Message Inspector for Service Endpoint Behavior

Listing 5.23 implements a logging behavior by printing out every message sent and received by an endpoint. The code shows a message inspector called from an endpoint behavior. This also shows how the endpoint behavior is manually added to the service description in a custom hosted service.

> **■TIP   Implementing Custom Behavior for Tracing**
>
> In practice, if you're implementing a message inspector for diagnostic purposes, see Chapter 10, "Exception Handling," for tracing techniques.

The class myMessageInspector implements the IDispatchMessageIn-spector interface. In its BeforeSendRequest and AfterReceiveReply it prints out the message to the console. The class myEndPointBehavior imple-ments the IEndpointBehavior interface. In its AddDispatchBehavior method it adds the myMessageInspector class to the list of message inspec-tors to be called with each message. Finally, the main program adds the myEndpointBehavior class to the list of behaviors on all endpoints. Note that because the service also has a MEX endpoint, the request and response to that endpoint is also printed by myEndpointBehavior.

LISTING 5.23 Message Inspector in a Service Endpoint Behavior

```
using System;
using System.Text;
using System.ServiceModel;
using System.ServiceModel.Description;
using System.ServiceModel.Dispatcher;
using System.IO;

namespace EssentialWCF
{
    public class myEndpointBehavior : IEndpointBehavior
    {
        public void AddBindingParameters
                    (ServiceEndpoint endpoint,
                        System.ServiceModel.Channels.
                            BindingParameterCollection
                                    bindingParameters)
        {
        }

        public void ApplyClientBehavior
                    (ServiceEndpoint endpoint,
                        ClientRuntime clientRuntime)
        {
        }
        public void ApplyDispatchBehavior
                    (ServiceEndpoint endpoint,
                        EndpointDispatcher endpointDispatcher)
        {
            endpointDispatcher.DispatchRuntime.MessageInspectors.Add(
                    new myMessageInspector());
        }
```

```
        public void Validate(ServiceEndpoint endpoint)
        {
        }
}
public class myMessageInspector : IDispatchMessageInspector
{
        public object AfterReceiveRequest
                    (ref System.ServiceModel.Channels.Message request,
                     IClientChannel channel,
                     InstanceContext instanceContext)
        {
            Console.WriteLine(request.ToString());
            return request;
        }

        public void BeforeSendReply
                    (ref System.ServiceModel.Channels.Message reply,
                     object correlationState)
        {
            Console.WriteLine(reply.ToString());
        }
}

[ServiceContract]
public interface IStockService
{
        [OperationContract]
        double GetPrice(string ticker);
}

public class StockService :IStockService
{
        public double GetPrice(string ticker)
        {
            return 94.85;
        }
}
public class service
{
        public static void Main()
        {
            ServiceHost serviceHost = new
                    ServiceHost(typeof(StockService));

            foreach (ServiceEndpoint endpoint in
                        serviceHost.Description.Endpoints)
                endpoint.Behaviors.Add(new myEndpointBehavior());
```

LISTING 5.23 continued

```
        serviceHost.Open();

        // The service can now be accessed.
        Console.WriteLine("The services is ready\n\n");
        Console.ReadLine();

        // Close the ServiceHostBase to shut down the service.
        serviceHost.Close();

    }
  }
}
```

Exposing a Parameter Inspector for Service Operation Behavior as an Attribute

Listing 5.24 implements a behavior for validating parameters against regular expressions. It can be applied to any operation and enables the developer to define a regular expression and an error message to return if the parameter is invalid.

The code shows a parameter inspector called from an operation behavior and shows the operation behavior implementing an attribute. It also shows how the operation behavior is added to the service description by referencing the attribute in the service definition.

The class myParameterInpsector implements the IParameterInspector interface. The class stores two local properties, _pattern and _message, that are used to validate parameters in the BeforeCall method. In that method, the parameter value is compared to the parameter pattern using regular expression matching. If the value does not fit the pattern, an error is thrown.

The class myOperationBehavior implements the IEndpointBehavior and Attribute interfaces. In its AddDispatchBehavior method it adds the myParameterInspector class to the list of parameter inspectors to be called for each operation. Finally, when the service operation, GetPrice, is defined, the myOperationBehavior attribute is used to validate its parameters at runtime.

LISTING 5.24 Custom Parameter Inspector in an Operation Behavior Exposed as an Attribute

```csharp
using System;
using System.Text;
using System.Text.RegularExpressions;
using System.ServiceModel;
using System.ServiceModel.Channels;
using System.ServiceModel.Description;
using System.ServiceModel.Dispatcher;
using System.IO;

namespace EssentialWCF
{
    [AttributeUsage(AttributeTargets.Method)]
    public class myOperationBehavior : Attribute, IOperationBehavior
    {
        public string pattern;
        public string message;

        public void AddBindingParameters
                    (OperationDescription operationDescription,
                    BindingParameterCollection bindingParameters)
        {
        }

        public void ApplyClientBehavior
                    (OperationDescription operationDescription,
                    ClientOperation clientOperation)
        {
        }

        public void ApplyDispatchBehavior
                        (OperationDescription operationDescription,
                        DispatchOperation dispatchOperation)
        {
            dispatchOperation.ParameterInspectors.Add(
                        new myParameterInspector(
                            this.pattern, this.message));
        }

        public void Validate(OperationDescription operationDescription)
        {
        }
    }

    public class myParameterInspector : IParameterInspector
    {
        string _pattern;
```

LISTING 5.24 continued

```csharp
        string _message;
        public myParameterInspector(string pattern, string message)
        {
            _pattern = pattern;
            _message = message;
        }

        public void AfterCall(string operationName,
                              object[] outputs,
                              object returnValue, object
                              correlationState)
        {
        }

        public object BeforeCall(string operationName, object[] inputs)
        {
            foreach (object input in inputs)
            {
                if ((input != null) &&
                            (input.GetType() == typeof(string)))
                {
                    Regex regex = new Regex(_pattern);
                    if (regex.IsMatch((string)input))
                        throw new FaultException(string.
                            Format("Parameter out of range:{0}, {1}",
                                    (string) input, _message));
                }
            }
            return null;
        }
    }

[ServiceContract]
public interface IStockService
{
    [OperationContract]
    double GetPrice(string ticker);
}

public class StockService : IStockService
{
    [myOperationBehavior(pattern="[^a-zA-Z]",
                        message="Only alpha characters allowed")]
    public double GetPrice(string ticker)
    {
```

```
                if (ticker == "MSFT") return 94.85;
                else return 0.0;
            }
        }
    }
```

Exposing a Service Behavior Through Configuration

Listing 5.25 implements a behavior for validating that a software license key is installed in the service configuration. If it is not present or if it is invalid, the service will not start. It shows an endpoint behavior that validates configuration information as the service runtime is built. It also shows a behavior extension that is called as the service runtime is being built and how that extension adds the behavior to the service runtime. The result is that a custom behavior is used in the configuration file (app.config or web.config) and added to the service runtime so that configuration information can be validated as the service starts.

The class myServiceBehavior implements the IServiceBehavior interface. The class has two local properties, _EvaluationKey and _EvaluationType. The Validate method of myEndpointBehavior compares those properties against predetermined values.

The class myBehaviorExtensionElement implements the IBehaviorExtensionElement interface. It defines two [ConfigurationProperties] that can be represented in the configuration file. It overrides the BehaviorType and CreateBehavior methods so that it returns and creates the custom behavior, myServiceBehavior, during runtime startup. The constructor of myServiceBehavior takes two arguments, one for each property, so it can do the validation.

LISTING 5.25 Endpoint Behavior Exposed in Configuration

```
using System;
using System.Text;
using System.ServiceModel;
using System.ServiceModel.Channels;
using System.ServiceModel.Description;
using System.ServiceModel.Dispatcher;
using System.ServiceModel.Configuration;
using System.Configuration;
```

LISTING 5.25 continued

```
namespace EssentialWCF
{
    public class myServiceBehavior : IServiceBehavior
    {
        string _EvaluationKey;
        string _EvaluationType;
        public myEndpointBehavior( string EvaluationKey,
                                   string EvaluationType)
        {
            _EvaluationKey = EvaluationKey;
            _EvaluationType = EvaluationType;
        }

        public void AddBindingParameters
                    (ServiceDescription serviceDescription,
                     ServiceHostBase serviceHostBase,
                     System.Collections.ObjectModel.
                            Collection<ServiceEndpoint> endpoints,
                     BindingParameterCollection bindingParameters)
        {
        }

        public void ApplyClientBehavior(ServiceEndpoint endpoint,
                     ClientRuntime clientRuntime)
        {
        }

        public void ApplyDispatchBehavior(ServiceEndpoint endpoint,
                     EndpointDispatcher endpointDispatcher)
        {
        }

        public void Validate( ServiceDescription serviceDescription,
                              ServiceHostBase serviceHostBase)
        {
            if ((_EvaluationType == "Enterprise") &
                (_EvaluationKey != "SuperSecretEvaluationKey"))
                    throw new Exception
                        (String.Format("Invalid evaluation key.
                                        Type:{0}",_EvaluationType));
        }
    }

    public class myBehaviorExtensionElement : BehaviorExtensionElement
    {
        [ConfigurationProperty("EvaluationKey", DefaultValue = "",
```

```
                                                IsRequired = true)]
        public string EvaluationKey
        {
            get { return (string)base["EvaluationKey"]; }
            set { base["EvaluationKey"] = value; }
        }
        [ConfigurationProperty("EvaluationType",
                            DefaultValue = "Enterprise",
                            IsRequired = false)]
        public string EvaluationType
        {
            get { return (string)base["EvaluationType"]; }
            set { base["EvaluationType"] = value; }
        }

        public override Type BehaviorType
        {
            get { return typeof(myServiceBehavior); }
        }

        protected override object CreateBehavior()
        {
            return new myServiceBehavior( EvaluationKey,
                                        EvaluationType);
        }
    }

}
[ServiceContract]
public interface IStockService
{
    [OperationContract]
    double GetPrice(string ticker);
}

public class StockService : IStockService
{
    public double GetPrice(string ticker)
    {
        if (ticker == "MSFT") return 94.85;
        else return 0.0;
    }
}
}
```

Listing 5.26 shows the configuration file for the service. In the configuration file a <behaviorExtension> is added, pointing to the extension implementation. Notice that the implementation is fully qualified, including its type name and assembly information (title, version, culture, and public key). In this example, the assembly name and DLL that houses the extensions is Server.

LISTING 5.26 Configuration File for Exposing an Endpoint Behavior

```xml
<?xml version="1.0" encoding="utf-8" ?>
<configuration>

  <system.serviceModel>

    <extensions>
      <behaviorExtensions>
        <add name ="FreeTrial"
             Type = "EssentialWCF.myBehaviorExtensionElement, Server,
                     Version=1.0.0.0, Culture=neutral,
                     PublicKeyToken=null"/>
      </behaviorExtensions>
    </extensions>

    <services>
      <service name="EssentialWCF.StockService"
               behaviorConfiguration="customBehavior">
        <host>
          <baseAddresses>
            <add baseAddress="http://localhost:8000/EssentialWCF"/>
          </baseAddresses>
        </host>
        <endpoint address=""
                  binding="basicHttpBinding"
                  contract="EssentialWCF.StockService" />
      </service>
    </services>

    <behaviors>
      <serviceBehaviors>
        <behavior name="customBehavior">
          <FreeTrial EvaluationKey="SuperSecretEvaluationKey"
                     EvaluationType="Enterprise"/>
        </behavior>
      </serviceBehaviors>
    </behaviors>

  </system.serviceModel>
</configuration>
```

Security Behaviors

There are some important behaviors that handle security. These are covered in detail in Chapter 8, "Security," but it's worth understanding their role as behaviors.

The ServiceCredentials behavior is a service behavior used to specify the credentials of a service. This class is useful for accessing client security information, such as the user's Windows authentication settings, and client certificates. It's implemented as a behavior so that it can inspect incoming messages for their security information.

The Impersonation attribute of an operation behavior enables impersonation from the client to the service. When impersonation is allowed (or required), client credentials that are passed in the channel are used by the WCF runtime to impersonate the client for the duration of the service operation.

The ServiceAuthorization behavior, scoped at either the service or operation level, is used to authorize the caller to access the service or operation. Using this behavior, you can set an AuthorizationManager that is responsible for inspecting claims that the user presents and determining whether to grant access to the service.

The ServiceSecurityAudit behavior is accessible in the <serviceBehaviors> section of a configuration file and determines what, if any, information is automatically logged with each service request. If not defined, no audit information is logged.

SUMMARY

Behaviors are a fundamental extensibility point in the WCF architecture. They are used when the client or service runtime is being constructed and with each service call. When the runtime starts, it looks for behaviors by inspecting the type structures passed into the ClientChannel or ServiceHost, and then looks in configuration files. Behaviors can also be defined in code and added to the ServiceDescription object before opening the ServiceHost, or in code by using attributes, or in configuration files.

Behaviors implement inspectors—code that inspects objects presented to them. There are message inspectors that work at the message level and parameter inspectors that work on operation parameters. At the operation level, behaviors are involved with selecting which method to invoke to run for a given SOAP input message and again to invoke that method.

Behaviors control the instancing and concurrency of service classes and their operations. Instancing is controlled by the `InstanceContextMode` setting and can be `Single`, `PerCall`, or `PerSession`. Concurrency is controlled by the `ConcurrencyMode` setting and can be `Single Multiple` or `Reentrant` (single, but thread-safe code). Together, these two settings control the level of concurrency of a service, from a singleton on one end of the spectrum to creating a new instance per call on the other end. Service behaviors also enable you to throttle the number of concurrent calls, instances, or sessions.

One important service behavior is the `serviceMetaData` behavior. This behavior exposes the WCF type system and `ServiceDescription` model in WSDL so that clients know the where, how, and what to communicate with a service. More generally, the `serviceMetaData` endpoint uses the WS-MEX protocol so that it can communicate with clients on different platforms and return metadata information in a variety of formats. Only if a service includes this behavior will it expose WSDL. This is a different experience from what many developers are used to with ASMX, which exposes WSDL by default.

WCF implements short-lived, ACID-style transactions in behaviors. Transactions can exist within a service or can flow across service boundaries. Transactions are implemented at the operation behavior level, although certain conditions must be met at the endpoint and service level. For instance, to flow transactional context from the client to the service, the service endpoints must use a protocol that supports sessions, such as `wsHttpBinding`. Sessions must be allowed at the service level to flow transactions across service boundaries. Operation behaviors enable developers to specify the isolation level of transactions, and administrators can control the timeout properties.

WCF supports three transaction managers, one for local transactions within a process, one for Vista-only resources, and the Distributed Transaction Coordinator. In addition, communication across service boundaries can use either a Windows-only transaction protocol that leverages RPC, or it can use the standards-based WS-AT protocol.

Custom behaviors enable developers to create new behaviors at the service, endpoint, contract, or operation level. These behaviors enable the inspection and modification of messages as they flow in and out of clients or services. They also enable developers or system administrators to validate or modify the WCF runtime as services are started.

■ 6 ■
Serialization and Encoding

I N CHAPTER 2, "CONTRACTS," WE discussed serialization by using `DataContract` serialization to convert CLR types to standards-based XML for transmission between client and service. However, many scenarios exist where `DataContract` serialization is not sufficient. This includes serialization of existing CLR types that do not support `DataContract` serialization, legacy Web services, interoperability, code migration (such as .NET Remoting), and *data shaping.* Data shaping is the process of controlling the serialized XML of a .NET type used for performance optimization and contract-first development. In these situations, it is important to know how to work with the serialization facilities that WCF and the .NET Framework provide.

Encoding is another important topic related to serialization. WCF makes a distinction between the serialization of objects and the conversion of messages into an array of bytes that can be sent using a transport protocol.

Serialization Versus Encoding

There are important differences between serialization and encoding in WCF. The terms serialization and encoding have slightly different meanings in the WCF world when compared with other distributed computing technologies (such as ASP.NET Web services and COM).

Serialization is the term often used to describe the process of converting an object graph into an array of bytes. This is a very useful feature for representing the state of an object. Serialization can be used to persist an object's state to a file or a database, copy an object to the clipboard, or transfer objects across a network to another application. WCF does not follow the standard definition of serialization, though. WCF defines serialization as the process of converting an object graph into an XML Information Set (XML Infoset). This definition is not new, because ASP.NET Web services followed this same approach. The XML Infoset is the data model WCF uses internally to represent a message. The `System.ServiceModel.Channels.Message` class is a representation of an XML Infoset. The XML Infoset is the data model for representing an XML document. It is also the base abstraction from which the XML specification is derived. Figure 6.1 shows the relationship of Extensible Markup Language (XML) to the XML Infoset.

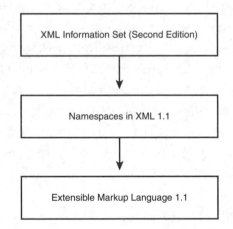

FIGURE 6.1 XML Information Set

A key distinction between XML and XML Infosets is that XML Infosets do not specify a specific format. So although the XML standard uses a text format, the XML Infoset has no such restriction. There are significant advantages to working with XML Infosets instead of XML directly. For example, WCF can represent messages in different formats as long as they are based on an XML Infoset. This includes the text format specified by the XML 1.1 specification as well as other formats such as a binary XML format.

This allows WCF to work with XML, but always using the most appropriate format based on interoperability and performance requirements.

Encoding is the term used to describe the process of converting a WCF message into an array of bytes. This is done so that the message can be sent across a transport protocol. WCF provides five types of encoding formats: binary, text, Message Transmission Optimization Mechanism (MTOM), JavaScript Object Notation, and Plain-Old-XML (POX). Which one you use will depend on your application's requirements. For example, you may want to use the `BinaryMessageEncoder` encoder for optimal performance between .NET applications, use the `TextMessageEncoder` or `MtomMessageEncoder` encoder for interoperability based on WS-* Web services, or use the `JsonMessageEncoder` encoder for AJAX-based Web applications. Encoders are one of the extensibility mechanisms provided by WCF; therefore, WCF can be extended to support new encoders if the encoders provided do not satisfy your requirements.

The rest of this chapter looks at how WCF uses serialization and encoding to transmit messages across a transport. We will examine the different forms of serialization and encoding and present scenarios where each option should be used.

Comparing WCF Serialization Options

There are many ways to use serialization objects using WCF. Determining which mechanism to use for serialization depends on a number of factors. These include whether you want to share types or contracts, support existing .NET types, preserve references, and more.

DataContractSerializer

The default serialization mechanism for WCF is the `DataContractSerializer`. This class can be found in the `System.Runtime.Serialization` namespace. The `DataContractSerializer` is built to support the sharing of contracts based on XSD schema. It maps Common Language Runtime (CLR) types to types defined in XSD. This means that XSD is the common schema that is used to exchange data between two applications. For example, you could exchange data between a .NET and Java application using XSD. An example of this is using a string.

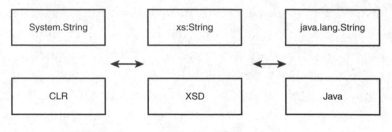

FIGURE 6.2 XSD types

Notice that type information, other than XSD types, is not exchanged between a server and a client. So in Figure 6.2, the notion of either System.String or java.lang.String is not exchanged as a part of the communication. This allows either side to map XSD types to specific types in their respective environments. This works well for primitive types. Complex types then become an extension of primitive types. So how does one describe mapping a .NET CLR type to an XSD schema using the DataContractSerializer?

As described in Chapter 2, the [DataContract] attribute can be used to mark a type as serializable. Members and properties can then be marked with the [DataMember] attribute as being part of the data contract. This is very much an opt-in scenario where the developer defines how the type is serialized. This means that the contract is explicit, unlike the XmlSerializer, which is very much an opt-out mode. Listing 6.1 shows an example of a complex type, Employee, using the DataContractSerializer. We will use the Employee type to examine the schema and the serialized output using the DataContractSerializer. This will form the basis for comparison with the other serialization mechanisms available with WCF.

LISTING 6.1 Employee Class Using DataContractSerialization

```
using System.Runtime.Serialization;

[DataContract]
public class Employee
{
    private int employeeID;
    private string firstName;
    private string lastName;

    public Employee(int employeeID, string firstName, string lastName)
    {
```

```
        this.employeeID = employeeID;
        this.firstName = firstName;
        this.lastName = lastName;
    }

    [DataMember]
    public int EmployeeID
    {
        get { return employeeID; }
        set { employeeID = value; }
    }

    [DataMember]
    public string FirstName
    {
        get { return firstName; }
        set { firstName = value; }
    }

    [DataMember]
    public string LastName
    {
        get { return lastName; }
        set { lastName = value; }
    }
}
```

The Employee complex type shown in Listing 6.1 is represented in an XSD schema in Listing 6.2.

LISTING 6.2 Employee XSD Schema

```
<xs:schema xmlns:tns=http://schemas.datacontract.org/2004/07/
➥elementFormDefault="qualified" targetNamespace=
➥"http://schemas.datacontract.org/2004/07/"
➥xmlns:xs="http://www.w3.org/2001/XMLSchema">
  <xs:complexType name="Employee">
    <xs:sequence>
      <xs:element minOccurs="0" name="EmployeeID" type="xs:int" />
      <xs:element minOccurs="0" name="FirstName" nillable="true"
        type="xs:string" /
      <xs:element minOccurs="0" name="LastName" nillable="true"
        type="xs:string" />
    </xs:sequence>
  </xs:complexType>
  <xs:element name="Employee" nillable="true" type="tns:Employee" />
</xs:schema>
```

Listing 6.3 shows how the schema of the Employee class was exported.

LISTING 6.3 Export XSD Schema

```
using System.IO;
using System.Runtime.Serialization;
using System.Xml.Schema;

namespace EssentialWCF
{
    class Program
    {
        static void Main(string[] args)
        {
            XsdDataContractExporter xsdexp =
                new XsdDataContractExporter();
            xsdexp.Options = new ExportOptions();
            xsdexp.Export(typeof(Employee));

            // Write out exported schema to a file
            using (FileStream fs = new FileStream("sample.xsd",
                                        FileMode.Create))
                foreach (XmlSchema sch in xsdexp.Schemas.Schemas())
                    sch.Write(fs);
        }
    }
}
```

The final task that forms the basis for our comparison with other serialization mechanisms is to serialize an Employee instance using the DataContractSerializer. Listing 6.4 shows how this is done.

LISTING 6.4 Serialization Using DataContractSerializer

```
using System.IO;
using System.Runtime.Serialization;

namespace EssentialWCF
{
    class Program
    {
        static void Main(string[] args)
        {
            Employee e = new Employee(101,"John","Doe");
            FileStream writer = new FileStream("sample.xml",
                                        FileMode.Create);
            DataContractSerializer ser =
                new DataContractSerializer(typeof(Employee));
```

```
        ser.WriteObject(writer, e);
        writer.Close();
    }
  }
}
```

The serialized output from the `DataContractSerializer` of the `Employee` class is shown in Listing 6.5.

LISTING 6.5 Serialized Employee Class Using `DataContractSerializer`

```
<Employee xmlns="http://schemas.datacontract.org/2004/07/"
xmlns:i="http://www.w3.org/2001/XMLSchema-instance">
  <EmployeeID>101</EmployeeID>
  <FirstName>John</FirstName>
  <LastName>Doe</LastName>
</Employee>
```

NetDataContractSerializer

The `NetDataContractSerializer` is an alternative serialization mechanism available in WCF that allows for the sharing of types. This class can be found in the `System.Runtime.Serialization` namespace. This serialization can be used when type fidelity is required between client and server. The `NetDataContractSerializer` supports type fidelity by adding additional information for CLR type information and reference preservation. Besides this, there is no difference between the `NetDataContractSerializer` and the `DataContractSerializer`.

The sharing of type information goes against the principles of sharing just contracts. Because of this the `NetDataContractSerializer` is not meant for designing services between different applications and should be used within the confines of a single application. This is also why the capability to use the `NetDataContractSerializer` was left out of WCF. This means that this feature is available only if you write additional code. How to enable this feature will be discussed in the "Sharing Type with the `NetDataContractSerializer`" section.

Let's look at a particular instance of an `Employee` class serialized using the `DataContractSerializer` and the `NetDataContractSerializer`. We already saw how to serialize the `Employee` contract using the `DataContractSerializer` in Listing 6.4. Listing 6.6 shows how to serialize the same class using the `NetDataContractSerializer`. Notice that the `NetDataContractSerializer` does not require a type passed into the constructor. This is because the `NetDataContractSerializer` will determine the CLR type of the `Employee` class at runtime.

LISTING 6.6 Serialization Using `NetDataContractSerializer`

```
using System.IO;
using System.Runtime.Serialization;

namespace EssentialWCF
{
    class Program
    {
        static void Main(string[] args)
        {
            Employee e = new Employee(101,"John","Doe");
            FileStream writer =
                new FileStream("sample.xml", FileMode.Create);
            NetDataContractSerializer ser =
                new NetDataContractSerializer();
            ser.WriteObject(writer, e);
            writer.Close();
        }
    }
}
```

Listing 6.7 shows the serialized output of the `Employee` class. Notice that the `NetDataContractSerializer` includes the name of the `Assembly` and `Type` of the type that was serialized. This additional information can be used to deserialize the XML into the specified type. This allows the same type to be used by both the client and the server. The other information that is different is the `z:Id` attribute on various elements. This has to do with reference types and whether references are preserved when the XML is deserialized. We will discuss how to preserve references in the "Preserving References and Cyclical References" section. The final observation is that the output contains more information than the output from the `DataContractSerializer`.

LISTING 6.7 Serialized Employee Class Using `NetDataContractSerializer`

```
<Employee z:Id="1" z:Type="Employee" z:Assembly="DataContract,
➥Version=1.0.0.0, Culture=neutral, PublicKeyToken=null"
➥xmlns="http://schemas.datacontract.org/2004/07/"
```

```
➥xmlns:i="http://www.w3.org/2001/XMLSchema-instance"
➥xmlns:z="http://schemas.microsoft.com/2003/10/Serialization/">
  <EmployeeID>101</EmployeeID>
  <FirstName z:Id="2">John</FirstName>
  <LastName z:Id="3">Doe</LastName>
</Employee>
```

XmlSerializer

The XmlSerializer is the third option available for serialization in WCF. The XmlSerializer is a serialization mechanism already built in to .NET 2.0. There are several advantages to using the XmlSerializer, including support for existing .NET types, compatibility with ASP.NET Web Services, and the capability to shape the XML output.

WCF supports the XmlSerializer so that it can work with existing types, whereas the DataContractSerializer is specifically meant for use with new types. Support for existing types is often the case with existing applications or third-party components where you do not have the source code or you cannot recompile your application to support DataContract serialization. The XmlSerializer is also the serialization used by ASP.NET Web Services. This means that the XmlSerializer can be used to help convert ASP.NET Web Services to WCF. Finally, the XmlSerializer offers the most control over the serialized XML output and can be used in scenarios where the DataContractSerializer is not sufficient to shape the serialized XML.

There are three approaches to using the XmlSerializer. The first is to rely on the default serialization. The XmlSerializer requires a public constructor and serializes any public fields and/or public read/write properties. The assumption is that your class can be reconstituted by creating an instance of the class with a default constructor and then set the appropriate fields and properties. Although simple, this approach almost never works unless you design your classes to support this method of serialization. It also means that you cannot serialize any of the internals of a class without exposing it to the rest of the world. The second approach is to use the [XmlElement] and [XmlAttribute] attributes to mark up public fields and public read/write properties. These attributes, and more attributes to control the resulting XML, can be found in the System.Xml.Serialization namespace. The attribute approach allows for control over how public fields and public read/write properties are expressed in XML. Although simple, this approach still limits how you can serialize your objects and may force you to expose internal data structures that you would otherwise not expose to a consumer of your class. The third approach is to use the `IXmlSerializable` interface to completely customize the serialization using the `XmlSerializer`. This approach allows for complete customization of the serialization process.

We will take a look at custom serialization using the `XmlSerializer` later in this chapter. For now we will concentrate on the simplest example using the `XmlSerializer`. Listing 6.8 uses the `XmlSerializer` using the same `Employee` class without support for `DataContractSerializer` by removing the `[DataContract]` or `[DataMember]` attributes present in Listing 6.1. A default constructor is also needed.

LISTING 6.8 Employee Class Using `XmlSerializer`

```csharp
public class Employee
{
    private int employeeID;
    private string firstName;
    private string lastName;

    public Employee()
    {
    }

    public Employee(int employeeID, string firstName, string lastName)
    {
        this.employeeID = employeeID;
        this.firstName = firstName;
        this.lastName = lastName;
    }

    public int EmployeeID
    {
        get { return employeeID; }
        set { employeeID = value; }
    }

    public string FirstName
    {
        get { return firstName; }
        set { firstName = value; }
    }

    public string LastName
```

```
        {
            get { return lastName; }
            set { lastName = value; }
        }
    }
```

Listing 6.9 shows how to serialize the Employee instance using the XmlSerializer.

LISTING 6.9 Serialization Using XmlSerializer

```
using System.IO;
using System.Xml.Serialization;

namespace EssentialWCF
{
    class Program
    {
        static void Main(string[] args)
        {
            Employee e = new Employee(101,"John","Doe");
            FileStream writer =
                new FileStream("sample.xml", FileMode.Create);
            XmlSerializer ser = new XmlSerializer((typeof(Employee)));
            ser.Serialize(writer, e);
            writer.Close();
        }
    }
}
```

The output from the XmlSerializer is shown in Listing 6.10. Notice that the output is similar to the output from the DataContractSerializer. Both serialization mechanisms output XML that looks similar. The big difference is in what is not shown. The XmlSerializer does not support as many types as the DataContractSerializer but allows for greater control over the resulting XML.

LISTING 6.10 Serialized Employee Class Using XmlSerializer

```
<?xml version="1.0"?>
<Employee xmlns:xsi="http://www.w3.org/2001/XMLSchema-instance"
          xmlns:xsd="http://www.w3.org/2001/XMLSchema">
  <EmployeeID>101</EmployeeID>
  <FirstName>John</FirstName>
  <LastName>Doe</LastName>
</Employee>
```

The Employee class in Listing 6.8 is not serializable without the XmlSerializer. The [XmlSerializerFormat] attribute can be used to attribute a service contract, operation contract, or service to instruct WCF to use the XmlSerializer. Listing 6.11 uses the [XmlSerializerFormat] attribute on a service contract to instruct WCF to use the XmlSerializer. You will typically want to apply the [XmlSerializerFormat] attribute if you are exposing any contract that uses the XMLSerializer. Doing so instructs Visual Studio and the svcutil.exe tool to generate proxies that rely on the XMLSerializer. Without this attribute you need to generate proxies using the svcutil.exe tool with the /Serializer:XmlSerializer flag.

> **■ TIP**   The DataContractFormat Attribute
>
> Conversely, there is an equivalent attribute to the [XmlSerializerFormat] attribute for the DataContractSerializer called the [DataContractFormat] attribute. WCF uses the DataContractSerializer by default, so there should be no reason to use this attribute.

LISTING 6.11 Using XmlSerializerFormat Attribute

```
using System.Collections.Generic;
using System.ServiceModel;

namespace EssentialWCF
{
    [ServiceContract]
    [XmlSerializerFormat]
    public interface IEmployeeInformation
    {
        [OperationContract]
        List<Employee> GetEmployees();
    }
}
```

DataContractJsonSerializer

The DataContractJsonSerializer supports the use of JavaScript Object Notation as a serialization format and is available with .NET Framework 3.5. This serialization works well if you are calling services from a Web application using JavaScript, especially ASP.NET AJAX and Silverlight Web applications. The `DataContractJsonSerializer` is used when the `WebScriptEnablingBehavior` behavior is used. Alternatively, it can be used if the `WebHttpBehavior` behavior is configured to use JSON encoding. These endpoint behaviors instruct WCF to support REST/POX style services. See Chapter 13, "Programmable Web," for more information about these attributes. For now, we will examine how to use the `DataContractJsonSerializer` directly and compare it to the other serialization mechanisms mentioned previously. Listing 6.12 shows how to serialize an Employee instance using the `DataContractJsonSerializer`.

LISTING 6.12 Serialization Using `DataContractJsonSerializer`

```
using System.IO;
using System.Runtime.Serialization.Json;

namespace EssentialWCF
{
    class Program
    {
        static void Main(string[] args)
        {
            Employee e = new Employee(101,"John","Doe");
            FileStream writer = new FileStream("sample.xml",
                FileMode.Create);
            DataContractJsonSerializer ser =
                new DataContractJsonSerializer(typeof(Employee));
            ser.WriteObject(writer, e);
            writer.Close();
        }
    }
}
```

The `DataContractJsonSerializer` follows the same rules of serialization as the `DataContractSerializer` except that the output is JSON and not XML. The serialized output from the `DataContractJsonSerializer` of the Employee class is shown in Listing 6.13. The output in this case is much smaller and more compact than using the `DataContactSerializer`, `NetDataContractSerializer`, or the `XmlSerializer`, and the output is more readable compared to the previous XML examples.

LISTING 6.13 Serialized Employee Class Using DataContractJsonSerializer

```
{"EmployeeID":101,
"FirstName":"John",
"LastName":"Doe"}
```

Choosing a Serializer

Deciding whether to use the DataContractSerializer, NetDataContract-Serializer, XmlSerializer, or the DataContractJsonSerializer is often an easy decision. The DataContractSerializer should be the default serialization mechanism used because it is the native serialization mechanism for WCF. However, if you have the need to support existing types or custom serialization not supported by the DataContractSerializer, you will most likely want to use the XmlSerializer. Although the NetDataContractSerializer is interesting, no direct support exists for using it without having to write code. Although some benefits exist to using the NetDataContractSerializer, its use is discouraged because it requires the sharing of types between the client and server. Finally, the DataContractJsonSerializer is used mostly in Web scenarios where services are being called from AJAX applications. If you plan to develop ASP.NET AJAX or Rich Internet Applications (RIAs) using Silverlight, you will most likely want to support JSON serialization using the DataContractJsonSerializer. Although JSON serialization is predominantly used within Web applications from JavaScript, its use is extended beyond Web applications because of its popularity. In these situations, the choice to use JSON becomes mostly a matter of personal preference. Finally, WCF provides a number of extensibility points that allow serialization to be completely replaced.

Preserving References and Cyclical References

Two important issues exist regarding references and serialization: preserving references and *cyclical references*. Both of these issues are addressed through *reference preservation*. Reference preservation may help significantly when you are trying to optimize the amount of data that gets serialized or when sharing type information between client and server.

Reference preservation allows for the same data to be referred to more than once in a data contract without duplicating the data. This is a common scenario when working with data structures such as lists, arrays, and hash tables where data may appear more than once. With reference preservation, data is serialized the first time it appears in a data contract and a reference to the data is used for all subsequent appearances. This can have the desired effect of significantly reducing the amount of data that gets serialized if it is referred to multiple times.

Cyclical references are when an object maintains a reference to descendant objects that then refer back to it. An example of a cyclical reference is a parent-child relationship where a child object maintains a reference to the parent object. These types of situations are common when doing object-oriented programming. The issue of objects that maintain cyclical references is that serialization is not possible without support for reference preservation. Any serialization mechanism would end up in an endless loop trying to serialize the object. Reference preservation allows for a reference to data to be used instead of continuing to serialize the data over and over again.

The `DataContractSerializer` does not enable reference preservation by default. Reference preservation is enabled with both the `NetDataContract-Serializer` and the `XmlSerializer`. Use one of these serialization mechanisms if you plan to share type information between client and server. Otherwise, you can use a custom attribute to support reference preservation with the `DataContractSerializer`.

■ **TIP** Reference Preservation with `IXmlSerializable`

Support for reference preservation needs to be implemented in code if you plan to use custom serialization using the `IXmlSerializable` interface.

Let's look at an example in Listing 6.14. First, a list is created from `List<Employees>`. Then several `Employee` objects are added to the list.

LISTING 6.14 The Need for Reference Preservation

```
using System.Collections.Generic;
using System.ServiceModel;

[ServiceContract]
public interface IEmployeeInformation
{
    [OperationContract]
    Employee[] GetEmployeesOfTheMonth();
}

[ServiceContract]
public class EmployeeInformation
{
    public EmployeeInformation()
    {
    }

    public Employee[] GetEmployeesOfTheMonthForLastSixMonths()
    {
        List<Employee> list = new List<Employee>(6);
        Employee Employee1 = new Employee(1,"John","Doe");
        Employee Employee2 = new Employee(2,"Jane","Doe");
        Employee Employee3 = new Employee(3,"John","Smith");

        list.Add(Employee1);
        list.Add(Employee2);
        list.Add(Employee3);
        list.Add(Employee1);
        list.Add(Employee2);
        list.Add(Employee3);

        return list.ToArray();
    }
}
```

By default, the DataContractSerializer will serialize each reference as a separate copy of the data. The output in Listing 6.15 shows that Employee1, Employee2, and Employee3 appear multiple times.

LISTING 6.15 Serialized List Without Reference Preservation

```
<s:Envelope xmlns:s="http://www.w3.org/2003/05/soap-envelope"
➥xmlns:a="http://www.w3.org/2005/08/addressing">
  <s:Header>    <a:Actions:mustUnderstand="1">
➥http://tempuri.org/IEmployeeInformation/
➥GetEmployeesOfTheMonthForLastSixMonthsResponse</a:Action>
    <a:RelatesTo>urn:uuid:0a35e6da-1dad-47f6-bb95-bfcdf3fe856c</a:RelatesTo>
```

```
   </s:Header>
   <s:Body>
    <GetEmployeesOfTheMonthForLastSixMonthsResponse xmlns=
➥"http://tempuri.org/">
     <GetEmployeesOfTheMonthForLastSixMonthsResult
➥xmlns:i="http://www.w3.org/2001/XMLSchema-instance">
      <Employee xmlns="http://schemas.datacontract.org/2004/07/">
       <EmployeeID>1</EmployeeID>
       <FirstName>John</FirstName>
       <LastName>Doe</LastName>
      </Employee>
      <Employee xmlns="http://schemas.datacontract.org/2004/07/">
       <EmployeeID>2</EmployeeID>
       <FirstName>Jane</FirstName>
       <LastName>Doe</LastName>
      </Employee>
      <Employee xmlns="http://schemas.datacontract.org/2004/07/">
       <EmployeeID>3</EmployeeID>
       <FirstName>John</FirstName>
       <LastName>Smith</LastName>
      </Employee>
      <Employee xmlns="http://schemas.datacontract.org/2004/07/">
       <EmployeeID>1</EmployeeID>
       <FirstName>John</FirstName>
       <LastName>Doe</LastName>
      </Employee>
      <Employee xmlns="http://schemas.datacontract.org/2004/07/">
       <EmployeeID>2</EmployeeID>
       <FirstName>Jane</FirstName>
       <LastName>Doe</LastName>
      </Employee>
      <Employee xmlns="http://schemas.datacontract.org/2004/07/">
       <EmployeeID>3</EmployeeID>
       <FirstName>John</FirstName>
       <LastName>Smith</LastName>
      </Employee>
     </GetEmployeesOfTheMonthForLastSixMonthsResult>
    </GetEmployeesOfTheMonthForLastSixMonthsResponse>
   </s:Body>
  </s:Envelope>
```

To preserve references, apply a custom behavior to create an instance of the `DataContractSerializer` by passing a value of `true` for the `preserveObjectReferences` parameters to its constructor. A behavior is an extensibility mechanism within WCF that allows you to modify the default behavior of the runtime; it will be covered in detail in Chapter 5, "Behaviors." In this situation it is allowing us to modify the default behavior of the

DataContractSerializer to support reference preservation. Listing 6.16 implements a custom behavior to demonstrate this.

LISTING 6.16 Implementing Reference Preservation Using a Custom Behavior

```
using System;
using System.Collections.Generic;
using System.Runtime.Serialization;
using System.ServiceModel.Channels;
using System.ServiceModel.Description;
using System.ServiceModel.Dispatcher;
using System.Xml;

namespace EssentialWCF
{
    public class ReferencePreservingDataContractFormatAttribute :
                Attribute, IOperationBehavior
    {
        public void AddBindingParameters(
                    OperationDescription description,
                    BindingParameterCollection parameters)
        {
        }

        public void ApplyClientBehavior(
                    OperationDescription description,
                    ClientOperation proxy)
        {
            IOperationBehavior innerBehavior = new
➥ReferencePreservingDataContractSerializerOperationBehavior(description);
            innerBehavior.ApplyClientBehavior(description, proxy);
        }

        public void ApplyDispatchBehavior(
                    OperationDescription description,
                    DispatchOperation dispatch)
        {
            IOperationBehavior innerBehavior = new
➥ReferencePreservingDataContractSerializerOperationBehavior(description);
            innerBehavior.ApplyDispatchBehavior(description, dispatch);
        }

        public void Validate(OperationDescription description)
        {
        }
    }

    public class
➥ReferencePreservingDataContractSerializerOperationBehavior :
```

```
                        DataContractSerializerOperationBehavior
    {
        public ReferencePreservingDataContractSerializerOperationBehavior(
            OperationDescription operationDescription)
            : base(operationDescription)
        {
        }

        public override XmlObjectSerializer CreateSerializer(Type type,
            string name, string ns, IList<Type> knownTypes)
        {
            return CreateDataContractSerializer(type, name, ns,
                                                knownTypes);
        }

        private static XmlObjectSerializer
            CreateDataContractSerializer(Type type, string name,
                string ns, IList<Type> knownTypes)
        {
            return CreateDataContractSerializer(type, name, ns,
                    knownTypes);
        }

        public override XmlObjectSerializer CreateSerializer(Type type,
                XmlDictionaryString name, XmlDictionaryString ns,
                IList<Type> knownTypes)
        {
            return new DataContractSerializer(type, name, ns,
                knownTypes, 0x7FFF, false, true, null);
        }
    }
}
```

The result of applying the attribute to our operation contract is shown
in Listing 6.17. The output shows that the Employee1, Employee2, and
Employee3 appear only once, but they are now marked with an attribute,
z:Id, which is used as a reference identifier. Additional references to these
objects refer back to the reference identifier using the z:Ref attribute.

LISTING 6.17 Serialized List with Reference Preservation

```
<s:Envelope xmlns:s="http://www.w3.org/2003/05/soap-envelope"
➥xmlns:a="http://www.w3.org/2005/08/addressing">
  <s:Header>
    <a:Action s:mustUnderstand="1">http://tempuri.org/IEmployeeInformation/
➥GetEmployeesOfTheMonthForLastSixMonthsResponse</a:Action>
    <a:RelatesTo>urn:uuid:9331e9f4-9991-447e-812d-db1b129bfb25</a:RelatesTo>
  </s:Header>
```

LISTING 6.17 continued

```
  <s:Body>
    <GetEmployeesOfTheMonthForLastSixMonthsResponse
➡xmlns="http://tempuri.org/">
      <GetEmployeesOfTheMonthForLastSixMonthsResult z:Id="1" z:Size="6"
➡xmlns:i="http://www.w3.org/2001/XMLSchema-instance"
➡xmlns:z="http://schemas.microsoft.com/2003/10/Serialization/">
        <Employee z:Id="2" xmlns="http://schemas.datacontract.org/2004/07/">
          <EmployeeID>1</EmployeeID>
          <FirstName z:Id="3">John</FirstName>
          <LastName z:Id="4">Doe</LastName>
        </Employee>
        <Employee z:Id="5"
                  xmlns="http://schemas.datacontract.org/2004/07/">
          <EmployeeID>2</EmployeeID>
          <FirstName z:Id="6">Jane</FirstName>
          <LastName z:Id="7">Doe</LastName>
        </Employee>
        <Employee z:Id="8"
                  xmlns="http://schemas.datacontract.org/2004/07/">
          <EmployeeID>3</EmployeeID>
          <FirstName z:Id="9">John</FirstName>
          <LastName z:Id="10">Smith</LastName>
        </Employee>
        <Employee z:Ref="2" i:nil="true"
                  xmlns="http://schemas.datacontract.org/2004/07/"/>
        <Employee z:Ref="5" i:nil="true"
                  xmlns="http://schemas.datacontract.org/2004/07/"/>
        <Employee z:Ref="8" i:nil="true"
                  xmlns="http://schemas.datacontract.org/2004/07/"/>
      </GetEmployeesOfTheMonthForLastSixMonthsResult>
    </GetEmployeesOfTheMonthForLastSixMonthsResponse>
  </s:Body>
</s:Envelope>
```

Sharing Type with the NetDataContractSerializer

The default serialization mechanism for WCF is the DataContractSerializer. This is the serialization mechanism that the WCF team intends for
most developers to use because it enforces the sharing of contracts and not
types. This is one of the principles for building service-oriented architectures. However, if your intent is to support type fidelity and share type
information between client and service and this does not pose a problem

to your design, you can use the NetDataContractSerializer for serialization. As mentioned previously in the "Comparing WCF Serialization Options" section, the NetDataContractSerializer is essentially the same as the DataContractSerializer, but with additional support for sharing of type information and reference preservation.

Although support exists for the NetDataContractSerializer in WCF, there is no support for attributing your data contracts to use this serialization. This was done on purpose so that the sharing of types would not be proliferated easily. To use the NetDataContractSerializer, you must use a custom behavior (see Listing 6.18) and annotate your operation contracts (see Listing 6.19).

LISTING 6.18 Using NetDataContractFormatAttribute

```
using System;
using System.Collections.Generic;
using System.Runtime.Serialization;
using System.ServiceModel.Channels;
using System.ServiceModel.Description;
using System.ServiceModel.Dispatcher;
using System.Xml;

namespace EssentialWCF
{
    public class NetDataContractFormatAttribute :
➥Attribute, IOperationBehavior
    {
        public void AddBindingParameters(OperationDescription
➥description, BindingParameterCollection parameters)
        {
        }

        public void ApplyClientBehavior(OperationDescription
➥description, ClientOperation proxy)
        {
            ReplaceDataContractSerializerOperationBehavior(description);
        }

        public void ApplyDispatchBehavior(OperationDescription
➥description, DispatchOperation dispatch)
        {
            ReplaceDataContractSerializerOperationBehavior(description);
        }
```

LISTING 6.18 continued

```
        public void Validate(OperationDescription description)
        {
        }

        private static void ReplaceDataContractSerializerOperationBehavior
➥(OperationDescription description)
        {
            DataContractSerializerOperationBehavior dcs =
➥description.Behaviors.Find<DataContractSerializerOperationBehavior>();

            if (dcs != null)
                description.Behaviors.Remove(dcs);

            description.Behaviors.Add(new
➥NetDataContractSerializerOperationBehavior(description));
        }

        public class NetDataContractSerializerOperationBehavior :
➥DataContractSerializerOperationBehavior
        {
            private static NetDataContractSerializer serializer = new
➥NetDataContractSerializer();

            public NetDataContractSerializerOperationBehavior(
➥OperationDescription operationDescription) :
➥base(operationDescription) { }

            public override XmlObjectSerializer CreateSerializer(Type
➥type, string name, string ns, IList<Type> knownTypes)
            {
                return NetDataContractSerializerOperationBehavior.
➥serializer;
            }

            public override XmlObjectSerializer CreateSerializer(Type type,
➥XmlDictionaryString name, XmlDictionaryString ns, IList<Type> knownTypes)
            {
                return NetDataContractSerializerOperationBehavior.
➥serializer;
            }
        }
    }
}
```

To use the NetDataContractSerializer, specify the [NetDataContract-
Format] attribute on an operation, as shown in Listing 6.19.

LISTING 6.19 Using **NetDataContract** Serialization

```
using System.Collections.Generic;
using System.ServiceModel;

namespace EssentialWCF
{
    [ServiceContract]
    public interface IEmployeeInformation
    {
        [OperationContract]
        [NetDataContractFormat]
        List<Employee> GetEmployees();
    }
}
```

Applying this attribute to an operation contract will instruct WCF to use the `NetDataContractSerializer`. If we look at the output on the network, we can see that the XML sent includes type information and additional information for reference preservation, as shown in Listing 6.20.

LISTING 6.20 Serialized Output Using **NetDataContract** Serialization

```
<s:Envelope xmlns:s="http://www.w3.org/2003/05/soap-envelope"
➥xmlns:a="http://www.w3.org/2005/08/addressing">
  <s:Header>
    <a:Action s:mustUnderstand="1">http://tempuri.org/IEmployeeInformation/
➥GetEmployeesResponse</a:Action>
    <a:RelatesTo>urn:uuid:12c35e16-52ed-4b81-a4d4-2cabd9f2c7c2</a:RelatesTo>
  </s:Header>
  <s:Body>
    <GetEmployeesResponse xmlns="http://tempuri.org/">
      <ArrayOfEmployee z:Id="1" z:Type="System.Collections.Generic.List`1
➥[[Employee, App_Code.5cwz4hgr, Version=0.0.0.0, Culture=neutral,
➥PublicKeyToken=null]]" z:Assembly="0"
➥xmlns="http://schemas.datacontract.org/2004/07/"
➥xmlns:i="http://www.w3.org/2001/XMLSchema-instance"
➥xmlns:z="http://schemas.microsoft.com/2003/10/Serialization/">
        <_items z:Id="2" z:Size="4">
          <Employee z:Id="3">
            <EmployeeID>1</EmployeeID>
            <FirstName z:Id="4">John</FirstName>
            <LastName z:Id="5">Doe</LastName>
          </Employee>
          <Employee z:Id="6">
            <EmployeeID>2</EmployeeID>
            <FirstName z:Id="7">Jane</FirstName>
            <LastName z:Id="8">Doe</LastName>
```

LISTING 6.20 continued

```
            </Employee>
            <Employee z:Id="9">
              <EmployeeID>3</EmployeeID>
              <FirstName z:Id="10">John</FirstName>
              <LastName z:Id="11">Smith</LastName>
            </Employee>
            <Employee i:nil="true"/>
          </_items>
          <_size>3</_size>
          <_version>3</_version>
        </ArrayOfEmployee>
      </GetEmployeesResponse>
    </s:Body>
  </s:Envelope>
```

Roundtrip Serialization Using `IExtensibleDataObject`

Data contract versioning is an important aspect of service orientation of support service-oriented architectures over time. Over time, it is likely that new versions of new services are created that have new versions of the same data contracts, just with additional information. Rather than recompiling all previous clients and services that were built using the older data contracts versions, you would hope that they would gracefully degrade to sharing the data they have in common. This is exactly the case with the `DataContractSerializer`. If there is additional data, the `DataContractSerializer` will discard the extra information. This does not work in all situations. Ignoring any additional data could mean a loss of information if the data is received and then sent back to a client. An example might be a new client that sends data to an old service that stores information into a database for retrieval at some future point in time. In this situation, if there is any additional information that the client sends to the server, it will be lost when the data is sent back to the client. This is exactly the issue the `IExtensibleDataObject` interface is meant to solve. It provides an interface for working with external data not known to the data contract. It does this by storing any data not known during deserializing in an instance of an `ExtensibleDataObject` class.

The default behavior for the `DataContractSerializer` is to ignore any unexpected data unless the `IExtensibleDataObject` interface is implemented on the contract. Here is an example of two data contracts for an Employee class. The first data contract shown in Listing 6.21 has three fields: `FirstName`, `LastName`, and `EmployeeID`. The second data contract shown in Listing 6.22 is a newer version of the same data contract with an additional field, `SSN`.

> **■ TIP Make Sure to Implement `IExtensibleDataObject`**
>
> It is possible to share your data contracts without generating proxy classes using svcutil.exe or Add Service Reference. This is done by adding a reference to the assembly that contains your data contracts. In this situation, make sure that the data contracts implement `IExtensibleDataObject` or else they will not support roundtrip serialization.

LISTING 6.21 Original Employee Contract

```
using System.Runtime.Serialization;

[DataContract]
public class Employee
{
    private int employeeID;
    private string firstName;
    private string lastName;

    public Employee(int employeeID, string firstName, string lastName)
    {
        this.employeeID = employeeID;
        this.firstName = firstName;
        this.lastName = lastName;
    }

    [DataMember]
    public int EmployeeID
    {
        get { return employeeID; }
        set { employeeID = value; }
    }

    [DataMember]
    public string FirstName
    {
```

LISTING 6.21 continued

```
            get { return firstName; }
            set { firstName = value; }
    }

    [DataMember]
    public string LastName
    {
        get { return lastName; }
        set { lastName = value; }
    }
}
```

Listing 6.22 shows a newer version of the Employee contract that contains an additional field, SSN, which represents the employee's social security number.

LISTING 6.22 New Employee Contract

```
using System.Runtime.Serialization;

[DataContract]
public class Employee
{
    private int employeeID;
    private string firstName;
    private string lastName;
    private string ssn;

    public Employee()
    {
    }

    public Employee(int employeeID, string firstName, string lastName,
     string ssn)
    {
        this.employeeID = employeeID;
        this.firstName = firstName;
        this.lastName = lastName;
        this.ssn = ssn;
    }

    [DataMember]
    public int EmployeeID
    {
        get { return employeeID; }
        set { employeeID = value; }
    }
```

```csharp
        [DataMember]
        public string FirstName
        {
            get { return firstName; }
            set { firstName = value; }
        }

        [DataMember]
        public string LastName
        {
            get { return lastName; }
            set { lastName = value; }
        }

        [DataMember]
        public string SSN
        {
            get { return ssn; }
            set { ssn = value; }
        }
    }
```

The data contracts in Listing 6.21 and Listing 6.22 are different. You might expect that a server using the original data contract would not accept communication from a client using the newer data contract. In fact, everything still works. The reason is that all the fields in the newer data contract are present in the original data contract. This means that all the information that the server needs is present. What happens at this point is the server will ignore the additional data. This can be seen using the following `UpdateEmployee` service shown in Listing 6.23. This service takes an `Employee` instance, does something with it, and then returns that same `Employee` instance back to the client.

LISTING 6.23 Employee Update Service

```csharp
    using System.ServiceModel;

    namespace EssentialWCF
    {
        [ServiceContract]
        public interface IEmployeeInformation
        {
            [OperationContract]
            Employee UpdateEmployee(Employee employee);
        }

        public class EmployeeInformation : IEmployeeInformation
```

LISTING 6.23 continued

```
    {
        public Employee UpdateEmployee(Employee emp)
        {
            // Pretend to do something here...
            // Not really important for this demo.

            // We return the employee instance back to the client.
            return emp;
        }
    }
}
```

The corresponding client code is shown in Listing 6.24.

LISTING 6.24 Employee Update Client

```
using System;

namespace EssentialWCF
{
    class Program
    {
        static void Main(string[] args)
        {
            Employee e = new Employee() { EmployeeID = 123456,
                    FirstName ="John", LastName ="Doe",
                    SSN ="000-00-0000" };
            Console.WriteLine("{0} {1}, {2}, {3}", new object[] {
                                            e.FirstName,
                                            e.LastName,
                                            e.EmployeeID,
                                            e.SSN });

            using (EmployeeInformationClient client =
                    new EmployeeInformationClient())
                e = client.UpdateEmployee(e);

            Console.WriteLine("{0} {1}, {2}, {3}", new object[] {
                                            e.FirstName,
                                            e.LastName,
                                            e.EmployeeID,
                                            e.SSN });

            Console.WriteLine("Press [ENTER] to exit.");
            Console.ReadLine();
        }
    }
}
```

The result returned from the server does not return the SSN field. This means that we could not roundtrip our data contract to the server and back because of the version incompatibility. So how do we modify our service to accept unknown data and return it appropriately? Fortunately, WCF provides a facility for accepting unknown data and storing it. We can change our data contract on the server to allow for additional data that it does not know about. To do this you must implement the `IExtensibleDataObject` interface on the data contract, which is done by default when generating the client-side proxy through svcutil.exe or Add Service Reference. Listing 6.25 shows the original `Employee` contract with support for the `IExtensibleDataObject` interface.

LISTING 6.25 Original Employee Contract with `IExtensibleDataObject`

```
using System.Runtime.Serialization;

[DataContract]
public class Employee : IExtensibleDataObject
{
    private ExtensionDataObject extensionData;

    private int employeeID;
    private string firstName;
    private string lastName;

    public Employee()
    {
    }

    public Employee(int employeeID, string firstName, string lastName)
    {
        this.employeeID = employeeID;
        this.firstName = firstName;
        this.lastName = lastName;
    }

    public ExtensionDataObject ExtensionData
    {
        get { return extensionData; }
        set { extensionData = value; }
    }

    [DataMember]
    public int EmployeeID
    {
```

LISTING 6.25 continued

```
        get { return employeeID; }
        set { employeeID = value; }
    }

    [DataMember]
    public string FirstName
    {
        get { return firstName; }
        set { firstName = value; }
    }

    [DataMember]
    public string LastName
    {
        get { return lastName; }
        set { lastName = value; }
    }
}
```

With this change the client now receives the SSN member back from the server. Given that this behavior would be an expected result in a service-oriented architecture, you probably should implement IExtensible-DataObject interface on all data contracts as a best practice.

Serializing Types Using Surrogates

At times you might need to implement serialization on behalf of a type that is either not serializable or that requires a change in how it is serialized. An example is a type that is provided by a third-party component vendor or a component that you no longer have the source code to. The following example (see Listing 6.26) shows a nonserializable class, Employee. This class intentionally does not have a default constructor and it does not have any writable fields or properties. This means that it is not serializable using any of the serialization techniques we have mentioned so far. To serialize this class we need to provide a surrogate that serializes this class on its behalf.

LISTING 6.26 Nonserializable Employee Class

```
namespace EssentialWCF.Serialization.Surrogate
{
    public class Employee
    {
```

```
        private int employeeID;
        private string firstName;
        private string lastName;

        public Employee(int employeeID, string firstName,
                        string lastName)
        {
            this.employeeID = employeeID;
            this.firstName = firstName;
            this.lastName = lastName;
        }

        public int EmployeeID
        {
            get { return employeeID; }
        }

        public string FirstName
        {
            get { return firstName; }
        }

        public string LastName
        {
            get { return lastName; }
        }
    }
}
```

You need to take two steps to develop a surrogate. The first is to define the data contract that will represent the serialized type. The second is to implement a data contract surrogate based on the IDataContractSurrogate interface. The three main methods that we will examine are the GetDataContractType, GetDeserializedObject, and GetObjectToSerialize methods. The GetDataContractType returns the serialized type to the DataContractSerializer, and the GetDeserializedObject and GetObjectToSerialize perform the deserialization and serialization, respectively. The EmployeeSurrogate class is shown in Listing 6.27.

LISTING 6.27 Employee Surrogate Class

```
using System;
using System.CodeDom;
using System.Collections.ObjectModel;
using System.Runtime.Serialization;
```

LISTING 6.27 continued

```
namespace EssentialWCF.Serialization.Surrogate
{
    [DataContract]
    internal class EmployeeSurrogated
    {
        [DataMember]
        private int employeeID;
        [DataMember]
        private string firstName;
        [DataMember]
        private string lastName;

        public EmployeeSurrogated(int employeeID, string firstName,
            string lastName)
        {
            this.employeeID = employeeID;
            this.firstName = firstName;
            this.lastName = lastName;
        }

        public int EmployeeID
        {
            get { return employeeID; }
        }

        public string FirstName
        {
            get { return firstName; }
        }

        public string LastName
        {
            get { return lastName; }
        }
    }

    public class EmployeeSurrogate : IDataContractSurrogate
    {
        public object GetCustomDataToExport(Type clrType,
            Type dataContractType)
        {
            return null; // NotImplemented
        }

        public object GetCustomDataToExport(
            System.Reflection.MemberInfo memberInfo,
            Type dataContractType)
        {
```

```
        return null; // NotImplemented
}

public Type GetDataContractType(Type type)
{
    if (typeof(Employee).IsAssignableFrom(type))
    {
        return typeof(EmployeeSurrogated);
    }
    return type;
}

public object GetDeserializedObject(object obj, Type targetType)
{
    if (obj is EmployeeSurrogated)
    {
        EmployeeSurrogated oldEmployee =
            (EmployeeSurrogated)obj;
        Employee newEmployee =
          new Employee(oldEmployee.EmployeeID,
                    oldEmployee.FirstName,
                    oldEmployee.LastName);
        return newEmployee;
    }
    return obj;
}

public void GetKnownCustomDataTypes(
    Collection<Type> customDataTypes)
{
    throw new NotImplementedException();
}

public object GetObjectToSerialize(object obj, Type targetType)
{
    if (obj is Employee)
    {
        Employee oldEmployee = (Employee)obj;
        EmployeeSurrogated newEmployee =
          new EmployeeSurrogated(oldEmployee.EmployeeID,
                oldEmployee.FirstName,
                oldEmployee.LastName);
        return newEmployee;
    }
    return obj;
}

public Type GetReferencedTypeOnImport(string typeName,
    string typeNamespace, object customData)
{
```

LISTING 6.27 continued

```
                if
(typeNamespace.Equals("http://schemas.datacontract.org/2004/07/
➥EmployeeSurrogated"))
            {
                if (typeName.Equals("EmployeeSurrogated"))
                    return typeof(Employee);
            }
            return null;
        }

        public CodeTypeDeclaration ProcessImportedType(CodeTypeDeclaration
➥typeDeclaration,
            CodeCompileUnit compileUnit)
        {
            return typeDeclaration;
        }
    }
}
```

We put this all together by letting the DataContractSerializer know
about the surrogate class. You need to instantiate the DataContractSerializer and pass in the EmployeeSurrogated class to the constructor, as shown
in Listing 6.28.

LISTING 6.28 Using the Employee Surrogate Class with the DataContractSerializer

```
using System;
using System.IO;
using System.Runtime.Serialization;
using System.Xml;

namespace EssentialWCF.Serialization.Surrogate
{
    class Program
    {
        static void TryToSerialize(Employee e)
        {
            DataContractSerializer dcs =
                new DataContractSerializer(typeof(Employee));

            using (StringWriter sw = new StringWriter())
            {
                using (XmlWriter xw = XmlWriter.Create(sw))
                {
                    try
                    {
                        dcs.WriteObject(xw, e);
```

```
                    }
                    catch (InvalidDataContractException)
                    {
                        Console.WriteLine("Cannot serialize without
                            a surrogate!");
                    }
                }
            }
        }

        static string SerializeUsingSurrogate(
            DataContractSerializer dcs, Employee e)
        {
            using (StringWriter sw = new StringWriter())
            {
                using (XmlWriter xw = XmlWriter.Create(sw))
                {
                    dcs.WriteObject(xw, e);
                    xw.Flush();
                    return sw.ToString();
                }
            }
        }

        static Employee DeserializeUsingSurrogate(
            DataContractSerializer dcs, string employeeAsString)
        {
            using (StringReader tr = new StringReader(employeeAsString))
                using (XmlReader xr = XmlReader.Create(tr))
                    return dcs.ReadObject(xr) as Employee;
        }

        static void Main(string[] args)
        {
            Employee e = new Employee(12345,"John","Doe");

            TryToSerialize(e);

            DataContractSerializer dcs =
                    new DataContractSerializer(typeof(Employee),
                    null, int.MaxValue, false, false,
                    new EmployeeSurrogate());

            string employeeAsString = SerializeUsingSurrogate(dcs, e);

            e = DeserializeUsingSurrogate(dcs, employeeAsString);

            Console.ReadLine();
        }
    }
}
```

Streaming Large Data

WCF supports two modes for processing messages: *buffered* and *streamed*. Buffered mode is the default way in which WCF processes messages. In this mode, the entire message is in memory before it is sent or after it is received. In most scenarios, buffering of messages is sufficient and is sometimes required to support features such as reliable messaging and digital signatures. However, buffering large messages can easily exhaust system resources and limit scalability. WCF supports another mode for processing messages using streaming. In this mode, data is sent between client and server using a `System.IO.Stream`. Streaming is typically enabled on either a binding or a transport channel. Listing 6.29 shows how to enable streaming on the `netTcpBinding` binding by setting the `transferMode` attribute on the binding configuration. The acceptable values for the `transferMode` attribute are `Buffer`, `Streamed`, `StreamedResponse`, and `StreamedRequest`. This allows for granular control of streaming between the client and the server.

LISTING 6.29 Enabling Streaming on `netTcpBinding`

```
<system.serviceModel>
  <services>
    <service name="EssentialWCF.FileDownload">
      <endpoint address=""
                binding="netTcpBinding"
                bindingConfiguration="EnableStreamingOnNetTcp"
                contract="EssentialWCF.IFileDownload" />
    </service>
  </services>
  <bindings>
    <netTcpBinding>
      <binding name="EnableStreamingOnNetTcp" transferMode="Streamed" />
    </netTcpBinding>
  </bindings>
</system.serviceModel>
```

To take advantage of streaming, the operation contract needs to use an instance of a `System.IO.Stream` or return a message contract that uses a stream. Listing 6.30 shows an example of a file download service contract that returns a `System.IO.Stream`.

LISTING 6.30 FileDownload Service Contract

```
using System.IO;
using System.ServiceModel;

namespace EssentialWCF
{
    [ServiceContract]
    public interface IFileDownload
    {
        [OperationContract]
        Stream GetFile(string fileName);
    }
}
```

Streaming does not work in all scenarios where large amounts of data are being used. For example, if reliable messaging, digital signatures, or resuming after failure are needed, streaming is not acceptable. In these scenarios, manually chunking the data into small messages and sending many small messages that eventually get reconstituted by the recipient is preferred. This can easily be layered on top of WCF.

Using the XmlSerializer for Custom Serialization

The DataContractSerializer is the preferred serialization mechanism in WCF. However, at times you might want to go beyond the default serialization. One option to change the serialization is to work with the XmlSerializer. There are many reasons to use the XmlSerializer, including the capability to implement custom serialization, sharing of types, and support for legacy Web services. As with the DataContractSerializer, the XmlSerializer is an integral part of WCF. This section looks at the XmlSerializer and discusses how it can be used to shape the resulting XML output.

The DataContractSerializer always serializes data using XML elements rather than XML attributes. Listing 6.31 shows an instance of an Employee class using the DataContractSerializer.

LISTING 6.31 Serialized Employee Instance Using DataContract Serialization

```
<Employee xmlns="http://schemas.datacontract.org/2004/07/TestSerialization"
xmlns:i="http://www.w3.org/2001/XMLSchema-instance">
  <EmployeeID>101</EmployeeID>
  <FirstName>John</FirstName>
  <LastName>Doe</LastName>
</Employee>
```

Examining the serialized XML, you can see that the data contract could be rewritten using XML attributes. An example using XML attributes rather than XML elements is shown here:

```
<Employee EmployeeID="101" FirstName="John" LastName="Doe" />
```

XML attributes are not possible using the DataContractSerializer. The DataContractSerializer does offer limited control of the XML by allowing the names of XML elements to be specified using the [DataMember] attribute. The NetDataContractSerializer is essentially the same as the DataContractSerializer but with support for sharing type information. This means that the XmlSerializer is the only serializer where you can completely control output of serialization. Listing 6.32 shows a schema for the Employee class using XML attributes.

LISTING 6.32 Employee XSD Schema

```
<?xml version="1.0" encoding="utf-8"?>
<xs:schema targetNamespace="http://tempuri.org/XMLSchema.xsd"
elementFormDefault="qualified" xmlns="http://tempuri.org/XMLSchema.xsd"
xmlns:mstns="http://tempuri.org/XMLSchema.xsd"
xmlns:xs="http://www.w3.org/2001/XMLSchema">
  <xs:element name="Employee">
    <xs:complexType>
      <xs:attribute name="EmployeeID" type="xs:int" />
      <xs:attribute name="FirstName" type="xs:string" />
      <xs:attribute name="LastName" type="xs:string" />
    </xs:complexType>
  </xs:element>
</xs:schema>
```

Custom XmlSerialization Using Attributes

You can shape the XML output using the XmlSerializer in two ways. The first and most direct approach is to use the attributes provided in the .NET

Framework under the System.Xml.Serialization namespace to instruct the XmlSerializer how to shape the XML output. By default, the XmlSerializer will output public fields and public read/write properties as XML elements. These can be changed to XML attributes by attributing them with the [XmlAttribute] attribute. Also, the XmlSerializer is an opt-out serialization model. By default the XmlSerializer will serialize public fields and public read/write properties unless instructed not to do so with the [XmlIgnore] attribute. Additional attributes, such as the [XmlElement], [XmlRoot], [XmlArray], and [XmlArrayItem] attributes, help instruct the XmlSerializer how to serialize types.

Custom XmlSerialization Using IXmlSerializable

The second approach to using the XmlSerializer is to use the IXmlSerializable interface, which is generally used in advanced scenarios where complete control over serialization is needed. The IXmlSerializable interface supports three methods: GetSchema, ReadXml, and WriteXml. With .NET 2.0, the GetSchema method was deprecated and replaced with the [XmlSchemaProvider] attribute. The other two methods are ReadXml and WriteXml. These methods correspond to methods used to deserialize and serialize from and to XML. Listing 6.33 demonstrates this.

LISTING 6.33 Employee Class Using XML Serialization

```
using System.IO;
using System.Xml;
using System.Xml.Schema;
using System.Xml.Serialization;

[XmlSchemaProvider("MySchema")]
public class Employee : IXmlSerializable
{
    private const string ns ="http://essentialwcf/xmlserialization/";

    private int employeeID;
    private string firstName;
    private string lastName;

    public Employee()
    {
    }

    public Employee(int employeeID, string firstName, string lastName)
```

Listing 6.33 continued

```
    {
        this.employeeID = employeeID;
        this.firstName = firstName;
        this.lastName = lastName;
    }

    public int EmployeeID
    {
        get { return employeeID; }
        set { employeeID = value; }
    }

    public string FirstName
    {
        get { return firstName; }
        set { firstName = value; }
    }

    public string LastName
    {
        get { return lastName; }
        set { lastName = value; }
    }

    public static XmlQualifiedName MySchema(XmlSchemaSet schemaSet)
    {
        XmlSchema shema = XmlSchema.Read(new StringReader(
            @"<xs:schema elementFormDefault=""qualified""" +
            @" xmlns:tns="" + namespace +""" +
            @" targetNamespace="" + namespace +""" +
            @" xmlns=""http://www.w3.org/2001/XMLSchema""" +
            @" xmlns:xs=""http://www.w3.org/2001/XMLSchema"">" +
            @" <xs:element name=""Employee"">" + @"<xs:complexType>" +
            @"<xs:attribute name=""EmployeeID"" type=""xs:int"" />" +
            @"<xs:attribute name=""FirstName"" type=""xs:string"" />" +
            @"<xs:attribute name=""LastName"" type=""xs:string"" />" +
            @"</xs:complexType>" +
            @" </xs:element>" +
            @"</xs:schema>"), null);
        schemaSet.XmlResolver = new XmlUrlResolver();
        schemaSet.Add(shema);

        return new XmlQualifiedName("Employee", ns);
    }

    public XmlSchema GetSchema()
    {
        return null;
```

```
        }

        public void ReadXml(XmlReader reader)
        {
            reader.ReadStartElement("Employee");
            reader.MoveToAttribute("ID");
            this.employeeID = reader.ReadContentAsInt();
            reader.MoveToAttribute("FirstName");
            this.firstName = reader.ReadContentAsString();
            reader.MoveToAttribute("LastName");
            this.LastName = reader.ReadContentAsString();
            reader.ReadEndElement();
        }

        public void WriteXml(XmlWriter writer)
        {
            writer.WriteStartElement("Employee");

            writer.WriteStartAttribute("ID");
            writer.WriteString(this.employeeID.ToString());
            writer.WriteEndAttribute();

            writer.WriteStartAttribute("FirstName");
            writer.WriteString(this.firstName);
            writer.WriteEndAttribute();

            writer.WriteStartAttribute("LastName");
            writer.WriteString(this.lastName);
            writer.WriteEndAttribute();

            writer.WriteEndElement();
        }
    }
```

The result of using the XmlSerializer is that we can work with XSD schemas as the starting point for our contracts. The drawback to this approach is that there could potentially be much more code to write.

Choosing an Encoder

At the beginning of this chapter we mentioned that there are two steps in WCF to prepare an object for transmission over a network. The first step is serialization, which takes an object graph and transforms it into an XML Infoset. The second step is encoding, which takes an XML Infoset and transforms it into a set of bytes that can be sent across a network. WCF provides three types of encoding: text, binary, and MTOM. This section focuses on when to use each of these encoders.

Text Versus Binary Encoding

Prior to WCF, you had a number of choices for building distributed applications. Two of those options were .NET Remoting and ASP.NET Web Services. .NET Remoting was great for communicating between .NET applications because it optimized the transmission of data using binary encoding. This offered better performance than ASP.NET Web Services, which leveraged text encoding for interoperability. Text encoding was acceptable for ASP.NET Web Services because it allowed for interoperability across platforms. WCF abstracts out the encoding mechanism and allows for bindings that allow for both styles of encoding. This allows WCF to provide functionality that replaces both .NET Remoting and ASP.NET Web Services.

Encoding is not something that you work with directly. Instead, it is specified by the binding used to expose a service. Chapter 4, "Bindings," highlighted bindings for use between .NET applications and those used for interoperability. The `netTcpBinding` binding, which is used between .NET applications, leverages the `binaryMessageEncoding` encoder. The `binaryMessageEncoding` encoder offers the best performance, but it does not support interoperability. Conversely, bindings such as the `wsHttpBinding` binding use the `textMessageEncoding` encoder, which offers interoperability using the WS-* specifications. Listing 6.34 shows an example of a custom binding using the `textMessageEncoding` encoder.

LISTING 6.34 Custom Binding Using `textMessageEncoding`

```xml
<?xml version="1.0" encoding="utf-8" ?>
<configuration>
    <system.serviceModel>
        <bindings>
            <customBinding>
                <binding name="Custom">
                    <textMessageEncoding />
                    <httpTransport />
                </binding>
            </customBinding>
        </bindings>
        <client>
```

```
            <endpoint
            address="http://localhost/SerializationExample/Service.svc"
            binding="customBinding"
            bindingConfiguration="Custom"
            contract="Serialization.localhost.IEmployeeInformation"
            name="IEmployeeInformation" />
        </client>
    </system.serviceModel>
</configuration>
```

Listing 6.35 shows the configuration of a custom binding using the binaryMessageEncoding encoder.

LISTING 6.35 Custom Binding Using binaryMessageEncoding

```
<?xml version="1.0" encoding="utf-8" ?>
<configuration>
    <system.serviceModel>
        <bindings>
            <customBinding>
                <binding name="Custom">
                    <binaryMessageEncoding />
                    <httpTransport />
                </binding>
            </customBinding>
        </bindings>
        <client>
            <endpoint
            address="http://localhost/SerializationExample/Service.svc"
            binding="customBinding"
            bindingConfiguration="Custom"
            contract="Serialization.localhost.IEmployeeInformation"
            name="IEmployeeInformation" />
        </client>
    </system.serviceModel>
</configuration>
```

Sending Binary Data Using MTOM Encoding

The textMessageEncoding encoder converts messages into text-based XML. This is great for interoperability, but it is not efficient at transmitting large chunks of binary data. MTOM is used to send large amounts of binary data as raw bytes in interoperable scenarios. As mentioned previously, MTOM refers to Message Transmission Optimization Mechanism. This is standard for optimizing the binary data by sending the binary data as attachments to the SOAP message. This means that binary data can be transmitted using a SOAP message without the overhead of Base64 text encoding. To benefit from the use of MTOM, a service must contain a byte array or a `Stream` object in the operation contract.

WCF provides support for MTOM through the `mtomMessageEncoding` encoder. The use of the `mtomMessageEncoding` encoder is typically specified by the binding. Listing 6.36 shows how to specify the MTOM encoder using the `wsHttpBinding` binding.

LISTING 6.36 wsHttpBinding Using mtomMessageEncoding

```xml
<?xml version="1.0" encoding="utf-8" ?>
<configuration>
    <system.serviceModel>
        <bindings>
          <wsHttpBinding>
            <binding name="MTOMBinding" messageEncoding="Mtom" />
          </wsHttpBinding>
        </bindings>
        <client>
            <endpoint
            address="http://localhost/SerializationExample/Service.svc"
            binding="wsHttpBinding"
            bindingConfiguration="MTOMBinding"
            contract="EssentialWCF.IEmployeePicture"
            name="IEmployeePicture" />
        </client>
    </system.serviceModel>
</configuration>
```

Getting to Know the WebMessageEncoder

The `WebMessageEncoder` encoder is available with WCF in .NET Framework 3.5 and provides support for JSON and POX encoding. This encoder does not provide a specific type of encoding, but aggregates a set of encoding styles that are used on the Web today. The `WebMessageEncoder` encoder is enabled by using either the `WebHttpBehavior` or the `WebScriptEnablingBehavior` endpoint behaviors.

The `WebHttpBehavior` endpoint behavior instructs the `WebMessageEncoder` encoder to use the `TextMessageEncoder` encoder. This is done internally by using the `TextMessageEncoder` encoder and setting the message version to `MessageVersion.None`. This instructs the `TextMessageEncoder`

encoder to not include any SOAP or WS-Addressing information in the XML output. The `WebMessageEncoder` encoder supports request and responses messages in either XML or JSON. The default for the `WebHttp-Behavior` endpoint behavior is to have the request and response message formats set to `WebMessageFormat.Xml`. This can be controlled in code by setting the request and/or response message formats on the `[WebGet]` attribute to `WebMessageFormat.Xml` or `WebMessageFormat.Json`.

Although both the request and response formats can be specified independently, they are typically set to the same value. The `WebScriptEnablingBehavior` endpoint behavior does exactly this by setting the default for the request and response formats to `WebMessageFormat.Json`. This in turn instructs the `WebMessageEncoder` encoder to use the `JsonMessageEncoder` encoder to encode messages. The `WebScriptEnablingBehavior` is used for AJAX-enabled Web applications that call services from JavaScript. It also enables support for ASP.NET AJAX client proxies.

Refer to Chapter 13 for more information on the `WebHttpBehavior` behavior, `WebScriptEnablingBehavior` behavior, and the `[WebGet]` attribute.

SUMMARY

This chapter describes the serialization and encoding capabilities of WCF. As with the rest of WCF, many features allow you to customize and extend serialization. Some guiding principles for working serialization and WCF are the following:

- Try to use `DataContract` serialization whenever and wherever possible. This is the default serialization in WCF and is meant to be used for service-oriented development by forcing contracts to be explicit.
- In many situations, you will need to rely on the `XMLSerializer`, such as support for existing .NET types, compatibility with ASP.NET Web Services, and control over the shape of the serialized XML. Place the `[XmlSerializerFormat]` on your contracts where appropriate if you rely on the `XMLSerializer`. Be sure to place this attribute on your service contract if all your operations require the use of XML Serialization.

- All of the out-of-the-box bindings specify their default encoder. If you are looking to change the default encoder for a binding, look instead to a more appropriate binding that suits your needs.
- When creating custom bindings, be aware of the default encoder that the underlying transport uses. If you don't specify one, the default encoder for that transport will be used.
- Use streaming support built in to WCF when working with large amounts of data that cannot be worked with in memory. If streaming is not acceptable, use a chunking technique to break up the data into multiple messages that can be sent.

■7■
Hosting

A *SERVICE HOST* IS AN OPERATING SYSTEM process responsible for the lifetime and context of a WCF service. The service host, or just "host," is responsible for starting and stopping the WCF service and providing some basic management functions for controlling it. Other than that, the host knows very little about the WCF service that runs in its memory space.

Any operating system process can be a service host. Both IIS and Windows Process Activation Services (WAS) have the built-in infrastructure that makes this easy. Together with ASP.NET, they provide a common service hosting environment. In addition to IIS and WAS, you can host a WCF service in a Managed Windows Service (NT Service) that starts and stops with the operating system. You can host a service in a Windows application running full screen or minimized as a tray icon, or you can even host a service in a custom console application that runs on the system console. Regardless of how you host a service, the method of configuring a service address, binding, contract, and behaviors will be almost the same.

Choosing the right hosting environment for a service should be based on operational requirements, such as availability, reliability, and manageability. For example, hosting in a Managed Windows Service provides an interface for starting and stopping the service that is familiar to most Windows system administrators. Hosting in a Windows application running on the desktop, on the other hand, is something very familiar to most end users. Regardless of the hosting environment, the WCF programming model doesn't change. In fact, just as developers can design and implement a service without explicit concern about its binding or address, they can also be agnostic to the hosting environment.

All hosts are required to do three things: instantiate a `ServiceHost` class from `System.ServiceModel`, add endpoints to the host, and start listening for messages. The logic in Listing 7.1 is the core logic for hosting a service in your own programs. It's also automatically provided when hosting in IIS or WAS.

LISTING 7.1 Basic Logic for Hosting a Service

```
ServiceHost myHost = new ServiceHost( typeof( MyService ) );
myHost.AddServiceEndpoint (typeof( IMyService ),
                someBinding,
                someUri);
myHost.Open();
```

In this chapter, we cover the common techniques for hosting services. For IIS, the technique is pretty simple and is demonstrated in Chapter 1, "Basics." Specifically, we'll cover the details of how the new Windows Process Activation Service (WAS) process relates to the IIS infrastructure. We'll also cover self-hosting services in NT Services and client-side applications.

Hosting a Service in Windows Process Activation Services

Windows Process Activation Services (WAS) is the hosting infrastructure built into Vista and Windows Server 2008. Features previously available only in IIS, such as process activation, recycling, and identity management, have been moved into WAS and made available to protocols other than HTTP.

WAS enables you to host services in a robust environment that doesn't rely on the HTTP protocol. The HTTP protocol is widely deployed and understood, but there are cases when it's not the best option.

For example, imagine a service that receives one-way messages for the purpose of tracking and analysis, and the messages are sent by clients that are occasionally disconnected from the network. To provide the capability to send messages while disconnected, a queuing mechanism is needed. The MSMQ protocol will accomplish this, whereas the HTTP protocol will not. Or, imagine a very "chatty" service, one that quickly sends numerous small messages as part of a larger conversation. For this, the TCP protocol is more efficient than HTTP because it will keep a connection open when sending the multiple messages. In both of these examples, WAS can host the service where IIS cannot.

WAS supports multiple protocols through a *listener adapter* architecture where *listeners* are abstracted from the process management function. By defining an interface between WAS and the listeners, WAS can support multiple listeners without introducing extra complexity into the system. This way, WAS can communicate over HTTP, TCP, MSMQ, and named pipes using a consistent mechanism, thereby improving system reliability. Figure 7.1 depicts the WAS architecture.

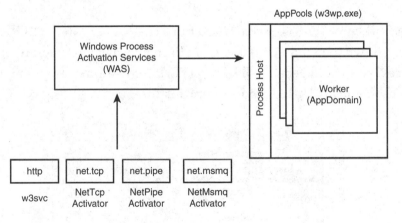

FIGURE 7.1 WAS architecture

WAS is automatically installed in Vista and Windows 2008 when IIS is installed, because IIS is dependent on it. When IIS is installed, it registers w3svc as an HTTP listener adapter with WAS. When .NET 3.5 is installed, it registers listener adapters for TCP, MSMQ, and named pipes with WAS. It's also possible to use WAS without installing IIS. To do this, you must enable two Windows features. First, you must enable the Windows Process Activation Services as shown in Figure 7.2. You get to this screen in

Windows by clicking Start, Control Panel, Programs, Turn Windows Features On or Off.

FIGURE 7.2 Enabling Windows Process Activation Services

Second, after WAS is enabled, you must check WCF Non-HTTP Activation as shown in Figure 7.3. If you want to enable HTTP activation for WCF services, you should enable the WCF HTTP Activation component, which will automatically enable required IIS7 features.

FIGURE 7.3 Enabling WCF non-HTTP activation

Hosting a service in WAS is similar to hosting in IIS, as shown in Chapter 1. You need a virtual application, an SVC file, and/or entries in the `<system.serviceModel>` section of the `web.config` file. To enable protocols other than HTTP, you need to complete two additional steps.

First, add the protocol binding information to the corresponding Web site in the WAS configuration. For example, with TCP you need to configure a specific port. The default binding information for `net.tcp` is 808:*, which means that the port number is 808 and the listener uses a wildcard mechanism for listening. Then you need to update the virtual application to enable that alternative protocol. Both of these settings are in the `ApplicationHost` config file in %windir\System32\inetsrv\config and can be set using the `appcmd.exe` utility, found in %windir\System32\inetsrv\. Listing 7.2 shows the commands to make both of these changes. The name of the virtual application is WASHosted and is defined under Default Web Site.

LISTING 7.2 Enabling `net.tcp` for a Virtual Application

```
appcmd.exe set site "Default Web Site" -
            +bindings.[protocol='net.tcp',bindingInformation='808:*']
appcmd.exe set app "Default Web Site/WASHosted"
            /enabledProtocols:http,net.tcp
```

In the same way that you can add a protocol, you can also remove one. For example, if you want to disable HTTP for that application, you can remove HTTP from the list of enabled protocols, as shown in Listing 7.3.

LISTING 7.3 Disabling HTTP from a Virtual Application

```
appcmd.exe set app "Default Web Site/WASHosted"
            /enabledProtocols:net.tcp
```

Second, enable the binding in the `web.config` any of the WCF-supported transports, including TCP, MSMQ, and named pipes. Listing 7.4 shows a `web.config` file configured for TCP binding.

LISTING 7.4 Configuration for WAS-Hosted Service

```
<?xml version="1.0" encoding="utf-8" ?>
<configuration>

  <system.serviceModel>
```

LISTING 7.4 continued

```
        <service name="EssentialWCF.StockService" >
          <endpoint address=""
                     binding="netTcpBinding"
                     contract="EssentialWCF.IStockService"/>
        </service>
      </services>
    </system.serviceModel>

  </configuration>
```

Hosting a Service in IIS 7

In IIS 6, available on Windows 2003 and Windows XP SP2, application pools were introduced as a runtime container for hosted applications. This enabled control over startup and shutdown, and identity and recycling services on a per-process basis. It naturally provided process isolation across applications, which led to greater reliability. Overall process management was handled by the application pool architecture.

In IIS7, available on Windows Vista and Windows Server 2008, process management has been generalized to support multiple protocols and was moved into WAS. ASP.NET is also extended to support process activation and service hosting in WAS.

Figure 7.4 depicts IIS7 on the WAS architecture.

The three minimum steps necessary to host a service in IIS7 are described in Chapter 1. For review, you must create an IIS Virtual Application, create an SVC file to define the service implementation, and include a `<system.serviceModel>` section in `web.config`.

To host a WCF service in IIS, you first need to define a virtual application. A virtual application is an IIS construct that combines a Web site, a protocol listener, and process activation. The Web site is a virtual directory that stores files. The listener process is w3svc for IIS and leverages `http.sys` for network I/O. Process activation maintains the runtime environment for code and is defined as an AppPool within IIS.

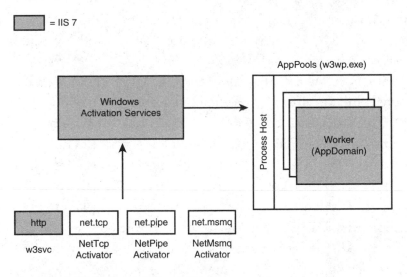

FIGURE 7.4 **IIS implemented on WAS**

After the virtual application is defined, you must place an SVC file and a web.config in the virtual directory. The SVC file includes a reference to the service implementation and the web.config defines the address, binding, and contract for the endpoints and the behaviors for the service.

The SVC file will look in three places for the implementation of the service: first in the SVC file itself, then in the /bin folder of the virtual directory, and finally in the GAC of the machine. The SVC file is similar in function to the ASMX file in IIS 6.

The web.config defines the service and endpoints, the ABCs of WCF, which are an address, a binding, and a contract. Because the service is hosted by IIS, and IIS only knows about the HTTP transport (in contrast to TCP or MSMQ), the endpoints in the web.config file must use a binding that specifies HTTP as the transport. Three of the built-in standard bindings, basicHttpBinding, wsHttpBinding, and wsDualHttpBinding, use this transport, so these can be used by endpoints defined by services hosted by IIS. If you define an endpoint that uses a binding based on a different transport, such as TCP or MSMQ (that is, netTcpBinding), a runtime error will be thrown when the service is first activated. The address should be a relative address because the base address of the service is determined by the protocol binding and the virtual path of the SVC file.

Let's consider what happens when a virtual application is created, when the first HTTP request arrives at that application, and how subsequent requests are handled.

When you create a virtual application using the IIS Manager, the URL associated with the virtual application is registered with IIS (w3svc). At that point, all requests received by the HTTP protocol listener adapter are sent for processing. The HTTP protocol listener adapter is HTTP.SYS, which is a system driver. The listener adapter architecture is described in the "Hosting a Service in Windows Process Activation Services" section of this chapter.

When the first request for a particular SVC file arrives from the protocol listener, IIS invokes WAS to start the worker process `w3wp.exe`, if it is not already started. The worker process is designated by the AppPool for that virtual application. The ASP.NET application manager sitting in the worker process receives the request from IIS/WAS and loads WCF hosting modules and handlers. The WCF hosting layer looks in the `<servicemodel>` section of the `web.config` and uses a `ServiceHostFactory` to create a `ServiceHost` for the class indicated in the `<Service>` element. It then adds the endpoints to the `ServiceHost` defined in the `<service>` section of `web.config`. Finally, it calls the `ServiceHost.Open` so that the service can start listening for incoming requests. When service starts, it registers the endpoint addresses with the protocol listener so that subsequent requests are sent directly from the protocol listener to the service itself.

Enabling ASMX Features in an IIS-Hosted Service

Prior to WCF, ASMX was a common approach to Web services in ASP.NET. It provided excellent support for the common Web service requirements and offered robust extensibility via the ASP.NET HTTP pipeline. With WCF, services are designed to be transport independent and agnostic to their hosting model. So WCF services cannot rely on an implementation within the HTTP pipeline, such as HTTP.SYS.

Like ASMX, WCF also provides a robust extensibility model. But rather than using the HTTP pipeline, it leverages the channel stack. Channels in

WCF are very flexible. They know about transports, like HTTP, but also about other protocol elements such as security and transactions. Channel stacks are described in Chapter 3, "Channels," and Chapter 4, "Bindings."

WCF supports a special hosting model within IIS: ASP.NET Compatibility mode. When running in this mode, ASP.NET provides the hosting environment for WCF services. Therefore, settings under `<system.web/hostingEnvironment>` and `<system.web/compilation>` are valid. However, not all ASP.NET HTTP features are enabled in this mode:

- **`HttpContext.Current`.** Set to `null` in the ASP.NET HTTP pipeline. In a WCF service, you can use the `OperationContext.Current` object to achieve similar purposes.
- **File/Url Authorization**
- **Impersonation**
- **Session state**
- **`<system.web/Globalization>`**
- **`ConfigurationManager.AppSettings`.** You can only get the settings in `web.config` at the root or above the virtual application, because `httpContext` is `null`.

To enable ASP.NET features by running in ASP.NET Compatibility mode, two settings must be adjusted. At the application level, you must set the attribute `<aspNetCompatibilityEnabled>` in `<serviceHostingEnvironment>` of `<system.serviceModel>` to `true` in the `web.config`. And because ASMX is an opt-in model at the service level, you must set the property `AspNetCompatibilityRequirements` to `Allowed` at the service level. With these two settings, almost all of the ASP.NET features are available to the WCF service. Table 7.1 describes the relationship between these two settings.

TABLE 7.1 Settings for Enabling ASMX Features in a WCF Service

aspNetCompatabilityEnabled in <web.config>	AspNetCompatibilityRequirementsMode in [ServiceBehavior]	ASMX Features Enabled
True	NotAllowed	No— Activation error
True	Allowed	Yes
True	Required	Yes
False (default)	NotAllowed	No
False (default)	Allowed	No
False (default)	Required	No— Activation error

However, there are few areas that need further explanation.

- **HttpContext.Current.** ConfigurationManager.AppSettings and ConfigurationManager.GetSection both work. Also, HttpContext.Current will flow among WCF threads.
- **Globalization.** You can set thread culture and access the Globalization section in <system.web>.
- **Impersonation.** WCF supports impersonation at the service and operation level using behaviors. This is in addition to what is implemented by ASP.NET. If the service enables impersonation through WCF, this overrides settings in ASP.NET. If the service does not implement impersonation, ASP.NET rules will be used.
- **Session state.** This is fully implemented and derived from ASP.NET configuration. You can save state with the process, server, or SQL persistence mechanism.

After ASP.NET Compatibility mode is enabled, services can take advantage of the features in ASP.NET. In Listing 7.5, we leverage two ASP.NET features. First, we use the SessionState feature of ASMX to store session-level state. Instancing can be scoped as `PerCall`, `PerSession`, or `Single`. These are further defined in Chapter 5, "Behaviors." In this example, we use `PerSession`, so that if a client uses the same proxy multiple times to invoke the service, session state will be preserved across calls. There are many other ways to store session-level data in WCF, but for those familiar with ASMX, this is a convenient mechanism. Second, we use the familiar AppSettings section in `web.config` to store application-specific configuration data. In the service code, the `AppSettings` collection of the `ConfigurationManager` object is used to retrieve these values.

LISTING 7.5 Accessing ASMX Session State and Configuration Settings

```
using System;
using System.Web;
using System.Web.Configuration;
using System.Configuration;
using System.ServiceModel;
using System.Runtime.Serialization;
using System.ServiceModel.Activation;

namespace EssentialWCF
{
    [DataContract]
    public class StockPrice
    {
        [DataMember] public string Source;
        [DataMember] public int calls;
        [DataMember] public double price;
    }

    [ServiceContract]
    public interface IStockService
    {
        [OperationContract]
        StockPrice GetPrice(string ticker);
    }

    [ServiceBehavior(InstanceContextMode =
                        InstanceContextMode.PerSession)]
    [AspNetCompatibilityRequirements
            (RequirementsMode=
                    AspNetCompatibilityRequirementsMode.Required)]
    public class StockService : IStockService
    {
        public StockPrice GetPrice(string ticker)
        {
```

Listing 7.5 continued

```
            StockPrice p = new StockPrice();
            int nCalls = 0;
            if (HttpContext.Current.Session["cnt"] != null)
                nCalls = (int)HttpContext.Current.Session["cnt"];
            HttpContext.Current.Session["cnt"] = ++nCalls;

            p.calls = nCalls;
            p.price = 94.85;
            p.Source = ConfigurationManager.AppSettings["StockSource"];
            return p;
        }
    }
}
```

For PerSession instancing to work, a session identifier must be preserved on the client so that subsequent calls from the client to the service
can pass the session ID back to the service. With ASP.NET, this is done with
a client-side cookie that is passed in the HTTP headers. For PerSession
instancing via ASMX to work, the client must enable cookies. Because
the standard HTTP bindings, basicHttpBinding and wsHttpBinding, dis-
allow cookies by default, you must define a binding configuration with
AllowsCookies=true in the client's app.config. Listing 7.6 shows enabling
aspNetCompatibility on the service.

Listing 7.6 Enabling ASP.NET Compatibility on the Service Configuration

```
<system.serviceModel>
  <serviceHostingEnvironment aspNetCompatibilityEnabled="true" />
  <services>
    <service behaviorConfiguration="MEXServiceTypeBehavior"
            name="EssentialWCF.StockService">
      <endpoint address="" binding="basicHttpBinding"
                contract="EssentialWCF.IStockService" />
      <endpoint address="mex" binding="mexHttpBinding"
                contract="IMetadataExchange" />
    </service>
  </services>
  <behaviors>
    <serviceBehaviors>
      <behavior name="MEXServiceTypeBehavior">
        <serviceMetadata httpGetEnabled="true" />
      </behavior>
    </serviceBehaviors>
  </behaviors>
</system.serviceModel>
```

Listing 7.7 shows how to enable cookies in the client-side configuration. This listing was generated by Add Service Reference in Visual Studio. Note that the default value for allowCookies is set to true.

LISTING 7.7 Enabling Cookies in the Client Configuration

```xml
<?xml version="1.0" encoding="utf-8" ?>
<configuration>
    <system.serviceModel>
        <bindings>
            <basicHttpBinding>
                <binding name="BasicHttpBinding_IStockService"
                    closeTimeout="00:01:00"
                    openTimeout="00:01:00" receiveTimeout="00:10:00"
                    sendTimeout="00:01:00"
                    allowCookies="true"
                    bypassProxyOnLocal="false"
                    hostNameComparisonMode="StrongWildcard"
                    maxBufferSize="65536" maxBufferPoolSize="524288"
                    maxReceivedMessageSize="65536"
                    messageEncoding="Text" textEncoding="utf-8"
                    transferMode="Buffered"
                    useDefaultWebProxy="true">
                    <readerQuotas maxDepth="32"
                        maxStringContentLength="8192"
                        maxArrayLength="16384"
                        maxBytesPerRead="4096"
                        maxNameTableCharCount="16384" />
                    <security mode="None">
                        <transport clientCredentialType="None"
                                    proxyCredentialType="None"
                            realm="" />
                        <message clientCredentialType="UserName"
                                    algorithmSuite="Default" />
                    </security>
                </binding>
            </basicHttpBinding>
        </bindings>
        <client>
            <endpoint
                address="http://myserver/WCFASMXState/StockService.svc"
                binding="basicHttpBinding"
                bindingConfiguration="BasicHttpBinding_IStockService"
                contract="localhost.IStockService"
                name="BasicHttpBinding_IStockService" />
        </client>
    </system.serviceModel>
</configuration>
```

Enabling ASP.NET impersonation is done the same way in WCF as it was in .NET 1.X. This is accomplished by including <identity imperson-ate="true"/> in the <system.web> section of the web.config file. When you do this, client credentials are automatically passed to the service, and the service executes operations using the client's credentials.

Enabling impersonation can be done in one of two ways. To set it at the service level, use impersonateCallerForAllOperations=true in the service behavior and ImpersonationOption.Allowed in the operation behavior. To enable it at the operation level, use ImpersonationOption.Required in the operation behavior without any reference at the service behavior.

Listing 7.8 shows setting impersonation at the operation level, assuming it is not disallowed at the service level in web.config. When a client accesses this service, the logged-on identity of the user is returned in the RequestedBy member. If the operation behavior is removed, the RequestedBy member defaults to the network service. Impersonation is covered in more detail in Chapter 8, "Security."

LISTING 7.8 Enabling Impersonation

```
namespace EssentialWCF
{
    [DataContract]
    public class StockPrice
    {
        [DataMember] public string RequestedBy;
        [DataMember] public double price;
    }


    [ServiceContract]
    public interface IStockService
    {
        [OperationContract]
        StockPrice GetPrice(string ticker);
    }

    [ServiceBehavior]
    [AspNetCompatibilityRequirements
            (RequirementsMode=
                        AspNetCompatibilityRequirementsMode.Required)]
    [ServiceContract]
    public class StockService : IStockService
```

```
    {
        [OperationBehavior(Impersonation =
                           ImpersonationOption.Required)]
        [OperationContract]
        public StockPrice GetPrice(string ticker)
        {
            StockPrice p = new StockPrice();
            p.RequestedBy = WindowsIdentity.GetCurrent().Name;
            p.price = 94.85;
            return p;
        }
    }
}
```

Self-Hosting

The most common environment for hosting WCF services is IIS or WAS. Built on a common architecture, they both provide robust process control and life cycle services, as well as a familiar management interface. This is the right solution for most scenarios where IIS infrastructure is already in place.

However, there may be cases where you don't want to host a service within IIS or WAS. You may want explicit control of the startup and shutdown events. Or you may want to provide a custom administration interface rather than using the IIS or WAS tools. For this, you can host a service in any program by using the ServiceHost class from the System.ServiceModel namespace. When you do that, you're *self-hosting* a WCF service.

A common scenario is to host a WCF service in a managed Windows service that starts when the system boots and shuts down with the system. A managed Windows service may run on an operating system that supports WCF, including Windows XP, Windows 2003 Server, Windows Vista, or Windows Server 2008. This is covered in detail in the "Self-Hosting in a Managed Windows Service" section of this chapter.

Another scenario is to host the service in a desktop application, using WinForms or Windows Presentation Framework or a command-line console application. The service could use peer networking, use a well- known address so that other clients can send it messages, or advertise its address in some other way. If the service uses a persistent queue as the transport, messages can be sent to this service even when the client isn't running. A persistent queue, implemented by MSMQ or tables in a relational database, is a good mechanism to facilitate communication between a client and service; the two may be temporarily disconnected from each other.

Implementing a self-hosted service is very straightforward. The three steps are listed in Listing 7.1. The *host*, the program that creates the ServiceHost object and calls its Open method, is responsible for staying alive until it's time to shut down. There are a few options when creating the ServiceHost, such as where to get the server base address from and whether to create a singleton, but that's about it.

Listings 1.1 and 1.2 in Chapter 1 demonstrate the bare minimum for self-hosting a service. Those listings show self-hosting from a console application that could be run on the console of a server or on an administrator desktop.

Self-Hosting in a Managed Windows Service

Managed Windows services are operating system processes that are controlled by the Service Control Manager (SCM). They are administered using the Services Microsoft Management Console (MMC), but Windows Management Instrumentation (WMI) and SCM APIs make them available to other configuration tools and scripting. Through these tools you can configure a variety of features, such as whether they start automatically with the OS and the Windows identity in which they run. Windows services are a common hosting environment for enterprise applications such as Microsoft SQL Server and Microsoft Exchange.

The managed Windows service infrastructure, available in unmanaged code via Win32 APIs and managed code derived from ServiceBase in the System.ServiceProcess namespace, provides a basic administration interface but does nothing for the actual hosting, scaling, security, and reliability of your code. You are responsible for implementing all communication (MSMQ, named pipes, TCP, and so on) as well as threading, instancing, and throttling. Fortunately, those features are implemented in WCF, so when you host a WCF service in a Windows service, this is done for you.

Visual Studio has a built-in template for defining a Windows service. When creating a project from this template, the skeleton has a static `main()` that starts the service and a class that derives from `ServiceBase` into which you put your code. The skeleton code needs to be completed in two ways: Add the WCF ServiceHost to instantiate your service and register the service with the SCM.

First, you need to add code to the `OnStart` method to start processing incoming messages. Prior to the introduction of WCF, this is where you would create thread pools, listeners, and a recycling mechanism, all typically driven off of configuration files. But by using WCF, all you need to do in the `OnStart` method is create the `ServiceHost` and start it listening. It's also helpful to use the `EventLog` to log an informational startup message.

Second, you need to implement a `ProjectInstaller`, which is defined and referenced in the `System.Configuration.Install` namespace. The `ProjectInstaller` class is used to install the managed service on the target machine. You could do this in a setup program or you can include it right within the service itself. To install the service, you then use the installutil.exe utility to register the service with the SCM. After running the utility, the service will be ready to run from the SCM.

Listing 7.9 shows the fully implemented Windows service.

LISTING 7.9 WCF Service Hosted in a Windows Service

```
using System;
using System.ComponentModel;
using System.Diagnostics;
using System.ServiceProcess;
using System.Configuration;
using System.Configuration.Install;
using System.ServiceModel;
using System.ServiceModel.Description;

namespace EssentialWCF
{
    [RunInstaller(true)]
    public class ProjectInstaller : Installer
    {
        private ServiceProcessInstaller process;
        private ServiceInstaller service;

        public ProjectInstaller()
        {
```

LISTING 7.9 continued

```
                    process = new ServiceProcessInstaller();
                    process.Account = ServiceAccount.LocalSystem;
                    service = new ServiceInstaller();
                    service.ServiceName = "EssentialWCF";
                    Installers.Add(process);
                    Installers.Add(service);
        }
    }


    [ServiceContract]
    public class StockService
    {
        [OperationContract]
        private double GetPrice(string ticker)
        {
            return 94.85;
        }
    }

    public partial class Service : ServiceBase
    {
        public Service()
        {
            InitializeComponent();
        }

        protected override void OnStart(string[] args)
        {
            ServiceHost serviceHost = new
                    ServiceHost(typeof(StockService));
            serviceHost.Open();
            ServiceEndpoint endpoint =
                        serviceHost.Description.Endpoints[0];

            EventLog.WriteEntry(endpoint.Contract.Name + " Started"
                            + " listening on " + endpoint.Address
                            + " (" + endpoint.Binding.Name + ")",
                        System.Diagnostics.
                                EventLogEntryType.Information);
        }

        protected override void OnStop()
        {
            EventLog.WriteEntry("EssentialWCF Stopping",
                            System.Diagnostics.
                                    EventLogEntryType.Information);
        }
    }
}
```

Figure 7.5 shows a screenshot of the Service Control Manager with the EffectiveWCF service started.

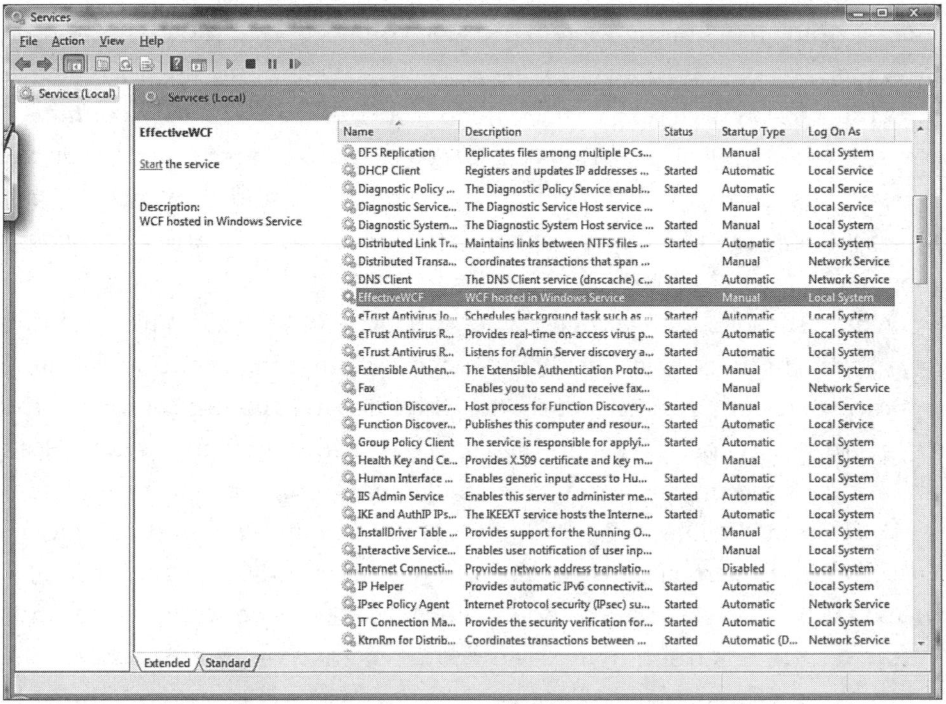

FIGURE 7.5 Service control manager

Hosting Multiple Services in One Process

Aggregating application capabilities to just the right service level is an essential element of system design. Build a system with too many interfaces and it becomes confusing. Build one with too few interfaces and it becomes monolithic and difficult to change.

In Chapter 2, "Contracts," we described how to aggregate multiple class interfaces into a single endpoint. This is accomplished through .NET interface aggregation. We also described how to expose multiple endpoints within a single service. This section takes an alternative approach. Rather than aggregating two interfaces into one and exposing the aggregate as a service, here we demonstrate how to expose two services independently within a single operating system process.

A ServiceHost exposes exactly one service. So, to expose multiple services within an operating system process, you need to implement multiple ServiceHost classes. This is precisely what WAS does—it creates a ServiceHost for each service activated via an SVC file. The SVC contains a service name that has endpoints described in the web.config for the application. The endpoint lists the address, binding, and contract, so the ServiceHost has everything it needs to begin listening for and dispatching messages.

When self-hosting services, you can similarly instantiate multiple ServiceHosts. Each host is truly independent, other than sharing the same operating system process. Each host has its own configuration in the <system.servicemodel> section of app.config file. After the ServiceHost is started, threading and instance management is managed independently by WCF so the hosting program does not need to implement that logic.

Listing 7.10 demonstrates a console application that is hosting two services. The GetStockPrice method of GoodStockService waits ten seconds before returning a result, whereas the same method of GreatStockService returns results immediately. Because the service behaviors are configured in WCF, this simple application is multithreaded, so when GoodStockService is sleeping, GreatStockService is responding to requests. And even the slow service is multithreaded, dispatching multiple inbound messages to new instances of GetStockPrice as needed.

LISTING 7.10 Multiple Self-Hosted Services in One Process

```
using System;
using System.ServiceModel;
using System.ServiceModel.Description;
using System.Configuration;
using System.Threading;

namespace EssentialWCF
{
    [ServiceContract]
    public class GoodStockService
    {
        [OperationContract]
        public double GetStockPrice(string ticker)
```

```
        {
            Thread.Sleep(10000);
            return 94.85;
        }
    }
    [ServiceContract]
    public class GreatStockService
    {
        [OperationContract]
        public double GetStockPrice(string ticker)
        {
            return 94.85;
        }
    }

    public class program
    {
        // Host the service within this EXE console application.
        public static void Main( )
        {
            ServiceDescription desc = null;
            ServiceHost serviceHost1 = new
                ServiceHost(typeof(GoodStockService));
            serviceHost1.Open();
            Console.WriteLine("Service #1 is ready.");

            ServiceHost serviceHost2 = new
                ServiceHost(typeof(GreatStockService));
            serviceHost2.Open();
            Console.WriteLine("Service #2 is ready.");

            Console.WriteLine("Press <ENTER> to terminate.\n\n");
            Console.ReadLine();

            // Close the ServiceHosts to shutdown the service.
            serviceHost1.Close();
            serviceHost2.Close();
        }
    }
}
```

The app.config file in Listing 7.11 has two entries in the <System. ServiceHost> section—one for each service. Each service has a unique base address. Note that each endpoint within each service has a blank address. An endpoint with a blank address listens for incoming messages on the service's base address. There can be, at most, one endpoint within a service that specifies a null address using the same URI scheme as the service's base address.

LISTING 7.11 Configuration for Multiple Self-Hosted Services in a Process

```xml
<?xml version="1.0" encoding="utf-8" ?>
<configuration>

  <system.serviceModel>
    <services>
      <service name="EssentialWCF.GoodStockService"
                      behaviorConfiguration="mexServiceBehavior">
        <host>
          <baseAddresses>
            <add baseAddress="http://localhost:8001/EssentialWCF/"/>
          </baseAddresses>
        </host>
        <endpoint address=""
                  binding="basicHttpBinding"
                  contract="EssentialWCF.GoodStockService" />
      </service>

      <service name="EssentialWCF.GreatStockService"
                      behaviorConfiguration="mexServiceBehavior">
        <host>
          <baseAddresses>
            <add baseAddress="http://localhost:8002/EssentialWCF/"/>
          </baseAddresses>
        </host>
        <endpoint address=""
                  binding="basicHttpBinding"
                  contract="EssentialWCF.GreatStockService" />
      </service>
    </services>

    <behaviors>
      <serviceBehaviors>
        <behavior name="mexServiceBehavior">
          <serviceMetadata httpGetEnabled="True"/>
        </behavior>
      </serviceBehaviors>
    </behaviors>

  </system.serviceModel>
</configuration>
```

Defining Service and Endpoint Addresses

A WCF service is a collection of endpoints, where each endpoint has a
unique address. The endpoint address and binding defines where and how

the endpoint listens for incoming requests. In addition to the endpoint addresses, the service itself has an address, which is called the base address.

The base address for a service is used as a base for relative addresses that may be defined in the endpoints. Using relative, rather than absolute, endpoint addresses makes it easier to manage endpoints in a service. With relative addresses, you can change all the endpoint addresses in a service by just changing the service's base address.

When using a relative address in an endpoint, the relative address is appended to the base address to form the service base address. For instance, if a service base address is http://localhost/foo and the endpoint's address is bar, the endpoint will listen at http://localhost/foo/bar for incoming messages.

When using absolute addresses in an endpoint, the endpoint address is unrelated to the service base address. For instance, a service base address can be http://localhost/foo, whereas an endpoint address within that is net.tcp://bar/MyOtherService/.

A service can have multiple base addresses, but only one per URI scheme. When a relative address is used in an endpoint, WCF finds the base address of the service with a transport that matches the protocol defined by the endpoint's binding. For instance, if a service defines two base addresses, http://localhost/ and net.tcp://bigserver/, and an endpoint uses a relative address of foo with a binding of basicHttpBinding, the endpoint's address is http://localhost/foo. If another endpoint in that service uses the same relative address foo, that endpoint's address is netc.tcp/bigserver/foo.

When hosting a service in IIS, the base address of the service is the address of the IIS virtual directory in which the SVC file resides. If the MyService.SVC file resides in the http://localhost/foo/, the base address of the service is http://localhost/foo. Endpoint addresses specified within the web.config must be relative when hosting in IIS.

Listing 7.12 shows a configuration file for a service. Note a few points:

- **Base addresses.** Two base addresses are defined for the service, each using a different protocol. If two base addresses are defined with the same protocol, it would be impossible to know how to build full addresses from relative addresses specified in the endpoints, so WCF will throw an error at service activation time.

- **Blank relative address.** The address of the first endpoint is blank. Combined with the base address of the service using the same protocol, the address of the endpoint is the same as the address of the service.

- **Nonblank relative address.** The address of the second endpoint is ws. Combined with the base address of the service using the same protocol, the address of the endpoint is http://localhost:8000/ EssentialWCF/ws.

LISTING 7.12 Service and Endpoint Addressing in Configuration

```xml
<?xml version="1.0" encoding="utf-8" ?>
<configuration>
  <system.serviceModel>
    <services>
      <service name="EssentialWCF.StockService">
        <host>
          <baseAddresses>
            <add baseAddress="http://localhost:8000/EssentialWCF/"/>
            <add baseAddress="net.tcp://localhost:8001/EssentialWCF/"/>
          </baseAddresses>
        </host>
        <endpoint address=""
                  binding="basicHttpBinding"
                  contract="EssentialWCF.IStockService" />
        <endpoint address="secure"
                  binding="wsHttpBinding"
                  contract="EssentialWCF.IStockService" />
        <endpoint address="fast"
                  binding="netTcpBinding"
                  contract="EssentialWCF.IStockService" />      </service>
    </services>
  </system.serviceModel>
</configuration>
```

Using the System.ServiceModel.Description namespace, you can access all the address and binding information from the ServiceHost. Listing 7.13 shows a code snippet to point out this information.

LISTING 7.13 Code Snippet to Print Address and Binding Information

```
foreach (Uri uri in serviceHost.BaseAddresses)
    Console.WriteLine("Base Addr Uri    : {0}", uri.AbsoluteUri);

foreach (ServiceEndpoint endpoint in serviceHost.Description.Endpoints)
{
    Console.WriteLine("\nEndpoint - address: {0}",
                                   endpoint.Address);
    Console.WriteLine("              binding: {0}",
                                   endpoint.Binding.Name);
    Console.WriteLine("              contract: {0}",
                                   endpoint.Contract.Name);
}
```

Figure 7.6 shows the output of this code when run against the configuration in Listing 7.12.

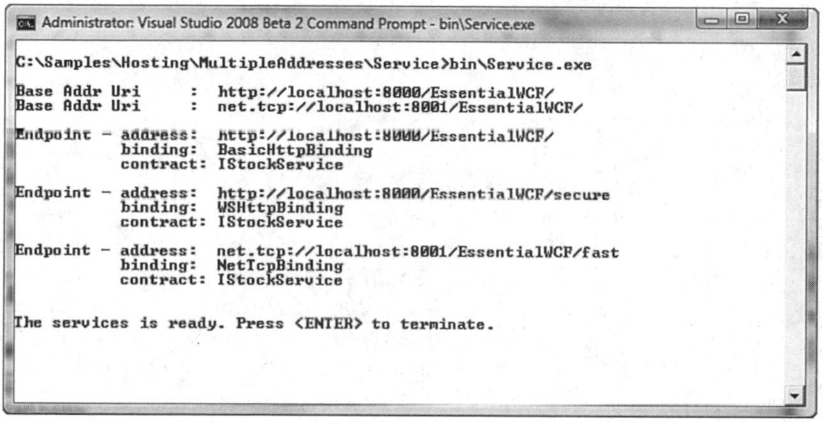

FIGURE 7.6 Viewing address and binding from a running service

SUMMARY

WCF has great flexibility when it comes to hosting. WCF services can be hosted in practically any operating system process. The service host, or just "host," is responsible for starting and stopping the service and providing some basic management functions for controlling it. Choosing the right hosting environment for a service is based on operational quality requirements such as availability, reliability, and manageability.

Both IIS and Windows Process Activation Services (WAS) have built-in infrastructure for hosting WCF services. Features previously available only in IIS, such as process activation, recycling, and identity management, have been moved into WAS and made available to protocols other than HTTP. This makes WAS a superset of IIS, but IIS is ideally suited for hosting HTTP-based WCF services. WCF supports many of the ASMX features through ASP.NET Compatibility mode.

In addition to IIS, managed Windows services is also a common technique for hosting WCF services. These processes are controlled by the Service Control Manager (SCM) and have a familiar administration interface. Visual Studio has a built-in template for defining a Windows Service, so between the ease of development and ease of management, Managed Windows Services make a good candidate for self-hosting WCF services.

Table 7.2 summarizes the common hosting choices.

TABLE 7.2 Hosting Choices

Host	When to Use
IIS	Host in IIS for unattended services that start and stop with the system. If you're deploying into an environment that already has IIS running, many of the administrative policies are already in place, and IT staff may already be trained. IIS hosting is limited to HTTP transports. Host in IIS if you want to leverage WCF for services (as opposed to ASMX) but want access to some of the ASMX/ASP.NET features.
WAS	Host in WAS for unattended services that start and stop with the system but that use TCP, MSMQ, named pipes, or other transports.
Managed Service	Host in a managed service (a.k.a. NT Service) if you want a custom administration interface for starting and stopping the host. Managed services can be configured to start and stop with the system. Many commercial grade applications run as managed services.

Host	When to Use
Desktop Application	Host a desktop application if you're implementing a service for user interaction. Peer networking is a common example.
Console Application	Console applications are great for testing services because debugging is very straightforward.

8
Security

I T'S HARD TO IMAGINE A facet of business applications in today's environment that is more critical than security. Certainly performance and availability are also central concerns, but there is little value in an application that is *sometimes* secure (in fact, it is probably more harmful than valuable). When we use an online banking service, we trust that the application providers have done their utmost to prevent abuse, corruption of data, hacking, and exposure of our financial details to others. The same is expected of us as we provide WCF-based services to consumers.

This chapter will focus on the concepts behind security and the practical means by which services are secured (when necessary) using WCF. We'll begin by introducing the major concepts, and then work our way into the details, showing many examples along the way.

After a description of concepts, to provide background necessary to work with the remainder of the chapter, we begin with an introduction to the creation and use of certificates to secure services. That in hand, we cover the details behind ensuring security from the transport and message perspectives.

A large part of the chapter focuses on practical approaches for security services in commonly encountered scenarios. These are categorized into two broad groups, modeling intranet and Internet environments.

Finally, we end the chapter by showing how to enable WCF's security auditing features, enabling us to track and diagnose issues related to authentication and authorization of callers to our service operations.

WCF Security Concepts

Before we get to the code, configuration, and processes for implementing secure services, let's begin by introducing four major tenets of service security: authentication, authorization, confidentiality, and integrity. With those defined, we'll then describe the concepts of transport and message security as they apply to WCF.

Authentication

One of the .most fundamental concepts of security is knowing who is knocking on your door. *Authentication* is the process of establishing a clear identity for an entity, for example, by providing evidence such as username and password. Although this is clearly important for a service to understand of its callers, it is equally important that callers have an assurance that the service being called is the expected service and not an impostor.

WCF provides several options for this mutual authentication by both the service and the caller—for example, certificates and Windows accounts and groups. By using these and other options, as we'll show throughout this chapter, each side can have firm trust that they are communicating with an expected party.

Authorization

The next step in .security, after identity has been established, is to determine whether the calling party should be permitted to do what they are requesting. This process is called *authorization* because the service or resource authorizes a caller to proceed. Note that you can choose to authorize anonymous users for actions as well, so although authorization is not strictly dependent on authentication, it does normally follow.

Authorization can be performed by custom code in the service, native or custom authorization providers, ASP.NET roles, Windows groups, Active Directory, Authorization Manager, and other mechanisms.

Confidentiality

When dealing with sensitive information, there is little use in establishing identity and authorization if the results of a call will be broadcast to anyone who is interested. *Confidentiality* is the concept of preventing others from reading the information exchanged between a caller and a service. This is typically accomplished via encryption, and a variety of mechanisms for this exist within WCF.

Integrity

The final basic concept of security is the assurance that the contents of a message have not been tampered with during transfer between caller and service, and vice versa. This is typically done by digitally signing or generating a signed hash for the contents of the message and having the receiving party validate the signature based on the contents of what it received. If the computed value does not match the embedded value, the message should be refused.

Note that integrity can be provided even when privacy is not necessary. It may be acceptable to send information in the clear (unencrypted) as long as the receiver can be assured that it is the original data via digital signature verification.

Transport and Message Security

There are two major classifications of security within WCF; both are related to the security of what is transferred between a service and caller (sometimes called *transfer security*). The first concept is of protecting data as it is sent across the network, or "on the wire." This is known as *transport security*. The other classification is called *message security* and is concerned with the protection that each message provides for itself, regardless of the transportation mechanism used.

Transport security provides protection for the data sent, without regard to the contents. A common approach for this is to use Secure Sockets Layer (SSL) for encrypting and signing the contents of the packets sent over HTTPS. There are other transport security options as well, and the choice of options will depend on the particular WCF binding used. In fact, you will see that many options in WCF are configured to be secure by default, such as with TCP.

One limitation of transport security is that it relies on every "step" and participant in the network path having consistently configured security. In other words, if a message must travel through an intermediary before reaching its destination, there is no way to ensure that transport security has been enabled for the step after the intermediary (unless that intermediary is fully controlled by the original service provider). If that security is not faithfully reproduced, the data may be compromised downstream. In addition, the intermediary itself must be trusted not to alter the message before continuing transfer. These considerations are especially important for services available via Internet-based routes, and typically less important for systems exposed and consumed within a corporate intranet.

Message security focuses on ensuring the integrity and privacy of individual messages, without regard for the network. Through mechanisms such as encryption and signing via public and private keys, the message will be protected even if sent over an unprotected transport (such as plain HTTP).

The option to use transport and message security is typically specified in configuration; two basic examples are shown in Listing 8.1.

LISTING 8.1 Transport and Message Security Examples

```
<basicHttpBinding>
  <binding name="MyBinding">
    <security mode="Transport">
      <transport clientCredentialType="Windows"/>
    </security >
  </binding>
</basicHttpBinding>

<wsHttpBinding>
  <binding name="MyBinding">
    <security mode="Message">
      <transport clientCredentialType="None"/>
    </security >
  </binding>
</wsHttpBinding>
```

As you progress through this chapter, you'll see scenarios with examples using transport or message security, and in some cases, a mixture of both.

Certificate-Based Encryption

Certificates, and the claims they represent, are a secure, general-purpose method for proving identity. They embody a robust security mechanism that makes them a great option for encryption and authentication. WCF uses industry-standard X.509 certificates, which are widely adopted and used by many technology vendors. Internet browsers and Internet servers use this format to store encryption keys and signatures for SSL communication on the Web. Certificates provide strong encryption and are well understood and documented.

The primary disadvantages of certificates are the expense of acquiring them for production from a third-party authority and the complexity associated with provisioning them. How do you distribute them? What do you do if one is stolen? How do you recover data after one is lost? If you store them on a client computer, how can you access information from the road? A variety of solutions address these problems, from storing certificates in a directory within an intranet or on the public Internet, to storing them in Smart Cards that we can carry in our wallets. Regardless of the provisioning solution, certificates are a good option for encryption and authentication.

Concepts

The overall concept of message encryption with asymmetric keys is fairly simple. Imagine an algorithm that can encrypt an arbitrary string using one key and that can decrypt it with another key. Now imagine that I have a pair of those keys, and I make one of them public so that everyone on the Internet can see it, but I keep the other one private so that only I can see it. If my friend wants to send me a message, he looks up my public key, runs the algorithm to encrypt the message, and sends it. If the encrypted message is intercepted by my enemy, that person can't read it because only I, with my private key, can decrypt it. When I send a response back to my friend, I look up his public key, run the algorithm to encrypt the response, and send it. Again, only he can decrypt the encrypted messages, so it will be kept confidential between us.

Digital signatures use message encryption, but in reverse. A digital signature is simply a string that is encrypted with a private key so that it can only be decrypted with a corresponding public key. The correct decryption of the string (for example, my name) is public information, so after someone decrypts the string using my public key, the person can verify that my name was stored in the message.

Trust is another important aspect of certificates. In our example of exchanging messages with a friend, how do we know that we have the public key of our friend and not of our enemy? For a client and service to trust that each other's certificates are correct, valid, and have not been revoked, they must trust a common authority. It's okay if the client and service use certificates issued by different authorities, as long as those authorities both trust a third, common authority. The common authority is often referred to as the root authority, which typically is self-signed, meaning that it doesn't trust anyone else. When a client receives a certificate from a service, it looks at the certification path of the service certificate to see if the path is valid and terminates at a trusted authority. If so, the client trusts that the certificate is valid; if not, it rejects it. There are provisions in WCF for disabling the certification path validation so that untrusted certificates can be used in development and testing.

Setup

Certificates can be used for transport- or message-level security. A commonly used transport-level encryption option, SSL, is applied to the transport by using a certificate on the server. Message-level encryption works on individual messages. Whereas transport-based encryption requires a certificate to be installed with the service, message-based encryption supports a variety of modes with client and/or server certificates.

The examples in the "Transport-Level Security" and "Message-Level Security" sections of this chapter will use two machines: a Vista desktop and a Windows 2003 server. The desktop has a certificate, MyClientCert. The server has a certificate, MyServerCert. Listing 8.2 shows the commands that run on Vista to generate the necessary certificates. Makecert.exe creates a certificate. The -pe switch makes the private key exportable. The -n switch defines the name of the certificate that will be the name that is used for authentication. The -sv switch defines the private key file. The -sky switch can be "exchange" or a digital signature. Pvt2pfx is a utility that combines the private key and public key into a single file.

If you're developing on one machine, change the name MyServer to localhost. All other instructions will remain the same.

> ■ **NOTE**   Production Certificates
>
> Keep in mind that certificates generated in this fashion should *not* be used in production scenarios. Certificates for use in production environments should be requested from a trusted third-party certificate authority.

LISTING 8.2 Generating Certificates

```
makecert.exe  -r -pe -sky exchange
              -n "CN=MyClientCert"  MyClientCert.cer
              -sv MyClientCert.pvk
pvk2pfx.exe   -pvk MyClientCert.pvk
              -spc MyClientCert.cer
              -pfx MyClientCert.pfx

makecert.exe  -r -pe -sky exchange
              -n "CN=MyServer.com"  MyServerCert.cer
              -sv MyServerCert.pvk
pvk2pfx.exe   -pvk MyServerCert.pvk
              -spc MyServerCert.cer
              -pfx MyServerCert.pfx
```

The .cer file is the public key, the .pvk file is the private key, and the .pfx file is a key exchange file that contains both. The following keys must be installed using the Certificates snap-in in the Microsoft Management Console.

1. Install the following on the server, in the local computer certificate store:

   a. **Import MyServerCert.pfx to the Personal folder.** This enables the server to decrypt messages that have been encrypted with its public key. It also enables the server to encrypt messages with its private key.

b. **Import `MyClientCert.cer` to the Trusted People folder.** This enables the server to decrypt messages that have been encrypted with the MyClientCert private key, such as data messages and digital signatures for authentication. It also enables the server to encrypt messages with the MyClientCert public key.

2. Install the following on the client, in the current user certificate store:

a. **Import `MyClientCert.pfx` to the Personal folder.** This enables the client to decrypt messages that have been encrypted with its public key. It also enables the client to encrypt messages with its private key.

b. **Import `MyServerCert.cer` to the Trusted People folder.** This enables the client to decrypt messages that have been encrypted with the MyServerCert private key, such as data messages and digital signatures for authentication. It also enables the client to encrypt messages with the MyServerCert public key.

Transport-Level Security

Transport-level security, as its name implies, provides security in the communication channel between the client and the service. Security at this level can include both encryption and authentication. The channel stack (binding) determines the types of encryption and authentication protocols available.

At a minimum, transport-level security ensures that communication is encrypted between the client and the service so that only the client or service can understand the messages exchanged. The specific algorithm used for encryption is either a function of the underlying protocol (HTTPS uses SSL, for example) or it can be specified in the binding. (MSMQ can use RC4Stream or AES.)

In addition to encryption, transport-level security can include client authentication by requiring credentials to be passed from the client to the service when establishing the communication channel. Credentials may be digital certificates, SAML tokens, Windows tokens, or a shared secret such as a username and password. Transport-level security also validates the service identity before establishing a secure channel between client and service. This validation protects against man-in-the-middle and spoofing attacks.

Encryption Using SSL

SSL is a convenient, secure way to encrypt communications. It's well understood by IT organizations, it is firewall friendly, and there are many management and performance tools on the market. Using SSL with `BasicHttpBinding` enables the broadest reach of a secure Web service.

SSL requires a digital certificate with an asymmetrical (public/private) key to establish an encrypted pathway. After it is established, SSL uses this pathway, with a more efficient symmetric encryption algorithm, to encrypt messages going both ways on the channel.

A digital certificate can be obtained from a number of sources. There are public entities, such as Verisign, that issue certificates for testing and production purposes. Windows Server itself ships with a certificate issuing service, so you can generate your own certificates that can be trusted by your organization or partners. In addition, .NET ships with a utility, MakeCert, which generates certificates for testing purposes.

SSL over HTTP

SSL can be applied to most transport protocols (a notable exception being queued transports), but it is most commonly used with HTTP. When using a binding based on the HTTP transport, whether you're hosting the services in IIS or self-hosting in another process, HTTP.SYS must be configured for SSL. For IIS, you can add the binding using the IIS Administration tool. For IIS 7, this is done by selecting the Web site under which the virtual root is defined, and then selecting the Bindings link in the Actions pane. This will launch a dialog from which you can select the certificate to use for SSL communications (see Figure 8.1).

For self-hosting a service on Windows Server 2008 or Vista, you can use the *netsh* tool. Listing 8.3 shows the command line to configure HTTP.SYS to allow SSL traffic on port 8001. Specifying IP address 0.0.0.0 indicates all IP addresses. The 40-digit hex number is the thumbprint of a certificate installed on the machine. The thumbprint can be found by using the Certificates Add-In in the Microsoft Management Console and viewing the certificate details. The final GUID is an application identifier, representing who enabled this access. Any GUID that you generate is acceptable here and will be associated with your application.

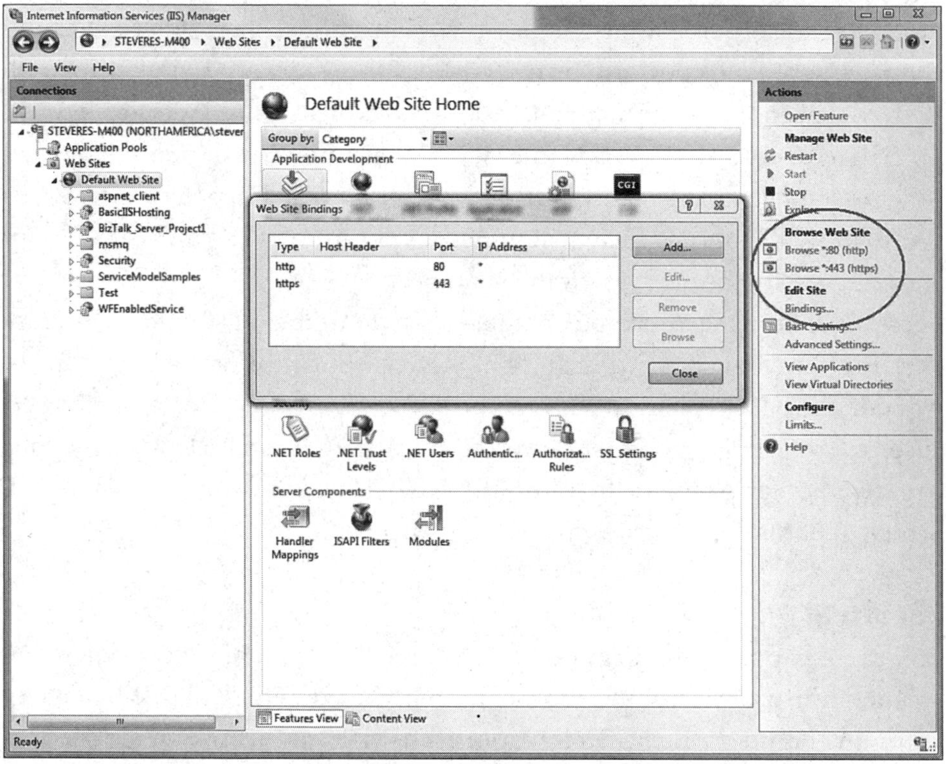

FIGURE 8.1 Configuring IIS 7 for SSL

LISTING 8.3 Using NetSh to Configure HTTP.SYS to Allow SSL on Different Ports

```
netsh http add sslcert 0.0.0.0:8001
    1db7b6d4a25819b9aa09c8eaec9275007d562dcf
    {4dc3e181-e14b-4a21-b022-59fc669b0914}
```

After you've registered the certificate with HTTP.SYS, you can then configure a service to use SSL encryption. Listing 8.4 shows a service configuration file that is using the basicHttpBinding binding, transport-level encryption, and no client authentication. Note that two base addresses are specified in this self-hosted configuration file, one for encrypted and one for non-encrypted communication. This enables the MEX endpoint to use a non-encrypted channel and the subsequent communication to be encrypted. If you don't want to expose a MEX endpoint, or if it is okay to expose it on a secure channel, you don't need the non-encrypted address.

LISTING 8.4 Encryption with basicHttpBinding

```
<system.serviceModel>
  <services>
    <service name="EffectiveWCF.StockService"
             behaviorConfiguration="MyBehavior">
      <host>
        <baseAddresses>
          <add baseAddress="http://localhost:8000/EffectiveWCF" />
          <add baseAddress="https://localhost:8001/EffectiveWCF"/>
        </baseAddresses>
      </host>
      <endpoint address=""
                binding="basicHttpBinding"
                bindingConfiguration="MyBinding"
                contract="EffectiveWCF.IStockService" />
      <endpoint address="mex"
                binding="mexHttpBinding"
                contract="IMetadataExchange" />
    </service>
  </services>
  <behaviors>
    <serviceBehaviors>
      <behavior name="MyBehavior">
        <serviceMetadata httpGetEnabled="true" />
      </behavior>
    </serviceBehaviors>
  </behaviors>
  <bindings>
    <basicHttpBinding>
      <binding name="MyBinding">
        <security mode="Transport">
          <transport clientCredentialType="None"/>
        </security >
      </binding>
    </basicHttpBinding>
  </bindings>
</system.serviceModel>
```

SSL over TCP

Like HTTP, the TCP transport can be used with SSL for encrypted communication. Configuration options for specifying transport security for TCP are similar to HTTP. To configure a service to use the TCP security, three changes must be made to Listing 8.4.

First, the binding specified for the non-MEX endpoint is `NetTcpBinding` rather than `basicHttpBinding`. Second, the base address of the service should be a TCP URI address rather than an HTTP URI, of the form `net.tcp://{hostname}[:port]/{service location}`. Third, a `NetTcpBinding` configuration should be used rather than a `basicHttpBinding` configuration to specify the `<Security mode="transport">` setting. Listing 8.5 shows this configuration.

LISTING 8.5 Encryption with `NetTcpBinding`

```
<system.serviceModel>
  <services>
    <service name="EffectiveWCF.StockService"
             behaviorConfiguration="MyBehavior">
      <host>
        <baseAddresses>
          <add baseAddress="http://localhost:8000/EffectiveWCF" />
          <add baseAddress="net.tcp://localhost:8002/EffectiveWCF" />
        </baseAddresses>
      </host>
      <endpoint address=""
                binding="netTcpBinding"
                bindingConfiguration="MyBinding"
                contract="EffectiveWCF.IStockService" />
      <endpoint address="mex"
                binding="mexHttpBinding"
                contract="IMetadataExchange" />
    </service>
  </services>
  <behaviors>
    <serviceBehaviors>
      <behavior name="MyBehavior">
        <serviceMetadata httpGetEnabled="true" />
      </behavior>
    </serviceBehaviors>
```

```
        </behaviors>
        <bindings>
          <netTcpBinding>
            <binding name="MyBinding">
              <security mode="Transport">
                <transport clientCredentialType="None"/>
              </security >
            </binding>
          </netTcpBinding>
        </bindings>
      </system.serviceModel>
```

Client Authentication

A client authenticates with a service by presenting a set of claims that the service trusts. The claims can be in any format, as long as both the client and the service understand the format and trust its source.

If the client and service share a secret, such as a username and password, as long as the client sends over a valid credentials, the service trusts that the client is who it says it is. This is the mechanism for basic authentication with HTTP. In a Windows-only environment where the client machine and services are running under accounts defined in Active Directory or in a domain, both the client and the services are already in a trust relationship. In this case, Windows authentication can be specified, whereby Kerberos or NTLM tokens will be used. If the client and service each trust some third party and are not part of a Windows domain, certificate authentication is most appropriate, in which the client sends a certificate from a source that the service trusts.

A service specifies a client authentication requirement in the `client-CredentialType` attribute on the `transport` element while setting the security mode to `Transport`. This is done within the binding configuration in the service description of the service, whether defined in configuration file or in code. Different client authentication schemes are available for different bindings. Table 8.1 summarizes the options for the built-in bindings.

TABLE 8.1 Client Authentication with Transport Security

	None	User/Pswd	Windows	Certificate
basicHttpBinding	✓	✓	✓	✓
wsHttpBinding	✓	✓	✓	✓
wsDualHttpBinding				
netTcpBinding	✓		✓	✓
netNamedPipeBinding	✓		✓	✓
netMsmqBinding	✓		✓	✓
netPeerTcpBinding		✓		✓
msmqIntegrationBinding	✓		✓	✓
wsFederationHttpBinding				

When using client authentication with transport security, the client must attach claims to the channel before sending messages. The client must attach claims that match the service requirement. For instance, if basic authentication is required with an HTTP-based binding, the client must send a username and password. If certificate authentication is required with any binding, the client must sign the message with its private key and send a digital certificate from an authority trusted by the service (if the service does not already have it).

Authenticating with Basic Credentials and basicHttpBinding

Listing 8.4, "Encryption with basicHttpBinding," depicts a service configuration that uses basicHttpBinding transport mode security to implement encryption via SSL. To add username/password authentication to this example, the clientCredentialType attribute is changed to Basic. Listing 8.6 shows a fragment of the changed configuration that implements a service that requires authentication at the transport layer. This service would be appropriate for Internet communication because the credentials are passed over a secured transport.

LISTING 8.6 Basic Authentication with basicHttpBinding

```
<basicHttpBinding>
  <binding name="MyBinding">
    <security mode="Transport">
      <transport clientCredentialType="Basic"/>
    </security >
  </binding>
</basicHttpBinding>
```

When using basic authentication, the client must pass a username and password to the service. This is done using a proxy class or directly on the channel. Listing 8.7 shows client code that passes credentials to a service whose endpoint is using basicHttpBinding and Basic credentials.

LISTING 8.7 Passing Username and Password from a Client

```
proxy.ClientCredentials.UserName.UserName = "MyDomain\\Me";
proxy.ClientCredentials.UserName.Password = "SecretPassword";
```

Basic, or username/password, authentication is appropriate when it's feasible for a client and service to share a secret and when security risks aren't that great. Because passwords tend to be stored on sticky notes on people's desks, in database tables, or in configuration files, they're easily copied or viewed without notice. To keep them "fresh," they're frequently invalidated ("your password will expire in 10 days") so there's additional overhead involved. In addition, because people often reuse the same passwords for multiple accounts, compromise of one account can lead to compromises on other systems.

Authenticating with Windows Credentials

Other authentication schemes are more secure than username/password. If you're working in a Windows environment that has Active Directory deployed, Windows authentication can be used. This leverages the identity of the user/process of the client and sends those credentials to the service. This is a single-sign-on solution, in that after the user signs on to the Windows domain, the user's credentials can automatically be passed from the client machine to the service. When using Windows authentication, the client code shown in Listing 8.7 is not needed. Listing 8.8 shows net.tcp binding using Windows authentication.

LISTING 8.8 Windows Authentication with *basicHttpBinding*

```
<basicHttpBinding>
  <binding name="MyBinding">
    <security mode="Transport">
      <transport clientCredentialType="Windows"/>
    </security >
  </binding>
</basicHttpBinding>
```

Authenticating with Certificates and netTcpBinding

Digital certificates provide a more comprehensive form of authentication than passwords. For scenarios requiring secure, fast, certificate-based communication, netTcpBinding is a good choice. Certificates work with mixed security models found on complex intranets, including Windows, UNIX, and third-party LDAP authentication. On the Internet, if you need fast, secure server-to-server communication, and you can specify which firewall ports are open, netTcpBinding can prove very valuable. Using NetTcpBinding with certificate authentication combines fast communication and robust security.

Listing 8.9 shows a service configuration using transport-level security with certificate-based client authentication. There are a few points worth noting. First, the service is configured to require client certificates by using the clientCredentialType in the NetTcpBinding binding. Second, the server's certificate is specified in the <serviceCredential> node. This is necessary so that the server knows which certificate and key pair to use in the SSL handshake. Third, the service is configured to bypass verifying the certification path of the client's certificates by specifying PeerTrust as the certificationValidationMode. This is necessary when working with certificates generated by MakeCert.exe, rather than real certificates obtained or generated from a trusted authority.

LISTING 8.9 Certificate Authentication with NetTcpBinding

```
<?xml version="1.0" encoding="utf-8" ?>
<configuration>
  <system.serviceModel>

    <services>
      <service name="EffectiveWCF.StockService"
               behaviorConfiguration="MyBehavior">
```

```xml
      <host>
        <baseAddresses>
          <add baseAddress="http://localhost:8000/EffectiveWCF" />
          <add baseAddress="net.tcp://localhost:8001/EffectiveWCF" />
        </baseAddresses>
      </host>
      <endpoint address=""
                binding="netTcpBinding"
                bindingConfiguration="MyBinding"
                contract="EffectiveWCF.IStockService" />

      <endpoint address="mex"
                binding="mexHttpBinding"
                contract="IMetadataExchange" />
    </service>
  </services>

  <behaviors>
    <serviceBehaviors>
      <behavior name="MyBehavior">
        <serviceMetadata httpGetEnabled="true" />
        <serviceCredentials>
          <serviceCertificate findValue="localhost"
                      storeLocation="LocalMachine" storeName="My"
                      x509FindType="FindBySubjectName"/>
          <clientCertificate>
            <authentication certificateValidationMode="PeerTrust"/>
          </clientCertificate>
        </serviceCredentials>

      </behavior>
    </serviceBehaviors>
  </behaviors>

  <bindings>
    <netTcpBinding>
      <binding name="MyBinding">
        <security mode="Transport">
          <transport clientCredentialType="Certificate"/>
          <message clientCredentialType="None"/>
        </security>
      </binding>
    </netTcpBinding>
  </bindings>

  </system.serviceModel>
</configuration>
```

To initiate communication between the client and service, the client must specify a certificate for authentication. This can be done in configuration or in code. Listing 8.10 shows client-side code that attaches a certificate to the channel for the service to use in authentication. Under peer trust, the service will look up the certificate in its Trusted People folder. If found, access will be granted; if not, access will be denied.

LISTING 8.10 Client Code for Certificate Authentication

```
StockServiceClient proxy = new StockServiceClient();
proxy.ClientCredentials.ServiceCertificate.
                        Authentication.CertificateValidationMode =
                System.ServiceModel.Security.
                        X509CertificateValidationMode.PeerTrust;
proxy.ClientCredentials.ClientCertificate.SetCertificate(
                StoreLocation.CurrentUser,
                StoreName.My,
                X509FindType.FindBySubjectName,
                "MyClientCert");
try
{
  double p = proxy.GetPrice("msft");
  Console.WriteLine("Price:{0}", p);
}
catch (Exception ex)
{
  Console.WriteLine("Message:{0}", ex.Message);
  if (ex.InnerException != null)
    Console.WriteLine("Inner:{0}", ex.InnerException.Message);
}
```

Service Identity

When establishing a secure communication channel between the client and the service, the client can authenticate with the service through a variety of methods described in this chapter. The client can be authenticated with a username/password, Windows, or certificate credentials. Equally important, however, is authenticating the service. If a client is going to exchange sensitive information with the service, then service authentication is just as important as client authentication. Failure to do so enables the popular spoofing scams on the Internet to occur in services. To guard against this, WCF checks the service identity before establishing a secure communication channel through transport-level security.

When the MEX endpoint of a service is called to generate WSDL, it returns the identity of the service. If the binding supports the WS-Security protocol (all preconfigured bindings do, except basicHttpBinding), the WSDL will include information about the identity of the service. Depending on the binding and service authentication mechanism, different identity information is returned.

When svcutil is used to generate a client proxy and client configuration file from a running service, the identity of the service is written into the configuration file. At runtime, the identity of the service is verified to ensure that the client is communicating to the proper service. If the runtime service has a different identity from what the client is expecting, WCF will not establish the secure channel.

Listing 8.11 shows a configuration file generated by svcutil for a service using wsHttpBinding with certificate-based client authentication for message-level security. Note that the server's encrypted certificate is included. If the client attempts to initiate secure communication with a service but the service does not have that certificate, WCF will throw an error.

LISTING 8.11 Service Identity Generated for Certificate-Based Authentication

```
<client>
  <endpoint address="http://localhost:8000/EffectiveWCF"
            binding="wsHttpBinding"
            bindingConfiguration="WSHttpBinding_IStockService"
            contract="IStockService"
            name="WSHttpBinding_IStockService">
    <identity>
      <certificate encodedValue=
➡"AwAAAAEAAAAUAAAAHbe21KJYGbmqCcjq7JJ1AH1WLc8gAAAAQAAAL
➡0BAAAwggG5MIIBY6ADAgECAhAN4tyIi6rOqEYmrBcPIOHPMA0GCSqGS
➡Ib3DQEBBAUAMBYxFDASBgNVBAMTC1Jvb3QgQWdlbmN5MB4XDTA3MDky
➡ODIyMzgxOVoXDTM5MTIzMTIzNTk1OVowFDESMBAGA1UEAxMJbG9jYWx4
➡ob3N0MIGfMA0GCSqGSIb3DQEBAQUAA4GNADCBiQKBgQCwYocYLHnP+c
➡hgEurathCfwIxGhqL86lOdbEMuf1dfYjgkAhUBmkwVMhH8TVxyZkujp
➡09FKprT/beuzWmZVRjucaa/4yzOTsbrma0NGPI8V31Z+TYcU9zhNXn9
➡4d5eNH9Bc7QOhgwlRbl74I18iPC9WGFB1V1PS/KYoYyCqNC8AwIDAQA
➡Bo0swSTBHBgNVHQEEQDA+gBAS5AktBh0dTwCNYSHcFmRjoRgwFjEUMB
➡IGA1UEAxMLUm9vdCBBZ2VuY3mCEAY3bACqAGSKEc+41KpcNfQwDQYJK
➡oZIhvcNAQEEBQADQQB+1CX4+Jk8L6NSQ8YjR51mkFSu6u3XZst/j5wq
➡gPIukU812/GEE4N/b8jXIXo6hyQqpvl9HKXnlTmYNivwXH2Q" />
    </identity>
  </endpoint>
</client>
```

Listing 8.12 shows a configuration file generated by svcutil for a service using wsHttpBinding with Windows-based client authentication. Note that the server's Windows credentials are included. If the client attempts to initiate secure communication with a service but the service is running under a different Windows account, WCF will throw an error. It may be the case that the service account that generated the WSDL in the development environment had one set of credentials, but in production a different Windows account is used. In that case, the client-side configuration file must be changed to match the new identity of the service.

LISTING 8.12 Service Identity Generated for Certificate-Based Authentication

```
<client>
  <endpoint address="http://localhost:8000/EffectiveWCF"
            binding="wsHttpBinding"
            bindingConfiguration="WSHttpBinding_IStockService"
            contract="IStockService"
            name="WSHttpBinding_IStockService">
    <identity>
      <userPrincipalName value="MyDomain\Me"/>
    </identity>
  </endpoint>
</client>
```

If the client cannot verify that the service is running on the configured account for any reason, it will throw an error. For instance, if you're doing development offline and do not have access to Active Directory, the client may time out waiting to verify the services credentials. In that case, you can change the identity of the service from `<userPrincipalName>` to `<servicePrincipalName>` and change the value from MyDomain\Me to host/localhost in the client configuration file.

Message-Level Security

Message-level security ensures confidentiality of messages by encrypting and signing messages before sending them out over the transport. This way, only the parties who know how to decrypt the message can read them.

In some scenarios, message-level security can provide a longer confidentiality lifetime than transport-level security. A common example involves intermediaries. For instance, when a message is sent from a client to a service, what if the message is actually sent to an intermediary for queuing or routing rather than the ultimate recipient endpoint? Transport-level security would ensure confidentiality up until the intermediary but not further. After the intermediary, the client loses control of the confidentiality because encryption was used only until the intermediary. By using message-level security, the intermediary can read header information but not the contents of the message. Only the intended recipient, whose public key was used to encrypt the message, can decrypt the message with the corresponding private key and access its contents. In this way, confidentiality is maintained end-to-end.

Like transport-level security, message-level security is based on X.509 certificates, though custom implementations are possible. The service must have a certificate installed so that a client can send an encrypted message to the service to initiate communication. This is necessary when negotiating communication so that if credentials are required, those credentials are protected. By default, most predefined WCF bindings, with the exception of `basicHttpBinding` and `netNamedPipeBinding`, use message-level encryption. This helps to ensure that default WCF communications are secure.

Authenticating with `wsHttpBinding`

The `wsHttpBinding` uses message-level security. It uses the WS-Security protocol to send the encrypted messages between client and service over the HTTP transport channel. You do not need to configure HTTP.SYS or IIS to support SSL, because WS-Security enables secure communication on any protocol. Because of this, the service endpoint and its MEX sibling can be on the same port, making secure IIS hosting very simple. A potential disadvantage of `wsHttpBinding` is that because it uses port 80 rather than 443 for SSL, it can be more difficult to use hardware-based encryption accelerators.

The `wsHttpBinding` binding supports numerous methods for client authentication. The default is Windows authentication, but other options available include including None, Basic, and Certificate.

Windows Authentication

Listing 8.13 shows `wsHttpBinding` being used to secure messages. Note that only one base address is present, because an SSL channel isn't needed as it is with transport-level security. By default, `wsHttpBinding` uses Windows authentication for transport security. Therefore, this configuration would work well on an intranet where both client and service belong to the same Windows domain, but it will not work on the Internet or across untrusted Windows machines.

LISTING 8.13 Encryption with `wsHttpBinding` and Windows Authentication

```
<system.serviceModel>
  <services>
    <service name="EffectiveWCF.StockService"
             behaviorConfiguration="MyBehavior">
      <host>
        <baseAddresses>
          <add baseAddress="http://localhost:8000/EffectiveWCF" />
        </baseAddresses>
      </host>
      <endpoint address=""
                binding="wsHttpBinding"
                contract="EffectiveWCF.IStockService" />
      <endpoint address="mex"
                binding="mexHttpBinding"
                contract="IMetadataExchange" />
    </service>
  </services>
  <behaviors>
    <serviceBehaviors>
      <behavior name="MyBehavior">
        <serviceMetadata httpGetEnabled="true" />
      </behavior>
    </serviceBehaviors>
  </behaviors>
</system.serviceModel>
```

No Authentication

If you don't want any client authentication, specify None for the `client-CredentialType` attribute. Listing 8.14 shows the binding configuration used to specify no client authentication.

LISTING 8.14 Encryption with `wsHttpBinding` and No Client Authentication

```
<system.serviceModel>
  <services>
    <service name="EffectiveWCF.StockService"
             behaviorConfiguration="MyBehavior">
      <host>
```

```
              <baseAddresses>
                <add baseAddress="http://localhost:8000/EffectiveWCF" />
              </baseAddresses>
            </host>
            <endpoint address=""
                      binding="wsHttpBinding"
                      bindingConfiguration="MyBinding"
                      contract="EffectiveWCF.IStockService" />
          </service>
        </services>
        <bindings>
          <wsHttpBinding>
            <binding name="MyBinding">
              <security mode="Message">
                <transport clientCredentialType="None"/>
              </security >
            </binding>
          </wsHttpBinding>
        </bindings>
      </system.serviceModel>
```

Certificate Authentication

Using certificates for authentication with the wsHttpBinding binding ensures a good reach for secure Internet applications. Configuring certificate-based authentication is similar to other authentication schemes at the message level.

Listing 8.15 shows a service configuration file that uses certificate-based authentication. There are a few points worth noting. First, the service is configured to require client certificates by using the clientCredentialType in the wsHttpBinding binding. Second, the server's certificate is specified in the <serviceCredential> node. This is necessary so that the client can encrypt messages with the server's public key. Third, the service is configured to bypass verifying the certification path of the client's certificates by specifying PeerTrust as the certificationValidationMode. This is necessary when working with certification generated by MakeCert.exe, rather than real certificates obtained or generated from a trusted authority.

LISTING 8.15 Service Configuration for Client Certificate Authentication

```
<system.serviceModel>
  <services>
    <service name="EffectiveWCF.StockService"
             behaviorConfiguration="MyBehavior">
```

LISTING 8.15 continued

```
      <host>
        <baseAddresses>
          <add baseAddress="http://localhost:8000/EffectiveWCF" />
        </baseAddresses>
      </host>
      <endpoint address=""
                binding="wsHttpBinding"
                bindingConfiguration="MyBinding"
                contract="EffectiveWCF.IStockService" />
    </service>
  </services>

  <behaviors>
    <serviceBehaviors>
      <behavior name="MyBehavior">
        <serviceMetadata httpGetEnabled="true" />
        <serviceCredentials>
          <serviceCertificate findValue="localhost"
                  storeLocation="LocalMachine" storeName="My"
                  x509FindType="FindBySubjectName"/>
          <clientCertificate>
            <authentication certificateValidationMode="PeerTrust"/>
          </clientCertificate>
        </serviceCredentials>
      </behavior>
    </serviceBehaviors>
  </behaviors>

  <bindings>
    <wsHttpBinding>
      <binding name="MyBinding">
        <security mode="Message">
        <message clientCredentialType="Certificate"/>
        </security>
      </binding>
    </wsHttpBinding>
  </bindings>
</system.serviceModel>
```

To communicate with a service that requires certificate-based authentication, clients must attach a certificate to each message. This can be done in code or in configuration. If done in configuration, the configuration file generated by svcutil must be modified to include the certificates. Specifically, an endpoint behavior must be added in which the client certificate is specified. And if nontrusted certificates are used, the behavior must also indicate that PeerTrust should be used for the certificate validation method.

Listing 8.16 shows an updated client-side configuration file that attaches a certificate to messages.

LISTING 8.16 Client Configuration for Certificate Authentication

```xml
<?xml version="1.0" encoding="utf-8"?>
<configuration>
    <system.serviceModel>
        <bindings>
            <wsHttpBinding>
                <binding name="WSHttpBinding_IStockService"
                    .
                    .
                    <security mode="Message">
                        <transport clientCredentialType="Windows"
                                proxyCredentialType="None"
                                realm="" />
                        <message clientCredentialType="Certificate"
                                negotiateServiceCredential="true"
                                algorithmSuite="Default"
                                establishSecurityContext="true" />
                    </security>
                </binding>
            </wsHttpBinding>
        </bindings>
        <client>
            <endpoint address="http://localhost:8000/EffectiveWCF"
                    binding="wsHttpBinding"
                    bindingConfiguration="WSHttpBinding_IStockService"
                    contract="IStockService"
                    behaviorConfiguration="ClientCert"
                name="WSHttpBinding_IStockService">
                <identity>
                    <certificate encodedValue=
"AwAAAAEAAAAUAAAAHbe21KJYGbmqCcjq7JJ1AH1WLc8gAAAAAQAAAL
0BAAAwggG5MIIBY6ADAgECAhAN4tyIi6rOqEYmrBcPIOHPMA0GCSqGS
Ib3DQEBBAUAMBYxFDASBgNVBAMTC1Jvb3QgQWdlbmN5MB4XDTA3MDky
ODIyMzgxOVoXDTM5MTIzMTIzNTk1OVowFDESMBAGA1UEAxMJbG9jYWx
ob3N0MIGfMA0GCSqGSIb3DQEBAQUAA4GNADCBiQKBgQCwYocYLHnP+c
hgEurathCfwIxGhqL86lOdbEMuf1dfYjgkAhUBmkwVMhH8TVxyZkujp
09FKprT/beuzWmZVRjucaa/4yzOTsbrma0NGPI8V31Z+TYcU9zhNXn9
4d5eNH9Bc7QOhgwlRbl74Il8iPC9WGEB1V1PS/KYoYyCqNC8AwIDAQA
Bo0swSTBHBgNVHQEEQDA+gBAS5AktBh0dTwCNYSHcFmRjoRgwFjEUMB
IGA1UEAxMLUm9vdCBBZ2VuY3mCEAY3bACqAGSSKEc+41KpcNfQwDQYJK
oZIhvcNAQEEBQADQQB+lCX4+Jk8L6NSQ8YjR51mkFSu6u3XZst/j5wq
gPIukU812/GEE4N/b8jXIXo6hyQqpvl9HKXnlTmYNivwXH2Q" />
                </identity>
            </endpoint>
        </client>
```

LISTING 8.16 continued

```
<behaviors>
  <endpointBehaviors>
    <behavior name="ClientCert">
      <clientCredentials>
        <serviceCertificate>
          <authentication certificateValidationMode="PeerTrust"/>
        </serviceCertificate>
        <clientCertificate
         findValue="MyClientCert"
         storeLocation="CurrentUser"
         storeName="My"
         x509FindType="FindBySubjectName"/>
      </clientCredentials>
    </behavior>
  </endpointBehaviors>
</behaviors>
</system.serviceModel>
</configuration>
```

The client-side certificate can also be added to the service description in code. The client-side code looks up the certificate in the local certificate store and adds it to the service description via the proxy before making calls to the service. WCF will attach the certificate to each message sent to the service. Listing 8.10 shows the client-side code necessary to do this.

When svcutil is used to generate the client-side configuration from a service with no client authentication, it inserts an `<identity>` element in the endpoint definition of the service description. This element contains the signature of the service from which the configuration was generated. At runtime, this signature is checked against the identity of the running service. If the client attempts to communicate with a service with a different signature, an error will be thrown:

```
"The expected identity is 'identity(http://schemas.xmlsoap.org/ws/2005/05/
identity/right/possessproperty: http://schemas.xmlsoap.org/ws/2005/05/
identity/claims/thumbprint)' for the 'http://localhost:8000/EffectiveWCF'
target endpoint."
```

Securing Services with Windows Integrated Security

In this section, we'll focus on the issues and opportunities faced when deploying and consuming services internally to an organization or other trusted environment. As the service may be called by another machine on a Windows network, we can take advantage of shared authentication and authorization systems that are not natively available for Internet-based deployments.

Because we are on a local network, we can take advantage of binding types, such as TCP (NetTcpBinding), and on the same machine, named pipes (NetNamedPipeBinding), to improve performance and efficiency. We can also leverage reliability mechanisms such as MSMQ (via the NetMsmqBinding).

Section Examples Introduction

The examples in this section are modeled to reflect having WCF-based services and callers communicating over a LAN behind a corporate firewall. We follow the basic model of having a contract/implementation class library, host console application (SampleHost), and client console application (ClientConsole). The topology is shown in Figure 8.2, where the client, host, and other resources such as the database are all behind a corporate firewall separating communications from the open Internet.

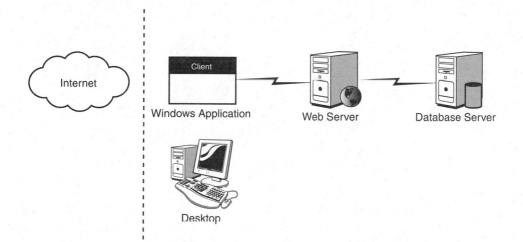

FIGURE 8.2 Services over corporate LAN with Windows application

The service implementation is SampleService and has an ISamples.cs defining three simple operations, GetSecretCode, GetMemberCode, and GetPublicCode, as shown in Listing 8.17.

LISTING 8.17 ISamples.cs Service Contract Interface

```
using System.ServiceModel;

namespace SampleService
{
    [ServiceContract]
    public interface ISamples
    {
        [OperationContract]
        string GetSecretCode();
        [OperationContract]
        string GetMemberCode();
        [OperationContract]
        string GetPublicCode();
    }
}
}
```

The ISamples interface is implemented in the Samples.cs class file shown in Listing 8.18.

LISTING 8.18 Samples.cs Service Implementation Class

```
using System;
using System.Security.Principal;
using System.ServiceModel;
using System.Threading;

namespace SampleService
{
    public class Samples : ISamples
    {
        public string GetSecretCode()
        {
            DisplaySecurityDetails();
            return "The Secret Code";
        }

        public string GetMemberCode()
        {
            DisplaySecurityDetails();
            return "The Member-Only Code";
        }

        public string GetPublicCode()
```

```
        {
            DisplaySecurityDetails();
            return "The Public Code";
        }

        private static void DisplaySecurityDetails()
        {
            Console.WriteLine("Windows Identity = " +
➥WindowsIdentity.GetCurrent().Name);
            Console.WriteLine("Thread CurrentPrincipal Identity = " +
➥Thread.CurrentPrincipal.Identity.Name);
            Console.WriteLine("ServiceSecurityContext Primary Identity
➥= " + ServiceSecurityContext.Current.PrimaryIdentity.Name);
            Console.WriteLine("ServiceSecurityContext Windows Identity
➥= " + ServiceSecurityContext.Current.WindowsIdentity.Name);
        }
    }
}
```

We have also created two local test accounts in Windows to be used in the next few examples. Use the Computer Management console and open the Local Users and Groups node. Under Users, create two accounts. In our case, we created Peter Admin (username "peter") and Jessica Member (username "jessica").

Authenticating Users with Windows Credentials

Let's begin by looking at the default behavior for a TCP-based service using Windows credentials for authentication. The service has been configured with NetTcpBinding, as shown in Listing 8.19. Note that we have also enabled metadata exposure for proxy generation.

LISTING 8.19 Service Configuration for TCP with Default Security Settings

```xml
<?xml version="1.0" encoding="utf-8" ?>
<configuration>
  <system.serviceModel>
    <services>
      <service behaviorConfiguration="ServiceBehavior"
               name="SampleService.Samples">
        <endpoint address="" binding="netTcpBinding" name="netTcp"
                  contract="SampleService.ISamples" />
        <endpoint address="mex" binding="mexHttpBinding" name="mex"
                  contract="IMetadataExchange" />
```

LISTING 8.19 continued

```
        <host>
          <baseAddresses>
            <add baseAddress="http://localhost:8080/Samples" />
            <add baseAddress="net.tcp://localhost:8090/Samples" />
          </baseAddresses>
        </host>
      </service>
    </services>
    <behaviors>
      <serviceBehaviors>
        <behavior name="ServiceBehavior" >
          <serviceMetadata httpGetEnabled="true" />
        </behavior>
      </serviceBehaviors>
    </behaviors>
  </system.serviceModel>
</configuration>
```

The ClientConsole application simply creates an instance of the generated proxy class and makes calls sequentially to each operation, shown in Listing 8.20.

LISTING 8.20 ClientConsole Application Calling SampleService via TCP

```
using System;

namespace ClientConsole
{
    class Program
    {
        static void Main(string[] args)
        {
            Console.WriteLine("Press ENTER to make service calls");
            Console.ReadLine();

            Samples.SamplesClient proxy =
                    new Samples.SamplesClient("netTcp");

            try
            {
                Console.WriteLine(proxy.GetPublicCode());
                Console.WriteLine(proxy.GetMemberCode());
                Console.WriteLine(proxy.GetSecretCode());
            }
            catch (Exception e)
```

```
        {
            Console.WriteLine("Exception = " + e.Message);
        }

        Console.ReadLine();
        }
    }
}
```

When `ClientConsole` is run against the `SampleHost`, each call is made successfully and the `SampleHost` writes identity details to its console (via the `DisplaySecurityDetails` method). All identities are reported as the Windows user running the `ClientConsole` application. This is expected because we haven't introduced any other identities yet.

Specifying Alternative Identities

Generated WCF proxies support a mechanism for specifying alternative credentials to services. This can be useful in a variety of scenarios. For example, if a client application supports multiple user identities, those identities can be supplied at runtime by the client through the proxy so the service can determine which actions may be taken by the current user.

Using the `Samples.SamplesClient` proxy, we supply the username and password for the "peter" account we created earlier, as shown in Listing 8.21.

LISTING 8.21 Providing Alternative Credentials via the Client-Generated Proxy

```
using System;
using System.Net;

namespace ClientConsole
{
    class Program
    {
        static void Main(string[] args)
        {
            Console.WriteLine("Press ENTER to make service calls");
            Console.ReadLine();

            Samples.SamplesClient proxy =
                    new Samples.SamplesClient("netTcp");
```

LISTING 8.21 continued

```
        proxy.ClientCredentials.Windows.ClientCredential =
            new NetworkCredential("MACHINENAME\\peter", "p@ssw0rd1");

        try
        {
            Console.WriteLine(proxy.GetPublicCode());
            Console.WriteLine(proxy.GetMemberCode());
            Console.WriteLine(proxy.GetSecretCode());
        }
        catch (Exception e)
        {
            Console.WriteLine("Exception = " + e.Message);
        }

        Console.ReadLine();
    }
  }
 }
```

Running the application now results in all three services being called successfully, but the console `DisplaySecurityDetails` method shows us that while the host identity (`WindowsIdentity.GetCurrent().Name`) remains as the system user, the other displays of identity show MACHINENAME\peter. WCF has automatically mapped the credentials we supplied on the client side into the security context and thread identity.

> **■ NOTE**   Non-Windows Usernames and Passwords
>
> It is possible to provide basic usernames and passwords that are not specific to Windows. Certain bindings, such as `WsHttpBinding`, support this option (see Table 8.1 for a list of binding options). To enable this, configure message security with `clientCredentialType="UserName"`.
>
> In these cases, however, WCF will require transport security (for example, a certificate) to protect the confidentiality and integrity of those credentials on the wire. Certificates were described earlier in this chapter.

Authorizing Users with Windows Credentials

We've shown that we can identify users via Windows credentials; now let's focus on determining access permissions (authorization) for the same scenario. To begin, we'll use the standard security `PrincipalPermission-Attribute`. This attribute can be used to decorate members and restrict or permit access to callers.

To begin, let's decorate methods with attributes to limit access only to Peter (`GetSecretCode`) and both Peter and Jessica (`GetMemberCode`). Add the following to `GetSecretCode` (where `MACHINENAME` should be replaced with your own system's name):

```
[PrincipalPermission(SecurityAction.Demand, Name = @"MACHINENAME\peter")]
```

Now add the following to `GetMemberCode`:

```
[PrincipalPermission(SecurityAction.Demand, Name = @"MACHINENAME\peter")]
[PrincipalPermission(SecurityAction.Demand, Name = @"MACHINENAME\jessica")]
```

Run the service and client applications, ensuring Peter remains specified in the proxy's ClientCredentials property. The result should be that all three service operations are called successfully. Now change "peter" to "jessica" in the client code, updating the password if necessary. Running the client this time should result in an Access Is Denied exception for the `GetSecretCode` method.

Certainly this approach works and provides a mechanism for authenticating and authorizing known Windows accounts for specific service operations. However, for almost all production systems, you will need an easier way to configure and maintain access lists for a variety of users.

The `PrincipalPermissionAttribute` also supports a `Role` parameter that lets us specify a specific Windows group rather than a named user. Before proceeding, use the Computer Management console to create temporary Sample Admins and Sample Members local Windows groups, adding Peter to the former and both Peter and Jessica to the latter. Now, adjust the attributes as shown in Listing 8.22.

LISTING 8.22 Specifying Access by Security Role

```
using System;
using System.Security.Permissions;
using System.Security.Principal;
using System.ServiceModel;
using System.Threading;
```

LISTING 8.22 continued

```
namespace SampleService
{
    public class Samples : ISamples
    {
        [PrincipalPermission(SecurityAction.Demand,
                             Role="Sample Admins")]
        public string GetSecretCode()
        {...}

        [PrincipalPermission(SecurityAction.Demand,
                             Role="Sample Members")]
        public string GetMemberCode()
        {...}

        public string GetPublicCode()
        {...}

        private static void DisplaySecurityDetails() {...}
    }
}
```

Running the client again should produce similar results, but now you can rely on membership in Windows groups to determine which users are authorized to make calls to WCF operations.

> **■ NOTE   Using Native Windows Groups**
>
> To use the standard Windows groups as roles with the `PrincipalPermissionAttribute`, prepend the word BUILTIN as a machine name before the group name. For example, the Administrators group is referenced by `@"BUILTIN\Administrators"` and Users by `@"BUILTIN\Users"`. Also note that, in C#, you'll need the @ symbol to unescape the embedded backslashes, or else you'll need to double the backslash to avoid a compilation error.

Authorization Using AzMan

Windows Authorization Manager (AzMan) is a system that provides centralized (and therefore easier to maintain) role-based authorization services to applications, including WCF, based on policies defined in authorization stores. AzMan features an MMC-based utility for managing both the authorization stores and related access levels. The runtime of Authorization

Manager is independent of the physical authorization stores, which may be based on SQL Server, Active Directory, ADAM, or XML, depending on the operating system used.

In this section, we'll use a simple XML authorization store to configure role-based access to our prior service example. To work with Authorization Manager, use the Microsoft Management Console (MMC) and ensure Authorization Manager has been added via the File, Add/Remove Snap-In option.

To create an authorization store, you must be in Developer mode (versus Administrator mode), which enables access to all features. From the Action menu, choose Options, then Developer Mode. In Developer mode, right-click the Authorization Manager node and choose New Authorization Store, which will open a dialog similar to Figure 8.3.

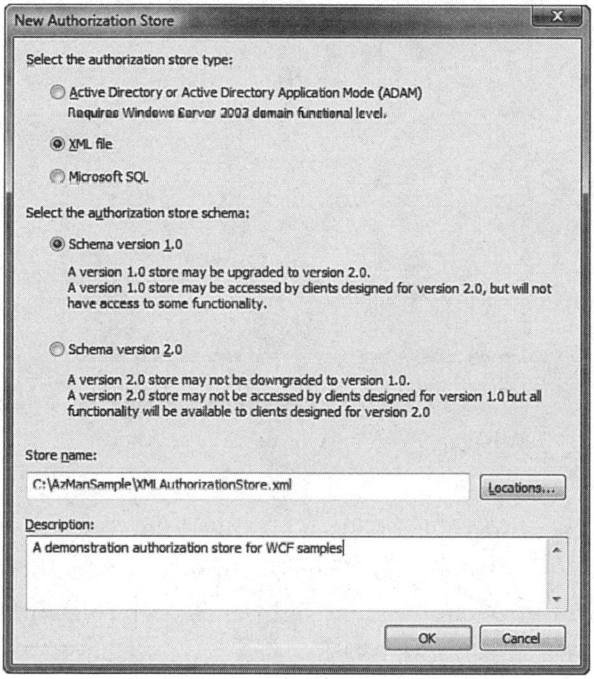

FIGURE 8.3 Configuring an XML Authorization store

For our example, choose XML file, leave the schema version as 1.0, and give the store a name and description. Note that, depending on your operating system, you may also use Active Directory, ADAM, or SQL Server.

Having created the store, ensure that the XML file is highlighted, then right-click and choose New Application. Name the application **AzManDemo** and click OK.

To define the roles to which we'll assign user permissions, expand the AzManDemo node in the left pane, and then expand Definitions. Right-click Role Definitions and choose New Role Definition. We'll create two roles, Member Role and Admin Role; however, for the latter, click Add on the New Role Definition dialog and choose the Member Role to include that role as part of the Admin Role definition, shown in Figure 8.4.

FIGURE 8.4 Creating a role definition with Authorization Manager

To assign users to roles, right-click the Role Assignments node and choose New Role Assignment. The Admin and Member roles should appear beneath Role Assignments. Right-click each role and choose Assign Users and Groups, then From Windows and Active Directory. Add the sample "Peter" account to Admin Role and "Jessica" to Member Role. The final configuration should appear similar to Figure 8.5.

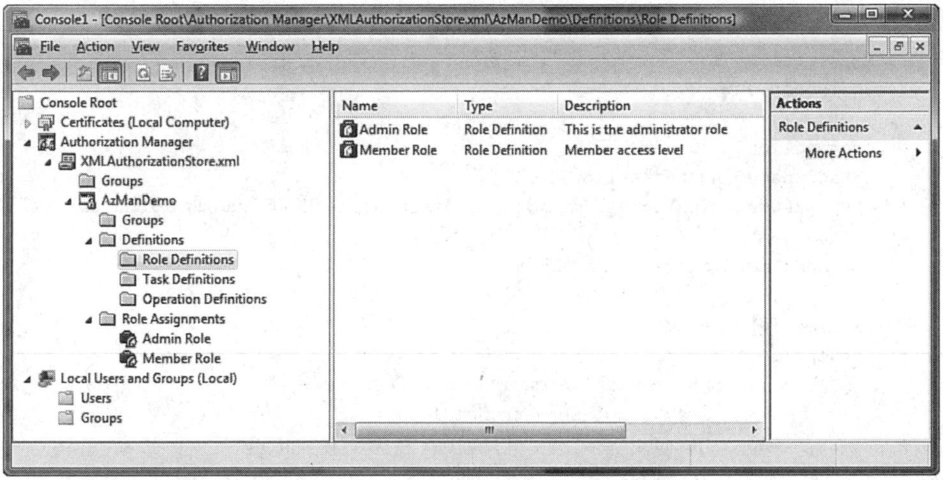

FIGURE 8.5 Authorization Manager showing example configuration

Now that Authorization Manager has been configured with a role and user assignment, we can tell WCF to leverage AzMan for authorization. The flexibility of WCF combined with the capability to access the AzMan runtime via the AzRoles assembly gives us a number of options. For example, we could create a custom `ServiceAuthorizationManager` and manually call the AzRoles assembly for role and operation verification. However, by leveraging existing ASP.NET 2.0 functionality, we can integrate AzMan authorization and WCF with less effort.

The role-based provider system of ASP.NET is useful to us here because WCF can automatically integrate with its services and because there is a native `AuthorizationStoreRoleProvider` that we can use to communicate with our AzMan-created authorization store.

To enable use of Authorization Manager, in the `SampleHost` project's `App.config` file, we need to add the `<roleManager>` node under `<system.Web>`. The service's behavior needs to include a `<serviceAuthorization>` to enable use of ASP.NET roles with the `AuthorizationStoreRoleProvider`. We also need to specify the path to the XML authorization store in the `<connectionStrings>` node. These settings are shown in Listing 8.23.

LISTING 8.23 Service Configuration for TCP with Authorization Manager Integration

```xml
<?xml version="1.0" encoding="utf-8" ?>
<configuration>

  <connectionStrings>
    <add name="AuthorizationStore"
         connectionString="msxml://C:\AzManSample\XMLAuthorizationStore.xml"
    />
  </connectionStrings>

  <system.serviceModel>
    <services>
      <service behaviorConfiguration="ServiceBehavior"
               name="SampleService.Samples">
        <endpoint address="mex" binding="mexHttpBinding"
                  bindingConfiguration=""
          name="mex" contract="IMetadataExchange" />
        <endpoint address="" binding="netTcpBinding" bindingConfiguration=""
          name="netTcp" contract="SampleService.ISamples" />
        <host>
          <baseAddresses>
            <add baseAddress="http://localhost:8080/Samples" />
            <add baseAddress="net.tcp://localhost:8090/Samples" />
          </baseAddresses>
        </host>
      </service>
    </services>
    <behaviors>
      <serviceBehaviors>
        <behavior name="ServiceBehavior" >
          <serviceAuthorization
              principalPermissionMode="UseAspNetRoles"
              roleProviderName="AuthorizationStoreRoleProvider" />
          <serviceMetadata httpGetEnabled="true" />
        </behavior>
      </serviceBehaviors>
    </behaviors>
  </system.serviceModel>

  <system.web>
    <roleManager
        defaultProvider="AuthorizationStoreRoleProvider"
        enabled="true"
        cacheRolesInCookie="true"
        cookieName=".ASPROLES"
        cookiePath="/"
        cookieProtection="All"
        cookieRequireSSL="false"
        cookieSlidingExpiration="true"
```

```
               cookieTimeout="30"
          >
          <providers>
            <clear />
            <add
              name="AuthorizationStoreRoleProvider"
              type="System.Web.Security.AuthorizationStoreRoleProvider"
              connectionStringName="AuthorizationStore"
              applicationName="AzManDemo" />
          </providers>
        </roleManager>
      </system.web>
    </configuration>
```

Finally, to bind operations to specific Authorization Manger groups, modify the `PrincipalPermisionAttribute` to reference the role definitions contained in the authorization store. Modifying the Windows groups example from before, change the role names from Sample Admins and Sample Members to **Admin Role** and **Member Role**, respectively, matching the names given via the AzMan utility.

```
[PrincipalPermission(SecurityAction.Demand, Role="Admin Role")]
[PrincipalPermission(SecurityAction.Demand, Role="Member Role")]
```

Running the application again for each user (Peter and Jessica) should again result in Peter having unrestricted access while Jessica is unable to call the `GetSecretCode` method. However, now that AzMan is configured for access, we can use the convenient tools and authentication stores to maintain the roles, users, tasks, and operations for our application with limited modification to the service code itself.

Impersonating Users

By default, WCF services access local and remote resources using the credentials under which the service host is executing. It is up to the service to authenticate callers to verify who they are, then perform authorization checks to ensure that they can access other resources (which would be accessed as the host identity). When running services that receive Windows credentials, we have another option called *impersonation*.

Impersonation is the process by which an alternative credential is used for execution of program logic. A service may impersonate a caller by assuming that caller's identity. This is typically for the duration of a single call, but the impersonation token could be retained and reused by the service. The thread under which the call is executing is assigned to the impersonated identity, and operations are performed under the authorization and roles of that assumed identity.

Impersonation is important because, by adopting the identity of a caller, the service is only able to access resources for which the caller has permissions. By running under the privileges of the caller, it is easier to ensure that only the data and resources appropriate for that user are accessed.

Impersonation is an agreement between the service and its callers. Higher levels of impersonation require permission from both the client and, in some cases, system permissions on the host machine. To begin, let's configure the service code to support impersonation. This is done via the `OperationBehaviorAttribute`, which has an `Impersonation` parameter. This parameter is given a selection from the `ImpersonationOption` enumeration. An example of this is shown in Listing 8.24.

LISTING 8.24 Requiring Impersonation via the `OperationBehaviorAttribute`

```
[OperationBehavior(Impersonation = ImpersonationOption.Required)]
public string GetSecretCode()
{
    DisplaySecurityDetails();
    return "The Secret Code";
}
```

`ImpersonationOption` can be `NotAllowed`, which disables impersonation, `Required`, which demands that the client agree to be impersonated (otherwise the call will fail), and `Allowed`, which will use impersonation if agreed to by the client, but will continue without impersonation if the client does not agree, although doing so is uncommon and typically avoided.

It is possible to configure `OperationBehavior` for impersonation on all necessary operations, but you may also enable impersonation for all operations in configuration. Listing 8.25 shows how to use the `ImpersonateCallerForAllOperations` option, which is `false` by default.

LISTING 8.25 Enabling Impersonation via ImpersonateCallerForAllOperations

```xml
<?xml version="1.0" encoding="utf-8" ?>
<configuration>
  <system.serviceModel>
    <services>
      <service behaviorConfiguration="ServiceBehavior"
               name="SampleService.Samples">
        <endpoint address="mex" binding="mexHttpBinding"
                  bindingConfiguration=""
          name="mex" contract="IMetadataExchange" />
        <endpoint address="" binding="netTcpBinding" bindingConfiguration=""
          name="netTcp" contract="SampleService.ISamples" />
        <host>
          <baseAddresses>
            <add baseAddress="http://localhost:8080/Samples" />
            <add baseAddress="net.tcp://localhost:8090/Samples" />
          </baseAddresses>
        </host>
      </service>
    </services>
    <behaviors>
      <serviceBehaviors>
        <behavior name="ServiceBehavior" >
          <serviceAuthorization
            principalPermissionMode="UseWindowsGroups"
            impersonateCallerForAllOperations="true" />
          <serviceMetadata httpGetEnabled="true" />
        </behavior>
      </serviceBehaviors>
    </behaviors>
  </system.serviceModel>
</configuration>
```

> **NOTE Impersonation via Code**
>
> It is also possible to invoke impersonation manually through code. The WindowsIdentity exposed via ServiceSecurityContext.Current features an Impersonate method that can be invoked to activate impersonation. Ensure you have first verified that the WindowsIdentity is not null before attempting the call.

Next, the client (in cases where full impersonation or delegation is necessary) must explicitly designate that it supports impersonation. This can be done via configuration or code. For configuration, ensure that the client has settings similar to those shown in Listing 8.26.

LISTING 8.26 Specifying SupportedImpersonation Level in Client Configuration

```
<?xml version="1.0" encoding="utf-8" ?>
<configuration>
  <system.serviceModel>
    <behaviors>
      <endpointBehaviors>
        <behavior name="EndBehave">
          <clientCredentials>
            <windows allowedImpersonationLevel="Impersonation" />
          </clientCredentials>
        </behavior>
      </endpointBehaviors>
    </behaviors>
    <bindings>
      <netTcpBinding>...</netTcpBinding>
    </bindings>
    <client>
      <endpoint address="net.tcp://localhost:8090/Samples"
          behaviorConfiguration="EndBehave"
          binding="netTcpBinding"
          bindingConfiguration="netTcp"
          contract="ClientConsole.Samples.ISamples"
          name="netTcp">
        <identity>...</identity>
      </endpoint>
    </client>
  </system.serviceModel>
</configuration>
```

You can also specify a specific impersonation level via the service proxy in the client code, as shown in Listing 8.27.

LISTING 8.27 Specifying Impersonation via Client-Side Proxy

```
using System;
using System.Net;
using System.Security.Principal;

namespace ClientConsole
{
    class Program
    {
```

```
static void Main(string[] args)
{
    Samples.SamplesClient proxy =
        new Samples.SamplesClient("netTcp");
    proxy.ClientCredentials.Windows.AllowedImpersonationLevel =
        TokenImpersonationLevel.Delegation;


        ...

    }
  }
}
</configuration>
```

The AllowedImpersonationLevel property, whether set in configuration or code, supports the following options from the TokenImpersonation-Level enumeration:

- **None.** No impersonation performed.
- **Anonymous.** Impersonation is used for access checks, but the service code does not know who the caller is. Can be used only for same-machine bindings such as NetNamedPipeBinding.
- **Identify.** No impersonation is performed, but the service code knows who the caller is and can make access decisions based on that identity.
- **Impersonate.** The service can identify the caller as with Identify, but in this mode, impersonation can be used for resources on the same machine.
- **Delegate.** The same as Impersonate; however, the credentials can be used for network-based resource access.

Use caution when enabling impersonation, and consider the effects of having part of the overall system compromised by attackers. For example, if you enable delegation (in this case via configuration and Active Directory permissions, which by default would not allow this scenario,) and a user with domain administrator access calls your service (via a client that has opted to enable delegation), should your service logic be compromised, those administrator credentials could be used to access arbitrary resources on the domain with elevated permissions. Clearly, the risks are high, and you should invest time to fully understand the options around impersonation and the ability to deny permissions via the `PrincipalPermissionAttribute` introduced earlier.

If you understand the risks, impersonation remains a powerful concept that can be used to effectively manage access to resources by service code according to the permissions of callers to that service.

Securing Services over the Internet

This section will focus on securing services over the Internet. Figure 8.6 shows a Windows application that accesses services over the Internet. This figure begins to highlight the Software + Services model from Microsoft, where you have client applications that run on the desktop that accesses services over the Internet. These types of applications need mechanisms for managing users that come from the Internet. This includes authenticating and authorizing users that come from the Internet. The typical approach for this style of application is to use a database to store usernames, passwords, and roles. This is done for a variety of reasons, including account management, security scope, and ease of backup and restore. ASP.NET 2.0 offers these capabilities through application-level services such as Membership and Role-Based Authorization. WCF integrates with these application-level services for authentication and authorization of users. This means that developers can reuse several of the out-of-the-box providers available in ASP.NET to manage access to WCF services.

We will look at a sample application to understand the integration with ASP.NET. This application just happens to be a Web application built using ASP.NET. The use of these capabilities is not tied solely to Web applications and could have easily been a Windows desktop application. Figure 8.7 shows a sample application built using ASP.NET that will be used to highlight features in this section. This application displays a list of games and allows users to log in and provide reviews on their favorite games. The premise behind this application is that both anonymous and registered users can view the games and their reviews. Only registered users that are logged in can add reviews, and only administrators can moderate reviews. More details about this application will be given in Chapter 13, "Programmable Web."

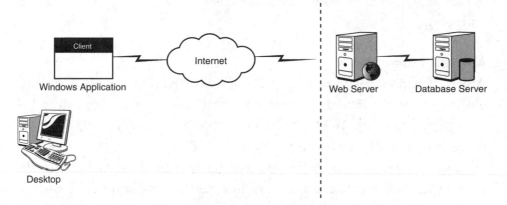

FIGURE 8.6 Services over Internet with Windows application

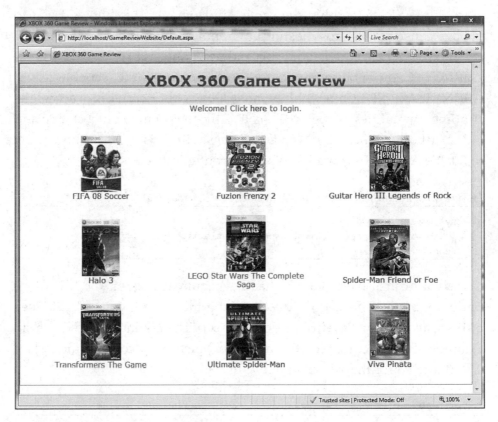

FIGURE 8.7 Sample Internet application

Because this is a Web application, we will also look into Forms Authentication and how to authenticate requests using the Forms Authentication

HTTP cookie that is based to a service hosted over an HTTP-based endpoint.

ASP.NET Integration

ASP.NET and WCF support slightly different activation and hosting models. WCF was designed to support activation of services using a variety of transports, such as TCP, HTTP, and MSMQ, whereas ASP.NET was designed primarily for activation over the HTTP protocol. WCF was also designed to support multiple different hosting models, including self-hosting as well as hosting inside of Internet Information Services (IIS). When hosted inside of IIS, WCF can either receive messages directly or using an ASP.NET Compatibility mode. The default mode is to run side-by-side with ASP.NET within the same AppDomain. This allows WCF to behave consistently across hosting environments and transport protocols. If you are not concerned about this and need only HTTP, WCF can leave ASP.NET Compatibility mode to access some of the capabilities of ASP.NET. ASP.NET Compatibility mode allows WCF services to access the runtime capabilities of ASP.NET, such as the `HttpContext` object, File and URL Authorization, and `HTTPModule` Extensibility. Listing 8.28 shows how to enable ASP.NET compatibility within configuration.

LISTING 8.28 Setting ASP.NET Compatibility Mode (in `web.config`)

```
<system.serviceModel>
  <serviceHostingEnvironment aspNetCompatibilityEnabled="true" />
</configuration>
```

Services can also register whether they require the use of ASP.NET Compatibility mode. This is done by specifying the `AspNetCompatibilityRequirementsAttribute` attribute on the service. Listing 8.29 shows an example of a service that sets this attribute. Much of the code for the service was removed for the sake of brevity.

LISTING 8.29 `ASP.NETCompatibleRequirements` Attribute (in `web.config`)

```
namespace EssentialWCF
{
  [ServiceContract(Namespace="EssentialWCF")]
  [AspNetCompatibilityRequirements(RequirementsMode=
    AspNetCompatibilityRequirementsMode.Required)]
```

```
public class GameReviewService
{
  [OperationContract]
  [WebGet]
  public GameReview[] Reviews(string gameIdAsString)
  {
  }

  [OperationContract]
  [WebInvoke]
  [PrincipalPermission(SecurityAction.Demand, Role = "User")]
  public void AddReview(string gameIdAsString, string comment)
  {
  }
 }
}
```

It is important to understand that ASP.NET Compatibility mode is not always needed. For example, we will be examining how to use the ASP.NET Membership Provider to authenticate access to WCF services. This feature does not require the use of ASP.NET Compatibility mode. However, if you want to be able to access the Principal and Identity of a user from the ASP.NET HttpContext, or use other security-related features such as File and URL Authorization, you will need to use ASP.NET Compatibility mode. In this scenario, WCF services act more like ASP.NET Web Services because they have similar capabilities. One important point is that you should not use ASP.NET Compatibility mode if your intent is to host services outside of IIS or use other transports besides HTTP.

Authentication Using Membership Providers

ASP.NET 2.0 provides a number of services such as Membership, Roles, Profiles, and more. These services are prebuilt frameworks that developers can use without the need for writing additional code. For example, the Membership service provides the capabilities to manage users, including the creation, deletion, and updating of users. ASP.NET also allows for Forms Authentication to use the Membership service to authenticate users for Web applications.

WCF provides a similar mechanism to authenticate user access to services against the Membership services. This capability can be used whether or not there is an ASP.NET Web application to consider. This means that any

ASP.NET Membership service can be used to authenticate access to a WCF service. Because the Membership service provides its own mechanism for managing users, we need to use UserName tokens. Listing 8.30 gives an example of a binding that uses the UserName tokens to authenticate its users. UserName tokens are unencrypted, therefore they need to be encrypted using either transport-level or message-level encryption. This example shows the use of transport-level encryption, which is the more common scenario. It is important to mention that WCF requires the use of encryption in this scenario, so skipping the encryption is not optional.

LISTING 8.30 Use UserName/Password Credentials (in `web.config`)

```
<system.serviceModel>
  <bindings>
    <wsHttpBinding>
      <binding name="MembershipBinding">
        <security mode="TransportWithMessageCredential">
          <message clientCredentialType="UserName"/>
        </security>
      </binding>
    </wsHttpBinding>
  </bindings>
</system.serviceModel>
```

The next step to using the ASP.NET Membership service is to configure a service behavior that specifies username authentication to be performed using a membership provider. We will use the `System.Web.Security.SqlMembershipProvider`, which uses SQL Server as the mechanism for storing and retrieving user information. Listing 8.31 shows how to specify a service behavior that validates users against an ASP.NET Membership Provider.

LISTING 8.31 Service Credentials Using SQL Membership Provider (in `web.config`)

```
<system.serviceModel>
  <behaviors>
    <serviceBehaviors>
      <behavior name="ServiceBehavior">
        <serviceCredentials>
          <userNameAuthentication
            userNamePasswordValidationMode="MembershipProvider"
            membershipProviderName="AspNetSqlMembershipProvider"
          />
```

```
        </serviceCredentials>
      </behavior>
    </serviceBehaviors>
  </behaviors>
</system.serviceModel>
```

Listing 8.31 uses the default ASP.NET Membership Provider for SQL Server. Listing 8.32 shows the default configuration for the ASP.NET Membership Providers in `machine.config`.

LISTING 8.32 Membership Provider Configuration (in `machine.config`)

```
<system.web>
  <processModel autoConfig="true"/>
  <httpHandlers/>
  <membership>
    <providers>
      <add name="AspNetSqlMembershipProvider"
          type="System.Web.Security.SqlMembershipProvider,
➥System.Web, Version=2.0.0.0, Culture=neutral,
➥PublicKeyToken=b03f5f7f11d50a3a"
          connectionStringName="LocalSqlServer"
          enablePasswordRetrieval="false"
          enablePasswordReset="true"
          requiresQuestionAndAnswer="true"
          applicationName="/"
          requiresUniqueEmail="false"
          passwordFormat="Hashed"
          maxInvalidPasswordAttempts="5"
          minRequiredPasswordLength="7"
          minRequiredNonalphanumericCharacters="1"
          passwordAttemptWindow="10"
          passwordStrengthRegularExpression=""/>
    </providers>
  </membership>
</system.web>
```

A common development task is setting up transport encryption using a self-signed certificate. WCF will attempt to validate this certificate and fail with the following error:

```
"Could not establish trust relationship for the SSL/TLS secure channel with
authority 'localhost'."
```

Looking to the inner exception shows that the remote certificate failed validation. The following was the original exception thrown:

```
"The remote certificate is invalid according to the validation procedure."
```

Listing 8.33 shows how to force a validation of a certificate that cannot be validated, such as a self-signed certificate. This code should be implemented by the client and should be used only in development for testing purposes.

LISTING 8.33 Developing Using Self-Signed Certificate

```
private void Window_Loaded(object sender, RoutedEventArgs e)
{
    System.Net.ServicePointManager.ServerCertificateValidationCallback
        += new System.Net.Security.RemoteCertificateValidationCallback(
        RemoteCertValidate);
}

static bool RemoteCertValidate(object sender,
                    X509Certificate cert, X509Chain chain,
                    System.Net.Security.SslPolicyErrors error)
{
    return true;
}
```

Role-Based Authorization Using Role Providers

ASP.NET role-based authorization allows developers to perform authorization checks based on roles. It also uses a provider model, which abstracts the details of user role storage from the application's code. There are several provider models in ASP.NET for roles, including the `SqlRoleProvider`, `WindowsTokenRoleProvider`, and `AuthorizationStoreRoleProvider`. Because we are assuming an Internet-facing application, we will examine how to use the `SqlRoleProvider` to perform authorization checks. There are several steps to using an ASP.NET role provider. The first step is to enable the use of roles. This is done via configuration within either `app.config` or `web.config` using the `roleManager` element.

```
<roleManager enabled ="true" />
```

This allows the application to use roles, but it does not specify which role provider to use. The next step is to configure a service behavior that specifies which role provider to use. Listing 8.34 shows a service behavior that specifies the `principalPermissionMode` and the `roleProviderName` attributes on the `serviceAuthorization` configuration element. The `principalPermissionMode` is used to specify how authorization checks are performed. In this situation we are using `"UseAspNetRoles"`, which means to use ASP.NET roles for authorization checks. We also specify the provider name.

LISTING 8.34 Service Authorization Using ASP.NET Roles

```
<system.serviceModel>
    <behaviors>
        <serviceBehaviors>
            <behavior name="ServiceBehavior">
                <serviceAuthorization
                    principalPermissionMode="UseAspNetRoles"
                    roleProviderName ="AspNetSqlRoleProvider"
                    />
            </behavior>
        </serviceBehaviors>
    </behaviors>
</system.serviceModel>
```

Listing 8.34 uses the default ASP.NET Role Provider for SQL Server. Listing 8.35 shows the default configuration for the ASP.NET Role Providers in `machine.config`.

LISTING 8.35 Role Providers (in `machine.config`)

```
<roleManager>
  <providers>
    <add name="AspNetSqlRoleProvider"
        connectionStringName="LocalSqlServer"
        applicationName="/"
        type="System.Web.Security.SqlRoleProvider,
➥System.Web, Version=2.0.0.0, Culture=neutral,
➥PublicKeyToken=b03f5f7f11d50a3a"
        />
    <add name="AspNetWindowsTokenRoleProvider"
        applicationName="/"
        type="System.Web.Security.WindowsTokenRoleProvider,
➥System.Web, Version=2.0.0.0, Culture=neutral,
➥PublicKeyToken=b03f5f7f11d50a3a"
      />
  </providers>
</roleManager>
```

For ASP.NET Web applications, the typical approach for performing access checks is to call User.IsInRole method. This approach works well for Web pages that often show or hide access to features based on authorization checks, but it does not work well for WCF services. WCF performs authorization checks at the service level using the PrincipalPermissionAttribute attribute. Listing 8.36 shows an example of a service that specifies permission checks. The attributes look to see whether the user is in the Administrator role. If the user does not belong to the role, the user is denied the ability to call the service.

LISTING 8.36 Principal Permission

```
namespace EssentialWCF
{
    [ServiceContract(Namespace="EssentialWCF")]
    [AspNetCompatibilityRequirements(RequirementsMode
        =AspNetCompatibilityRequirementsMode.Allowed)]
    public class GameReviewApprovalService
    {
        [OperationContract]
        [PrincipalPermission(SecurityAction.Demand,
            Role = "Administrator")]
        public void Approve(int gameReviewId, bool approved)
        {
        }

        [OperationContract]
        [PrincipalPermission(SecurityAction.Demand,
            Role = "Administrator")]
        public GameReview[] ReviewsToApprove()
        {
        }
    }
}
```

Using Forms Authentication

All the approaches so far show how services can be accessed over the Internet from a Windows-based application. Figure 8.8 shows a Web application that accesses services over the Internet from the browser. We will now consider how Web applications can access WCF services securely using a Web-centric approach. This means that we want to use standard HTTP approaches for securely accessing our services. This includes using

HTTP cookies for authentication and SSL for encryption. SSL for encryption has been covered earlier in this chapter, so we will focus on the use of HTTP cookies for authentication.

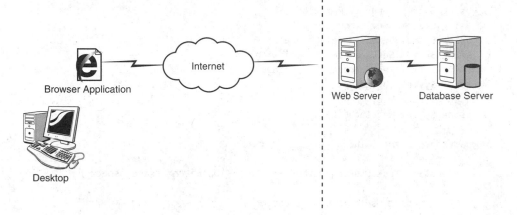

FIGURE 8.8 Services over Internet with Web application

ASP.NET provides a feature known as Forms Authentication, which uses HTTP cookies for authentication. Forms Authentication allows a developer to build a Web application that uses an HTML form for user login. After the user types in the username and password, the form is submitted to the Web server for authentication. After the user is authenticated, an HTTP cookie is sent down to the browser and used as an authentication token. Successive calls from the browser can then use this token to authenticate the user. By default, Forms Authentication works directly with the ASP.NET Membership to perform authentication checks. Using Forms Authentication and Membership, developers can write little or no code to secure their Web applications. This is great for Web applications, but it does nothing to help us for WCF services.

Unfortunately, there is no direct integration between WCF and Forms Authentication at this time. Fortunately, a simple fix solves this problem. Listing 8.37 shows a custom attribute that allows Forms Authentication to be used with a WCF service. This attribute sets the principal on the current thread to the principal specified in the current `HttpContext`. This simple attribute allows for access checks using `PrincipalPermissionAttribute` to work with Forms Authentication.

LISTING 8.37 UseFormsAuthentication Attribute

```
using System;
using System.Collections.ObjectModel;
using System.Data;
using System.Configuration;
using System.Security.Principal;
using System.ServiceModel;
using System.ServiceModel.Channels;
using System.ServiceModel.Description;
using System.ServiceModel.Dispatcher;
using System.Threading;
using System.Web;
using System.Web.Security;

namespace EssentialWCF
{
    public class UseFormsAuthentication : IDispatchMessageInspector
    {
        public UseFormsAuthentication()
        {
        }

        #region IDispatchMessageInspector Members

        public object AfterReceiveRequest(ref Message request,
            IClientChannel channel,
            InstanceContext instanceContext)
        {
            IPrincipal currentUser =
            System.Web.HttpContext.Current.User;

            if ((currentUser is System.Web.Security.RolePrincipal) &&
                (currentUser != Thread.CurrentPrincipal))
                    Thread.CurrentPrincipal = currentUser;

            return null;
        }

        public void BeforeSendReply(ref Message reply,
            object correlationState)
        {
        }

        #endregion
    }

    [AttributeUsage(AttributeTargets.Class)]
    public class UseFormsAuthenticationBehaviorAttribute : Attribute,
                                                IServiceBehavior
```

```
    {
        #region IServiceBehavior Members

        public void AddBindingParameters(
            ServiceDescription serviceDescription,
            ServiceHostBase serviceHostBase,
            Collection<ServiceEndpoint> endpoints,
            BindingParameterCollection bindingParameters)
        {
        }

        public void ApplyDispatchBehavior(
            ServiceDescription serviceDescription,
            ServiceHostBase serviceHostBase)
        {
            foreach (ChannelDispatcher channelDispatch in
                serviceHostBase.ChannelDispatchers)
            {
                foreach (EndpointDispatcher endpointDispatch in
                    channelDispatch.Endpoints)
                {
                endpointDispatch.DispatchRuntime.MessageInspectors.Add(
            new UseFormsAuthentication());
                }
            }
        }

        public void Validate(ServiceDescription serviceDescription,
            ServiceHostBase serviceHostBase)
        {
        }

        #endregion
    }
}
```

Listing 8.38 shows a service that uses the Forms Authentication attribute. It should be mentioned that the attribute is intended to be used with ASP.NET Compatibility mode. The GameReviewService service shown in Listing 8.38 is exposed using the new `webHttpBinding` binding. It allows all users to retrieve reviews on games from the browser, but only authenticated users can add reviews. This binding is used to expose WCF services using a REST/POX style endpoint. It also integrates well with the ASP.NET AJAX Extensions. For more information about these features, refer to Chapter 13.

LISTING 8.38 Services Using UseFormsAuthentication Attribute

```
using System;
using System.Data.Linq;
using System.Linq;
using System.Net;
using System.Security.Permissions;
using System.Security.Principal;
using System.ServiceModel;
using System.ServiceModel.Activation;
using System.ServiceModel.Web;
using System.Threading;

namespace EssentialWCF
{
    [UseFormsAuthenticationBehaviorAttribute]
    [ServiceContract(Namespace="EssentialWCF")]
    [AspNetCompatibilityRequirements(RequirementsMode
        =AspNetCompatibilityRequirementsMode.Required)]
    public class GameReviewService
    {
        public GameReviewService()
        {
        }

        [OperationContract]
        [WebGet]
        public GameReview[] Reviews(string gameIdAsString)
        {
            WebOperationContext wctx = WebOperationContext.Current;
            wctx.OutgoingResponse.Headers.Add(
            HttpResponseHeader.CacheControl,"no-cache");

            int gameId = Convert.ToInt32(gameIdAsString);
            GameReview[] value = null;

            try
            {
                using (GameReviewDataContext dc =
                  new GameReviewDataContext())
                {
                    var query = from r in dc.GameReviews
                                where (r.GameID == gameId) &&
                                      (r.Approved)
                                orderby r.Created descending
                                select r;
                    value = query.ToArray();
                }
            }
            catch
```

```
        {
            wctx.OutgoingResponse.StatusCode =
                System.Net.HttpStatusCode.InternalServerError;
        }

        return value;
    }

    [OperationContract]
    [WebInvoke]
    [PrincipalPermission(SecurityAction.Demand, Role = "User")]
    public void AddReview(string gameIdAsString, string comment)
    {
        string userName = Thread.CurrentPrincipal.Identity.Name;
        int gameId = Convert.ToInt32(gameIdAsString);
        bool bAutomaticApproval =
            Thread.CurrentPrincipal.IsInRole("Administrator");

        using (GameReviewDataContext dc =
            new GameReviewDataContext())
        {
            dc.GameReviews.Add(new GameReview()
            { GameID = gameId,
              Review = comment, Approved = bAutomaticApproval,
              User = userName, Created = System.DateTime.Now });
            dc.SubmitChanges();
        }
    }
  }
 }
}
```

Logging and Auditing

As you've seen in this chapter, there are many options for configuring security with WCF services and client applications. Given so many configuration possibilities, the ability to diagnose authentication and authorization issues is of great importance. In addition, the ability to create audit trails to record the calls (whether successful or not) to the security infrastructure is critically important for many industries, such as banking and health care, and also for companies seeking to maintain compliance with Sarbanes-Oxley and other regulatory requirements.

Fortunately, WCF supports an easy-to-configure mechanism for creating logs and audit trails of the security-related activities involving services.

Security auditing can be enabled via configuration using the ServiceSecurityAuditBehavior as shown in Listing 8.39.

LISTING 8.39 Configuring a Service to Audit Security Events via
ServiceSecurityAuditBehavior

```xml
<?xml version="1.0" encoding="utf-8" ?>
<configuration>
  <system.serviceModel>
    <services>
      <service behaviorConfiguration="ServiceBehavior"
               name="SampleService.Samples">
        <endpoint address="" binding="netTcpBinding" name="netTcp"
                  contract="SampleService.ISamples" />
        <endpoint address="mex" binding="mexHttpBinding" name="mex"
                  contract="IMetadataExchange" />
        <host>...</host>
      </service>
    </services>
    <behaviors>
      <serviceBehaviors>
        <behavior name="ServiceBehavior" >
          <serviceSecurityAudit
            auditLogLocation ="Application"
            messageAuthenticationAuditLevel="SuccessOrFailure"
            serviceAuthorizationAuditLevel="SuccessOrFailure"
            suppressAuditFailure="false" />
          <serviceMetadata httpGetEnabled="true" />
        </behavior>
      </serviceBehaviors>
    </behaviors>
  </system.serviceModel>
</configuration>
```

The auditLogLocation specifies which event log should be used for auditing; it can be Default, Application, or Security. The messageAuthenticationAuditLevel and serviceAuthorizationAuditLevel properties can be None, Success, Failure, or SuccessOrFailure. Finally, the suppressAuditFailure property can be set to true to prevent an exception from being thrown when the system fails to log an audit message.

Running a service with the ServiceSecurityAuditBehavior options shown in Listing 8.39 will result in MessageAuthentication and ServiceAuthorization events (for both failing and successful authentications/authorizations) being written to the system's Application log. Each entry will contain information such as the caller identity, time, target service URI, and protocol. Should any message fail to be written to the event log, an exception will be thrown.

By combining an auditing policy with the detailed options for message logging and system tracing described in Chapter 9, "Diagnostics," you can more effectively and reliably track the behavior and usage of your WCF applications.

SUMMARY

Security is clearly not an easy "feature" to provide in applications, especially when they are distributed over various programs, machines, and even companies. The penalty for overlooking a proper security policy and infrastructure is severe, and the loss of public trust associated with failure is difficult, if not impossible, to reverse. Therefore, a careful consideration of where, when, and how to apply security should never be overlooked.

By ensuring authentication of both the caller and service, parties can be assured they are exchanging information with an expected party. Authorization allows a service to verify that a caller should be granted access to functionality or data directly or indirectly accessible through the service. Finally, the privacy of the data exchanged can be protected via encryption, and the integrity of the data can be preserved by digital signatures.

You've seen how to leverage certificates for message- and transport-level security, which are especially useful for authentication as well as the protection of exchanged data. Besides certificates, you saw a variety of other options for configuring transport and message security, ensuring overall transfer security between callers and services.

Several scenarios related to intranet and Internet-based service exposure and consumption were introduced and detailed, helping to categorize your own requirements and providing a practical basis for implementation.

Finally, you saw how to enable WCF's native support for security-event auditing and logging. Through logging security events, your organization can quickly diagnose security issues in addition to creating a durable record of requests made for authentication and authorization.

Despite the potential complexities of security, you've seen that WCF offers many options to protect WCF services, as well as the consumers of those services. Details at times may be daunting, especially to those new to the underlying concepts, but with WCF, many of these features come at little more expense than enabling basic options in configuration or code.

▛ 9 ▗
Diagnostics

A s you've seen in the previous chapters, WCF offers numerous options for configuring your distributed applications and for extending WCF with custom code. Combine that with the complexities of cross-machine and even cross-company interactions and you have many places to look for sources of unexpected behavior.

Debugging distributed applications can be a challenging prospect. Even if you do have access to the processes and symbol tables necessary for stepping through flow across service call boundaries, remote logic might have been created by a different team with different coding and execution practices. There is also the difficulty of filtering diagnostic information to isolate a particular flow of execution—for example, a single user's session across multiple services and machines.

However, the challenge of any distributed system is not only its initial development, but ensuring ease of maintenance as that application is utilized in production scenarios. IT administrators need efficient means for finding root causes of issues so that the responsible company and development team can be notified.

Fortunately, WCF has a number of built-in features and tools for diagnosing causes of issues, often without much more effort than electing to enable those features in your configuration files. As you'll see in this chapter, WCF utilizes and builds on the native tracing and diagnostics features of the .NET Framework. This allows you to leverage your existing knowledge, and it enables integration of WCF applications' diagnostics with those of other applications.

In this chapter, we describe how to use tracing facilities to capture WCF events and logging to capture details of exchanged messages. Trace listeners are described, along with examples that show how to configure the settings for different events. The Service Trace Viewer, a powerful tool that is included with WCF, is also described, which enables you to inspect activities across service call boundaries.

Sample WCF Application

This chapter uses the SelfHost sample application that is included with the Windows SDK. Details on obtaining, configuring, and running the sample can be found on MSDN at http://msdn2.microsoft.com/en-us/library/ms750530.aspx. If you have the SDK installed, you'll find the SelfHost application under Basic\Service\Hosting\SelfHost\ with both C# and VB.NET versions available.

SelfHost is an introductory sample consisting of simple service and client Windows console projects. The client console application makes several calls to the WCF service, and results are displayed on both the client and service consoles.

Tracing

The core diagnostics capabilities of WCF build on the existing tracing facilities provided by the .NET Framework itself. The `System.Diagnostics` namespace includes classes that enable applications to easily emit tracing information and store those details in a variety of formats and locations.

`System.Diagnostics` features tracing capabilities organized around the concepts of trace sources and trace listeners. *Trace sources* are configured using the `System.Diagnostics.TraceSource` class and enable applications to emit details of execution, such as data or events. The traces emitted by a trace source can be received and processed by one or more *trace listeners*,

classes derived from the abstract base class System.Diagnostics.
TraceListener.

WCF natively utilizes these features to emit details about the actions
occurring during the processing of service calls and responses. No custom
code is required to create these details and the developer or IT administrator need only add configuration to enable the source and listener, as
described next. However, developers are free to add their own tracing calls
to emit additional details as desired.

End-to-End Tracing

A central feature for monitoring WCF applications is called *end-to-end (E2E)
tracing*. This concept utilizes System.Diagnostics features of the .NET
Framework to pass identifiers between the various entities of a distributed
application so that their actions can be correlated into a logical flow. Using
E2E tracing, it is possible to follow a sequence of actions across service and
machine boundaries—for example, from request origination on the client
through the business logic invoked by the target service.

E2E tracing uses a specific XML schema to persist details of processing
across logical boundaries. The XML is created by registering an instance of
the System.Diagnostics.XMLWriterTraceListener, which processes trace
information into the E2E XML format (defined at http://schemas.
microsoft.com/2004/06/E2ETraceEvent).

Listing 9.1 shows an abridged E2E trace XML fragment.

LISTING 9.1 End-to-End Trace Sample

```
<E2ETraceEvent xmlns="...">
 <System xmlns="...">
   <EventID>131085</EventID>
   <TimeCreated SystemTime=
➥"2007-05-06T15:28:11.4178040Z" />
   <Source Name="System.ServiceModel" />
   <Correlation ActivityID=
➥"{7175a87f-b796-4f8a-a416-f2b284d4df39}" />
   <Execution ProcessName="Host.vshost"
➥ProcessID="533" ThreadID="5"/>
   <Computer>LAERTES</Computer>
 </System>
```

LISTING 9.1 continued

```
  <ApplicationData>
   <TraceData><DataItem><TraceRecord>
     <Description>Activity boundary.</Description>
     <AppDomain>Host.vshost.exe</AppDomain>
     <ExtendedData>
      <ActivityName>Construct ServiceHost
➥'service'.</ActivityName>
      <ActivityType>Construct</ActivityType>
     </ExtendedData>
    </TraceRecord></DataItem></TraceData>
  </ApplicationData>
 </E2ETraceEvent>
```

Note in particular the `Correlation` node and the `ActivityID` property. These are the keys to combining individual trace fragments from a variety of sources into a unified logical flow. The concepts behind correlation are described next.

Activities and Correlation

A WCF *activity* is a logical subset of functionality used to group traces for ease of identification and monitoring. An example is the processing of a call into a service endpoint. Although activities are independently useful, effective monitoring requires a mechanism to track flow between multiple activities.

Correlation is the concept of associating multiple activities to create a logical sequence of flow in a distributed application. Correlation is performed via *transfers*, linking activities within an endpoint, and *propagation*, linking activities across multiple endpoints.

Activities are correlated by the interchange of an identifier called the *activity ID*. This identifier, a GUID, is generated by the `System.Diagnostics.CorrelationManager` class. `CorrelationManager` is associated with a trace and can be retrieved via the static property `System.Diagnostics.Trace.CorrelationManager`. It has two primary methods, `StartLogicalOperation()` and `StopLogicalOperation()`, used to link associated actions into a logical unit for tracing purposes.

Enabling Tracing

Tracing is disabled by default and can be enabled by configuring a trace source to emit information and trace listeners to process and save the final trace details.

Listing 9.2 shows the relevant portions of the `SelfHost App.config` file configured for tracing.

LISTING 9.2 Enabling Tracing in Configuration

```
<configuration>
  <system.serviceModel ... />
  <system.diagnostics>
    <sources>
      <source name="System.ServiceModel" propagateActivity="true"
              switchValue="Warning,ActivityTracing">
        <listeners>
          <add type="System.Diagnostics.DefaultTraceListener"
               name="Default">
            <filter type="" />
          </add>
          <add initializeData="app_tracelog.svclog"
               type="System.Diagnostics.XmlWriterTraceListener"
               name="tracelog" traceOutputOptions="Timestamp">
            <filter type="" />
          </add>
        </listeners>
      </source>
    </sources>
  </system.diagnostics>
</configuration>
```

In Listing 9.2, the `<source>` node references the `System.ServiceModel` trace source, which is the source used by WCF to emit tracing details. In the `<listeners>` node, we can add one or more trace listeners to process those details. The `type` property indicates the listener class to invoke and the `initializeData` contains arguments to that listener, such as a file location. An `XmlWriterTraceListener` is configured to write details to the `app_tracelog.svlog` file.

> ### ■ NOTE   Service Configuration Editor
>
> To avoid having abstractions hide the mechanics of WCF diagnostics, we're enabling tracing and message logging by manually specifying settings in the respective App.config files. Later in this chapter, we'll show how to use the Service Configuration Editor to quickly and accurately make such changes without editing the configuration files directly.

The trace source has a switchValue property that is used to specify the level of detail that should be captured. Table 9.1 shows the possible values for the switchValue property when configuring the trace source.

TABLE 9.1 Tracing Source switchValue Options

Option	Purpose
Off	Disables the trace source.
Critical	Tracks the most serious application and environmental failures, such as a service failing or a service being unable to start.
Error	Issues with application logic or the environment—for example, an unrecoverable exception.
Warning	Scenarios that may result in an exception or failure in the future, or notifications that the application recovered from an exception.
Information	Details about system events that may be helpful for debugging, simple auditing, and overall monitoring.
Verbose	Full information at each processing step. Useful for pinpointing sources of issues.
ActivityTracing	Uses correlation to track flow between logically connected components of the distributed application.

Note that `ActivityTracing` can be combined with a verbosity selector (for example, `switchValue="Warning, ActivityTracing"`).

Verbosity Recommendations

Using the more verbose options for tracing can quickly lead to large amounts of traced information, which can add to system overhead and increase the challenge of separating the relevant data from extraneous data. When diagnosing an issue, we recommend that you begin tracing at the `Warning` level.

When operating under normal production conditions, consider leaving tracing off or at `Critical` or `Error` until conditions require further information for diagnostics or monitoring.

Message Logging

Tracing is used to record the flow and individual actions of the various components of a distributed application. Another feature, message logging, is used to record the contents of the messages from or to clients and services. Message logging can be configured to capture messages at the service level, the transport level, and to record messages that are malformed. The data captured via message logging can be useful for a variety of situations, from diagnostics to creating audit trails of service utilization.

Enabling Message Logging

Like tracing, message logging is based on `System.Diagnostics` and is disabled by default. It can be enabled first by adding a trace listener (for example, `XMLWriterTraceListener`) to process messages from the `System.ServiceModel.MessageLogging` trace source.

Listing 9.3 shows our SelfHost application, configured for message logging.

LISTING 9.3 Enabling Message Logging in Configuration

```
<configuration>
  <system.serviceModel>
  <services ... />
  <behaviors ... />
  <diagnostics>
    <messageLogging
      logEntireMessage="true"
      logMessagesAtServiceLevel="true"
      maxMessagesToLog="4000"/>
  </diagnostics>
  </system.serviceModel>

<system.diagnostics>
  <sources>
    <source name="System.ServiceModel.MessageLogging">
      <listeners>
        <add name="messages"
             type="System.Diagnostics.XmlWriterTraceListener"
             initializeData="messages.svclog" />
      </listeners>
    </source>
  </sources>
</system.diagnostics>
</configuration>
```

The `<system.diagnostics>` section looks similar to that used for enabling tracing. We have added a source using `System.ServiceModel.MessageLogging`, the mechanism through which messages are emitted for logging, and are processing that source with the same listener class, `XmlWriterTraceListener`, used earlier for tracing.

Unlike tracing, however, the format and verbosity of messages emitted by the `MessageLogging` source is specified in a `<messageLogging>` element added to the `<system.serviceModel><diagnostics>` configuration node. Table 9.2 shows the `messageLogging` options along with descriptions of their purposes. Any number of these options may be specified in configuration, and those that are not will use the default values shown in Table 9.2.

TABLE 9.2 `messageLogging` Options

Option	Default	Purpose
`logEntireMessage`	False	If true, both the message header and body are logged. If false, only the message header will be logged.
`logMalformedMessages`	False	Logs incorrectly formatted messages.
`logMessagesAtServiceLevel`	False	Logs messages as received or sent by the service itself.
`logMessagesAtTransportLevel`	False	Logs messages either just before encoding for transport or directly after being received from transport.
`maxMessagesToLog`	10,000	Number of logged messages after which further logging will be suspended.
`maxSizeOfMessageToLog`	262,144	Maximum message size, in bytes, that will be logged. If a message exceeds this limit, it will be ignored and a warning trace will be emitted.

Note that messages logged at the transport level may be encrypted, depending on the binding or configuration options you have selected.

Additional Configuration Options

The previous sections described basic approaches for configuring logging and tracing. In this section, we'll describe several other options that you should be aware of for configuring your WCF application.

Shared Listeners

The previous examples have used dedicated listeners for each of the sources (messages and tracing.) You may choose to configure a shared listener and assign multiple sources, unifying the output to a single item, such as an XML file. Listing 9.4 shows how to configure both tracing and message logging to use the same output file.

LISTING 9.4 Tracing and Message Logging to a Shared Listener

```
<configuration>
  <system.serviceModel ... />
  <system.diagnostics>
    <sources>
      <source name="System.ServiceModel" propagateActivity="true"
              switchValue="Warning,ActivityTracing">
        <listeners>
          <add name="diagnostics" />
        </listeners>
      </source>
      <source name="System.ServiceModel.MessageLogging">
        <listeners>
          <add name="diagnostics" />
        </listeners>
      </source>
    </sources>
    <sharedListeners>
      <add name="diagnostics"
           type="System.Diagnostics.XmlWriterTraceListener"
           initializeData="diagnostics.svclog" />
    </sharedListeners>
  </system.diagnostics>
</configuration>
```

For each source, add a listener whose name matches the name of one of the shared listeners. In this case, we're matching the "diagnostics" listener, which will write traces and messages to the same `diagnostics.svclog` file.

Message Filters

By default, all messages appropriate for the level specified in the `<messageLogging>` configuration element are logged. However, to reduce the overhead associated with logging and to decrease the size of log files, you might want to include only messages that match a set of rules you configure.

Message filters are XPath expressions that must be satisfied before a message will be logged. Messages that do not match the XPath queries are excluded, except for malformed messages, which are not affected by filters.

Specify the filters by adding a `<filters>` node to `<messageLogging>` as shown in Listing 9.5.

LISTING 9.5 Adding a Filter for Message Logging

```
<configuration>
<system.serviceModel>
   <services ... />
   <behaviors ... />
   <diagnostics>
      <messageLogging logMalformedMessages="true"
                      logMessagesAtTransportLevel="true">
       <filters>
         <add nodeQuota="1000"
              xmlns:s12="http://www.w3.org/2003/05/soap-envelope"
              xmlns:wsa10="http://www.w3.org/2005/08/addressing">
/s12:Envelope/s12:Header/wsa10:Action[starts-
with(text(),'http://Microsoft.ServiceModel.Samples/ICalculator')]
         </add>
       </filters>
      </messageLogging>
   </diagnostics>
 </system.serviceModel>

 <system.diagnostics ... />
 </configuration>
```

This example may seem complex, but the bulk of it defines the namespaces used in the XPath expression. The namespaces are for the SOAP envelope and addressing schemas. The expression checks the header of each message to ensure it is directed to one of the ICalculator services defined in our SelfHost example. Messages for other services are ignored.

Trace Source Auto Flushing

If you want each tracing or message logging operation to automatically complete (write to disk,) after each trace, enable auto flushing in the `<trace>` element of the `<system.diagnostics>` configuration node as shown in Listing 9.6.

LISTING 9.6 Enabling Auto Flushing

```
<configuration>
  <system.serviceModel ... />
  <system.diagnostics>
    <sources ... />
      <trace autoflush="true" />
    </system.diagnostics>
</configuration>
```

Trace auto flushing is off by default. Before enabling auto flushing in production scenarios, be certain to measure the impact in a test environment because it can add overhead, especially as message traffic increases.

Performance Counters

Three sets of WCF-related performance counters are installed with the .NET Framework 3.0. In Performance Monitor, you can see these counters under ServiceModelService, ServiceModelEndpoint, and ServiceModelOperation. You can choose to enable these for your application via configuration, shown in Listing 9.7.

LISTING 9.7 Enabling Performance Counter Updates

```
<configuration>
  <system.serviceModel>
    <diagnostics performanceCounters="ServiceOnly">
      <messageLogging logMalformedMessages="true"
      logMessagesAtTransportLevel="true" />
    </diagnostics>
  </system.serviceModel>
</configuration>
```

Enable performance counters by including the performanceCounters attribute in the <system.serviceModel><diagnostics> node. Valid settings are Off (the default), ServiceOnly, and All. Enabling all performance counters is recommended for development and diagnostic purposes, but because performance counters do come with some cost of overhead, ServiceOnly is recommended for normal production operations, which will enable only those in the ServiceModelService category.

> **▪ NOTE Observing Performance Counters**
>
> You need a running instance of a WCF service or client to add performance counters in the Performance Monitor application. Ensure performance counters are enabled in configuration and start your service, then add the counters you want to observe, and then run your client application.

Windows Management Instrumentation (WMI)

WCF supports the capability to expose settings and status via Windows Management Instrumentation, or WMI. Many popular application administration and management applications, such as Microsoft Operations Manager and HP OpenView, use WMI to access various systems across an enterprise. Windows PowerShell also has native WMI capabilities, enabling you to write custom scripts for specific management and monitor scenarios.

You can enable the WMI provider for your WCF application in configuration as shown in Listing 9.8.

LISTING 9.8 Enabling the WMI Provider

```
<configuration>
  <system.serviceModel>
    <diagnostics wmiProviderEnabled="true">
      <messageLogging logMalformedMessages="true"
       logMessagesAtTransportLevel="true" />
    </diagnostics>
  </system.serviceModel>
</configuration>
```

Enabling WMI is similar to enabling performance counters. Add the `wmiProviderEnabled` attribute to the `<system.serviceModel><diagnostics>` node. After it is enabled, administration applications will be able to monitor and manage your WCF application.

Using the Service Configuration Editor

So far in this chapter, we've been specifying the manual XML-based methods of updating configuration files to enable tracing and message logging.

In practice, there's an easier and less error-prone way to add and modify configuration settings using the SDK tool, Service Configuration Editor. If the Window SDK has been installed, this editor can be found under All Programs, Microsoft Windows SDK, Tools. However, in Visual Studio you can quickly launch the editor by right-clicking a configuration file and choosing Edit WCF Configuration.

Let's use the Service Configuration Editor on the service project's App.config file. Right-click the SelfHost service project's App.config file, choose Edit WCF Configuration, and select the Diagnostics node from the Configuration pane.

To enable message logging and tracing, click the Enable MessageLogging and Enable Tracing hyperlinks. Doing so will configure the system as shown in Figure 9.1.

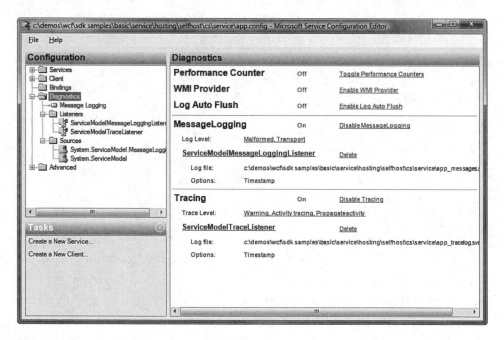

FIGURE 9.1 Tracing and MessageLogging enabled

Notice that the listeners and sources are now displayed in the left panel. You can now click the hyperlinks in each section to configure other related options.

Tracing Options

Once tracing is enabled, explore the available options by clicking the link next to the Trace Level label.

Here you can elect to enable activity propagation and tracing (described earlier in this chapter, and both are typically enabled) as well as the verbosity level from Off through Verbose. Remember that the trace level will affect the amount of space consumed by trace logs. A large log is more difficult to navigate, so you should typically choose the least verbose level necessary.

Logging Options

To access the Message Logging Settings dialog, click the link next to the Log Level label in the MessageLogging section. As described earlier, you can choose to log any of three types of messages: those that are malformed, messages as they are received or sent by the service level, and messages as they are ready for transport or just received from transport.

Clicking the Message Logging item inside the Diagnostics node on the left panel will show the advanced logging settings options shown in Figure 9.2.

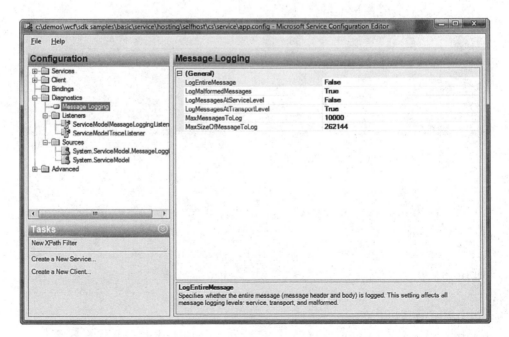

FIGURE 9.2 Advanced Message Logging settings

These options affect the behavior of the ServiceModel.MessageLogging source. They relate directly to the <messageLogging> configuration node, the defaults and purposes of which were shown previously in Table 9.2.

Earlier, we showed that message logging supports the concept of filters to log only those messages that pass specified XPath filters. The Message Logging node in the Service Configuration Editor exposes a New XPath Filter option in the Tasks pane. Figure 9.3 shows the same XPath filter we used earlier defined in the Service Configuration Editor.

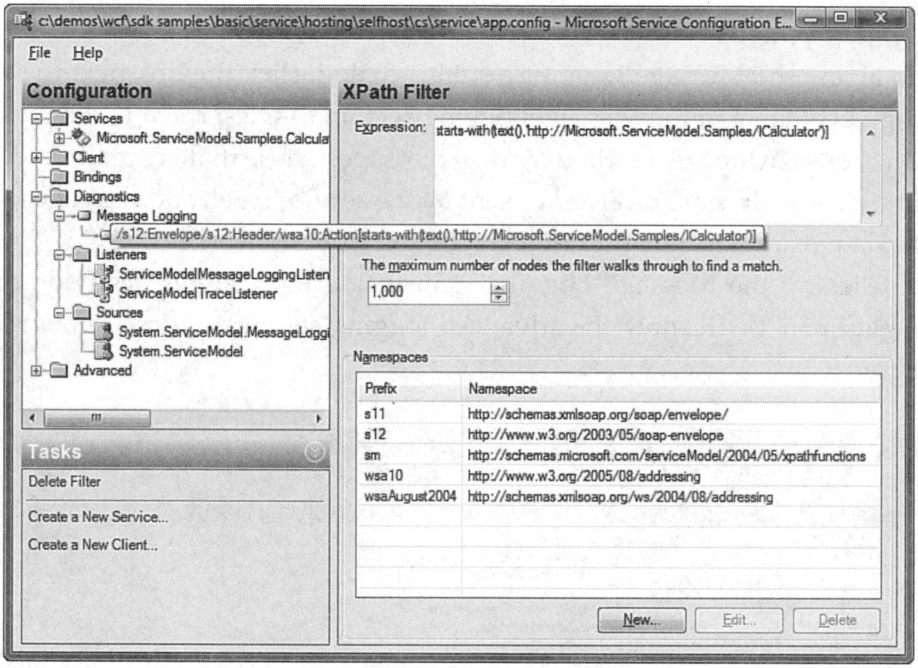

FIGURE 9.3 Message Logging XPath Filter

The tool lets you specify the maximum number of nodes to search (the nodeQuota attribute) and lists commonly used namespaces, along with the prefix for each. You can add more namespaces if you need and reference them via the prefix in your XPath expression.

Configuring Sources

Enabling tracing and logging via the Service Configuration Editor will automatically configure the System.ServiceModel and System.ServiceModel.

MessageLogging trace sources. To see them, expand the Diagnostics/Sources node in the Configuration pane. Select the System.ServiceModel source and you will see the settings shown in Figure 9.4.

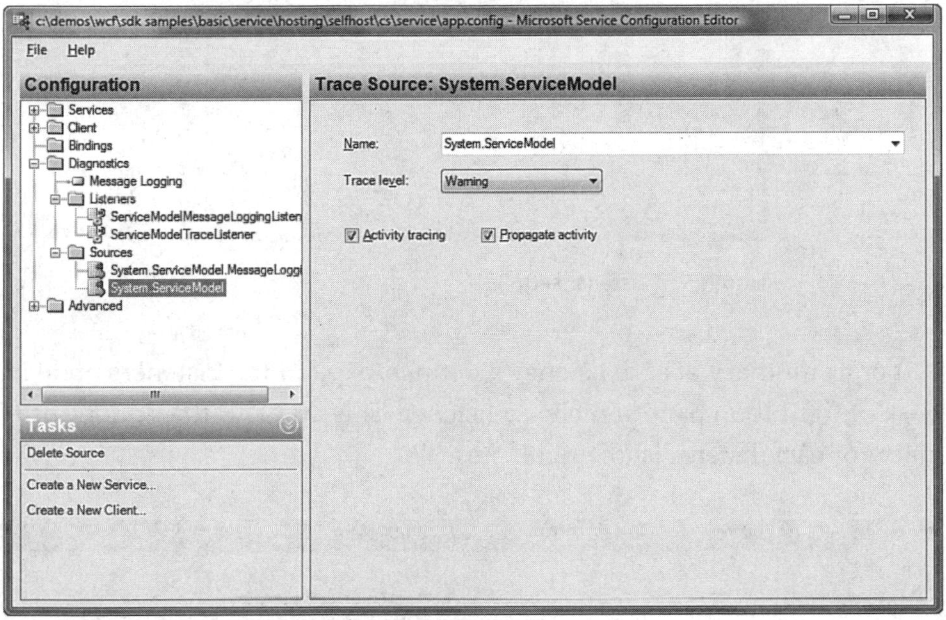

FIGURE 9.4 Trace Source settings

On this screen, you can view or change the verbosity level as well as whether activity tracing and propagation will be used. Note that activity tracing and propagation are available only for tracing listeners and not for message logging listeners.

Configuring Listeners

Returning to the main diagnostics screen (shown in Figure 9.1), you can access detailed listener settings by clicking the links for each listener name (for example, ServiceModelTraceListener.) These options, shown in Figure 9.5, enable you to specify the target file for the listener as well as multiple options for the details included with each trace or message.

The check boxes relate to the System.Diagnostics.TraceOptions enumeration. The basic options are to include Timestamp, Process ID, Thread ID, Callstack, and/or DateTime of the trace. The Logical Operation Stack includes the correlation "stack" of the trace, essentially the correlated history of the trace, which is not necessarily the same as the environmental callstack.

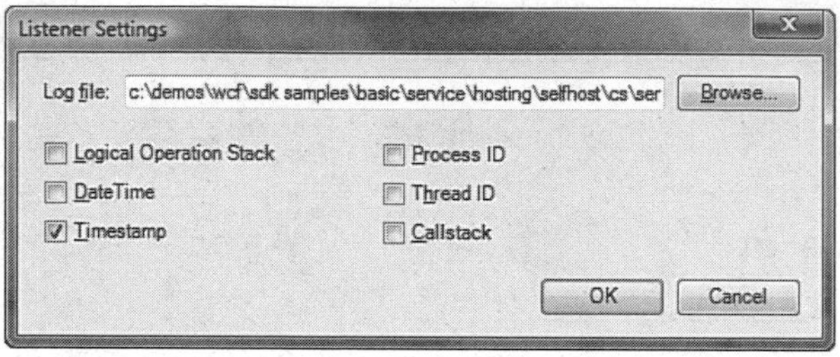

FIGURE 9.5 Listener settings

For a summary of each listener's settings, expand the Listeners node in the Configuration pane and click a listener. This displays the option summary for each listener, shown in Figure 9.6.

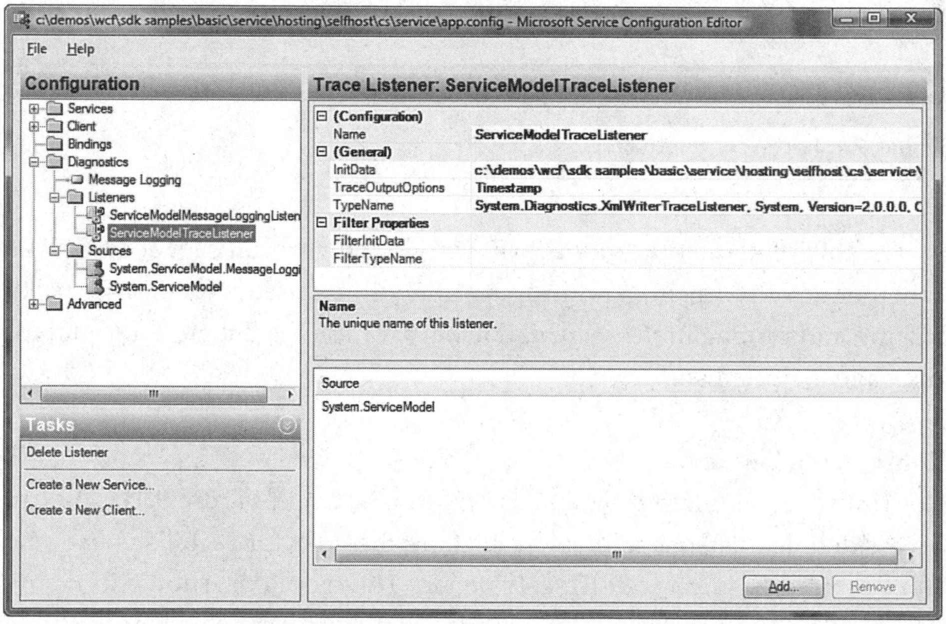

FIGURE 9.6 Detailed listener configuration

Here you can quickly review or change all the listeners' configuration options.

Service Trace Viewer

We've described how to enable various options for tracing and message logging, but how will the output of those diagnostic tools be put to effective use? Even over a brief period of time, tracing and message logging can emit large amounts of data.

WCF works with a powerful tool for analyzing diagnostics logs called the Service Trace Viewer. This tool can be used to import both trace and message log files from one or more components of a distributed application. After installing the Windows SDK, you can find the Service Trace Viewer via the All Programs, Microsoft Windows SDK, Tools menu.

■ TIP Configuring the SelfHost Example

In this section, we have enabled tracing and message logging for both the client and service projects. To follow along on your computer, use the Service Configuration Editor described earlier to enable tracing and message logging in both projects, selecting Information verbosity levels and defaults for all other settings. After it is configured, run the application to generate client and service log files.

Let's use the Service Trace Viewer to analyze the log files generated by the SelfHost example. Launch the Service Trace Viewer and choose File, Open from the menu. Find the SelfHost/client directory and select both the trace (`app_trace.svclog`) and message (`messages.svclog`) log files by holding the Shift key while clicking each. Be certain to select them both because subsequent uses of Open will clear any previously loaded information. (We'll later use File, Add to merge additional logs.)

Activity View

The Service Trace Viewer is able to merge the contents of multiple trace and log files. Figure 9.7 shows the Service Trace Viewer with the SelfHost client project's log files loaded.

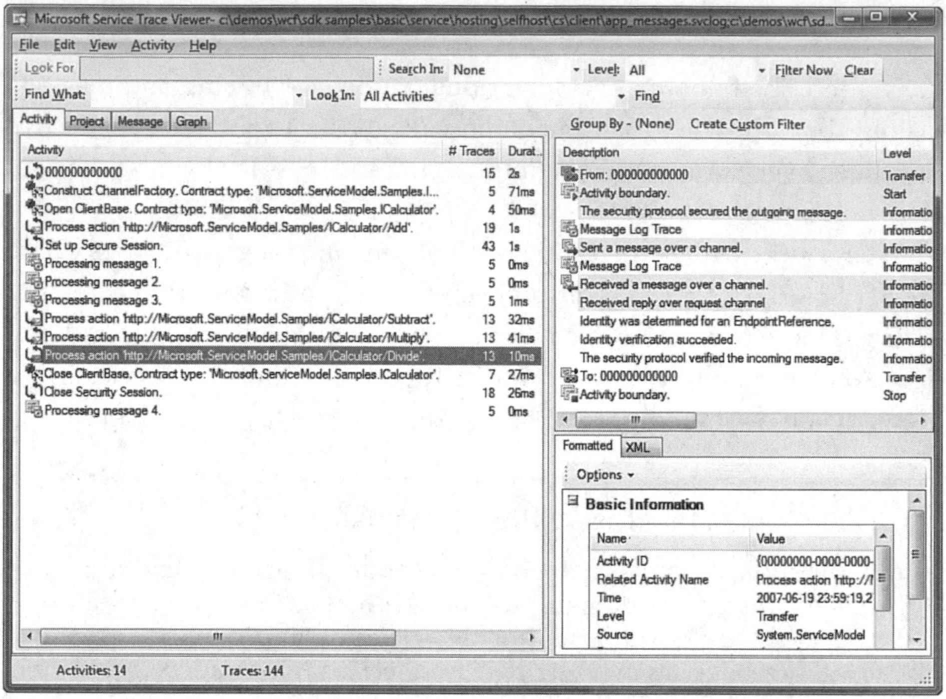

FIGURE 9.7 Service Trace Viewer with client trace and message logs

This screen shows the merged results in the default Activity view. The left pane lists each of the activities along with the number of traces they contain, the duration, the start time, and the end time. When one or more activities are selected, the upper-right pane shows the individual traces associated with the selected activities.

> **■ TIP   Warnings and Exceptions**
>
> Service Trace Viewer displays activities containing warning traces highlighted in yellow. Those with exceptions in their traces are shown with red text.

The first activity, 000000000000, is a dedicated root activity from which all others are linked. Moving down the list, we see the activities the client processed during the program run. First, `ChannelFactory` is constructed and opened, enabling communications with the service.

Each service call is shown as a Process action activity. There are four of these in our trace, relating to the Add, Subtract, Multiply, and Divide services that our client code invokes. The client also negotiates a secure session (Set Up Secure Session) as required by the service binding options.

Click the various activities and note the list of associated traces shown in the top-left pane. You can see the type of trace and a brief description. We'll see in a moment another option for inspecting these traces.

Project View

Another view, the Project view, can be shown by clicking the Project tab in the left pane. The Service Trace Viewer supports the concept of projects. A project enables you to specify multiple tracing and logging files that should be loaded when the project is opened. This is especially useful when you have multiple participants (for example, a client calling multiple services) that you are debugging together. From the File menu, choose Save Project after you have loaded the files you want to associate.

The Project view displays the files associated with the current project. Using this view, you can create or modify projects and add or remove associated files.

Message View

The Message view lists all the logged messages, independently of any correlated activities. This is useful for quickly finding a specific message—for example, the message sent to the Multiply service—and inspecting its contents.

Figure 9.8 shows the Message view, highlighting the message sent from the client to the Divide service.

Graph View

The Graph view is the most complex, yet potentially useful option in the Service Trace Viewer. You can access it by double-clicking any activity or message in the previous views or by selecting the Graph tab. The Graph view shown will be similar to Figure 9.9.

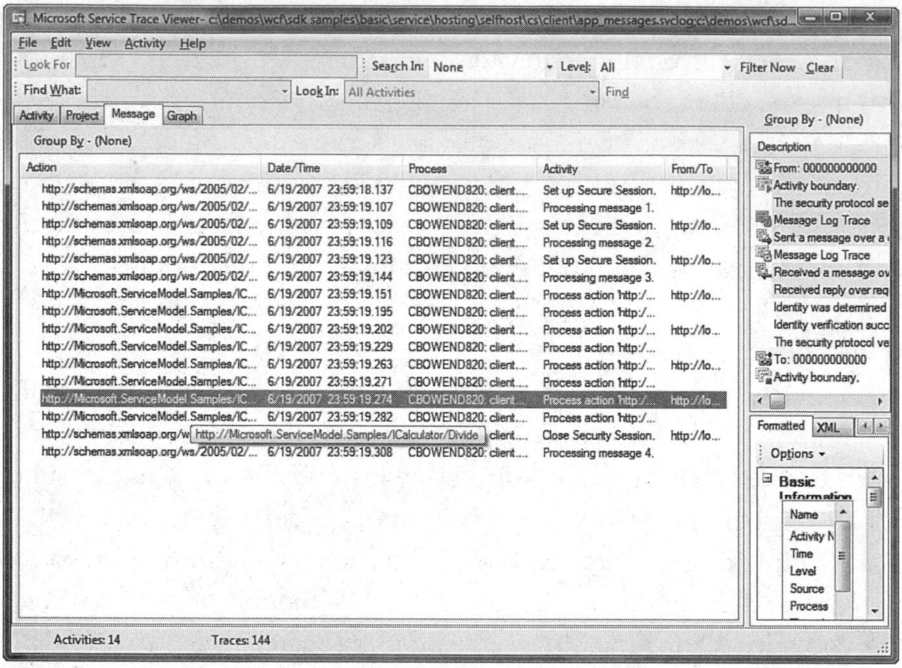

FIGURE 9.8 Service Trace Viewer Message view

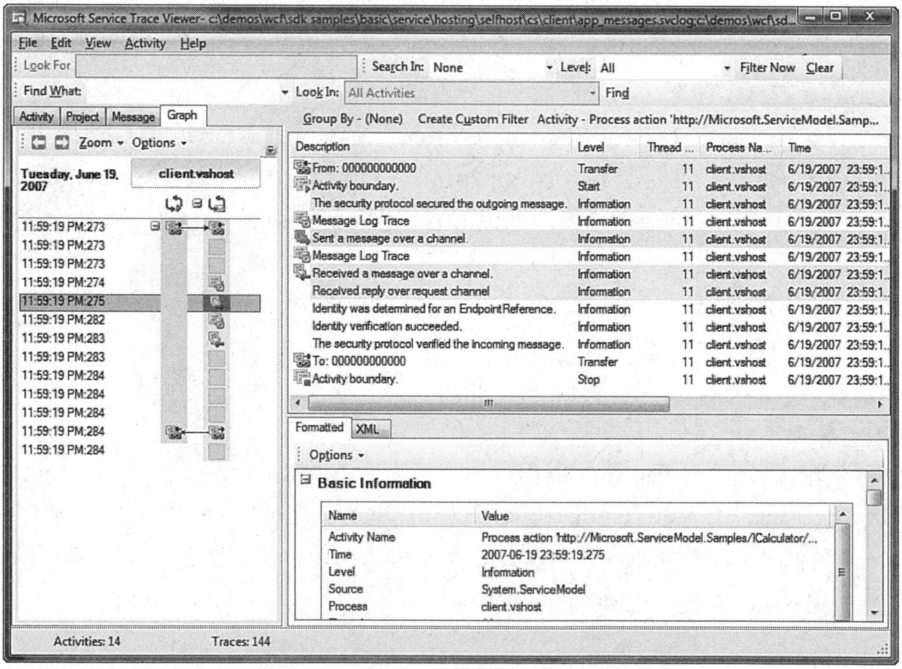

FIGURE 9.9 Service Trace Viewer Graph view

In this view, the activities are now arranged across the top of the left pane. The vertical "swimming lanes" show each trace within those activities, with connections between correlated activities. Select any trace on the left side and the right pane will highlight that trace among all traces for that activity.

The primary benefit of this view will be seen in a moment when we include trace files from the service project.

> ### ◼ TIP   Live Service Trace Viewer
>
> Although the Service Trace Viewer is excellent for after-the-fact analysis of service interactions, a sample tool, called the Live Service Trace Viewer, offers an alternative approach. This application uses a custom TraceListener and a Windows Presentation Foundation (WPF) interface to receive and display diagnostic information as it occurs, which can be very useful, especially during development to avoid the manual process of continually reloading log files between runs.
>
> Note that the Live Service Trace Viewer is not supported by Microsoft, but is an interesting example of how WCF diagnostics can be extended.
>
> Details and code can be found at http://blogs.msdn.com/ craigmcmurtry/archive/2006/09/19/762689.aspx.

Analyzing Logs from Multiple Sources

Although the Service Trace Viewer is helpful for viewing the logs for a single service or client, the real power of both the tool and of end-to-end tracing is realized when log files are added from more than one participant of a distributed application.

To see this, choose File, Add (which, unlike File, Open, merges new logs with currently loaded logs) and select the SelfHost service project's tracing and message logs. The service log files will be imported and correlated with the previously loaded client logs, as shown in Figure 9.10.

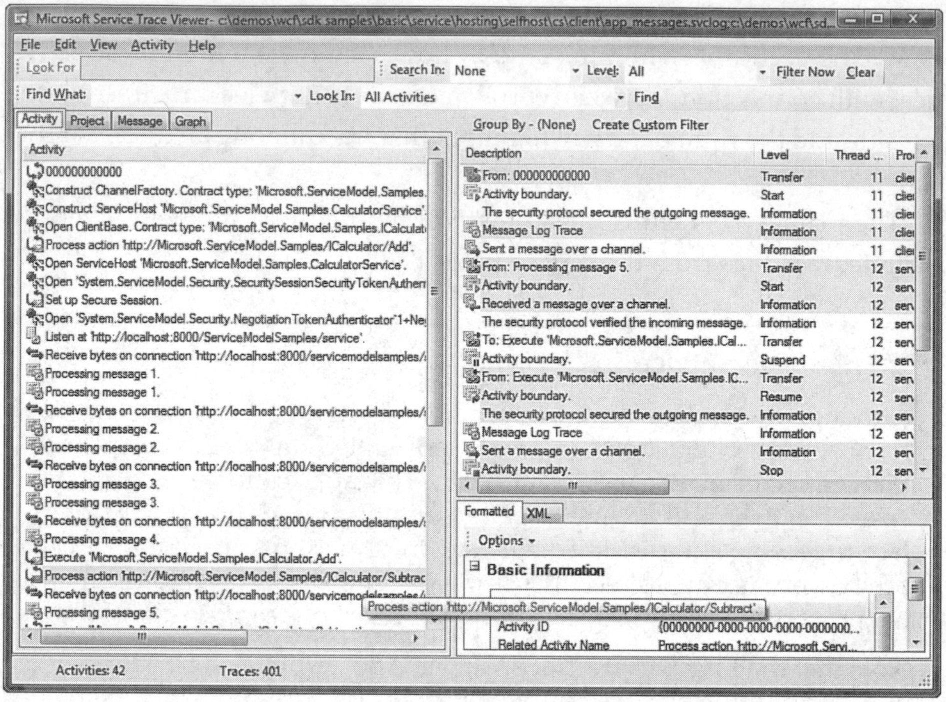

FIGURE 9.10 Service Trace Viewer with service and client logs loaded

As you can see, there is much more detail available to us. The activity list now displays activities for both the client and service projects.

Select the Process Action activity for the `Subtract` service call and either double-click it or click the Graph tab above. You should see the Graph view similar to Figure 9.11.

Now we can see how the Graph view can help us visualize otherwise complex interactions between services and callers. The top of the main pane organizes the activities by host, in our case service and client. Hover the mouse pointer over each activity to see its description. As you expand the traces within activities, you may see visual indicators of correlation between activities.

In Figure 9.11, you can see that the client sent a message to the service, the service processed that message by calling the `Subtract` method, and then a response message was created and sent back to the client. This visualization is possible because of end-to-end tracing and the use of correlation to link activities.

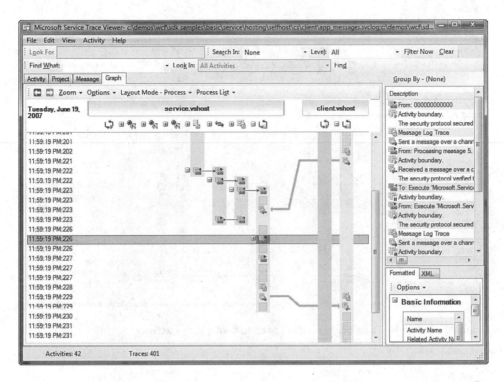

FIGURE 9.11 Service Trace Viewer graph of activity transfer

Clicking the plus symbol next to the highlighted trace in Figure 9.11 expands the display to show us another level of detail. Figure 9.12 shows the resulting detail.

A new activity is displayed under the service.vshost block, Execute 'Microsoft.ServiceModel.Samples.ICalculator.Subtract'. If there had been any exceptions or warnings traced, we would see them in the Graph view as yellow triangles or red circles, respectively. By expanding details to show contained activities and observing how interactions between activities and hosts are correlated, you can quickly use the Service Trace Viewer to locate the sources of unexpected behavior, whether you are a developer creating a distributed application or an IT professional investigating reported issues in production.

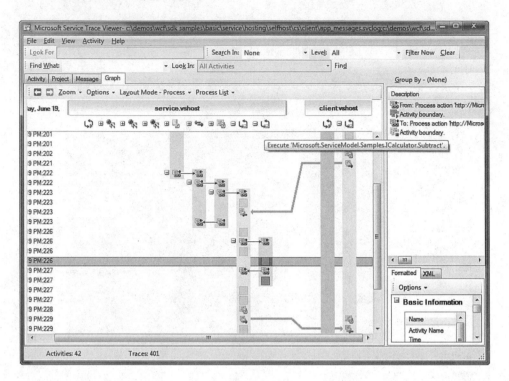

FIGURE 9.12 Service Trace Viewer with expanded subtract call activity

Filtering Results

You may find, especially with production-generated log files, that locating specific information in trace and message logs can become a challenge. For example, you may know that a particular user's session led to unexpected behavior (and for the sake of example, let's say there were no warnings or exceptions thrown, only incorrect data). This would be an extremely challenging prospect, but the Service Trace Viewer offers a flexible infrastructure for finding and filtering entries.

In the toolbar, the Find What option enables you to quickly search all traces for matching text. For example, type **Divide** and click Find. The trace list will highlight those traces containing that word.

You can use the Look For box to quickly limit the displayed traces to those matching your criteria. Click the Search In drop-down and select criteria (for example, Start Time). The Look For field becomes enabled. Enter the earliest time you are seeking and click Filter Now. The activities list displays only those activities that started on or after the selected time. You can also use the Level field to select the severity of messages you want to see (for example, Warning.) The Clear button returns the results to the unfiltered view.

The most powerful filtering option is the capability to create and save custom filters. Click the Create Custom Filter button at the top of the trace list to see a dialog similar to Figure 9.13.

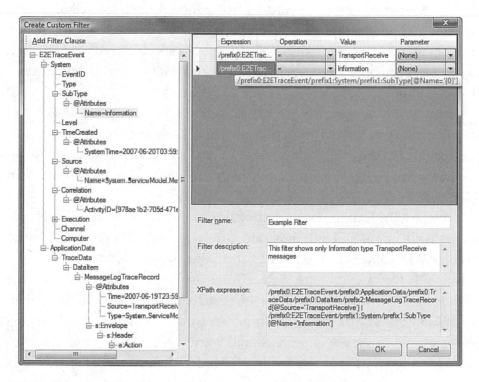

FIGURE 9.13 Creating a custom filter in the Service Trace Viewer

This editor allows composition of filters with one or more XPath expressions. The nodes and attributes in the left pane default to those of the activity or trace that was selected when the Create Custom Filter button was clicked. Select the attribute(s) you want to query and then give the filter a name and description. After clicking OK, you can select your custom filter from the Search In list on the top toolbar to constrain the display to show only entries matching your custom filter.

SUMMARY

In this chapter, we described how WCF utilizes much of the native functionality of the .NET Framework to improve developers' and IT professionals' abilities to diagnose issues in distributed applications.

End-to-end tracing is the concept where logically related actions in different areas of applications, and perhaps on different systems altogether, can be linked to improve our ability to follow specific scenarios through logged information. This correlation is performed by passing unique identifiers within and between endpoints of a WCF system.

Tracing and logging are simple to enable and configure, building on familiar concepts from the `System.Diagnostics` namespace. Tracing gives us insight into the actions occurring in our distributed applications. Message logging enables us to inspect the actual data being passed between clients and services.

The Service Configuration Editor is a useful Windows SDK tool that helps developers and administrators quickly and reliably inspect and change WCF configuration settings, including options for diagnostics.

Finally, we saw how the Service Trace Viewer, also included with the Windows SDK, is a powerful tool for visualizing and inspecting the often large amounts of data captured through tracing and message logging. It is especially useful when exceptions and warnings occur and multiple systems (or companies) are potentially involved. Developers or administrators can use the Service Trace Viewer to quickly isolate sources of unexpected behavior.

The diagnostic capabilities of WCF are an easy-to-use yet powerful way to ensure that your complex distributed applications can be effectively maintained and extended.

10
Exception Handling

THE HARSH REALITY of software development is that even carefully written systems break and unanticipated scenarios occur. It's the job of a good developer to ensure a balance between creating software that prevents problems and software that handles problems as they arise. Distributed service-based systems are no exception. In fact, service-based systems exacerbate the problem by introducing dependencies such as server availability, network conditions, and service version compatibility.

Exceptions are a critical component of a robust system and can be indicators of a variety of situations. For example, a caller may not have provided correct or complete information to a service, a service may have encountered an issue attempting to complete an operation, or a message may be formatted according to an unsupported version.

In this chapter, we'll talk about the effect exceptions have in WCF and the features WCF provides for communicating and processing exceptions. We'll describe the difference between exceptions and faults, the ways to create faults to send to a caller, and ways to process exceptions on both the service and caller. Finally, we'll describe ways to centralize exception processing in the service host, catching unexpected exceptions or performing additional processing on exceptions and faults, such as logging.

Introduction to WCF Exception Handling

Before we get to the details of properly handling exceptions in a WCF service and associated client applications, let's look at what happens when exceptions are thrown using default settings. Understanding what happens if you do not account for exceptions is important for all WCF developers.

A WCF service typically wraps calls to underlying business logic libraries, and as would be expected in any managed code, these libraries may raise standard .NET exceptions to their callers. Exceptions are raised up the call stack until either they are handled by a layer or reach the root application's context, at which point they are typically fatal to the calling application, process, or thread (depending on what type of application is running).

Although unhandled exceptions are not fatal to WCF itself, WCF makes the assumption that they indicate a serious issue in the service's capability to continue communications with the client. In those cases, WCF will fault the service channel, which means any existing sessions (for example, for security, reliable messaging, or state sharing) will be destroyed. If a session is part of the service call, the client channel will no longer be useful, and the client-side proxy will need to be re-created for the client to continue calling the service.

WCF Exception Communication via SOAP

Exceptions that occur either in the service implementation logic or within the mechanics of the service host itself are natively CLR-based `Exception` types. Because services need to support communication between any type of client and service regardless of technology, those .NET-specific details must be translated to a standardized format for interoperable communications.

Interoperability is ensured by serializing those platform-specific exception details to the common data schema described by the Simple Object Access Protocol (SOAP) specification. The SOAP specification provides for a fault element that may be present in a SOAP message's body.

In this chapter, we describe several ways in which exceptions can be communicated as faults from the service to the caller. Detailed knowledge of the SOAP fault schema is generally not necessary because the WCF infrastructure abstracts those details, providing a variety of ways to supply additional information that is then associated with the appropriate SOAP fault elements and properties.

Minimally, a SOAP fault must specify two values. The *reason* is a description of the error condition. The other required value is an error *code,* which can either be a custom indicator or one of the predefined codes enumerated in the SOAP specification. We'll return to these concepts later when we discuss the FaultException type.

More information on the SOAP specifications for fault management can be found on the W3C's website at www.w3.org/TR/2007/REC-soap12-part0-20070427/#L11549.

Unhandled Exception Example

To see how WCF behaves when unhandled exceptions are raised to the service host, create a basic WCF service and minimal Windows client. To demonstrate the effects of the server channel faulting, ensure your service involves a session, for example by choosing *wsHttpBinding*, which establishes a session for security.

In the service implementation, create an operation similar to the one shown in Listing 10.1.

LISTING 10.1 Sample Contract and Implementation

```
using System;
using System.ServiceModel;

namespace ServiceLibrary
{
    [ServiceContract()]
    public interface IService
    {
        [OperationContract]
        double Divide(double numerator, double denominator);
    }

    public class Service1 : IService
    {
        public double Divide(double numerator, double denominator)
```

LISTING 10.1 continued

```
        {
            if (denominator == 0)
                throw new ArgumentOutOfRangeException("denominator",
                    "Must be a numeric value less than or
                    ➥greater than zero");

            return numerator/denominator;
        }
    }
}
```

From the Windows client application, use the Add Service Reference option to create a proxy for the service. Create a simple form with two TextBoxes and two Buttons. Assign the first button to call the `Divide` Web service, passing the values from the TextBoxes as arguments. Assign the second button to refresh the local instance of the service proxy. Your client code might look similar to Listing 10.2.

LISTING 10.2 Client Windows Application Code

```
using System;
using System.ServiceModel;
using System.Windows.Forms;

namespace WindowsClient
{
    public partial class Form1 : Form
    {
        Service1.ServiceClient _serviceProxy = new
            WindowsClient.Service1.ServiceClient();

        public Form1() {InitializeComponent();}

        private void button1_Click(object sender, EventArgs e)
        {
            try
            {
                MessageBox.Show(_serviceProxy.Divide(
                    double.Parse(txtInputA.Text),
                    double.Parse(txtInputB.Text)).ToString());
            }
            catch (FaultException exp)
            {
                MessageBox.Show(exp.Code.Name + ": " +
                    exp.Message.ToString(),
                    exp.GetType().ToString());
```

```
        }
    }

    private void cmdNewProxy_Click(object sender, EventArgs e)
    {
        _serviceProxy = new WindowsClient.Service1.ServiceClient();
    }
  }
}
```

Run the application and pass functional arguments (for example, 10 and 5.) Assuming you've coded the sample correctly, the result of the division should be displayed (for example, 2). Now change the denominator value to zero and retry the call. You should see a result similar to Figure 10.1.

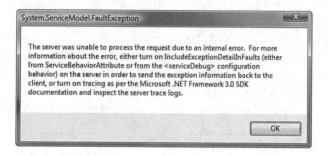

FIGURE 10.1 FaultException returned by calling service with zero denominator

Finally, return the denominator to a nonzero value and call the service again. Although the call would normally be successful, the call fails, receiving a CommunicationObjectFaultedException with a message similar to Figure 10.2.

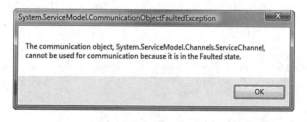

FIGURE 10.2 CommunicationObjectFaultedException for faulted channel

Because WCF received an unhandled exception at the service host, it assumed the exception was indicative of a fatal issue and therefore faulted the server channel. In our case with `wsHttpBinding`, the established security session is no longer valid, so communications must be reestablished by recreating the client proxy.

■ NOTE   One-Way Operations and Faults

Operations with one-way designations by design do not receive a message from the called service, regardless of whether that call was successful. Because no message is returned, there is no indication to the client that a fault has occurred.

In addition, if that fault was caused by an unhandled exception, the server channel will be considered faulted, but the client will not be aware of that fact. In a session-dependent interaction, continued calls will fail (with `CommunicationObjectFaultException`) until the proxy is re-created. Be certain to account for this behavior in your client and server logic when utilizing one-way operations.

Detecting and Recovering a Faulted Channel

Faulted channels can and should be detected by the client. Client code should inspect the channel after each fault to determine whether that fault resulted in faulting of the channel itself. This can be done by having the client code check the channel's `State` property in exception-handling code as shown in Listing 10.3.

LISTING 10.3 Verifying a Channel Is Not Faulted

```
private void button1_Click(object sender, EventArgs e)
{
   try
   {
      MessageBox.Show(_serviceProxy.Divide(double.Parse(txtInputA.Text),
                   double.Parse(txtInputB.Text)).ToString());
   }
   catch (FaultException exp)
   {
      MessageBox.Show(exp.Code.Name + ": " + exp.Message.ToString(),
exp.GetType().ToString());

      if (_serviceProxy.State == CommunicationState.Faulted)
```

```
        {
            MessageBox.Show("Communication channel has been faulted.
➥Attempting to recover.");
            cmdNewProxy_Click(null, null);
        }
    }
    catch (CommunicationException exp)
    {
        MessageBox.Show("Communication error: " +
                    exp.Message.ToString(), exp.GetType().ToString());
    }
    catch (Exception exp)
    {
        MessageBox.Show("General error: " +
                    exp.Message.ToString(),exp.GetType().ToString());
    }
}
```

If a faulted state is detected, you should log the conditions and cause, attempt to re-create the proxy, and continue. When that is not feasible, such as when a session was underway that you cannot manually re-create, the user should be notified and further calls with that proxy prevented.

Communicating Exception Details

In the earlier example, we called a service that raised an unhandled exception to the service layer, and the client received the minimal information shown in Figure 10.1. By default, WCF relays this message, rather than details about an exception, to a caller to prevent exposure of sensitive details about the system's implementation or infrastructure.

ServiceDebugBehavior has an IncludeExceptionDetailInFaults property that can be used to enable transmission of exception details to the client. To enable this behavior, modify your project's app.config file to be similar to Listing 10.4.

LISTING 10.4 Enabling `IncludeExceptionDetailsInFaults` Option via Configuration

```
<?xml version="1.0" encoding="utf-8" ?>
<configuration>
  <system.serviceModel>
    <services>
      <service name="ServiceLibrary.Service1"
behaviorConfiguration="MetadataAndExceptionDetail">
```

LISTING 10.4 continued

```
          <endpoint contract="ServiceLibrary.IService"
 binding="wsHttpBinding"/>
          <endpoint contract="IMetadataExchange" binding="mexHttpBinding"
 address="mex" />
       </service>
     </services>
     <behaviors>
       <serviceBehaviors>
         <behavior name="MetadataAndExceptionDetail" >
           <serviceMetadata httpGetEnabled="true" />
           <serviceDebug includeExceptionDetailInFaults="false" />
         </behavior>
       </serviceBehaviors>
     </behaviors>
   </system.serviceModel>
 </configuration>
```

After the `includeExceptionDetailInFaults` option has been enabled, run the sample service again and supply a zero denominator, which will result in the message shown in Figure 10.3.

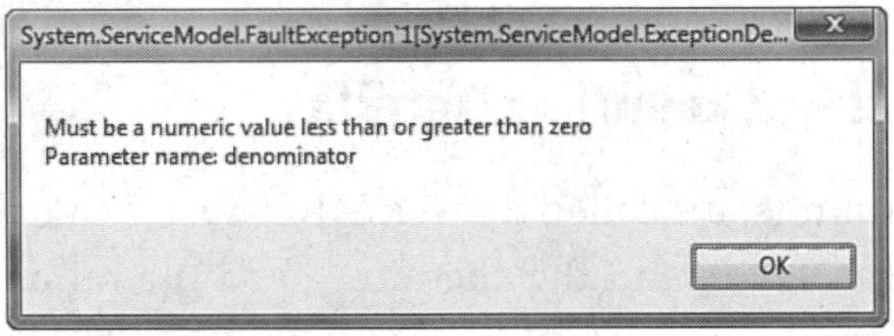

FIGURE 10.3 Exception detail included with ServiceDebugBehavior

Note that you can also set this behavior by using the `ServiceBehaviorAttribute` on the service definition. For example, we could enable the communication of debugging information by modifying the Service.cs definition to Listing 10.5.

LISTING 10.5 Using `ServiceBehaviorAttribute` to Enable `IncludeExceptionDetailsInFaults`

```
using System;
using System.ServiceModel;

namespace ServiceLibrary
```

```
{
    [ServiceBehavior(IncludeExceptionDetailInFaults=true)]
    public class Service1 : IService
    {
        public double Divide(double numerator, double denominator)
        {...}
    }
}
```

Note that using the attribute in this manner to enable exception detail will override any other settings in the configuration that may be intended to disable the feature. Therefore, we recommend you use a configuration-based approach for production applications, perhaps reserving the attribute usage for development purposes.

Whether you elect configuration- or attribute-based use of this feature, remember to disable the option when you do not actively require the details to be transmitted. Using this option only when necessary will help you to ensure that sensitive service details are not exposed.

Managing Service Exceptions with `FaultException`

The first example demonstrated the effect of allowing an unhandled exception to rise through the service implementation layers to the service host. Notice that in Figure 10.1, the type of exception returned to the caller is `FaultException`. This is a base `Exception`-derived type used in WCF to integrate with the SOAP fault specification.

By default, exceptions that reach the service host that are not derived from `FaultException` are considered indications of a potentially fatal condition. The exception is replaced by a `FaultException` and the original exception's details are omitted unless the `IncludeExceptionDetailInFaults` option is enabled. The `FaultException` is then serialized as a SOAP fault for communication back to the caller (save for one-way invocations.) Again, if the call was part of a session, that session will be destroyed and will need to be re-created.

The fatal condition created by unhandled exceptions can be prevented by catching exceptions before they reach the service host and throwing a `FaultException` manually. The `FaultException` class has a number of constructors and properties that allow you to specify different required and optional values that relate to the SOAP fault representation.

A recommended pattern is for the service code to catch any exceptions and extract the relevant details for inclusion in a new `FaultException` instance. An example of this is demonstrated in Listing 10.6.

LISTING 10.6 Catching an Exception and Throwing a `FaultException`

```
public bool ApproveInvoice(int invoiceId)
{
   try
   {
      Invoice invoice = InvoiceSystem.GetInvoice(invoiceId);
      return invoice.Approve();
   }
   catch (ArgumentException exp)
   {
      // Log details of the ArgumentException and context here

      // Raise a FaultException to the caller
      throw new FaultException(invoiceId + "is not valid.");
   }
   catch (Exception exp)
   {
      // Log details of the Exception and context here

      // Raise a FaultException to the caller
      throw new FaultException("Error processing invoice: " + exp.Message);
   }
}
```

Using `FaultCode` and `FaultReason` to Extend `FaultException`

Listing 10.5 is a good start, but it does not specify additional information that could be useful to the client. The `FaultException` constructor also supports `FaultReason` and `FaultCode` arguments, used to specify the reason and code elements of the SOAP fault, respectively.

There are three main options for the `FaultCode`. A `Sender` code indicates a problem with the message as sent by the caller. This is the default code if none is supplied to the `FaultException`. A `Receiver` code indicates that processing could not be completed because of an issue encountered by the service implementation. Alternatively, a custom code can be provided.

The FaultReason class is helpful for creating multiple reason messages featuring locale-based translations for localization of the application. The SOAP 1.2 specification provides for multiple reason nodes, each featuring a localeID (for example, en-US for English in the United States). The FaultReason class accepts a collection of FaultReasonText instances, which themselves include strings of translations with locale identifiers.

In Listing 10.7, we revisit the sample code in Listing 10.6 and utilize the FaultCode and FaultReason classes to enhance the fault information we're serializing back to the caller.

LISTING 10.7 Extending FaultException Using FaultCode and FaultReason

```
public bool ApproveInvoice(int invoiceId)
{
   try
   {
      Invoice invoice = InvoiceSystem.GetInvoice(InvoiceId);
      return invoice.Approve();
   }
   catch (ArgumentException exp)
   {
      throw new FaultException(invoiceId + "is not valid.");
   }
   catch (InvoiceNotFoundException exp)
   {
      throw new FaultException(invoiceId + "could not be loaded.",
FaultCode.CreateReceiverFaultCode(new FaultCode("GetInvoice")));
   }
   catch (Exception exp)
   {
      List<FaultReasonText> frts = new List<FaultReasonText>();
      frts.Add(new FaultReasonText("Error processing invoice"));
      frts.Add(new FaultReasonText("<French translation>",
            new CultureInfo("fr-FR")));
      frts.Add(new FaultReasonText("<Czech translation>",
            new CultureInfo("cs-CZ")));
      throw new FaultException(new FaultReason(frts),
            FaultCode.CreateReceiverFaultCode(
               new FaultCode("ApproveInvoice")));
   }
}
```

Because the ArgumentException indicates a problem with the value that was supplied to the service operation, we do not specify a FaultCode, so the default of Sender will be used. For the InvoiceNotFoundException, we want to indicate that there was a service-related problem, so the static method `CreateReceiverFaultCode()` was used to create a `Receiver` code.

In the catch-all section, we're demonstrating the use of the other `FaultReason` constructors to provide translated error messages to the caller. First, a generic `List` of `FaultReasonText` entries is created, supplying translations and associated culture codes. Then the `FaultException` is constructed, including that list of translations with the `FaultReason` constructor.

To access the translations on the client side, the `FaultException` class exposes a `Reason` property that features a `GetMatchingTranslation()` method. Call `<exception>.Reason.GetMatchingTranslation()` without arguments to automatically retrieve the translation for the current thread's culture, or supply a specific `CultureInfo` as an argument to retrieve a specific translation.

Limitations of Basic `FaultExceptions`

Using the base `FaultException` class is a simple way to prevent unhandled exceptions from reaching the service host and potentially canceling your sessions and invalidating the client proxy. However, `FaultExceptions` suffer from a lack of identity. If your service returns only `FaultExceptions`, you are making it difficult for client application developers to create robust exception-handling logic. Consider the example in Listing 10.8.

LISTING 10.8 Processing Untyped `FaultExceptions`

```
public double GetPrice(int itemId)
{
  try
  {
    // Call a service operation
  }
  catch (FaultException exp)
  {
    // Process WCF exceptions
    //    Process Reason, Code, Message, etc. to determine action
  }
  catch (Exception exp)
  {
    // Process any other exceptions, perhaps local to the proxy
  }
}
```

The challenge here is that there is no subclass of `FaultException` that can be used to create error handling `catch` regions specific to a set of scenarios. The next best approach that the client application developer can take is writing code to investigate each exception at runtime to parse information from the properties to hopefully determine the correct course of recovery or processing.

Creating and Consuming Strongly Typed Faults

As we just described, a basic `FaultException` does not provide a type-specific way to create robust `try/catch/finally` error-handling logic on the client side. To enable that kind of handling on the client, consider using the generic-based `FaultException< >` class.

`FaultException< >` accepts a type that defines the structure of exception data being serialized. This could be any type that can be serialized for transmission, but for the client to have strongly typed access to that type, it must have access to a definition of that type.

For example, we could use the `ArgumentException` from the example in Listing 10.6 and throw a `FaultException<ArgumentException>`. In the case where the client is a .NET application, this would indeed work, each side having strongly typed access to the details of the `ArgumentException`. However, what happens when a client based on non-.NET technology, such as Java, attempts to use the service? Java has no inherent knowledge of .NET's `ArgumentException`, so the Java proxy would not be able to provide strongly typed access to the fault details our service may return.

To ensure interoperability, the WSDL for the service should describe the structure of the type used to create the `FaultException<>` instance. This is done by providing a *fault contract*.

Declaring Fault Definitions with `FaultContract`

Remember that data contracts are used to define data structures that can be represented by a service's WSDL definition, enabling a client to know exactly the types and structures of data to supply or process when interacting with a service. Now we'll use the same concepts of data contracts to describe the structures used to convey fault information from a service to a caller.

One or more `FaultContract` attributes can be used to decorate a service operation. This indicates to WCF that a service's WSDL definition should include the details of fault-related information potentially thrown by the operation. This means that proxy-generating tools will be able to create strongly typed representations of the classes you use to convey fault information. Having well-defined proxies for the fault information will help developers create robust and reliable client applications that utilize your services. Note that because the details are contained in standard WSDL format, any type of tool can generate platform-specific proxies for your faults, not just .NET applications.

Let's create a data structure to convey details of an error condition back to a calling application. Create a `TrackedFault` class as shown in Listing 10.9.

LISTING 10.9 Creating a DataContract for Use from a FaultContract

```
using System;
using System.Runtime.Serialization;

namespace ServiceLibrary
{
    [DataContract]
    public class TrackedFault
    {
        Guid _trackingId;
        string _details;
        DateTime _dateTime;

        [DataMember]
        public Guid TrackingId
        {
            get { return _trackingId; }
            set { _trackingId = value; }
        }

        [DataMember]
        public string Details
        {
            get { return _details; }
            set { _details = value; }
        }

        [DataMember]
```

```
        public DateTime DateAndTime
        {
            get { return _dateTime; }
            set { _dateTime = value; }
        }

        public TrackedFault(Guid id, string details, DateTime dateTime)
        {
            _trackingId = id;
            _details = details;
            _dateTime = dateTime;
        }
    }
}
```

Defining a FaultContract

After you have one or more data contracts that you want to use to convey exception details to your callers, add the `FaultContract` attribute to your operation, specifying the name of the associated data contract(s).

For example, the `ApproveInvoice` operation in Listing 10.10 has been extended to potentially raise a `FaultException` based on the `TrackedFault` data contract we defined earlier.

LISTING 10.10 Extending an Operation Definition with a `FaultContract`

```
[OperationContract]
[FaultContract(TrackedFault)]
public bool ApproveInvoice(int invoiceId)
{
    ...
}
```

> ■ **NOTE**   One-Way Operations and FaultContracts
>
> As mentioned earlier, one-way operations do not return messages to callers, so there is no direct mechanism for returning faults. Because faults are not returned, an `InvalidOperationException` will be thrown at service load time if you decorate any one-way operations with a `FaultContract`.

Throwing a `FaultException<>` **with a Defined** `FaultContract`

Having indicated to WCF that the `ApproveInvoice` operation may throw an exception that serializes data within the `TrackedFault` data contract, we need only add the logic to populate that data contract and raise the exception. Listing 10.11 demonstrates this by extending the code from Listing 10.7.

LISTING 10.11 Throwing a `FaultException<>` with a `FaultContract`

```
[OperationContract]
[FaultContract(typeof(TrackedFault))]
public bool ApproveInvoice(int invoiceId)
{
   try
   {
      Invoice invoice = InvoiceSystem.GetInvoice(invoiceId);
      return invoice.Approve();
   }
   catch (ArgumentException exp)
   {
      throw new FaultException(invoiceId + "is not valid.");
   }
   catch (InvoiceNotFoundException exp)
   {
      TrackedFault tf = new TrackedFault(
                        Guid.NewGuid(),
                        invoiceId + "could not be loaded.",
                        DateTime.Now);

      throw new FaultException<TrackedFault>(
               tf,
               new FaultReason("InvoiceNotFoundException"),
               FaultCode.CreateReceiverFaultCode(new
                  FaultCode("GetInvoice")));
   }
   catch (Exception exp)
   {
      List<FaultReasonText> frts = new List<FaultReasonText>();
      frts.Add(new FaultReasonText("Error processing invoice"));
      frts.Add(new FaultReasonText("<French translation>",
            new CultureInfo("fr-FR")));
      frts.Add(new FaultReasonText("<Czech translation>",
            new CultureInfo("cs-CZ")));
      throw new FaultException(new FaultReason(frts),
            FaultCode.CreateReceiverFaultCode(
               new FaultCode("ApproveInvoice")));
   }
}
```

Fault Contract Strategies

A variety of strategies exist for describing your services with fault contracts. You could define a shared core library of contracts that are used by all your company's services. Fault contracts may be specific to a single service or application, including details specific to that system. You might decide to create a contract associated specifically with individual problems potentially encountered by your services.

We suggest that each time you create WCF service projects, you consider a comprehensive `FaultContract`-based approach to be your default exception policy. Careful decoration of your operations with `FaultContracts` for expected exceptions will enable creation of client applications with strongly typed representations of the exceptions that may be thrown by your services.

Whatever strategy you adopt, ensure that you consistently follow that strategy so that clients developed against your services will have improved maintainability and usability.

Implementing Client Fault Handlers

If you have declared your service's operations using the `FaultContract` attribute to define the data contracts included with any thrown faults, your service's WSDL description will include details of those data contracts. This will enable you or others to create client-side handlers that have full access to the details and types of those contracts.

Extending the earlier example of a basic client-side service invocation with exception handling, Listing 10.12 demonstrates how the strongly typed `FaultException` based on the `TrackedFault` data contract could be structured.

LISTING 10.12 Processing Untyped `FaultExceptions`

```
public double GetPrice(int itemId)
{
   try
   {
      // Call a service operation
   }
   catch (FaultException<TrackedFault> tfexp)
   {
```

LISTING 10.12 continued

```
        // Full and strongly typed access to TrackedFault details

        // TrackedFault properties are available via the Detail
        //   property of the FaultException<> type.

        MessageBox.Show("A problem has been encountered and recorded.
➥Please reference Id " + tfexp.Details.TrackingId + " when
➥contacting support.");
            }
    catch (FaultException fexp)
    {
        // Process other WCF exceptions

        // Inspect Reason, Code, Message, etc. to determine action
    }
    catch (Exception exp)
    {
        // Process any other exceptions, perhaps local to the proxy
    }
}
```

Exposing the details of TrackingFault via the service's WSDL allows a proxy generation tool to create strongly typed properties for each of the TrackingFault's members. A client exception handler can access the details of the embedded data contract by using the Details property of the FaultException<> instance. In Listing 10.12, the user is given the tracking ID by accessing the Details.TrackingId property of the typed exception instance.

Remember that, as with all .NET exception code, the ordering of the catch regions is significant. The FaultException<TrackedFault> is the most specific type and so should be first. Because FaultException is more specific than Exception (the type from which it derives), it should be next, followed by Exception, which should be last.

Full implementation details have been omitted from the example, but could include a variety of options from logging exception details, to informing the user and aborting, to retrying the service call.

Error-Handling Application Block

The Patterns and Practices team at Microsoft creates guidance and tools to help address gaps between available technologies and recommended best practices. The Enterprise Library is a free collection of integrated libraries of code, called *application blocks*, which can be used to quickly implement proven practices into an application.

The latest release of the Enterprise Library (currently version 3.1) includes new features that integrate with some of the capabilities of the .NET Framework 3.0 and 3.5. One of the application blocks contained in the Enterprise Library, called the *Exception Handling Application Block*, can be used to define policies for handling exceptions within an application. For example, you may create a policy where all data-related exceptions are logged and a new, generic `Exception` is rethrown in the original exception's place.

> **■ NOTE** **More on Enterprise Library**
>
> Full coverage of the Enterprise Library as it relates to .NET 3.x is beyond the scope of this book, but details can be found at http://msdn.com/practices.

Exception Shielding

The latest release of the Enterprise Library extends the functionality of the Exception Handling Application Block to provide a feature called *exception shielding*. It features a new attribute, `ExceptionShielding`, that can be used to invoke an exception policy when a service is accessed. Used in conjunction with the `FaultContractExceptionHandler`, you can fairly easily convert .NET exceptions thrown by your operations into strongly typed `FaultException<>` instances related to a target data contract.

In addition to the other handlers such as wrap, replace, and logging, the `FaultContractExceptionHandler`, based on configuration, can be used to perform a fielded mapping between a thrown exception and the data contract specified with a `FaultContract` attribute.

Consider using exception shielding as a way to catch and convert either all or a specific subset of exception types that are not already processed using one of the techniques described in this chapter.

Details and examples of using Enterprise Library for WCF exception shielding can be found on MSDN at http://msdn2.microsoft.com/en-us/library/aa480591.aspx.

SUMMARY

In this chapter, we introduced how WCF processes exceptions and the variety of options you have to influence those operations. The first and perhaps most important was to understand what happens when you do nothing. By default, unhandled exceptions may lead to interruptions of sessions and the invalidation of client proxies.

Knowing how to use the `FaultException` class is central to creating an effective exception-handling strategy and avoiding the potential issues associated with unhandled exceptions. `FaultException` is helpful for abstracting the details of the SOAP fault schema and how WCF converts exception information into that schema for transmission to callers. You saw that `FaultException` can be extended to provide detailed codes and reasons, even supplying locale-specific translations of exception messages to support a localized client application.

From unhandled exceptions and basic `FaultExceptions`, we moved on to the concept of strongly typed exceptions using the generic `FaultException<>`. By using data contracts to define data structures for conveying exception information, client applications can include effective type-driven exception-handling code without the need to parse individual `FaultException` instances at runtime to determine the correct course of action. Use of the `FaultContract` attribute enables proxy-generation tools to analyze a service's WSDL to create strongly typed representations of the source data contracts, regardless of the technology used by the client.

Finally, we introduced the concepts behind the WCF integration found in the Enterprise Library's Exception Handling Application Block. This enables you to easily create policies for handling exceptions at your services boundaries.

Having a well-defined and understood exception-handling strategy in your team, group, or company is of critical importance. As you create your WCF services and client applications, take the time to consider the mechanisms by which you'll ensure that your service will behave predictably while also enabling the development of robust and maintainable clients.

■ 11 ■
Workflow Services

AT THIS POINT IN THE BOOK, you already know that WCF is all about
services—it's about defining, building, and securing services. Services
have well-defined boundaries formally described in their contract, but the
inner workings are entirely opaque outside the service. WCF says little
about the service implementation; it simply provides the interfaces to reliably and securely exchange messages with clients.

Windows Workflow Foundation (WF) is complementary technology to
WCF. It's all about defining and executing activities of a multistep process
(a.k.a. workflow). WF can model workflows that are sequential or event-
driven in nature. The WF runtime executes activities by branching, looping,
forking, and joining the execution path. Workflows can be very short or can
run for a long time. They can implement a single transaction or coordinate
the work of many. WF says little about the interface to the workflow, which
makes it useful in a variety of applications.

> **■ TIP   New to .NET 3.5**
>
> WCF and WF shipped in .NET 3.0. Integration between the two, as
> described in this chapter, is new with .NET 3.5 and Visual Studio 2008.

Combining WCF and WF provides a robust platform for defining multistep processes and exposing them to clients in a secure, reliable way. There is a built-in activation model so that workflows can be started in response to a message being received. There is also a built-in persistence model so that the state of a running workflow can be saved between activities. And dispatcher support allows multiple instances of workflow to run simultaneously with incoming messages routed to the proper running instance.

Important: To fully understand the material in this chapter, you should have a good understanding of WF. This is not a tutorial on the subject of WF. Rather, it focuses on the integration points between WCF and WF with Visual Studio and .NET 3.5. A most excellent text on WF is the *Essential Windows Workflow Foundation* (Addison-Wesley; ISBN 0-321-39983-8), by Dharma Shukla and Bob Schmidt. In addition, because the integration WCF and WF relies heavily on bindings and behaviors, you should be sure to read Chapter 4, "Bindings," and Chapter 5, "Behaviors," of this book.

Integration Points

There are two ways to describe the integration between WCF and WF. From the WCF perspective, WF enables you to "implement a service as a workflow." From the WF viewpoint, WCF enables you to "service enable a workflow." Both are saying the same thing: That is, by combining WCF and WF, you model and implement logic that is exposed through a standards-based interface. Your logic can be compatible with many standards, such as SOAP, JSON, or X.509, and can be hosted by IIS, WAS, Windows Service, or any other WCF-supported hosting environment. In addition, the tracing, diagnostics, and unit testing tools available in Visual Studio can also be used with WCF and WF.

WF integrates with WCF by leveraging WCF extensibility. So although WF knows about WCF, WCF does not know about WF. The integration in .NET 3.5 is by WF plugging deeply into the WCF extensibility points. With .NET 3.5, WF updated its visual modeling tools in Visual Studio and added runtime support that leverages WCF.

Three elements are needed for integration between WCF and WF. First, you need a way to model service interactions. WF is good at defining a workflow as a set of activities, so all that's needed is a way to extend activities to interoperable services. With that, you can use WF to model interactions among services. Second, you need hosting an activation infrastructure for exposing a workflow as a service itself. This must support event-driven models, transactions, and persistence, so that the workflow can survive system reboots. Third, you need to support correlation between client and services, so that clients can communicate with the right instance of a service when there may be thousands running.

The integration built into .NET 3.5 and Visual Studio 2008 supports each of these scenarios. Each topic is briefly introduced here and covered in more detail in this chapter.

- Send and Receive activities are added to the WF designer.
- The `WorkflowServiceHost` class wraps the WCF hosting class.
- New bindings and behaviors add context information to the channel to support correlation and long-running workflows.

The Send activity is used to send a message to a WCF service endpoint. At design time, the WF designer maps the incoming and outgoing types in the WCF-generated proxy to WF variables. At runtime WF uses the proxy to communicate with the service endpoints. The Receive activity does the opposite of the Send activity. Rather being a client of an existing service, the Receive activity exposes the workflow as a service itself. At design time, the WF designer is used to specify a service endpoint and operation contracts for the workflow, including the messages it receives and returns. At runtime, when the endpoint receives a message, either a new workflow is instantiated or the message is routed to an already running workflow.

The `WorkflowServiceHost`, as its name implies, derives from WCF's `ServiceHost` class and is really the tip of the iceberg for the WF-WCF integration. It leverages a set of custom behaviors and bindings to accomplish WF-specific tasks relating to correlation and instance management. It also provides access to the WF runtime in the service host so that a persistence provider can enable long-running processes within a stateless WCF service.

As discussed in Chapter 5, WCF behaviors are a very flexible extensibility point in the WCF architecture. WCF uses service and operation behaviors to operate on messages and instances, as shown in Figure 11.1.

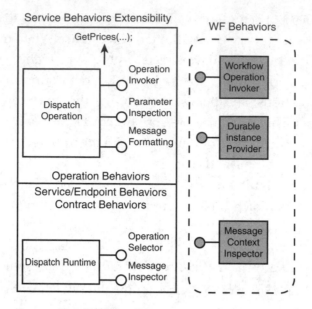

FIGURE 11.1 WF behaviors

Calling a WCF Service from WF

WF activities are the building block of workflow programs. Each activity typically performs one task, such as calling a method on a class, calling a Web service, or invoking another program. WF ships with a few built-in activities, and developers can create their own activities by inheriting from one of the activity base classes.

There are at least four ways to invoke a service from WF: use the Send activity, write a custom activity, use the InvokeWebService activity, or use the Code activity. The Send activity is best for calling WCF or other interoperable Web services and is introduced in .NET 3.5 for exactly this purpose. A custom activity is a lightweight mechanism for encapsulating code that can be easily reused across workflows. The InvokeWebService activity is useful when calling ASMX Web services but doesn't have any advantages over the Send activity. A Code activity is, well, code. Of these four, this chapter covers the Send activity and writing a custom activity. First we'll call a Web service using a Send activity, and then we'll write a very simple custom activity and use it instead.

Listing 11.1 shows the interface of the service that will be used in this example. `GetPrice` accepts a simple type as input and returns a complex type, `StockPrice`.

Create a project in Visual Studio 2008 using the "Sequential Workflow Console Application" template in the Workflow folder. This template includes a class file (`Workflow1.cs`) that implements the workflow and a main program (`Program.cs`) that initializes the workflow runtime and starts an instance of the workflow class.

LISTING 11.1 StockService Invoked by WF

```
[DataContract]
class StockPrice
{
    [DataMember] public double price;
    [DataMember] public int calls;
}

[ServiceContract]
interface IStockPrice
{
    [OperationContract]
    StockPrice GetPrice(string ticker);
}
```

Using a Send Activity

The Send activity is one of the built-in activities with Visual Studio 2008. Its purpose is to use a WCF proxy to call a Web service. The design environment supports the common properties that need to be configured to call a Web service, including endpoint information. The property sheet and designer is also used to bind WF variables to the service operation parameters. In addition, the activity can override the URI address of the service.

Before accessing the Web service, the project must first contain a proxy to the Web service you want to invoke. The proxy can be generated using the Add Service Reference tool in Visual Studio or by using the `svcutil.exe` tool.

To use the Send activity, drag it from the toolbox onto the workflow design surface as you would with any other activity. Figure 11.2 shows the workflow designer with the Send activity added to the workflow.

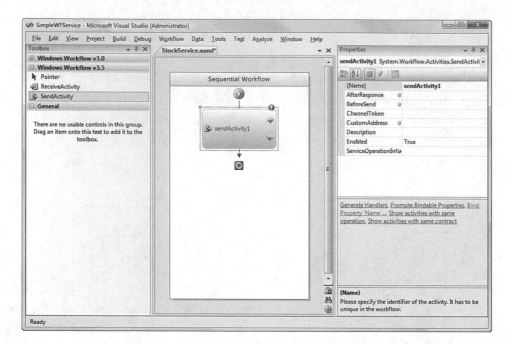

FIGURE 11.2 Adding a Send activity to a workflow design surface

The Send activity must be configured to specify the service operation to be called, the WF variables that will provide the input and receive the output of the service operation, and the endpoint name.

First, choose the service operation by setting the ServiceOperation property. When you select the ellipsis in the property sheet, a dialog will pop up from which you select the service operation. If this is the first time you're referencing the service from this workflow, you need to import the types from the WCF-generated proxy into WF. Select the Import button and then browse to the proxy in the project. Figure 11.3 shows the dialog after the proxy's type was imported from WF project. In this example, the GetPrice operation is selected. After the service operation is selected, the property sheet is expanded to include the parameters and return value of the service operation.

The next step is to bind WF variables to the proxy call. When you select the ellipsis in the property sheet next to variable names (in this example, Ticker and the ReturnValue) a dialog will pop up for you to select or create WF variables of the appropriate type. You can create a WF field or a WF property; a field is local to the workflow class, whereas a property has broader visibility within the WF design environment.

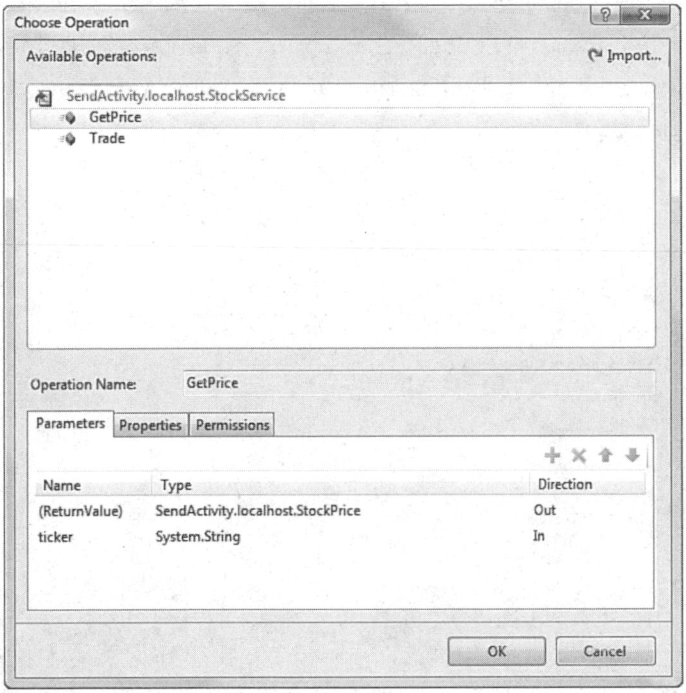

FIGURE 11.3 Proxy type was imported so an operation can be chosen.

> **▪ TIP   Property or Field**
>
> A property is a field that can be initialized when a workflow instance is started. You can send a value into the workflow on startup by defining a dictionary object and passing it as the optional second parameter of workflowRuntime.CreateWorkflow. If you define a property, the value passed into the workflow can be passed along to subsequent services or other activities invoked from the workflow.

Figure 11.4 shows the WF variable, sendActivity1_ReturnValue_1, bound to the return value from the getPrice operation.

Finally, you must configure the service endpoint properties so that the Send activity formats and sends the message to the right location. This is

done by configuring the ChannelToken property, which has three components: Name, EndpointName, and OwnerActivityName. The OwnerActivityName indicates the scope of the ChannelToken and is selected from a
drop-down list box. The EndpointName must match an endpoint configuration name in app.config such as one that was generated from Add Service
Reference or svcutil.exe.

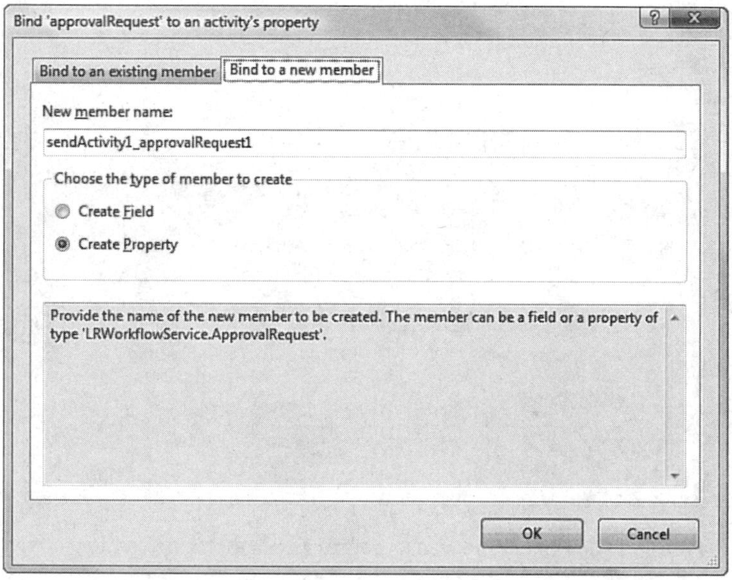

FIGURE 11.4 Binding WF variable to service operation parameters

Writing a Custom Activity

Custom activities in WF are a great way to encapsulate business capabilities. By providing the right level of abstraction and granularity in custom
activities, a WF developer can model an application by combining those
capabilities. Although using the Send activity is a great method for calling
any interoperable Web service, it requires the WF developer to know that
the business capability they want to consume is, in fact, a Web service. Custom activities encapsulate that knowledge so the WF developer can model
the application, not the plumbing.

In the simplest case, a custom activity is a .NET class that derives from
System.Workflow.ComponentModel.Activity. There are many subclasses
that derive from this, to specialize for sequential or state-machine models,

or composite activities. Only one method in that class, Execute, is required. The return value from the Execute method is an ActivityExecutionStatus enumeration. If set to Closed, the activity is done. If not, WF manages the activity instance until the activity notifies the WF runtime that it is complete.

Custom activities can expose properties to the WF designer at runtime. Properties can be set in Visual Studio at design time and can be bound to WF variables that are available at runtime. The properties are, in effect, the interface to the custom activity. The Execute method on the custom activity only requires context as a parameter, because the interface is done through properties. To create a custom activity, you can use the Workflow Activity Library template in Visual Studio 2008. The template creates a custom activity of SequenceActivity type, which derives from Activity.

Listing 11.2 shows a custom activity. Note that other than the constructor, there is only one method, Execute. This method is where you insert code to call the WCF service. In this example, we create the proxy and call the method off the proxy. When the proxy is generated, WCF creates an app.config file in the local project. At runtime, when the activity is called, WCF will look in the current application configuration file for service model information. Therefore, the service model configuration must be copied into the app.config file used for the workflow host.

There are two properties defined, ticker and price. Both are visible from the Visual Studio design surface and from code at runtime.

LISTING 11.2 Implementing a Custom WF Activity

```
namespace MyActivityLibrary
{
  public partial class GetPriceActivity: Activity
  {
    public GetPriceActivity(
    {
      InitializeComponent();
    }
    protected override ActivityExecutionStatus
            Execute(ActivityExecutionContext context)
        {
            localhost.StockServiceClient proxy =
              new ActivityLibrary1.localhost.StockServiceClient();
            price = proxy.GetPrice(ticker);
            return ActivityExecutionStatus.Closed;
```

LISTING 11.2 continued

```
            }

    public static DependencyProperty tickerProperty =
                    DependencyProperty.Register("ticker",
                    typeof(System.String),
                    typeof(GetPriceActivity));
    [DescriptionAttribute("Please specify a stock symbol ")]
    [DesignerSerializationVisibilityAttribute
        (DesignerSerializationVisibility.Visible)]
    [BrowsableAttribute(true)]
     public string ticker
     {
       get
         {
           return ((String)
                    (base.GetValue(GetPriceActivity.tickerProperty)));
         }
       set
         {
           base.SetValue(GetPriceActivity.tickerProperty, value);
         }
     }

    public static DependencyProperty priceProperty =
                    DependencyProperty.Register("price",
                    typeof(localhost.StockPrice),
                    typeof(GetPriceActivity));
    [DescriptionAttribute("tradePrice")]
    [DesignerSerializationVisibilityAttribute
            (DesignerSerializationVisibility.Visible)]
    [BrowsableAttribute(true)]
    public localhost.StockPrice price
    {
        get
        {
            return ((localhost.StockPrice)
                (base.GetValue(GetPriceActivity.priceProperty)));
        }
        set
        {
            base.SetValue(GetPriceActivity.priceProperty, value);
        }
    }
  }
}
```

After creating the activity library, the activity can be used in a workflow
project. The workflow is unaware the WCF is involved, because that

plumbing is encapsulated in the custom activity. Figure 11.5 shows a workflow using the `GetPrice` custom activity.

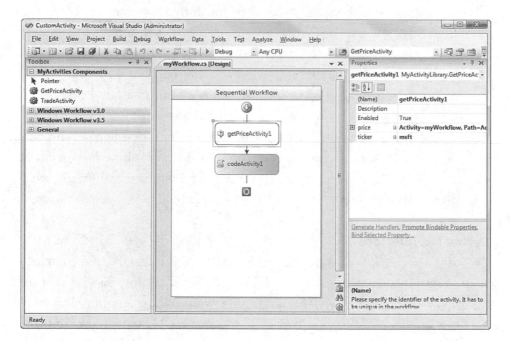

FIGURE 11.5 Using a custom activity in a workflow

Exposing a Service from WF

Developers typically use WF for building *reactive programs*. The program starts, does something useful, waits for input, does something else useful, waits for more input, and so on. At some deterministic point, the workflow program ends. Reactive programs may run for a very long time, during which the client or server computer may be shut down. There also may be many copies of the workflow instances running simultaneously, and each instance must be uniquely addressable so it can receive external input. Although these qualities are not unique to WF, they do require special attention.

The WF design and runtime environment taps into WCF extensibility points to support these key requirements. It handles long-running workflows that persist across system failure. It correlates incoming messages to existing workflows so that a scalable host can support many running instances. It exposes service endpoints from the workflow program so that standards-based messages can be used for communication.

This section, and the subsequent sections in this chapter, will cover the details of how WF exposes workflow programs as services. We will start by showing how to expose a simple workflow. We'll define an interface in C# and import that interface into the WF designer. We will configure a Receive activity to expose a workflow as a service endpoint and define one request-response operation. We'll then expand the workflow to have multiple steps, one of which waits for external input, and define a second service operation for the second Receive activity. We will show how a client can target messages to a particular running WF instance, and finally we'll add durability support to the workflow so it can survive system failures.

Define the Interface

To build a workflow that implements a particular interface, we created a new project in Visual Studio using the Sequential Workflow Service Library template, found in the WCF folder. In this example, the solution and project are named SimpleService. We deleted `IWorkflow1.cs` and `Workflow1.cs` and defined an interface, `IStockService`, shown in Listing 11.3. Note that the namespace in the file is `SimpleService`. The fully qualified interface name, `SimpleService.IStockService`, must be specified as the contract for the endpoint in the `app.config` for the project.

The service contract has two operations: `InitiateTrade` and `Approval`. The `InitiateTrade` operation places a fictitious stock order and returns a confirmation number in the `TradeRequestStatus` structure. The `Approval` operation is used after a potentially fraudulent stock order has been reviewed. This operation is called to restart a workflow that is waiting on an external event.

The interface shown Listing 11.3 is the interface that the workflow service exposes. Alternatively, we could have defined the interface from within the WF designer for more of a code-first style. By starting with the interface, we could publish it and iterate with other developers and then use that as the starting point to implement the service. Either way, starting with the interface or starting with the designer, would produce the same result but contract-first feels like a more deliberate method to building services.

LISTING 11.3 Service Interface Exposed from WF

```
namespace SimpleService {
  [ServiceContract]
  public interface IStockService
  {
    [OperationContract]
    TradeRequestStatus InitiateTrade(TradeRequest tradeRequest);

    [OperationContract]
    void Approval(ApprovalRequest approvalRequest);
  }

  [DataContract]
  public class TradeRequest
  {
    [DataMember] public string account;
    [DataMember] public string action;
    [DataMember] public string ticker;
    [DataMember] public double price;
  }

  [DataContract]
  public class ApprovalRequest
  {
    [DataMember] public string tradeNumber;
    [DataMember] public string approval;
    [DataMember] public string reason;
  }

  [DataContract]
  public class TradeRequestStatus
  {
    [DataMember] public string confirmationNumber;
    [DataMember] public string status;
  }

}
```

Receive Activity

A Receive activity models an operation contract. Because there are two operation contracts defined in Listing 11.3, there should be two Receive activities on the workflow. The properties of the Receive activity are the input and return messages of the operation contract.

To implement the workflow, we added a new item using the Sequential Workflow (with Code Separation) template. The code separation enables us to look at the XOML representation of the workflow, which is an XML grammar that defines the workflow and its activities. With the StockService.xoml file open in the WF designer, a Receive activity is placed on design surface and the result is shown in Figure 11.6.

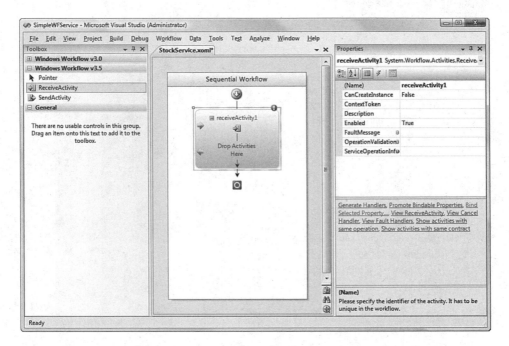

FIGURE 11.6 Adding a Receive activity to the workflow design surface

Selecting the ServiceOperationInfo property and clicking the ellipsis presents a dialog box for choosing or defining a contract. The first time that you launch that dialog box, there will be no operation contracts defined. Clicking the Import button in Figure 11.7 will show all the classes included in the project and referenced assemblies marked with the [ServiceContract] attribute. Only methods marked with [OperationContract] in those classes can be imported. A contract definition can be entered directly though the dialog, or you can select an existing class definition already present in the project. We included the IStockService interface in the project for exactly this purpose, and the resulting dialog is shown in Figure 11.7. Note that two operations are listed, along with the complex .NET types used as arguments.

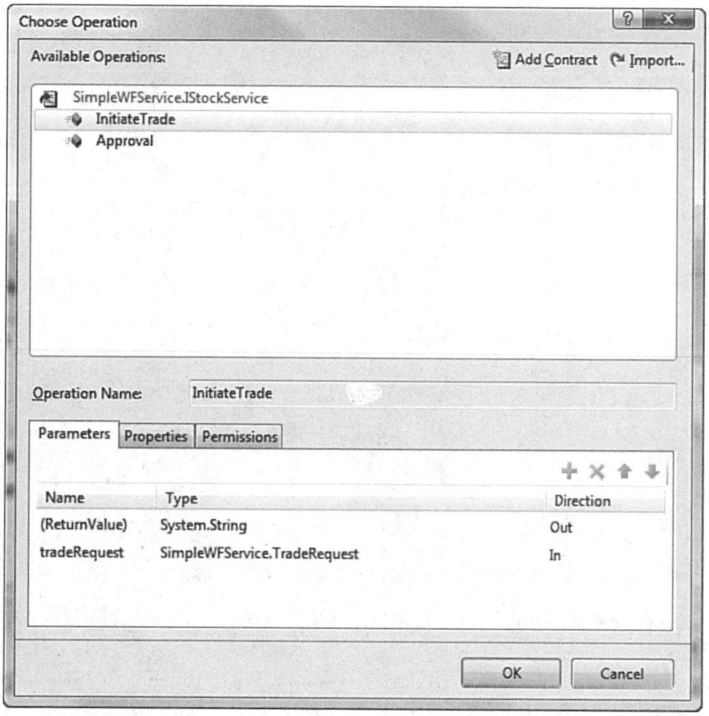

FIGURE 11.7 Entering or importing an interface for a Receive activity

A WF program is just like any other program, so service-enabling a WF program via WCF integration adds all the WCF capabilities afforded to other programs. When a WCF receives a message, it deserializes it to the .NET type and passes the type to the appropriate class method. In a WF program, the .NET type is assigned to a local variable in the workflow program.

Each parameter defined in the operation contract must be bound to a WF field or property. A dialog box is presented for this purpose where you can select an existing variable (field or property) or create a new one to bind to the parameter. The dialog pops up when you click the ellipsis next to a parameter name in the Receive activity's property sheet. Figure 11.8 shows the dialog box for binding workflow variables to operation contract parameters.

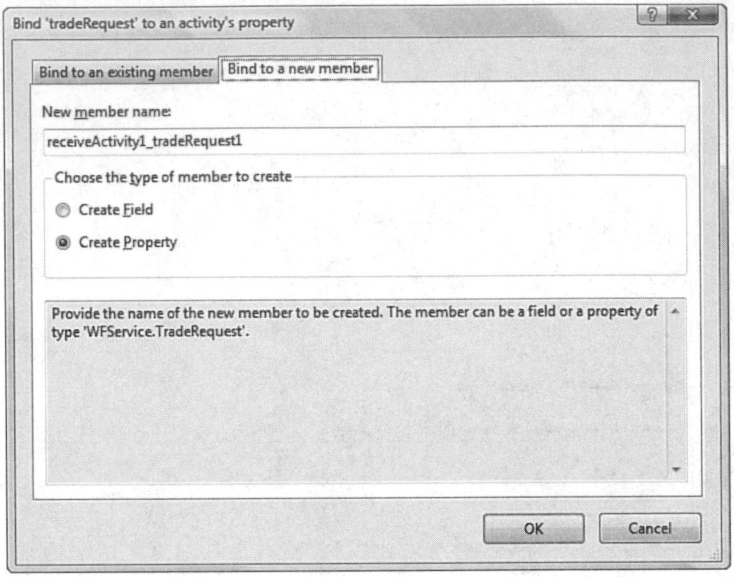

FIGURE 11.8 Binding operation contract parameters to workflow variables

At this point the service interface is completely defined. The service doesn't yet do anything, but its interface is defined. The next step is to update the Receive activity to include a Code activity to send a meaningful response back to the client. We will implement the Approval code later in this chapter. In this example, the code sets the return value of the operation contract to some text purporting to be a confirmation number. Note that a Receive activity is a composite activity, so you can place any activity within the Receive activity and it will execute before the response messages is sent back to the client. By keeping the code within the Receive activity to a minimum, the service operation will deliver fast performance to clients.

The final configured workflow is shown in Figure 11.9. Note that the return value and the input parameter for the `InitiateTrade` operation are bound to variables. Also note the `CanCreateInstance` property is set to true. This tells the hosting environment to spin up a new service instance within the WF runtime when it receives a message not associated with other instances.

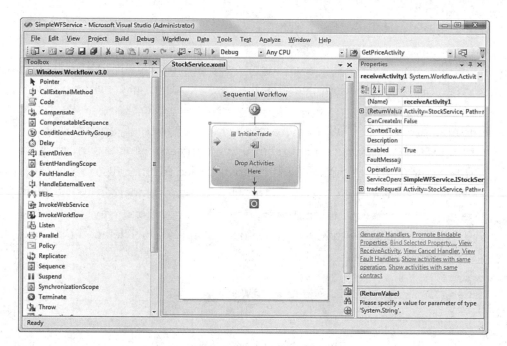

FIGURE 11.9 Workflow exposing one Receive activity

Configuration in `app.config`

As with most WCF services, information on endpoints and security and behavioral settings are stored in the `app.config` or `web.config` files.

When Visual Studio created the project using the Sequential Workflow Service template, it included an `app.config` file. But because the template included in the `IWorkflow1` and `Workflow1` interface and class and the example shown in this section use `IStockService` and `StockService`, these names need to be adjusted in the `app.config`. The updated WCF settings in the `app.config` file for this project is shown in Listing 11.4. A few settings are noteworthy.

First is the service name. This must match the class name that implements the service. Because the fully qualified class name was changed from `SimpleWFService.Workflow1` to `SimpleWFService.StockService` in the `StockService.XMOL.cs` file, the service name must match in the `app.config`. The same situation exists for the contract name in the endpoint, which must match the fully qualified interface name in the IStockService.cs file.

Finally, note the binding used in the endpoint. It defaults to wsHttpContextBinding. This binding contains the ContextBindingElement and supports sessions, which is necessary to support long-running workflows. Three bindings provided by WF implement the ContexBindingElement: wsHttpContextBinding, basicHttpContextBinding, and netTcpContextBinding. In addition, the ContextBindingElement can be added to other custom bindings so they can also be used to communicate with service-enabled workflows. Note that the ContextBindingElement does not support one-way operations, so it cannot be used with MSMQ bindings. Chapter 4 has detailed information on how to build custom bindings.

LISTING 11.4 app.config for Service-Enabled Workflow

```
<system.serviceModel>
  <services>
    <service name="SimpleWFService.StockService"
        behaviorConfiguration="SimpleWFService.Workflow1Behavior">
      <host>
        <baseAddresses>
          <add baseAddress="http://localhost:8080/Workflow1" />
        </baseAddresses>
      </host>
      <endpoint address=""
                binding="wsHttpContextBinding"
                contract="SimpleWFService.IStockService" />
      <endpoint address="mex"
                binding="mexHttpBinding"
                contract="IMetadataExchange" />
    </service>
  </services>
  <behaviors>
    <serviceBehaviors>
      <behavior name="SimpleWFService.Workflow1Behavior">
         .
         .
         .
      </behavior>
    </serviceBehaviors>
  </behaviors>
</system.serviceModel>
```

Hosting a Service-Enabled Workflow

Many options exist for hosting WCF services. Hosting is covered in detail in Chapter 7, "Hosting," but for a brief review, a WCF host is any process that instantiates the ServiceHost class. The most common hosting environment for services is IIS. There is direct support for IIS in WCF, so hosting and managing services in IIS is relatively easy. Vista and Windows Server 2008 generalized IIS to Windows Activation Services (WAS) for non-HTTP protocols, so hosting services through WAS is equally robust. Hosting services in Windows Services (a.k.a. NT Services) is also very common, with a familiar interface for system administrators. For testing or specialized scenarios, WCF services can be hosted in a command-line console or Windows applications.

Regardless of the hosting environment, the ServiceHost class adds endpoints to the service description at startup. At runtime, the ServiceHost requests the channel listeners specified in the bindings to listen for incoming messages. The ServiceHost reads the service description from the <servicemodel> node of the configuration file, from the attributes ([ServiceContract], [ServiceBehavior], [OperationContract], and so on) in code, and from class definitions. The ServiceHost can also be manipulated programmatically. The host program can also add behaviors to the service, which controls what happens when messages are received or sent and when instances are created or destroyed. As messages are received by the channel listeners, they are routed to the proper service contracts for processing. Much of this is implemented in behaviors, which is covered in detail in Chapter 5.

Hosting a service-enabled workflow is similar to hosting any other service. When hosting service-enabled workflows, WF provides a new class, WorkflowServiceHost, that derives from ServiceHost to address WF-specific needs. Whereas the ServiceHost constructor accepts any class marked with [ServiceContract], the WorkflowServiceHost constructor requires information (types derived from Activity or the XAML stream/file) that can be used to instantiate a workflow. The WorkflowServiceHost adds three behaviors to the service: WorkflowServiceBehavior, WorkflowOperationBehavior, and WorkflowRuntimeBehavior. It also adds a DurableInstanceProvider and MessageContextInspector. Combined, they manage service instances and dispatch messages into and out of work-flows. In addition, the WorkflowServiceHost requires that bindings used with a service endpoint include the ContextBindingElement.

Self-Hosting a Service-Enabled Workflow

Listing 11.5 shows a minimal self-hosting console application that exposes a service-enabled workflow. Compare this to Listing 1.2 in Chapter 1, "Basics," and you'll see that they're virtually identical. The only difference is that the WorkflowServiceHost class is used instead of the ServiceHost class.

LISTING 11.5 Self Hosting a Service-Enabled Workflow

```
WorkflowServiceHost serviceHost =
        new WorkflowServiceHost(typeof(StockService));

serviceHost.Open();

Console.WriteLine("Services is ready. Press <ENTER> to terminate.");
Console.ReadLine();

serviceHost.Close();
```

Listing 11.6 shows the configuration file associated with the self-hosted workflow. Compare this with Listing 1.5 in Chapter 1 and you'll see that they are virtually identical. The only difference here is the inclusion of authentication information in the behavior that is needed to enable the security features of service-enabled workflows. This security information is covered later in this section.

One housekeeping note: The app.config file created by Visual Studio is in the Sequential Workflow Library project. This file should be moved from the workflow library project to the console application project shown in Listing 11.5 because the WorkflowServiceHost will look in its own folder for configuration information.

LISTING 11.6 Configuration for a Workflow-Enabled Service

```
<?xml version="1.0" encoding="utf-8" ?>
<configuration>
  <system.serviceModel>
    <services>
```

```
      <service name="SimpleWFService.StockService"
              behaviorConfiguration="SimpleWFService.Workflow1Behavior">
        <host>
          <baseAddresses>
            <add baseAddress="http://localhost:8000/EffectiveWCF" />
          </baseAddresses>
        </host>
        <endpoint address=""
                  binding="basicHttpContextBinding"
                  contract="SimpleWFService.IStockService" />

        <endpoint address="mex"
                  binding="mexHttpBinding"
                  contract="IMetadataExchange" />
      </service>
    </services>
    <behaviors>
      <serviceBehaviors>
        <behavior name="SimpleWFService.Workflow1Behavior"  >
          <serviceMetadata httpGetEnabled="true" />
          <serviceCredentials>
            <windowsAuthentication
                allowAnonymousLogons="false"
                includeWindowsGroups="true" />
          </serviceCredentials>
        </behavior>
      </serviceBehaviors>
    </behaviors>
  </system.serviceModel>
</configuration>
```

Hosting a Service-Enabled Workflow in IIS

Hosting a workflow-enabled service in IIS is the same as hosting any other service. The steps needed to host a service in IIS are described in Chapter 1. There needs to be an IIS application, an SVC file that describes how to instantiate the service, a web.config file to include the <servicemodel> configuration, and the implementation in the /bin folder of the virtual root pointed to by the application.

Listing 11.7 shows a minimal SVC file associated with a service-enabled workflow. Comparing this to Listing 1.9 from Chapter 1 shows the similarity. The only difference is the inclusion of the Factory element, which tells IIS to use the WorkflowServiceHostFactory instead of the default ServiceHostFactory when creating the ServiceHost.

LISTING 11.7 SVC File for Hosting a Workflow-Enabled Service in IIS

```
<%@ ServiceHost
    Service="SimpleWFService.StockService"
    Factory="System.ServiceModel.Activation.WorkflowServiceHostFactory" %>
```

The web.config file is updated to include the <servicemodel> information from Listing 11.6, with the exception of the <host> node, because the base addresses for IIS are determined by the virtual root of the application.

Correlation and Durable Services

Workflows are often used to model business transactions. As in real-world business transactions, these may run for seconds (transfer money at the ATM machine) or considerably longer (purchase something from eBay, pay for it, receive it, and leave feedback). The transaction is modeled once and then thousands of instances may be launched, many running in parallel. While any of these transactions are running, the client, the server, or the network may be unavailable or rebooted along the way.

To support long-running transactions, two elements are needed: correlation and durability. Correlation allows a client to specify a particular workflow instance that it wants to communicate with. Durability allows a workflow instance to survive system failures and enables the workflow environment to efficiently use memory and CPU resources. The WorkflowServiceHost class implements extensions to support correlation and durability. It accomplishes these using two elements: a context class that is passed in the channel between the client and the service, and a durable instance provider that can dehydrate (write from memory to disk) and hydrate (read from disk to memory) a workflow instance.

The context passed between the client and service uniquely identifies the workflow instance. When the client sends a message to a WF-enabled service, the message is inspected to see if a context is present. If there is no context, a new workflow instance is created in the WF runtime. If a context is present on the message, the message is sent to an existing workflow instance. The WF runtime checks to see whether the instance is in memory, and if it's not, it calls the durable instance provider to read it from disk. The message is then deserialized to a .NET type and passed into the WF runtime and routed to the proper instance.

Note that the WF runtime is completely embedded in a single WCF service instance and is responsible for workflow instances and persistence. In other words, if 50 instances of a workflow are running, messages sent to all workflows flow into a single workflow runtime. The workflow runtime has its own internal mechanism for correlating and queuing messages to workflow instances. The Instance ID stored in the context, in conjunction with the Durable Instance Provider, is used to ensure that the workflow runtime has the right instance in memory.

Long-Running Workflow

In this section, we'll model a business process that accepts and executes stock trades. Fraud detection is done early in the workflow, for obvious reasons. If a trade is suspicious, it gets routed to an analyst for review. If it looks good to the analyst, the order goes through; if not, it's rejected. Most workflow instances in this example will complete within a few seconds because most trade requests are not fraudulent. But when a request is received that requires manual review, the process may take minutes or hours to complete. On a busy trading day, hundreds of stock trades might require review. The process is identical with each stock trade, but the details (the input and output) will be different.

In this scenario, our fictitious stock trader using a Web or rich-client application calls the `InitiateTrade` method to execute a new stock trade. If the status returned is `executed`, her trade is finished. If the status is `review`, then the trade is not complete and she should expect to receive a notification shortly (the example doesn't show any notification, but you can imagine e-mail, voice, SMS, or instant messaging here). If the status is `review`, somewhere else in the world, a financial analyst is notified that a stock trade requires review. The analyst uses a Web or rich-client application to review the trade request and then calls the `Approval` method indicating whether the system should execute trade.

Recall the interface for this scenario in Listing 11.3. It contains the three message formats and two service operations. The messages are `TradeRequest`, `TradeRequestStatus`, and `ApprovalRequest`. Clients send a `TradeRequest` to initiate a new trade and send an `ApprovalRequest` to approve or deny a dubious trade. Client communication with the workflow, from instantiation through termination, will be done exclusively with these messages. The interface contains two service operations: `InitiateTrade` and `Approval`, which each use the message's formats.

Figure 11.10 shows the start of the workflow. The Receive activity is named `InitiateTrade` and is a composite activity that has three code activities, two of which are embedded in an `IfThenElse` structure. The `CheckFraud` activity calls a routine to evaluate the trade for possible fraud. If it looks okay, the `ExecuteTrade` activity is called to execute the stock trade and return a `RequestTradeStatus` structure with a confirmation number and a `status = "executed"`. If the trade is potentially fraudulent, it is sent to a work queue (external to this workflow), and the return structure has a confirmation number and a `status = "review"`. These three code activities run synchronously (and presumably fast) within the Receive activity, so whichever branch is taken, a response is sent back in a timely manner.

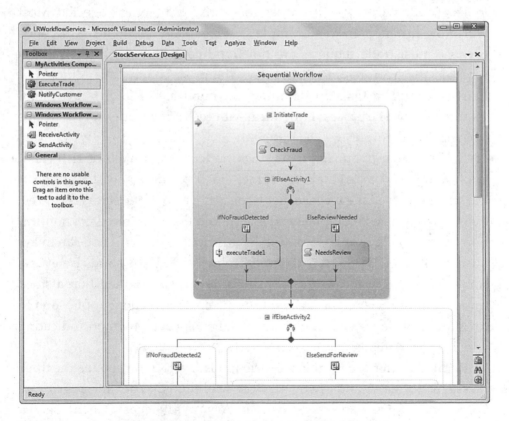

FIGURE 11.10 Composite Receive activity in a long-running workflow

The configuration file for this workflow is shown in Listing 11.6. As required by the service-enabled workflows, the ContextBinding element is used in the channel, and in this case the wsHttpContextBinding. When the TradeRequest message is received by the service, an internal WF behavior inspects the message to see if the context is present. If there is no context, the WorkflowRuntime creates a new instance of the workflow. When the synchronous TradeRequestStatus message is sent back from the Receive activity to the client, the WF behavior stamps the message with a context, indicating the Instance ID of the workflow.

Continuing with the example, if the trade request is not executed immediately, the workflow pauses, listening for the results of a manual review of the stock trade request. Figure 11.11 shows the remaining workflow. The Listen activity has two branches: one a Delay and the other a Receive activity. If the Receive activity is not called before the time indicated in the Delay activity, the workflow will continue without the input. Like the initial InitiateTrade activity, the Approval activity is also a composite activity, but this time it has only one code activity embedded. The ReviewReceived code looks at the ApprovalRequest message to see if the trade is okay. If so, it sets a flag indicating that the trade should be executed. Regardless of whether the trade is executed in ExecuteTrade2, the NotifyCustomer activity sends an e-mail to the customer who initiated the trade.

The workflow depicted in Figures 11.10 and 11.11 has two Receive activities, labeled InitiateTrade and Approval. The CanCreateInstance property of InitiateTrade is set to true, indicating that this operation can be called without passing an Instance ID in the context. When WF receives the message, it will create a new instance of the workflow program. The CanCreate-Instance of the Approval activity is set to false, indicating that this operation cannot be called without an Instance ID in the context. If a client attempts to call it without an instance ID, it will receive a SOAP fault.

Listing 11.8 shows the code that implements this workflow. A code activity, codeCheckFraud_ExecuteCode , is used for calling the internal validation routine and setting the return value from within the Receive location. Another code activity, codeNeedsReview_ExecuteCode_1, is used to call the internal routine to store the context. A third code activity, ReviewReceived_ExecuteCode, is used to inspect the approval message sent and set the validation flat accordingly. This internal routine, `saveContext`, is overly simple in this example and stores the `InstanceId` in a file. In production, this internal routine should be enhanced to store the name/value pair in a database or Web service that is accessible from the client and service.

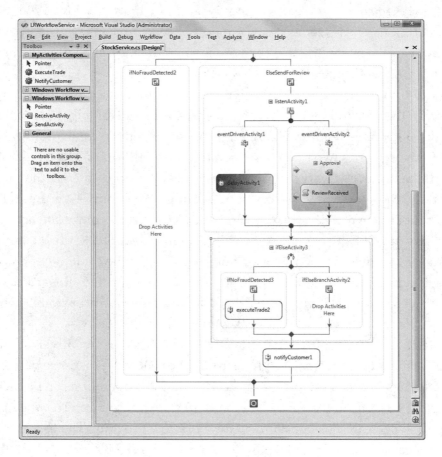

FIGURE 11.11   Completing a long-running workflow

LISTING 11.8 Code for a Long-Running Workflow

```
public sealed partial class StockService: SequentialWorkflowActivity
    {
      public StockService()
      {
       InitializeComponent();
      }
```

```
        public bool bValidation;
        public TradeRequestStatus receiveActivity1__ReturnValue_1;
        public ApprovalRequest receiveActivity2_approvalRequest1;
        public TradeRequest receiveActivity1_tradeRequest1;

        private void codeCheckFraud_ExecuteCode
                    (object sender, EventArgs e)
        {
            wfHelper h = new wfHelper();
            bValidation = h.Evaluate(receiveActivity1_tradeRequest1);
            receiveActivity1__ReturnValue_1 = new TradeRequestStatus();
            receiveActivity1__ReturnValue_1.confirmationNumber = "123";
            if (bValidation)
                receiveActivity1__ReturnValue_1.status = "OK";
            else
                receiveActivity1__ReturnValue_1.status = "Review";
        }

        private void codeNeedsReview_ExecuteCode_1
                    (object sender, EventArgs e)
        {
            wfHelper h = new wfHelper();
            h.SaveContext
                (receiveActivity1__ReturnValue_1.confirmationNumber,
                this.WorkflowInstanceId.ToString());
        }

        private void ReviewReceived_ExecuteCode
                    (object sender, EventArgs e)
        {
            wfHelper h = new wfHelper();
            bValidation = h.Evaluate(receiveActivity2_approvalRequest1);
        }

    }

public class wfHelper
{
  public const string INSTANCEFILENAME = "c:\temp\instanceID.txt";

  public bool Evaluate(TradeRequest tradeRequest)
    {
        if (tradeRequest.account == "000") return (false);
        else return (true);
    }

  public bool Evaluate(ApprovalRequest approvalRequest)
    {
        if (approvalRequest.approval == "OK") return (true);
        else return (false);
```

LISTING 11.8 continued

```
        }

        //this only works in demo/debug since the client and service
        // have access to the folder where key/instanceID is stored.
        // For real, it should use WS that the client and service
        // can reach
        public void SaveContext(string key, string instanceId)
        {
            if (File.Exists(INSTANCEFILENAME))
                File.Delete(INSTANCEFILENAME);
            string txt = string.Format("{0},{1}", key, instanceId);
            File.WriteAllText(INSTANCEFILENAME, txt);
        }
    }
```

Handling the Context

A long-running workflow may have multiple Receive activities, as shown in Figures 11.10 and 11.11. When the first Receive activity is called and a workflow instance is created, all subsequent calls to that workflow instance must attach a context to the binding channel to ensure proper correlation. This means that the client is responsible for tracking the context of workflow instances that it wants to communicate with. WF uses the ContextBinding element to make this available for the client.

By default, the context is available to the client in the channel. The pertinent information in the context is the InstanceId that uniquely identifies the workflow. The client can pull the InstanceId from the context, store it in memory or in a local file, and attach it to the channel on subsequent calls. This method works well as long as one client makes the initial and subsequent calls, and the client isn't restarted between calls. Figure 11.12 shows the sequence.

It is common, however, that multiple clients access a single workflow instance. These different clients may be different Web sites or two different people. In any case, clients making the subsequent calls to the workflow must obtain the context from the first client.

1. Client creates proxy/channel
and sends a message to service to
initiate a workflow.

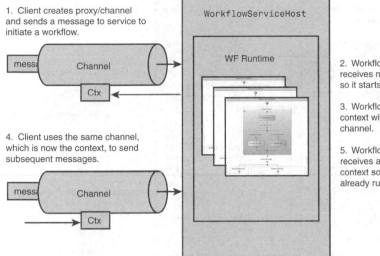

WorkflowServiceHost

WF Runtime

2. WorkflowServiceHost
receives message without context
so it starts a new WF instance.

3. WorkflowServiceHost places
context with Instance ID in
channel.

4. Client uses the same channel,
which is now the context, to send
subsequent messages.

5. WorkflowServiceHost
receives a message with a
context so it routes it to an
already running WF instance.

FIGURE 11.12 One client maintaining context with multiple calls to a workflow instance

To handle the case of multiple clients accessing a single workflow instance, the context, or `InstanceId`, must be stored separately from the client and workflow instance. Additionally, a friendly name should be associated with the `InstanceId` so that clients do not need to work with internally generated artifacts. In most business scenarios, this isn't a problem because the business transaction usually has a confirmation number or unique transaction number of some sort.

Figure 11.13 shows a design for enabling multiple clients to access a single workflow instance. In this design, the Receive activity in the workflow explicitly stores the WF `InstanceId` in a place that the client can later retrieve. It stores it with a friendly name, such as a confirmation number so that the client can easily look it up. The confirmation number is probably already returned from the initiating Receive activity or can be embedded in a URL.

Regardless of how the client gets the `InstanceId`, it must create a context and place it on the channel to make subsequent calls. Listing 11.9 shows client-side code to do this. It calls the `GetFromSomewhere` method to obtain the `InstanceId` and then places it in the context in the channel off of the proxy.

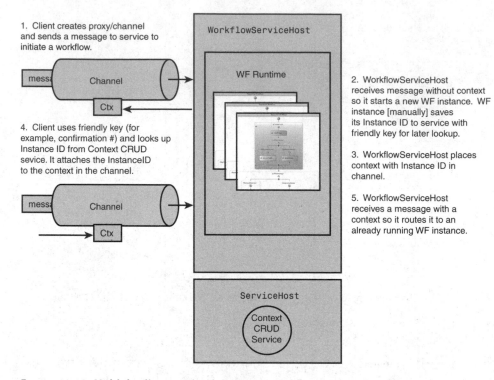

1. Client creates proxy/channel and sends a message to service to initiate a workflow.

4. Client uses friendly key (for example, confirmation #) and looks up Instance ID from Context CRUD sevice. It attaches the InstanceID to the context in the channel.

WorkflowServiceHost

WF Runtime

2. WorkflowServiceHost receives message without context so it starts a new WF instance. WF instance [manually] saves its Instance ID to service with friendly key for later lookup.

3. WorkflowServiceHost places context with Instance ID in channel.

5. WorkflowServiceHost receives a message with a context so it routes it to an already running WF instance.

ServiceHost

Context CRUD Service

FIGURE 11.13 Multiple clients maintaining context with multiple calls to a workflow instance

LISTING 11.9 Client Attaching Workflow Context ID onto the Channel

```
instanceID = GetFromSomewhere(myConfirmationNumber);
IContextManager cm =
        proxy.InnerChannel.GetProperty<IContextManager>();
IDictionary<string, string> context = new Dictionary<string,string>();
context.Add("InstanceId",instanceID);
cm.SetContext(context);
```

Persisting Workflow State on the Server

The state of a long-running workflow is stored within the WorkflowRuntime class. As events trigger activities within the workflow, the WorkflowRuntime executes those activities.

When a workflow is idle and waiting for an event, the WorkflowRuntime can persist the workflow state to external storage to free system resources such as memory and CPU. More importantly, when the WorkflowRuntime is shut down, the state of all active workflows must be written to external storage, or the workflow instances won't be able to resume when the runtime comes back up.

The WF runtime uses a persistence service to save state in external storage. It calls the persistence service when workflows are idle and again when the runtime shuts down. A persistence provider is registered with the runtime before workflows are initiated, and the runtime uses the service to serialize workflow instances to external storage. There is nothing WCF-specific about the persistence service, but it is mentioned here to support the scenario in this example.

A persistence service can register with the runtime in either code or configuration. If self-hosting a workflow within a WCF service, the host can register the service in code. Listing 11.10 shows the code to register the SQL persistence service with the runtime.

LISTING 11.10 Adding a Persistence Service in Code

```
WorkflowServiceHost serviceHost =
    new WorkflowServiceHost(typeof(StockService));

WorkflowPersistenceService persistenceService =
    new SqlWorkflowPersistenceService(
    "Initial Catalog=WFPersistence;Data Source=localhost;
                    Integrated Security=SSPI;",
    false,
    new TimeSpan(1, 0, 0),
    new TimeSpan(0, 0, 5));

WorkflowRuntime runtime =
    serviceHost.Description.Behaviors.Find
                    <WorkflowRuntimeBehavior>().WorkflowRuntime;
runtime.AddService(persistenceService);

serviceHost.Open();
```

To add a persistence service to a service-enabled workflow where you do not have access to the WorkflowServiceHost, you need to define the persistence store through configuration. This is done as a service behavior. Listing 11.11 shows the configuration file for a service. It is similar to Listing 11.6, with the addition of the persistence service in the behaviors section.

LISTING 11.11 Adding Persistence Service in web.config

```
<behaviors>
  <serviceBehaviors>
    <behavior name="Durable.Workflow1Behavior"  >
      <serviceMetadata httpGetEnabled="true" />
      <serviceDebug includeExceptionDetailInFaults="true" />
      <serviceCredentials>
        <windowsAuthentication
            allowAnonymousLogons="false"
            includeWindowsGroups="true" />
      </serviceCredentials>
      <workflowRuntime name="WorkflowServiceHostRuntime">
        <services>
          <add type="System.Workflow.Runtime.Hosting.
                        SqlWorkflowPersistenceService,
                  System.Workflow.Runtime,
                  Version=3.0.00000.0, Culture=neutral,
                  PublicKeyToken=31bf3856ad364e35"
              connectionString="Initial Catalog=WFPersistence;
                  Data Source=localhost;
                  Integrated Security=SSPI;"
              LoadIntervalSeconds="1" UnLoadOnIdle= "true" />
        </services>
      </workflowRuntime>
    </behavior>
  </serviceBehaviors>
</behaviors>
```

Controlling Access to Service-Enabled Workflows

Integration between WF and WCF occurs largely through behavior extensions. Behaviors can inspect and augment messages before they arrive at the WorkflowRuntime or after they leave. Behaviors have access to the full message, including the SOAP headers. Depending on the security model specified in the service description, different security information is passed from the client to the service in the SOAP header.

The example in Listing 11.6 shows that <windowsAuthentication> is used. This instructs WCF to serialize and send Windows Authentication information (encrypted over the wire) in the SOAP header. The includeWindowsGroups=true setting instructs WCF to include all the Windows groups that the current user belongs to. Together, these settings enable the workflow program to make decisions based on the user and group membership.

For workflow-specific access control, two mechanisms are built in to the Receive activity. First, a Receive activity can be configured to allow access for only certain users or users in certain groups. This is done declaratively. Second, a Receive activity can have an Operation Validation method that sets a flag to grant or deny access the operation. This is done programmatically. This section reviews these alternatives.

Declarative Access Control

There are many ways to control access to WCF services. Chapter 8, "Security," describes these in detail, including ASP.NET roles, certificates and Kerberos, and others. In addition to the WCF facilities, WF provides some in the Receive activity.

Remember that the Receive activity in WF exposes an operation contract of the service. When the operation contract is added into the project, a dialog box is presented for configuring parameters, properties, and permissions. Figure 11.14 shows this dialog. A domain\username can be entered in the Name field, or domain\group in the Role field. At runtime, after the message is received by the service but before it is dispatched to the `WorkflowRuntime`, a behavior will check membership permissions. It does this by looking at the message header and comparing the claims against what's indicated in this dialog box. If the message is coming from a valid user or group, then the operation is called. If not, a security exception is returned.

Programmatic Access Control

Each Receive activity can specify a method for authorizing access. The method is called before the operation contract is called and has the opportunity to grant or deny access. The method name is stored in the `OperationValidation` property of the Receive activity and can be generated from the WF designer. At runtime, the method is called by the WCF behavior before invoking the operation contract. It is passed an object containing all the claims configured by the client. This makes it relatively easy to do claims-based authorization.

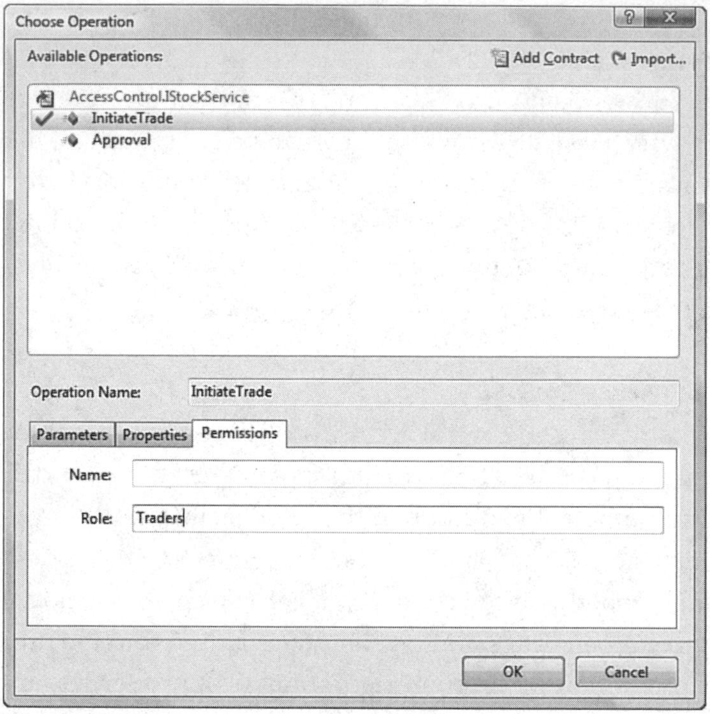

FIGURE 11.14 Declarative authorization within a Receive activity

Let's add a new requirement to the stock trade/approve example: *The person who initiates the trade cannot be the same person who approves it.* To implement this, we need to do two things. In the first Receive activity (Figure 11.10), an Operation Validation routine finds and stores the user-name who initiated the trade. In the second Receive activity (Figure 11.11) an Operation Validation routine compares the user requesting approval to the user who initiated the trade. If they're the same, or if either is blank, the authorization will be denied.

Listing 11.12 shows a small function for determining the user's name based on the `ClaimsSet` sent to the service. This function would be more robust working with more predictable claims, such as those in certificates, but to illustrate how access to service operations is controlled program-matically, it will suffice.

LISTING 11.12 Function to Find the Name Claim from a Windows ClaimSet

```
private string findClaimName(OperationValidationEventArgs e)
{
  string claimName="";
  if (e.ClaimSets.Count == 1)
  {
    IEnumerable myClaims = e.ClaimSets[0].
                      FindClaims("http://schemas.xmlsoap.org/
                              ws/2005/05/identity/claims/name",
                              Rights.PossessProperty);
    foreach (Claim c in myClaims) while (claimName =="")
        claimName = c.Resource.ToString();
  }
  return claimName;
}
```

Listing 11.13 shows how findClaimName is used. The two functions, receive1_OpValidation and receive2_OpValidation, are generated by the WF designer. The first one stores the username in a variable scoped to the workflow class. If it cannot find the username, it sets the **IsValid = false**, rejecting the call. The second function compares the current username to the previous one. If they are the same, it sets the **IsValid = false**, again rejecting the call. In both cases, when **IsValid = false**, the Receive activity does not call the operation contract.

LISTING 11.13 Operation Validation Methods

```
private void receive1_OpValidation(object sender,
                              OperationValidationEventArgs e)
{
  initiatedBy = findClaimName(e);
  if (initiatedBy == "") e.IsValid = false;
}

private void receive2_OpValidation(object sender,
                              OperationValidationEventArgs e)
{
  string reviewedBy = findClaimName(e);
  if (reviewedBy == initiatedBy)
      e.IsValid = false;
}
```

SUMMARY

Windows Workflow Foundation (WF) is complementary technology to WCF. Whereas WCF defines and implements the interface to a service, WF models and implements the business logic of the service. Visual Studio 2008 and .NET 3.5 provide deep integration between the two.

To invoke services from WF, you can use a Send Activity, Code activity, or a custom activity. The Send Activity requires the least code but a custom activity is by far the most flexible option.

The Receive activity is used in the WF designer to expose a workflow as a service. After it is configured, WF defines a [ServiceContract] for the service and an [OperationContract] for each Receive activity. You can either point the Receive activity at proxies imported or included in the project, or you can define interfaces using a WF designer. The Receive activity binds WF variables to the service operation. Using the WF designer, you can select or create WF-scoped variables to bind for each input variable in the operation.

The WF class, WorkflowServiceHost, is used to instantiate the WF runtime. This class is used instead of ServiceHost for service-enabled workflows. This class must be used when self-hosting. When hosting in IIS, a factory class must be specified in the SVC file to achieve the same result.

One of the context bindings must be used when exposing a service-enabled workflow: basicHttpContextBinding, wsHttpContextBinding, or netTcpContextBinding. These bindings use the context channel element, which adds context information to the channel. You can also add this channel element to custom bindings. The context information is required for correlating inbound messages with existing workflows.

Many workflow programs that model business processes must run for days, weeks, or months, during which time clients may be offline, services may be recycled, or networks may be down. To support the long-running nature of these processes, a persistence service is necessary. When a workflow instance is idle, or when the runtime is shutting down, the persistence service saves the state, or "dehydrates" it to durable storage. When the WF receives a message for a dehydrated instance, the WF "hydrates" it from the persistence service.

■ 12 ■
Peer Networking

MANY DEVELOPERS THINK of the client-server or n-tier models when building distributed applications. Another approach to building distributed applications that is often overlooked is the peer-to-peer (P2P) model. Some of the most popular Internet applications, including instant messaging, games, and file sharing, use the P2P approach. Unlike other types of applications, a P2P application assumes no central infrastructure, which means there is no distinction between client and server. This introduces a significant amount of complexity in the design of the application. Most developers shy away from building P2P applications because of the complexity and difficulty associated with building these types of application. If done properly, P2P applications can offer distinct advantages in terms of scalability and reliability. This chapter will focus on building P2P applications using WCF and Windows Vista. We will examine the capabilities in WCF and demonstrate new capabilities in the .NET Framework 3.5.

Approaches to Building Distributed Applications

Most distributed applications today are built using one of three types of network architectures: client/server, n-tier, and peer-to-peer. This section will compare the different approaches so that we can understand the motivation behind peer-to-peer applications.

Client/Server Applications

Many distributed applications in the past few decades have been built using the client/server approach. In this model, both the client and the server are participants in the distributed application, and each has a distinct role. Clients initiate requests and servers respond to those requests. Easily the most widely used client-server applications today are Web browsers such as Internet Explorer. A user initiates a request by typing a URL into the address bar of the Web browser and a server responds to that request. The URL contains the request as well as the location of the Web server to send that request to. Web servers such as Internet Information Services (IIS) handle the incoming request and send a response back to the client. Figure 12.1 shows the client/server model.

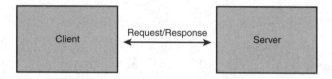

FIGURE 12.1 Client/server model

N-Tier Applications

Distributed applications then grew from client/server (two-tier) into n-tier configurations. The most common form of n-tier application is the three-tier model, where the user interface, business logic, and data layer are separated onto different physical tiers. Figure 12.2 shows the three-tier model. Many distributed applications are built using this model. There are many advantages to using this model. One of the most common reasons is encapsulating business logic onto a physically separate tier that can be secured. It also offers a way to scale applications, albeit with more hardware.

FIGURE 12.2 Three-tier model

Peer-to-Peer Applications

Another type of distributed application is the peer-to-peer (P2P) application. In a pure peer-to-peer application each participate *(node)* acts as both a client and a server to the other participants in the network. There is no distinction as to who can make or handle requests. P2P applications are often associated with collaboration applications. An example of a well-known P2P application is Gnutella, an Internet file-sharing application. Other examples of P2P applications include instant messaging, presentation, whiteboard, and document collaboration applications. Figure 12.3 shows the model for a P2P application with three nodes.

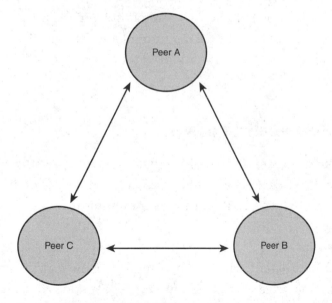

FIGURE 12.3 Peer model with three nodes

Comparison of Distributed Approaches

Client/server and n-tier applications are typically much easier to build than P2P applications. They have many advantages, including ease of development, centralized management, and securitdy. Disadvantages include scalability and reliability. Improvements in scalability can be achieved by using a scale-up (better, more costly hardware) or scale-out (more servers) approach. Reliability can be improved by adding redundant hardware. In either situation expensive hardware is needed, significantly adding to the overall cost of the solution. P2P applications are almost the opposite by comparison. Many of the advantages of a P2P application are disadvantages of a client/server application, and vice versa. For example, additional nodes can be added using commodity hardware to increase the scalability and reliability of a P2P application. This means that scalability and reliability can be improved without the costs associated with expensive server hardware. It also means that there is no central management or security that makes P2P applications harder to deploy, secure, and maintain. The reality is that each approach is no better than the other, but one may be more suitable, based on your requirements. Some applications may use multiple approaches to building distributed applications.

The remainder of this chapter will focus on building P2P applications using WCF.

Peer-to-Peer Applications

This section discusses the support that the Windows Communication Foundation (WCF) offers for creating P2P applications. To do this we examine the different ways P2P applications communicate.

Mesh Networks

P2P applications communicate to one another using a *mesh network* (a.k.a. peer mesh). A mesh network is a grouping of peer nodes that are connected together. A *peer node* is an instance of a P2P application. A *fully connected mesh* is one where all nodes in the mesh are connected to each other. An example of a fully connected mesh is shown in Figure 12.4.

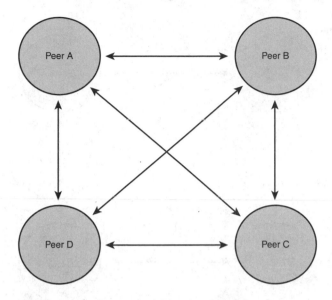

FIGURE 12.4 Fully connected mesh

Fully connected meshes make sense only for small mesh sizes. It would be impossible to have a fully connected mesh where the number of users is attempting to scale to the Internet. Instead, most meshes are only partially connected. These types of meshes are called *partially connected meshes*. In a partially connected mesh, peer nodes are connected to adjacent nodes, called neighbors. Figure 12.5 shows a partially connected mesh. Partially connected meshes reduce the number of resources needed on each node and in turn increase the scalability of the mesh. Scalability for a mesh network is measured by the number of participants in the mesh. The disadvantage to this type of mesh is that you cannot send messages directly to all nodes in the mesh. Instead, messages are forwarded between neighbors until all participants are sent the message. Messages traverse the mesh until all nodes have been contacted or messages reach a specified depth within the mesh.

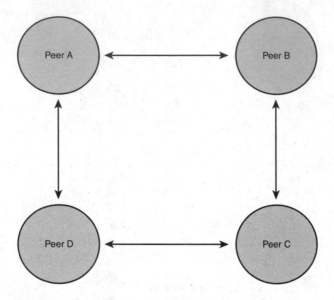

FIGURE 12.5 Partially connected mesh

Resolving Peer Meshes

P2P applications use mesh names to identify the mesh network to participate in. A mesh name is a logical network name that applications use to
address the mesh network. At some point a mesh name needs to be resolved
into a set of network addresses to connect to. This typically involves con-
necting to other participants in the mesh and exchanging information about
other participants connected to the mesh. There are many techniques used
by P2P applications to discover other nodes in the mesh. Examples include
the use of multicast protocols, such as UDP, or well-known servers, referred
to as bootstrap servers. The WCF uses a specific implementation known as
Peer Network Resolution Protocol (PNRP), which is available in both Windows XP SP2 and Windows Vista. PNRP uses a combination of techniques
that allow for discovery across a variety of networks. See "Resolving Peers
Using PNRP" for more information about PNRP.

Message Flooding Versus Directional Messaging

Communication over a mesh network is done using either message flooding
(a.k.a. multiparty messaging) or directional messaging. Message flooding

tries to send messages to all nodes in the mesh network. Messages propagate through a mesh network through nodes forwarding messages that are received to their neighbors. Directional messaging tries to send messages to a specific node in a mesh by routing a message across a set of connected nodes. Messages are sent from the originating node to one of its neighbors. Its neighbor then forwards the message to other nodes until the message reaches its destination. In either case, techniques are typically used to limit the number of messages sent across the mesh.

WCF supports building P2P applications that use message flooding. There is no out-of-the-box support for directional messaging; however, this type of communication can be layered on top of the existing peer networking capabilities using one or more of the extensibility features available in WCF.

Creating Peer-to-Peer Applications

WCF supports creating P2P applications using the `netPeerTcpBinding` binding. This binding allows for multiparty communication over a peer transport protocol. It also defines the means that nodes use to resolve neighbors within the mesh network. The default resolution protocol used by the peer transport channel is the PNRP. This technology is a part of the Windows operating system and has been available since Windows XP SP2. We discuss PNRP in more detail in the "Resolving Peers Using PNRP" section in this chapter.

netPeerTcpBinding

The `netPeerTcpBinding` binding offers support for peer communication with WCF. Peer communication is facilitated using the `PeerTransport-BindingElement`. This transport uses TCP and binary as the default transport protocol and message encoder.

The following code shows the addressing formats for the `netPeerTcp-Binding` binding:

```
net.peer://{meshname}[:port]/{service location}
```

The default port is set to 0. This means that the peer transport will randomly select a port for communication. A specific port is used if a port other than 0 is specified.

Table 12.1 lists the default binding properties for the `netPeerTcpBinding` binding.

TABLE 12.1 `netPeerTcpBinding` Binding Properties

Attribute Name	Description	Default
closeTimeout	The maximum time to wait for the connection to be closed.	00:01:00
listenIPAddress	The IP address for the peer transport to listen on.	n/a
port	The listener port for the peer transport. Specifying zero means that a randomly assigned port is used.	0
maxBufferSize	The maximum amount of memory used to store messages in memory.	65,536
maxConnections	The maximum number of outbound or inbound connections. Outbound and inbound connections are counted separately.	10
maxReceivedMessageSize	The maximum size of an incoming message.	65,536
name	The name of the binding.	n/a
openTimeout	The maximum time to wait for an open connection operation to complete.	00:01:00
readerQuotas	Specify the complexity of messages that can be processed (for example, size).	n/a
receiveTimeout	The maximum time to wait for a receive operation to complete.	00:01:00

Attribute Name	Description	Default
security	Specifies the security settings of the binding.	n/a
sendTimeout	The maximum time to wait for a send operation to complete.	00:01:00
resolver	The peer resolver used to register and to resolve other participants on a mesh network.	n/a

The minimal configuration to expose a service using the netPeerTcp-Binding binding is shown in Listing 12.1.

LISTING 12.1 netPeerTcpBinding Host Configuration

```xml
<?xml version="1.0" encoding="utf-8" ?>
<configuration>
  <system.serviceModel>
    <services>
      <service name="EssentialWCF.HelloWorld">
        <endpoint binding="netPeerTcpBinding"
                  contract="EssentialWCF.IHelloWorld"
                  address="net.peer://MyMeshName/HelloWorld/" />
      </service>
    </services>
  </system.serviceModel>
</configuration>
```

The minimal configuration to consume a service using the netPeerTcp-Binding binding is shown in Listing 12.2.

LISTING 12.2 netPeerTcpBinding Client Configuration

```xml
<?xml version="1.0" encoding="utf-8" ?>
<configuration>
  <system.serviceModel>
    <client>
      <endpoint binding="netPeerTcpBinding"
                contract="EssentialWCF.IHelloWorld"
                address="net.peer://MyMeshName/HelloWorld/" />
    </client>
  </system.serviceModel>
</configuration>
```

Resolving Peers Using PNRP

PNRP is a distributed name resolution protocol that enables publication and discovery of P2P resource information. WCF uses PNRP to resolve peer nodes in a mesh network. This allows for participants in a peer mesh to discover other participants so that they can communicate with one another. This protocol has been available for some time either as an optional download to Windows XP or as a part of Windows XP SP2. Windows Vista now includes PNRP v2.0 out of the box when you enable IPv6 support. PNRP is important to the peer transport channel in WCF because it is the default way that neighbors are discovered within a mesh network.

> **■ NOTE**　Get PNRP v2.0 for Windows XP SP2
>
> PNRP v2.0 comes with Windows Vista. This is a new version of PNRP that is *not* interoperable with older PNRP clients such as Windows XP SP2. Microsoft has provided a download on its support Web site (http://support.microsoft.com/kb/920342). This allows for peer applications using PNRP running on Windows XP SP2 to talk to Windows Vista clients.

PNRP is built on top of IPv6 and therefore requires IPv6 to be installed. You can still use the peer networking capabilities in WCF, even if your networks do not support IPv6, by implementing a custom peer resolver. Custom peer resolvers allow a custom resolution protocol to be used instead of PNRP. The section on "Implementing a Custom Peer Resolver" in this chapter goes into detail about how to do this.

PNRP works by exposing P2P resource information for discovery by other participants in a peer mesh. Resource information typically includes a list of clients and their associated IP addresses endpoints that are bound to a mesh names. PNRP can be used to store all sorts of information; however, we will focus only on the peer transport channel and how it leverages PNRP. The peer transport channel leverages PNRP to publish information on how to talk other P2P applications on the same mesh network. The information published to PNRP includes the name of the mesh as well as the services endpoints associated with each node. When another P2P application starts up, it uses PNRP to discover other applications that are on the same mesh network.

PNRP Bootstrap Process

PNRP uses multiple steps to bootstrap itself into a mesh network (a.k.a. PNRP Cloud). This approach allows participants in a mesh to register themselves in the mesh and subsequently discover one another. This multistep approach also helps PNRP scale on isolated networks such as corporate LANs or on the Internet because it tries to minimize the amount of network traffic needed to join a mesh:

1. **Check previously cached entries.** PNRP maintains a local cache of resource endpoints for each host. If a client previously registered itself with a particular mesh, PNRP will use those previously cached entries to try to reconnect to the mesh network.

2. **Simple Service Discovery Protocol (SSDP).** SSDP is a part of the Universal Plug-n-Play (UPnP) specification that allows for UPnP compliant devices to discover each other on a local network. This same technique allows for peer nodes to discover one another on the local network.

3. **PNRP seed nodes.** PNRP clients can be configured to look for another PNRP node that can be used as a bootstrap into a PNRP Cloud. These types of nodes are often referred to as a *seed node*. Microsoft provides a publicly available seed node on the Internet at pnrpv2.ipv6.microsoft.com. Users may also choose to host their own seed node on their own network.

Windows Internet Computer Names

Windows Vista allows for a name associated with your computer to be published using PNRP. This gets around the need for managing a domain name and adding records to the Domain Name System (DNS). These names are called Windows Internet Computer Names (WICN). You might find WICN referred to as PNRP Peer Names. There are two types of names: secured and unsecured. Unsecured names usually take a human readable form such as richshomecomputer.pnrp.net. These names are easy to remember but cannot be guaranteed to be secured. Figure 12.6 demonstrates using the `netsh` command to query a computer's WICN name. The command used is `netsh p2p pnrp peer show machine name`.

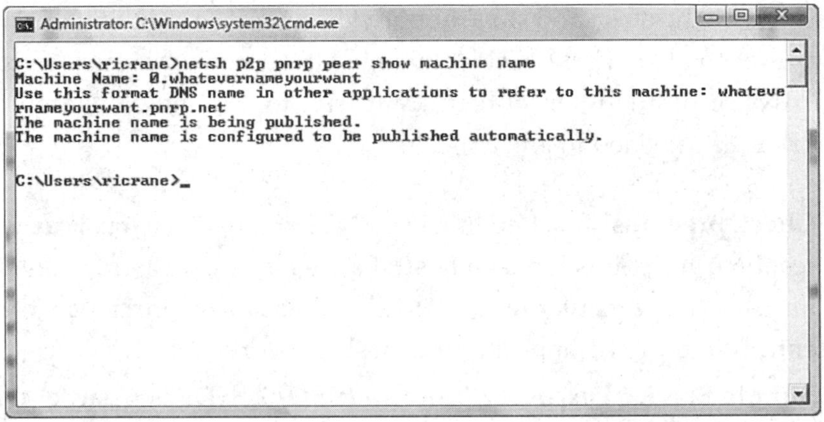

FIGURE 12.6 Windows Internet Computer Name (WICN)

Secure names, on the other hand, are secured using a private key, which is needed to prove ownership. Secure names are generated using a hash of the public key. To publish a secure name you must have the corresponding private key to the public key contained within the name. An example of a secure name is shown here:

```
p9962c5876ab48521cab41350013457109c1b0219
```

An interesting fact about WICN names is that they can be queried using the DNS APIs. The following code shows the same WICN name using a format that can be queried by DNS:

```
p.p9962c5876ab48521cab41350013457109c1b0219.pnrp.net
```

PnrpPeerResolver

Built in to the `netPeerTcpBinding` is the capability to specify a peer resolver that resolves other participants within a mesh network. By default, the

PnrpPeerResolver class is chosen by the netPeerTcpBinding binding if no other peer resolver is specified. The PnrpPeerResolver class is an implementation of the abstract class PeerResolver. These classes can be found in the System.ServiceModel.Channels namespace.

Mesh Authentication

Mesh networks can be protected by specifying a password or using an X.509 certificate associated with a mesh. For an application to participate on the mesh, it must specify the correct password for the mesh network. Mesh passwords allow applications to register on a mesh network and discover other participants in a mesh. They do not say whether a participant is an authenticated user. Mesh passwords need to be specified on both the server and the client. Listing 12.3 shows a mesh password being configured on the ServiceHost.

LISTING 12.3 Setting Mesh Password on ServiceHost

```
host = new ServiceHost(typeof(PeerChatService), baseAddresses);
host.Credentials.Peer.MeshPassword = meshPassword.ToString();
host.Open();
```

The corresponding client code for setting the mesh password is shown in Listing 12.4. This example uses the ChannelFactory approach described in Chapter 3, "Channels."

LISTING 12.4 Client Code for Setting Mesh Password on ServiceHost

```
using (ChannelFactory<IPeerChat> cf =
            new ChannelFactory<IPeerChat>(binding, ep))
{
        cf.Credentials.Peer.MeshPassword = meshPassword.ToString();

        IPeerChat chat = cf.CreateChannel();
        chat.Send(from, message);
}
```

Registering Names Using PNRP

WCF can use PNRP to discover other participants on a mesh network. In its implementation, the WCF peer channel abstracts away the use of PNRP so an application does not need to work with PNRP directly. However, some peer application might like to publish and resolve identifiers (peer names) themselves outside of the WCF peer channel. Unfortunately, prior to .NET Framework 3.5 there was no way from managed code to register PNRP names. A new namespace called `System.Net.Peer` was added in .NET Framework 3.5 to be able to work with the PNRP infrastructure using managed code.

System.Net.Peer

As mentioned previously, PNRP is used to publish and resolve peer names. To publish a peer name, we first need to create an instance of the `PeerName` class. The `PeerName` class specifies the identifier (peer name) and whether the identifier is secure or unsecure. From there we use the `PeerNameRegistration` class to register the peer name. To do this we are required to set the `PeerName` and `Port` properties and then call the `Start` method. The `Stop` method is used to unregister the peer name. Listing 12.5 shows an example of registering a peer name.

> **▪ NOTE Peer Names Are Owned by Applications**
>
> A peer name is owned by the application that registered it. If the application exits for any reason, the peer name is unregistered. This means that the application must be running in order to resolve a peer name.

LISTING 12.5 Publishing a Peer Name

```
using System;
using System.Collections.Generic;
using System.Linq;
using System.Net.PeerToPeer;
using System.Text;

namespace PublishName
{
    class Program
    {
        static void Main(string[] args)
        {
            PeerName peerName =
                    new PeerName("PeerChat", PeerNameType.Unsecured);
```

```
                PeerNameRegistration pnReg = new PeerNameRegistration();
                pnReg.PeerName = peerName;
                pnReg.Port = 8080;
                pnReg.Comment = "My registration.";
                pnReg.Data = Encoding.UTF8.GetBytes
    ➥("Some data to include with my registration.");


                pnReg.Start();

                Console.WriteLine("Hit ]Enter] to exit.");
                Console.ReadLine();
                pnReg.Stop();
            }
        }
    }
```

Listing 12.6 shows how we can resolve the same peer name shown in
Listing 12.5. In this example we use the PeerNameResolver class to get back
a collection of PeerNameRecord instances. We then enumerate over the collection and output the information contained within each record.

LISTING 12.6 Resolving a Peer Name

```
using System;
using System.Collections.Generic;
using System.Linq;
using System.Net;
using System.Net.PeerToPeer;
using System.Text;

namespace ResolveName
{
    class Program
    {
        static void Main(string[] args)
        {
            PeerNameResolver resolver = new PeerNameResolver();
            PeerName peerName = new PeerName("0.PeerChat");

            PeerNameRecordCollection results =
                resolver.Resolve(peerName);

            PeerNameRecord record;

            for (int i=0; i<results.Count; i++)
            {
                record = results[i];
```

LISTING 12.6 continued

```
                        Console.WriteLine("Record #{0}", i);
                        if (record.Comment != null)
                            Console.WriteLine(record.Comment);

                        Console.Write("Data: ");
                        if (record.Data != null)
    Console.WriteLine(Encoding.ASCII.GetString(record.Data));
                        else
                            Console.WriteLine();

                        Console.WriteLine("Endpoints:");

                        foreach (IPEndPoint endpoint in
                         record.EndPointCollection)
                            Console.WriteLine("Endpoint:{0}", endpoint);

                        Console.WriteLine();
                    }

                    Console.WriteLine("Hit ]Enter] to exit.");
                    Console.ReadLine();
                }
            }
        }
```

Implementing a Custom Peer Resolver

The peer transport channel allows developers to implement their own peer resolutions by specifying a custom peer resolver. There are many reasons to implement your own custom peer resolver rather than using the default PNRP resolver. PNRP requires the use of IPv6 and needs an additional download for Windows XP SP2 and Vista clients to work together. In these situations a custom peer resolver can be used to leverage an existing IPv4 infrastructure and to ease deployment. There are many examples of implementing a custom peer resolver. The Windows SDK shows an example of this approach using a WCF service. We will give a similar example of a custom peer resolver using a service, but backed by a SQL Server 2005 database. Many applications can leverage this implementation to have a number of computers collaborate on a network.

To create a new peer resolver, you must inherit from the abstract base class PeerResolver. This class has a number of methods on it that allow a client to register, update, and unregister a client from a mesh network. It also has a method to resolve other members of the mesh. Listing 12.7 shows the SqlPeerResolver class and the configuration classes associated with it.

LISTING 12.7 SqlPeerResolver

```
using System;
using System.Collections.Generic;
using System.Collections.ObjectModel;
using System.Configuration;
using System.ServiceModel;
using System.Runtime.Serialization;

namespace EssentialWCF.PeerNetworking
{
    public class SqlPeerResolver : PeerResolver
    {
        private static object dalLock = new object();
        private static SqlPeerResolverDatabase dal;

        private static SqlPeerResolverDatabase DAL
        {
            get
            {
                if (dal == null)
                {
                    lock (dalLock)
                    {
                        if (dal == null)
                            dal == new SqlPeerResolverDatabase();
                    }
                }

                return dal;
            }
        }

        public override bool CanShareReferrals
        {
            get { return true; }
        }

        public override object Register(string meshId,
            PeerNodeAddress nodeAddress, TimeSpan timeout)
```

LISTING 12.7 continued

```
        {
            MaskScopeId(nodeAddress.IPAddresses);
            int registrationId = DAL.Register(meshId, nodeAddress);
            return registrationId;
        }

        public override void Unregister(object registrationId,
            TimeSpan timeout)
        {
            DAL.Unregister((int)registrationId);
        }

        public override void Update(object registrationId,
            PeerNodeAddress updatedNodeAddress, TimeSpan timeout)
        {
            MaskScopeId(updatedNodeAddress.IPAddresses);
            DAL.Update((int)registrationId, updatedNodeAddress);
        }

        public override ReadOnlyCollection<PeerNodeAddress>
            Resolve(string meshId, int maxAddresses, TimeSpan timeout)
        {
            PeerNodeAddress[] addresses = null;

            addresses = DAL.Resolve(meshId, maxAddresses);

            if (addresses == null)
                addresses = new PeerNodeAddress[0];

            return new ReadOnlyCollection<PeerNodeAddress>(addresses);
        }

        void MaskScopeId(ReadOnlyCollection<IPAddress> ipAddresses)
        {
            foreach (IPAddress address in ipAddresses)
            {
                if (address.AddressFamily ==
                    AddressFamily.InterNetworkV6)
                    address.ScopeId = 0;
            }
        }
    }

    public class SqlPeerResolverBindingElement :
                    PeerResolverBindingElement
    {
        PeerReferralPolicy peerReferralPolicy =
                    PeerReferralPolicy.Share;
```

```csharp
            static SqlPeerResolver resolverClient = new SqlPeerResolver();

        public SqlPeerResolverBindingElement() { }
        protected
➥SqlPeerResolverBindingElement(SqlPeerResolverBindingElement
➥other) : base(other) { }

        public override PeerReferralPolicy ReferralPolicy
        {
            get { return peerReferralPolicy; }
            set { peerReferralPolicy = value; }
        }

        public override BindingElement Clone()
        {
            return new SqlPeerResolverBindingElement(this);
        }

        public override IChannelFactory<TChannel>
➥BuildChannelFactory<TChannel>(BindingContext context)
        {
            context.BindingParameters.Add(this);
            return context.BuildInnerChannelFactory<TChannel>();
        }

        public override bool
➥CanBuildChannelFactory<TChannel>(BindingContext context)
        {
            context.BindingParameters.Add(this);
            return context.CanBuildInnerChannelFactory<TChannel>();
        }

        public override IChannelListener<TChannel>
➥BuildChannelListener<TChannel>(BindingContext context)
        {
            context.BindingParameters.Add(this);
            return context.BuildInnerChannelListener<TChannel>();
        }

        public override bool
➥CanBuildChannelListener<TChannel>(BindingContext context)
        {
            context.BindingParameters.Add(this);
            return context.CanBuildInnerChannelListener<TChannel>();
        }

        public override PeerResolver CreatePeerResolver()
        {
            return resolverClient;
```

LISTING 12.7 continued

```
        }

        public override T GetProperty<T>(BindingContext context)
        {
            return context.GetInnerProperty<T>();
        }
    }

    public class SqlPeerResolverConfigurationBindingElement :
                    BindingElementExtensionElement
    {
        public override Type BindingElementType
        {
            get { return typeof(SqlPeerResolverBindingElement); }
        }

        protected override BindingElement CreateBindingElement()
        {
            return new SqlPeerResolverBindingElement();
        }
    }
}
```

Limiting the Number of Hops for a Message

Peer networks based on message flooding typically provide a way to limit the distance a message travels with the network. The distance a message travels is often referred to as the number of hops it makes when traveling on the network. The number of hops is determined by counting the number of times a message is sent between neighbors. For those familiar with socket programming, this is similar to the Time-to-Live (TTL) setting on the TCP protocol, which specifies the maximum number of routers a packet can traverse before being discarded. Figure 12.7 illustrates this point by representing nodes that are connected. Four nodes are labeled A, B, C, and D. A message sent by Node A will make three hops to be received by Node D. The number of hops can be significant when working with Internet-scale meshes. We look for ways to limit the number of hops when we encounter these situations.

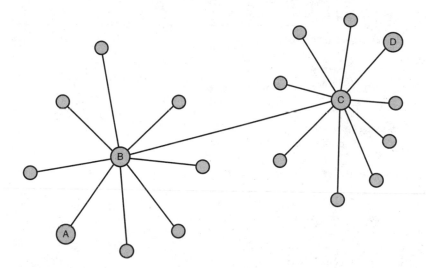

FIGURE 12.7 Number of hops across connected nodes

WCF provides a very simple mechanism using message contracts to limit the number of hops a message passes through in a peer mesh. Listing 12.8 shows the `SearchRequest` message contract for sending a request for a distributed search. One of the members of the contract is attributed with the `PeerHopCount` attribute. The `PeerHopCount` attribute can be associated with an integer value. This value is decremented each time the message is sent to a different node. The message will not be passed to any neighboring nodes when the message has passed through enough nodes to decrement the count to zero. A hop count essentially puts a stop condition on the number of nodes the message can travel through. In our case the number of hops is set to 3.

LISTING 12.8 Message Contract Using `PeerHopCount`

```
[MessageContract]
public class SearchRequest
{
    [PeerHopCount]
    private int _hopCount;

    [MessageBodyMember]
    private string _query;
```

LISTING 12.8 continued

```
    public string Query
    {
        get { return _query; }
        set { _query = value; }
    }

    [MessageBodyMember]
    private PeerInstance _participant;

    public PeerInstance Participant
    {
        get { return _participant; }
        set { _participant = value; }
    }

    public SearchRequest()
    {
    }

    public SearchRequest(string query)
    {
        _hopCount = 3;
        _query = query;
        _participant = new PeerInstance();
    }

    public SearchRequest(int hopCount, string query)
        : this(query)
    {
        _hopCount = hopCount;
    }
}
```

Collaboration Using Windows Vista

WCF provides the infrastructure for creating peer applications that can communicate across a mesh network. It does not provide capabilities for discovery and ad-hoc collaboration. For these we will rely on some new capabilities built in to Windows Vista and into the .NET Framework 3.5. These include People Near Me, Windows Contacts, and Invitations. This section examines these features and demonstrates how to use them using the classes found in the new System.Net.PeerToPeer namespace.

People Near Me

Windows Vista provides a capability to discover other people connected to the same local subnet and invite them to collaborate. This feature is available only in Windows Vista and is not available with Windows XP. People Near Me can be configured using the Control Panel or the associated tray application. Figure 12.8 shows the People Near Me Control Panel. The People Near Me Control Panel is also accessible from the system tray.

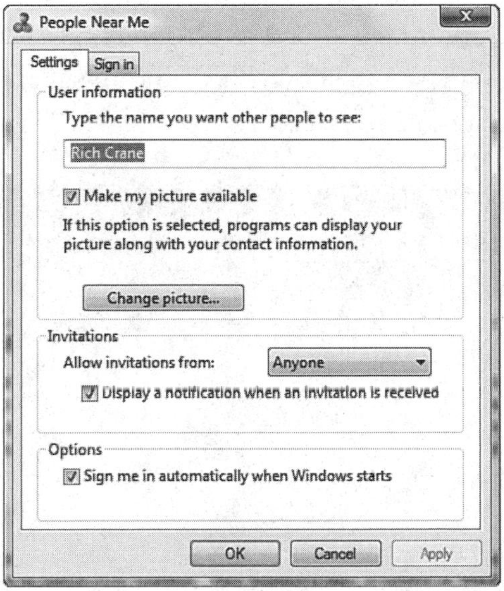

FIGURE 12.8 People Near Me Control Panel

The control panel allows you to configure your presence information, such as your name and picture. It also allows you to configure how you would like to collaborate with other people by specifying who can send you invitations. By default, anyone is allowed to send an invitation, but it can be configured to allow only trusted contacts or to disable invitations altogether. Figure 12.9 shows the available options for configuring who is allowed to send invitations.

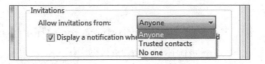

FIGURE 12.9 Allow invitations

Windows Contacts

You can use Windows Vista to keep track of your contacts using a new feature called Windows Contacts. Windows Contacts is a central place to store your contact list. Figure 12.10 shows the Windows Contacts folder, which shows a list of contacts.

FIGURE 12.10 Windows Contacts

By default a contact is created for each user and contains the username and an account picture. This contact is often referred to as the "Me" contact. The Windows Contacts can be used to collaborate with your contacts either through e-mail or other activities, such as ad-hoc meetings, using Windows Meeting Space. One of the most important concepts about Windows Contacts is trusted contacts. Trusted contacts are contacts that have exchanged their Me contact with trusted people. One of the most common ways to exchange Me contact information is through e-mail.

Windows Contacts can be edited by double-clicking the contact in the Windows Contacts folder. Figure 12.11 shows the Windows Contacts Properties page.

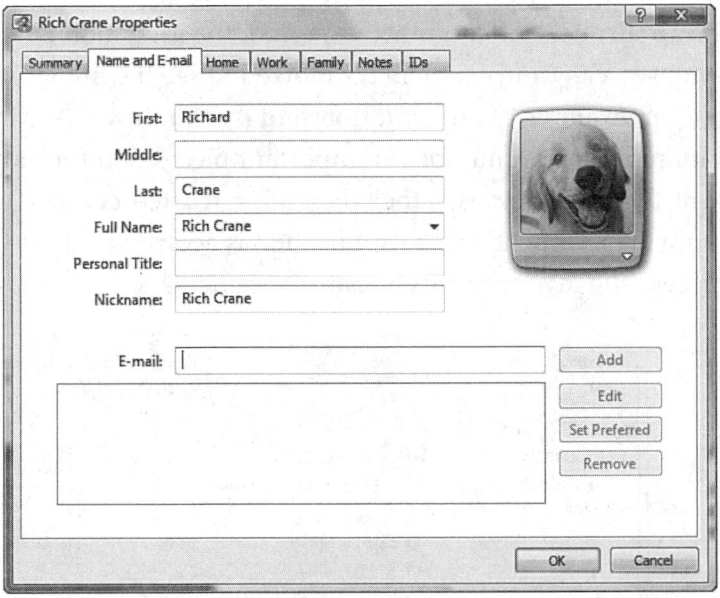

FIGURE 12.11 Windows Contact Properties

Invitations

Applications can use People Near Me to send invitations to people to start a collaborative activity. Figure 12.12 shows an invitation sent by Windows Meeting Space to start an ad-hoc meeting. When users receive the invitation they are asked to perform an action: View, Decline, or Dismiss.

FIGURE 12.12　Windows Meeting
Space invitation

If the user chooses Decline, a response is sent back to the application that sent the invitation saying that the invitation was declined. If the user chooses Dismiss, the invitation will be ignored and no response will be sent back to the application. After a timeout period, the invitation will expire. If the user chooses View, the user will be allowed to see the invitation. Figure 12.13 shows an example of an invitation sent by Windows Meeting Space. The invitation provides a number of important pieces of information, such as who sent the invitation, whether they are a trusted contact, and what application will be launched if the application is accepted. At this point the user can accept the invitation by choosing Accept.

FIGURE 12.13　Windows Meeting Space invitation details

System.Net.PeerToPeer.Collaboration

People Near Me, Windows Contacts, and Invitations all allow an application to start a collaborative activity. Prior to .NET Framework 3.5, developers needed to work with unmanaged APIs to use these features. This meant that they needed to be developing in either C++ or at the very least create interop assemblies (using P/Invoke) for use in .NET. .NET Framework 3.5 changed this by introducing managed libraries that can use the People Near Me, Windows Contacts, and Invitation infrastructure built in to Windows Vista. These libraries are provided in a new namespace called System.Net.PeerToPeer. A developer needs to add a reference to the System.Net assembly to use these new libraries. We will look at a sample application called Peer Chat to see how to use these new libraries. Figure 12.14 shows the Peer Chat application.

FIGURE 12.14 Peer Chat sample application

The first thing that an application should consider is registering itself with the collaboration infrastructure in Windows Vista. This is required if you would like to send an invitation to launch the application. Listing 12.9 shows how the Peer Chat application registers itself with the peer infrastructure. To do this we call the Register method on the PeerCollaboration static class found in the System.Net.PeerToPeer.Collaboration namespace. This method accepts an instance of PeerApplication class. An instance of this class is a description of the peer application, including an application identifier and a description.

LISTING 12.9 Registering a Peer Application

```
using System;
using System.Collections.Generic;
using System.Linq;
using System.Net.PeerToPeer;
using System.Net.PeerToPeer.Collaboration;
using System.Text;

namespace PeerChat
{
    public class PeerChatApplication
    {
        private static PeerApplication PeerChatPeerApplication;
        private static Guid PeerChatAppId =
            ➥new Guid("4BC6F59E-124E-4e75-8CD9-BB75BCA78CA8");
        private static string PeerChatDescription =
"A sample peer networking application.";

        static PeerChatApplication()
        {
            PeerChatPeerApplication =
                new PeerApplication(PeerChatAppId,
                        PeerChatDescription,
                        null,
                    System.Windows.Forms.Application.ExecutablePath,
                        null,
                        PeerScope.All);
        }

        public static void Register()
        {
            PeerApplicationCollection peerAppsColl =
                PeerCollaboration.GetLocalRegisteredApplications(
                PeerApplicationRegistrationType.AllUsers);

            // You gotta love LINQ!  It is so cool!
```

```
    IEnumerable<PeerApplication> findPeerApp =
        from peerApp in
        PeerCollaboration.GetLocalRegisteredApplications(
        PeerApplicationRegistrationType.AllUsers)
        where peerApp.Id == PeerChatAppId
        select peerApp;

    if (findPeerApp.Count<PeerApplication>() != 0)
        PeerCollaboration.UnregisterApplication(
            PeerChatPeerApplication,
            PeerApplicationRegistrationType.AllUsers);

    PeerCollaboration.RegisterApplication(
        PeerChatPeerApplication,
        PeerApplicationRegistrationType.AllUsers);
    }

    public static void UnRegister()
    {
        PeerCollaboration.UnregisterApplication(
            PeerChatPeerApplication,
            PeerApplicationRegistrationType.AllUsers);
    }
  }
}
```

The next thing an application might want to do is to display a list of people that are on its local subnet so the user can invite them to collaborative activity. This is done by enumerating the people signed into the People Near Me infrastructure. A user needs to be signed into People Near Me to retrieve this list of people near them. To help with this process, we created a helper class that ensures that the user is signed in before the first request. Listing 12.10 shows the `PeopleNearMeHelper` class. The class calls the `SignIn` method of the `PeerCollaboration` static class to ensure that the user is signed into People Near Me. After the user is signed in, the user is free to call the `GetPeersNearMe` static method, which returns a collection of `PeerNearMe` instances. A `PeerNearMe` instance is a description of a person logged into People Near Me on the local subnet.

LISTING 12.10 The People Near Me

```
using System;
using System.Collections.Generic;
using System.Linq;
using System.Net.PeerToPeer;
```

LISTING 12.10 continued

```
using System.Net.PeerToPeer.Collaboration;
using System.Text;

namespace PeerChat
{
    public class PeopleNearMeHelper
    {
        public PeopleNearMeHelper()
        {
            PeerCollaboration.SignIn(PeerScope.All);
        }

        public PeerNearMeCollection PeopleNearMe
        {
            get
            {
                return PeerCollaboration.GetPeersNearMe();
            }
        }
    }
}
```

Next we need to send an invitation to another user so he can collaborate. The Peer Chat application sends an invitation to other users to start a chat together. To do this, we not only need to send the invitation, we also need to send some additional information to bootstrap the communication process. Remember that the actual act of communication between peers is handled by WCF and the peer channel infrastructure. This means that we need additional information, such as the name of the mesh to communicate on and the mesh password. This additional information is sent with the invitation. Listing 12.11 shows how to send and receive invitations from the collaboration infrastructure in Windows Vista. An invitation is sent using either the `Invite` or `InviteAsync` method on an instance of a `PeerNearMe` class. It is recommended that you use the `InviteAsync` method; otherwise, the user interface is blocked, waiting for the user to accept the invitation. Both methods have an option to send additional data in the form of a byte array. In our situation, we package up the mesh name and password into a byte stream and send that along. Many might be concerned that information might be exposed by sending the mesh name and password with the invitation. No worries! The People Near Me infrastructure transmits this information over an encrypted connection.

LISTING 12.11 Sending and Receiving Invitations

```csharp
using System;
using System.Collections.Generic;
using System.Linq;
using System.IO;
using System.Net.PeerToPeer;
using System.Net.PeerToPeer.Collaboration;
using System.Text;

namespace PeerChat
{
    public class InvitationHelper
    {
        private static PeerApplication PeerChatPeerApplication;
        private static Guid PeerChatAppId =
            new Guid("4BC6F59E-124E-4e75-8CD9-BB75BCA78CA8");
        private static string PeerChatDescription =
            "A sample peer networking application.";

        static InvitationHelper()
        {
            PeerChatPeerApplication =
                new PeerApplication(PeerChatAppId,
                        PeerChatDescription,
                        null,
            System.Windows.Forms.Application.ExecutablePath,
                        null,
                        PeerScope.All);
        }

        public static PeerInvitationResponseType
            Invite(PeerNearMe personTo,
                    Guid chatId,
                    Guid meshPassword)
        {
            byte[] data;
            using (MemoryStream ms = new MemoryStream())
            {
                using (StreamWriter sw = new StreamWriter(ms))
                {
                    sw.Write(chatId.ToString());
                    sw.WriteLine();
                    sw.Write(meshPassword.ToString());
                }
                data = ms.ToArray();
            }

            PeerInvitationResponse response =
                personTo.Invite(PeerChatPeerApplication,
```

LISTING 12.11 continued

```csharp
            "You are being invited to chat.", data);
        return response.PeerInvitationResponseType;
}

public static void InviteAsync(PeerNearMe personTo,
        Guid chatId, Guid meshPassword)
{
    byte[] data;
    using (MemoryStream ms = new MemoryStream())
    {
        using (StreamWriter sw = new StreamWriter(ms))
        {
            sw.Write(chatId.ToString());
            sw.WriteLine();
            sw.Write(meshPassword.ToString());
        }
        data = ms.ToArray();
    }

    object userToken = Guid.NewGuid();
    personTo.InviteAsync(PeerChatPeerApplication,
        "You are being invited to chat.", data, userToken);
}

public static bool IsLaunched
{
    get
    {
        return
        (PeerCollaboration.ApplicationLaunchInfo != null) &&
        (PeerCollaboration.ApplicationLaunchInfo.Data != null);
    }
}

public static Guid ChatId
{
    get
    {
        Guid chatId;

        using (MemoryStream ms =
            new MemoryStream(
                PeerCollaboration.ApplicationLaunchInfo.Data))
        {
            using (StreamReader sr = new StreamReader(ms))
            {
```

```
                    string chatIdString = sr.ReadLine();
                    string meshPasswordString = sr.ReadToEnd();

                    chatId = new Guid(chatIdString);
                }
            }

            return chatId;
        }
    }

    public static Guid MeshPassword
    {
        get
        {
        Guid meshPassword;

        using (MemoryStream ms =
            new MemoryStream(
                PeerCollaboration.ApplicationLaunchInfo.Data))
        {
            using (StreamReader sr = new StreamReader(ms))
            {
                string chatIdString = sr.ReadLine();
                string meshPasswordString = sr.ReadToEnd();

                meshPassword = new Guid(meshPasswordString);
            }
        }

        return meshPassword;
        }
    }
}
```

The last thing to consider is how to determine whether an application was launched based on an invitation from People Near Me. To do this we need to get an instance of the PeerApplicationLaunchInfo class. This is available from the ApplicationLaunchInfo property on the PeerCollaboration static class. Listing 12.11 also shows how this class can be used to determine if the application was launched because of invitation and how to access any additional data sent with that invitation.

Directional Messaging Using Custom Binding

A common mistake when working with the peer transport channel is to assume that it supports directed communication over a peer mesh. Directional messaging means that a message can be sent to a particular node in a peer mesh by propagating it across a peer mesh to its destination (that is, routing). This is not possible using the peer transport channel. This limits the types of peer applications that can be built, because all messaging assumes that messages will be sent to every node. However, with a little know-how and very little effort, some of these limitations can be eliminated.

There are several ways directional messaging can be utilized, including one-to-one and many-to-one style communication. One-to-one communication is the capability to send a message to a particular node in a peer mesh. Many-to-one is the capability for a node to respond back to the originator of a request. One-to-one messages require the use of routing techniques to route the message through the peer mesh to its destination. This approach typically uses routing indices to rank neighbors by their likeliness to resolve the request to its destination. Unfortunately, the complexity of the solution and time prevent us from covering this form of directional messaging. Instead, we will focus on the easier form of directional messaging, which is the many-to-one scenario.

Many-to-one allows for a node to send a callback message back to the originator of a request. Two approaches can be used to implement this scenario. The first approach is to send a callback message to the originator of the message over the peer mesh. This is similar to the one-to-one approach. The second approach is for the originator to send an address on which it can receive callback messages. This approach is much easier to implement and is easily handled using the existing WCF infrastructure. The solution involves the creation of a composite transport channel. This takes two existing one-way transport channels and combines them to allow for request messages to be sent on one channel and callback messages to be received over a different channel. In our situation, we will use the peer transport channel to send messages while using the TCP transport channel to receive callback messages. We will also layer on a shape-changing channel using the CompositeDuplexBindingElement binding element to allow for duplex

messaging over the composite transport. Listing 12.12 shows the
CompositeTransportBindingElement binding element that is used to create
the asymmetric transport.

LISTING 12.12 CompositeTransportBindingElement

```
using System;
using System.Text;
using System.Collections.Generic;
using System.ServiceModel.Channels;

namespace EssentialWCF.PeerApplication.Bindings
{
    public class CompositeTransportBindingElement<TChannelBinding,
TListenerBinding>
        : TransportBindingElement
        where TChannelBinding : Binding, new()
        where TListenerBinding : Binding, new()
    {
        TChannelBinding channelBinding;
        TListenerBinding listenerBinding;

        public CompositeTransportBindingElement(TChannelBinding
channelBinding, TListenerBinding listenerBinding)
        {
            this.channelBinding = channelBinding;
            this.listenerBinding = listenerBinding;
        }

        public CompositeTransportBindingElement(
            CompositeTransportBindingElement<TChannelBinding,
                TListenerBinding>
            other)
            : base(other)
        {
            this.channelBinding =
(TChannelBinding)other.channelBinding;
            this.listenerBinding =
                (TListenerBinding)other.listenerBinding;
        }

        public TChannelBinding ChannelBinding
        {
            get { return this.channelBinding; }
        }

        public TListenerBinding ListenerBinding
        {
```

LISTING 12.12 continued

```
        get { return this.listenerBinding; }
    }

    public override bool CanBuildChannelFactory<TChannel>(
        BindingContext context)
    {
        ThrowIfContextIsNull(context);

        return channelBinding.CanBuildChannelFactory<TChannel>(
            context.BindingParameters);
    }

    public override bool CanBuildChannelListener<TChannel>(
        BindingContext context)
    {
        ThrowIfContextIsNull(context);

        return listenerBinding.CanBuildChannelListener<TChannel>(
            context.BindingParameters);
    }

    public override IChannelFactory<TChannel>
        BuildChannelFactory<TChannel>(BindingContext context)
    {
        ThrowIfContextIsNull(context);

        return channelBinding.BuildChannelFactory<TChannel>(
            context.BindingParameters);
    }

    public override IChannelListener<TChannel>
        BuildChannelListener<TChannel>(BindingContext context)
    {
        ThrowIfContextIsNull(context);

        return listenerBinding.BuildChannelListener<TChannel>(
            context.ListenUriBaseAddress,
            context.ListenUriRelativeAddress,
            context.ListenUriMode,
            context.BindingParameters);
    }

    public override BindingElement Clone()
    {
        return
            new CompositeTransportBindingElement<TChannelBinding,
            TListenerBinding>(this);
    }
```

```
public override T GetProperty<T>(BindingContext context)
{
    ThrowIfContextIsNull(context);

    T result =
        this.channelBinding.GetProperty<T>(
        context.BindingParameters);
    if (result != default(T))
        return result;

    result =
        this.listenerBinding.GetProperty<T>(
        context.BindingParameters);
    if (result != default(T))
        return result;

    return context.GetInnerProperty<T>();
}

public override string Scheme
{
    get
    {
        return listenerBinding.Scheme;
    }
}
    }
}
```

Leveraging the CompositeTransportBindingElement alone does not complete the solution. We must create a binding that combines several binding elements to create the composite transport binding. It is important to point out that the client and server do not use the same binding. The binding must be asymmetric because the transport is asymmetric. Listing 12.13 shows how these different bindings are created.

LISTING 12.13 Custom Bindings Using CompositeTransportBindingElement

```
using System;
using System.Collections.Generic;
using System.Net;
using System.ServiceModel;
using System.ServiceModel.Channels;
using System.ServiceModel.Description;

using EssentialWCF.PeerApplication.Bindings;
using EssentialWCF.PeerApplication.Helpers;
```

LISTING 12.13 continued

```
using EssentialWCF.PeerApplication.Encoder;

namespace EssentialWCF.PeerApplication.Helpers
{
    public static class BindingHelper
    {
        public static Binding CreateClientBinding()
        {
            Uri callbackUri = new
Uri(UriHelper.GetSearchCallbackUri());

            ListenUriBindingElement listenUri = new
                ListenUriBindingElement(callbackUri, "",
                ListenUriMode.Explicit);
            BinaryMessageEncodingBindingElement binaryEncoder =
                new BinaryMessageEncodingBindingElement();
            binaryEncoder.MessageVersion =
                MessageVersion.Soap12WSAddressingAugust2004;
            GZipMessageEncodingBindingElement encoder =
                new GZipMessageEncodingBindingElement(binaryEncoder);
            OneWayBindingElement oneWay = new OneWayBindingElement();
            CompositeDuplexBindingElement duplex =
                new CompositeDuplexBindingElement();
            TcpTransportBindingElement tcpTransport =
                new TcpTransportBindingElement();
            tcpTransport.ManualAddressing = false;
            tcpTransport.PortSharingEnabled = false;
            tcpTransport.TeredoEnabled = true;
            PeerTransportBindingElement peerTransport =
                new PeerTransportBindingElement();
            peerTransport.ManualAddressing = false;
            PnrpPeerResolverBindingElement pnrpResolver =
                new PnrpPeerResolverBindingElement();

            CustomBinding tcpBinding = new CustomBinding(oneWay,
                listenUri, encoder, tcpTransport);

            encoder.MessageVersion =
                MessageVersion.Soap12WSAddressing10;
            CustomBinding peerBinding = new CustomBinding(pnrpResolver,
                encoder, peerTransport);

            CompositeTransportBindingElement<CustomBinding,
            CustomBinding> compositeTransport =
                new CompositeTransportBindingElement<CustomBinding,
                CustomBinding>(peerBinding, tcpBinding);
```

```
            duplex.ClientBaseAddress = callbackUri;

            return new CustomBinding(duplex, compositeTransport);
        }

        public static Binding CreateServerBinding()
        {
            BinaryMessageEncodingBindingElement binaryEncoder =
                new BinaryMessageEncodingBindingElement();
            binaryEncoder.MessageVersion =
                MessageVersion.Soap12WSAddressingAugust2004;
            GZipMessageEncodingBindingElement encoder =
                new GZipMessageEncodingBindingElement(binaryEncoder);
            OneWayBindingElement oneWay = new OneWayBindingElement();
            CompositeDuplexBindingElement duplex =
                new CompositeDuplexBindingElement();
            TcpTransportBindingElement tcpTransport =
                new TcpTransportBindingElement();
            tcpTransport.ManualAddressing = false;
            tcpTransport.PortSharingEnabled = false;
            tcpTransport.TeredoEnabled = true;
            PeerTransportBindingElement peerTransport =
                new PeerTransportBindingElement();
            peerTransport.ManualAddressing = false;
            PnrpPeerResolverBindingElement pnrpResolver =
                new PnrpPeerResolverBindingElement();

            CustomBinding tcpBinding = new CustomBinding(oneWay,
                encoder, tcpTransport);
            encoder.MessageVersion =
                MessageVersion.Soap12WSAddressing10;
            CustomBinding peerBinding = new CustomBinding(pnrpResolver,
                encoder, peerTransport);

            CompositeTransportBindingElement<CustomBinding,
                CustomBinding> compositeTransport =
                new CompositeTransportBindingElement<CustomBinding,
                CustomBinding>(tcpBinding, peerBinding); ;

            return new CustomBinding(duplex, compositeTransport);
        }
    }
}
```

One final point is that this binding does not allow for automatic addressing to occur within WCF. There are two approaches to handling this. The preferred approach is to use a custom binding element or possibly a message inspector to handle the addressing. This would allow the addressing to be wired up properly within the channel stack and is the recommended approach. The simple and easy approach is to handle the addressing manually within application code, which we will demonstrate next. Listing 12.14 shows the client code needed to handle addressing. The manual addressing is handled by setting the `OutgoingMessageHeaders.ReplyTo` location to the `InnerChannel.LocalAddress`. The local address is the address that the client is listening on to receive callback messages.

LISTING 12.14 Manual Addressing on the Client

```
public void Search(SearchRequest request)
{

    SearchClient client = ClientHelper.GetSearchClient();

    using (OperationContextScope ctx =
        new OperationContextScope(client.InnerDuplexChannel))
    {
        string LocalAddress =
            client.InnerChannel.LocalAddress.ToString();
        OperationContext.Current.OutgoingMessageHeaders.ReplyTo =
            client.InnerChannel.LocalAddress;
        try
        {
            client.Search(request);
        }
        catch (CommunicationException ex)
        {
            Debug.WriteLine(ex.Message);
        }
    }
}
```

Listing 12.15 shows the same type of technique used by the server to take the `IncomingMessageHeaders.ReplyTo` address and set the `OutgoingMessageHeaders.To` location. This is needed to send messages back to the client using the callback contract.

LISTING 12.15 Manual Addressing on the Server

```
[OperationBehavior]
public void Search(SearchRequest search)
{
    OperationContext ctx = OperationContext.Current;
    ctx.OutgoingMessageHeaders.To =
```

```
        ctx.IncomingMessageHeaders.ReplyTo.Uri;
    ISearchCallback client = ctx.GetCallbackChannel<ISearchCallback>();

    List<SearchItem> results = _searchProvider.Execute(search.Query);

    if ((results != null) && (results.Count > 0))
        client.SendResults(results);
}
```

There is a drawback to the composite approach in that the client must instantiate a service to receive callback messages. The WCF channel infrastructure will instantiate a listener to receive these requests. However, we are leveraging a separate communication channel, which means that the client must be directly reachable to receive callback messages. This limits the use of clients that are behind network devices such as firewalls or NAT routers. One way this limitation can be diminished is by leveraging IPv6 addressing and enabling Teredo capabilities of the TCP transport channel. Teredo is a Network Address Translation (NAT) traversal technology for IPv6 traffic that allows IPv6 traffic to be tunneled across one or more NAT routers to access hosts on an IPv6 network. Listing 12.16 shows how to enable Teredo using a custom binding specified in configuration.

LISTING 12.16 Enabling Teredo Using Custom Binding

```xml
<?xml version="1.0" encoding="utf-8" ?>
<configuration>
  <system.serviceModel>
    <bindings>
      <customBinding>
        <binding name="CustomBindingWithTeredo">
          <tcpTransport teredoEnabled="true" />
        </binding>
      </customBinding>
    </bindings>
  </system.serviceModel>
</configuration>
```

Most home routers that can be purchased use NAT technology to let multiple computers share an Internet connection. For the TCP transport channel to use Teredo it must also be enabled at the computer level. Figure 12.15 shows how to enable Teredo using the netsh command from the command line.

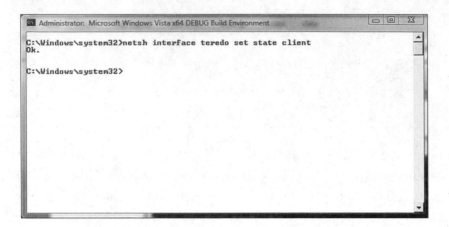

FIGURE 12.15 Enabling Teredo using NetSh

Teredo is a machinewide setting and therefore allows any IPv6 enabled service running on the client computer to be exposed. This includes services such as Remote Desktop and Internet Information Services (IIS). Because of this, using Teredo may be undesirable for security reasons and alternative methods may be needed. The final thing to mention about Teredo is that it relies on a centrally available server known as a Teredo server. This server can be hosted on the Internet or internally within a company. Microsoft provides a public server available at teredo.ipv6. microsoft.com. For more information about Teredo, visit www.microsoft. com/technet/network/ipv6/teredo.mspx and http://en.wikipedia.org/ wiki/Teredo_tunneling.

Another approach that can be used to address the issue of clients behind firewalls and NAT routers is to use a relay service that allows for computers to exchange messages between one another using a central server known as a *relay server*. The idea is that the relay server is available on the Internet to both computers and can facilitate the exchange of messages. This allows for developers to expose services to the Internet even if the server is behind a NAT router or a firewall. This approach requires a significant amount of effort and therefore requires much more detail than can be provided in this book. However, Microsoft is working on a set of products and technologies that help enable this approach. BizTalk Services are a new set of Internet services from Microsoft that provide identity and connectivity services. One of the connectivity services is a publicly available relay service. At the time of this writing, BizTalk Services are still experimental and will take some time to bring to market. They will eventually be a part of an effort Microsoft is working on, code named Oslo. Oslo is a combination of a number of Microsoft products to provide a better way of building model-driven and service-enabled applications. For more information about BizTalk Services and Oslo, visit http://labs.biztalk.net or http://www.microsoft.com/soa/products/oslo.aspx.

SUMMARY

Peer-to-peer (P2P) applications are a very compelling way to build distributed applications. P2P applications assume no central infrastructure, which means there is no distinction between client and server. If done properly, P2P applications can offer distinct advantages in scalability and reliability. Examples of peer applications include popular Internet applications such as instant messaging, games, and file sharing use the P2P approach.

The major hurdle to developing P2P applications has been the complexity and understanding needed to build them. WCF significantly reduces the complexity by providing the infrastructure for creating peer applications. The netPeerTcpBinding binding provides this capability by allowing communication across a mesh network. Windows Vista provides additional capabilities for discovery and collaboration using technologies such as Peer Name Resolution Protocol (PNRP), People Near Me, and Windows Contacts and Invitations. Using WCF and Windows Vista together provides a platform on which developers can build peer-to-peer applications.

■ 13 ■
Programmable Web

P ROGRAMMABLE WEB REFERS to a set of enabling technologies designed to help developers build the services for the Web. There are many ways of building services for the Web. We have already mentioned throughout the book how WCF can be used to build WS-* Web services, which use SOAP, HTTP, and XML. Services based on WS-* are typically built using a service-oriented architecture approach.

A service-oriented architecture approach follows four main tenants:

- Boundaries are explicit.
- Services are autonomous.
- Services share schema and contract, no class.
- Services compatibility is determined based on policy (see http://msdn.microsoft.com/msdnmag/issues/04/01/Indigo/default.aspx).

Services can be built from other styles of architectures, such as Representational State Transfer (REST). REST is an architectural style described in a dissertation from Roy Fielding (see www.ics.uci.edu/~fielding/pubs/dissertation/rest_arch_style.htm). REST follows a set of principles that are based on constraints:

- A client/server approach is used to separate user interface from data storage.
- Client/server interaction is stateless.
- Network efficiency is improved using caching.
- Components of the system interact using a uniform interface.
- The overall system can be composed using a layering approach.

The REST architectural style is often referred to as the architectural style of the Web because the constraints can easily be seen in modern Web architectures. We mention service orientation and REST because these are two common architectural styles for building services on the Web today. It is important to understand that WCF does not dictate the architectural style or manner in which to build services. Instead it exposes a set of features and capabilities that allow you to build services using a variety of architectural styles. The rest of this chapter will focus on the features that help developers build services for the Web. To help understand the motivation behind these new features, we will examine how developers use the Web today.

All About the URI

Most everyone should be familiar with URIs because this is how people browse the Web today. People access resources, such as HTML pages, via URIs typed into the address bar of their browsers. Browsers can access a variety of resources using URIs, including images, videos, data, applications, and more. Accessing of resources via a URI is also one of the principles behind the REST architectural style.

Table 13.1 shows several examples of resources on the Web that can be accessed in this manner.

TABLE 13.1 URI Examples

URI	Description
http://finance.yahoo.com/d/quotes?s=MSFT&f=spt1d	Microsoft (MSFT) stock quotes in comma-separated (CSV) format from Yahoo!
http://finance.google.com/finance/info?q=MSFT	Microsoft (MSFT) stock quote in custom JSON format from Google
http://en.wikipedia.org/wiki/Apple	A Wikipedia Web page about "Apples"
www.weather.com/weather/local/02451	Weather information for Waltham, MA from Weather.com
www.msnbc.msn.com/id/20265063/	News article on MSN.com
http://pipes.yahoo.com/pipes/pipe.run?_id=jlM12Ljj2xGAdeUR1vC6Jw&_render=json&merger=eg	Wall Street corporate events listing services (for example, stock splits, mergers, and so on) in JSON format
http://rss.slashdot.org/Slashdot/slashdot	Slashdot syndication feed in RSS format
http://api.flickr.com/services/rest/?method=flickr.photos.search&api_key=20701ea0647b482bcb124b1c80db976f&text=stocks	Flickr photo search in custom XML format

Each of the examples specifies a URI that takes a set of parameters that identifies a resource to retrieve. Parameters are sent either as query strings or embedded as a part of the path of the URI. This means that the URI is used to identify, locate, and access resources. To better understand what we mean, we look at the URL used to retrieve stock quotes from Google. It is obvious from the following URL that the parameter q represents the stock symbol and is passed into the service as a query string parameter.

```
http://finance.google.com/finance/info?q=MSFT
```

What is not represented is whether this URL is accessed using an HTTP GET or some other HTTP action. For now, we will assume that GET is being used. The URL can be rewritten with a parameter for the stock symbol in place of the MSFT stock symbol. Using this simplification of the URL, we can identify a number of resources.

```
http://finance.google.com/finance/info?q={StockSymbol}
```

This example helps form the basis for how we can identify and access resources on the Web.

The Ubiquitous GET

One thing in common with all the URIs in Table 13.1 is that they use the HTTP protocol to access resources. The HTTP protocol is considered the protocol of the Web. The original purpose of HTTP was to exchange HTML pages, but it has since been used to access all types of resources, including images, video, applications, and much more. The way in which it does this is by specifying a resource identifier and an action to be performed on that resource. URIs identify the resource. The action is defined by a set of HTTP verbs that specify the action to be performed on the resource. Table 13.2 shows a list of common HTTP verbs used on the Web today. There are many ways to interact with resources over the Web using the HTTP protocol, but none is as ubiquitous as GET. GET is by far the most widely used verb. POST comes in second, followed by other verbs such as PUT and DELETE.

TABLE 13.2 Common HTTP Verbs

Verb	Description
GET	Retrieve the resource identified by the URI.
POST	Send a resource to the server based on the resource identified by the URI.
PUT	Store a resource based on the resource identified by the URI.
DELETE	Delete a resource based on the resource identified by the URI.
HEAD	Identical to GET except that the response is not returned. This is used to retrieve metadata for the resource identified by the URI.

HTTP verbs form the basis for how we can interact with resources on the Web. GET is the most widely used HTTP verb because it is used to retrieve resources. HTTP verbs help to provide a uniform interface for interacting with resources, which is a constraint based on the REST architectural style.

Format Matters

The list of URIs in Table 13.1 demonstrates the vast number of formats available on the Web today. The content returned from these URIs includes HTML, XML, JSON, RSS, CSV, and custom formats. This means that developers have not found a single format that can represent all resources on the Web. For a while, it seemed that all roads would lead to XML as the single format. XML is a great mechanism for providing structure to data and for sharing information. For example, SOAP is a protocol for exchanging XML-based messages and is the foundation for traditional Web services. WCF provides support for the SOAP protocol. SOAP does more than provide structure to data, though. SOAP adds header information, which allows for advanced capabilities such as transport independence, message-level security, and transactions. Web developers are not necessarily concerned about such capabilities and need a way to exchange information. In these situations, formats such as Plain-Old-XML (POX) and JavaScript Object Notation (JSON) are often used.

POX is usually about developers not needing the capabilities that WS-* has to offer and not wanting the perceived overhead of SOAP. In these situations, using POX is a "good enough" format for their needs. JSON, on the other hand, is an efficient format for returning data to browser clients that leverage JavaScript. JSON as a format is more efficient than SOAP and can offer significant performance and scalability benefits when you are trying to reduce the number of bytes on the wires. What this comes down to is that format matters, and developers need to be able to work with a number of formats when using the Web.

Web Programming with WCF

Table 13.3 highlights some of the major features available to developers when they use WCF and .NET Framework 3.5. The remainder of this chapter focuses on the features within WCF that help enable the "programmable Web."

TABLE 13.3 Web Programming Features in .NET Framework 3.5

Verb	Description
Uri and UriTemplates	Enhanced support for working with URIs to support REST architectural patterns.
webHttpBinding Binding	A new binding that builds in support for POX and JSON, formal support for HTTP verbs including GET, and URI-based dispatching.
ASP.NET AJAX Integration	Integration with ASP.NET AJAX to support client-side service proxies.
Content Syndication	Classes for publishing and consuming RSS and ATOM syndication feeds.

URI and UriTemplates

Microsoft has provided support for URIs since .NET Framework v1.0. The System.Uri class allows developers to define and parse basic information within a URI. This class allows developers to access information such as the scheme, path, and hostname. This is great for passing a URI to Web clients such as the System.Windows.Forms.WebBrowser control or the System.Net.WebClient class. A companion to the System.Uri class is the System.UriBuilder class. This class provides a way to modify the System.Uri class without creating another System.Uri instance. These classes are the foundation for working with URIs based on the HTTP protocol. Additional capabilities are needed to support the REST architectural style used by developers today.

Table 13.1 showed that developers embed parameters in URIs as either query string parameters or as parts of the path. The System.Uri or System.UriBuilder classes do not allow building and parsing of URIs based on this approach. Another approach that has been used is to build and parse URIs based on patterns that specify named tokens. The tokens represent the parameters that are needed to build URIs using logical substitution. They also define how parameters can be parsed from URIs. .NET Framework 3.5

introduces a new class called the `System.UriTemplate` that provides a consistent way for building and parsing URIs based on patterns. This class defines a pattern based on named tokens. Tokens are represented in curly braces within a pattern. For example, the pattern `/finance/info?q={symbol}` specifies a stock symbol that is sent as a query string parameter. Named tokens can also be embedded as a part of the URI path and are not limited to query string parameters. For example, the following pattern, `/browse/{word}`, specifies a parameter within the URI path. `System.Uri` instances can be built or parsed based on these patterns. We will now examine how we can use the `System.UriTemplate` class do this.

Building URIs

Listing 13.1 shows two examples of how we can build `System.Uri` instances based on `System.UriTemplate` classes. The first example uses the `BindByPosition` method to create a `System.Uri` instance to retrieve Yahoo! stock quotes. The second example uses the `BindByName` method to pass a collection of name/value pairs to create a `System.Uri` instance to retrieve Google stock quotes.

LISTING 13.1 Binding Parameters with `UriTemplate`

```
using System;
using System.Collections.Specialized;

namespace EssentialWCF
{
    class Program
    {
        static void Main(string[] args)
        {
            string symbol = "MSFT";

            // BindByPosition
            Uri YahooStockBaseUri =
                new Uri("http://finance.yahoo.com");
            UriTemplate YahooStockUriTemplate =
                new UriTemplate("/d/quotes?s={symbol}&f=s1l1t1d1");
            Uri YahooStockUri =
                YahooStockUriTemplate.BindByPosition(
                    YahooStockBaseUri,
                    symbol);
            Console.WriteLine(YahooStockUri.ToString());
```

LISTING 13.1 continued

```
                    // BindByName
                    Uri GoogleStockBaseUri =
                        new Uri("http://finance.google.com");
                    UriTemplate GoogleStockUriTemplate =
                        new UriTemplate("/finance/info?q={symbol}");
                    NameValueCollection GoogleParams =
                        new NameValueCollection();
                    GoogleParams.Add("symbol", symbol);
                    Uri GoogleStockUri =
                        GoogleStockUriTemplate.BindByName(
                            GoogleStockBaseUri,
                            GoogleParams);
                    Console.WriteLine(GoogleStockUri.ToString());

                    Console.ReadLine();
                }
            }
        }
```

Parsing URIs

We just saw how easy it was to create System.Uri instances based on patterns. Listing 13.2 shows how we can take existing URIs and parse out parameters. Again we have two examples. The first example shows how we can parse out parameters based on query string parameters. The second example shows how we can parse out parameters based on a path. In both cases, we are able to extract a set of name/value pairs based on a pattern. We will see in the "Creating Operations for the Web" section how the UriTemplate can be used to dispatch Web service methods based on URIs.

LISTING 13.2 Matching Parameters with UriTemplate

```
using System;

namespace UriTemplate102
{
    class Program
    {
        static void Main(string[] args)
        {
            Uri YahooBaseUri = new Uri("http://finance.yahoo.com");
            UriTemplate YahooStockTemplate =
                new UriTemplate("/d/quotes?s={symbol}");
```

```
                Uri YahooStockUri =
        new Uri("http://finance.yahoo.com/d/quotes?s=MSFT&f=spt1d");
                UriTemplateMatch match =
                    YahooStockTemplate.Match(YahooBaseUri, YahooStockUri);

                foreach (string key in match.BoundVariables.Keys)
                    Console.WriteLine(String.Format("{0}: {1}", key,
                        match.BoundVariables[key]));

                Console.WriteLine();

                Uri ReferenceDotComBaseUri =
                    new Uri("http://dictionary.reference.com");
                UriTemplate ReferenceDotComTemplate =
                    new UriTemplate("/browse/{word}");

                Uri ReferenceDotComUri =
        new Uri("http://dictionary.reference.com/browse/opaque");
                match =
                    ReferenceDotComTemplate.Match(ReferenceDotComBaseUri
                    ReferenceDotComUri);

                foreach (string key in match.BoundVariables.Keys)
                    Console.WriteLine(String.Format("{0}: {1}", key,
                        match.BoundVariables[key]));

                Console.ReadLine();
            }
        }
    }
```

Creating Operations for the Web

Creating operations for the Web means that we will want to expose services based on URIs, encode messages without the overhead of SOAP, pass parameters using the HTTP protocol, and format data using JSON or POX. WCF provides the WebHttpBinding binding that supports these capabilities. The WebHttpBinding binding is constructed using two binding elements. The first binding element is a new message encoder called WebMessageEncodingBindingElement. This is a new binding element that allows for the encoding of messages using either JSON or POX. The second binding element is a transport binding element based on either the HttpTransportBindingElement or HttpsTransportBindingElement. These binding elements enable communication using the HTTP protocol. The `HttpsTransportBindingElement` binding element is used to support transport-level security.

Hosting Using `WebHttpBinding`

To examine how to use the `WebHttpBinding` binding, we will create a simple Echo Web service. We are going to keep this example simple because we will expand on how to use this binding later on in this chapter. Listing 13.3 shows the `IEchoService` interface. This interface defines a service contract that has a single operation contract called `Echo`. Notice that the `Echo` operation contract is also attributed with the `WebGet` attribute. This attribute tells the `webHttpBinding` binding to expose this operation over the HTTP protocol using the GET verb.

LISTING 13.3 **IEchoService** Interface

```
using System;
using System.ServiceModel;
using System.ServiceModel.Web;

[ServiceContract]
public interface IEchoService
{
    [OperationContract]
    [WebGet]
    string Echo(string echoThis);
}
```

Listing 13.4 shows the `EchoService` class that implements the `IEchoService` interface. This class implements the `Echo` operation by taking the `echoThis` parameter and returning it to the client.

LISTING 13.4 **EchoService** Class

```
using System;
using System.ServiceModel;

public class EchoService : IEchoService
{
    #region IEchoService Members

    public string Echo(string echoThis)
    {
```

```
        return string.Format("You sent this '{0}'.", echoThis);
    }

    #endregion
}
```

The last thing needed is to host the `EchoService` service within IIS. Listing 13.5 shows the configuration file that allows us to host this service using the `WebHttpBinding` binding. The `webHttpBinding` configuration element exposes services using the `WebHttpBinding` binding. One important point is that the `WebHttpBinding` binding does not specify the format to expose services. Instead we need to use an endpoint behavior to specify the format returned from services exposed with the `WebHttpBinding` binding. Two endpoint behaviors can be used: `WebHttpBehavior` and `WebScriptEnablingBehavior`. The `WebScriptEnablingBehavior` behavior will be discussed in the section "Programming the Web with AJAX and JSON" later in this chapter. For now we will discuss the `WebHttpBehavior` behavior. The `WebHttpBehavior` endpoint behavior is used with the `WebHttpBinding` to format messages using either JSON or XML. The default for this behavior is to use XML.

LISTING 13.5 EchoService Configuration

```
<system.serviceModel>
  <services>
    <service name="EchoService">
      <endpoint address=""
                behaviorConfiguration="WebBehavior"
                binding="webHttpBinding" contract="IEchoService"/>
    </service>
  </services>
  <behaviors>
    <endpointBehaviors>
      <behavior name="WebBehavior">
        <webHttp />
      </behavior>
    </endpointBehaviors>
  </behaviors>
</system.serviceModel>
```

Figure 13.1 shows the output from the `EchoService` service when exposed over the `WebHttpBinding` binding. Because we exposed the service using the `WebGet` attribute, we can call the service by typing the URI in a

browser. The URI that was used is http://localhost/SimpleWebService/
EchoService.svc/Echo?echoThis=helloworld.

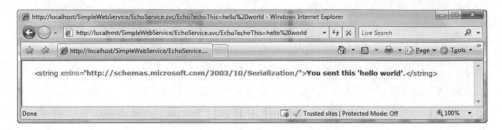

FIGURE 13.1 Response in browser using WebHttpBinding binding

Using WebGet and WebInvoke

Services can be exposed using the WebHttpBinding binding using either the
WebGet or WebInvoke attributes. Each of these attributes specifies the HTTP
verb, message format, and body style needed to expose an operation. We
will examine each of these attributes and reasons to use each.

WebGet

The WebGet attribute exposes operations using the GET verb. The GET has
significant advantages over other HTTP verbs. First, the endpoint is
directly accessible via a Web browser by typing the URI to the service into
the address bar. Parameters can be sent within the URI either as query
string parameters or embedded in the URI. Second, clients and other downstream systems such as proxy servers can easily cache resources based on
the cache policy for the service. Because of the caching capability, the
WebGet attribute should be used only for retrieval.

WebInvoke

The WebInvoke attribute exposes services using other HTTP verbs such as
POST, PUT, and DELETE. The default is to use POST, but it can be changed
by setting the Method property of the attribute. These operations are meant
to modify resources; therefore, the WebInvoke attribute is used to make
modifications to resources.

Listing 13.6 shows a service that defines services that are exposed in the WebGet and WebInvoke attributes. The WebGet attribute is used to retrieve customer information. The WebInvoke attribute is used for those operations that modify data such as adding or deleting customers. Last, the UriTemplate property is specified on WebGet and WebInvoke attribute to identify a customer resource using the URI.

LISTING 13.6 CustomerService

```
using System;
using System.ServiceModel;
using System.ServiceModel.Web;

namespace EssentialWCF
{
    [ServiceContract]
    public class CustomerService
    {
        [OperationContract]
        [WebGet(UriTemplate="/customer/{id}")]
        public Customer GetCustomer(int id)
        {
            Customer customer = null;

            // Get customer from database

            return customer;
        }

        [OperationContract]
        [WebInvoke(Method = "PUT", UriTemplate = "/customer/{id}")]
        public void PutCustomer(int id, Customer customer)
        {
            // Put customer in database
        }

        [OperationContract]
        [WebInvoke(Method = "DELETE", UriTemplate = "/customer/{id}")]
        public void DeleteCustomer(int id)
        {
            // Put customer in database
        }
    }
}
```

Programming the Web with AJAX and JSON

So far we have seen how to host services using the `WebHttpBinding` binding and the `WebHttpBehavior` endpoint behavior. This allows us to expose services using POX. Many Web developers want to forgo the use of XML and instead use JSON, a simpler format. JSON is well suited for browser applications that need an efficient means of parsing responses from services, and it has the added benefit of integration with JavaScript, the programming language most often used for client-side Web development. JSON is a subset of JavaScript's object literal notation, which means you can easily create objects in JavaScript. Because of this, it's a perfect alternative to using XML for use with AJAX applications.

AJAX stands for Asynchronous JavaScript and XML. AJAX-based Web applications have significant benefits over traditional Web applications. They allow for improved user experience and better bandwidth usage. This is done by improving browser-to-server communication so that the browser does not need to perform a page load. This in turn is done by communicating with a server asynchronously using the JavaScript and the `XMLHttpRequest` class. Because communication with the server can be done without the need for a page load, developers can create richer user interface experiences approaching that of desktop applications. These types of Web applications are often referred to as Rich Internet Applications, or RIAs.

ASP.NET AJAX Integration

Many frameworks exist for building these AJAX-based Web applications. One of the more popular frameworks is the ASP.NET AJAX framework. This framework has a great client-side and server-side model for building AJAX-enabled Web applications. It includes many capabilities such as a rich client-side class library, rich AJAX-enabled Web controls, and automatic client-side proxy generation for communication with services. It is also based on ASP.NET, which is Microsoft's technology for building Web applications using .NET. WCF already integrates with ASP.NET in .NET Framework 3.0. .NET Framework 3.5 introduces new support for ASP.NET AJAX applications using the `WebScriptEnablingBehavior` endpoint behavior. This replaces the `WebHttpBehavior` endpoint behavior. It adds support for using JSON by default and ASP.NET client-side proxy generation. These new capabilities can be used by replacing the `webHttp` endpoint behavior configuration element with the `enableWebScript` configuration element.

We created a sample ASP.NET AJAX application called the XBOX 360 Game Review to see how we can use the `WebHttpBinding` binding and the `WebScriptEnablingBehavior` to build AJAX-based applications. This simple Web application enables users to provide reviews about their favorite XBOX 360 game. The application was built using an ASP.NET AJAX Web site project template in Visual Studio 2008. Figure 13.2 shows a picture of this Web site.

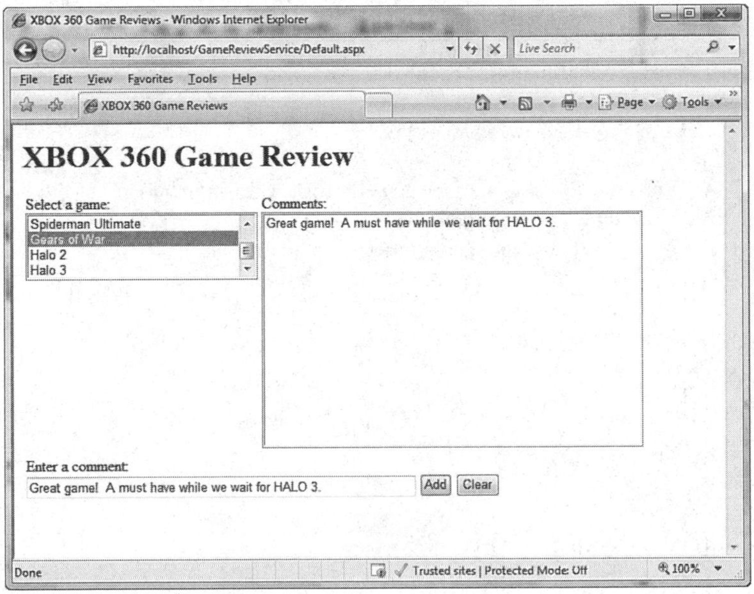

FIGURE 13.2 XBOX 360 Game Review AJAX-enabled application

This site has a number of features. First is a list of games that is displayed in a `ListBox` control to the user. Users can select a game and see a list of comments for each game. Then a user can add comments for the each game. Listing 13.7 lists the service that provides this functionality.

LISTING 13.7 `GameReviewService.cs`

```
using System;
using System.Collections;
using System.Collections.Generic;
using System.Runtime.Serialization;
using System.ServiceModel;
```

LISTING 13.7 continued

```
using System.ServiceModel.Activation;
using System.ServiceModel.Web;

namespace EssentialWCF
{
    [ServiceContract(Namespace="EssentialWCF")]
    [ServiceBehavior(InstanceContextMode = InstanceContextMode.Single)]
    [AspNetCompatibilityRequirements(RequirementsMode =
        AspNetCompatibilityRequirementsMode.Allowed)]
    public class GameReviewService
    {
        private string[] gamelist = new string[] { "Viva Pinata",
            "Star Wars Lego", "Spiderman Ultimate",
            "Gears of War", "Halo 2", "Halo 3" };
        private Dictionary<string, List<string>> reviews;

        public GameReviewService()
        {
            reviews = new Dictionary<string, List<string>>();
            foreach (string game in gamelist)
                reviews.Add(game, new List<string>());
        }

        [OperationContract]
        [WebGet]
        public string[] Games()
        {
            return gamelist;
        }

        [OperationContract]
        [WebGet]
        public string[] Reviews(string game)
        {
            WebOperationContext ctx = WebOperationContext.Current;
                ctx.OutgoingResponse.Headers.Add("Cache-Control",
                "no-cache");

            if (!reviews.ContainsKey(game))
                return null;

            List<string> listOfReviews = reviews[game];

            if (listOfReviews.Count == 0)
                return new string[] {
                    string.Format("No reviews found for {0}.",game) };
            else
                return listOfReviews.ToArray();
```

```
    }

    [OperationContract]
    [WebInvoke]
    public void AddReview(string game, string comment)
    {
        reviews[game].Add(comment);
    }

    [OperationContract]
    [WebInvoke]
    public void ClearReviews(string game)
    {
        reviews[game].Clear();
    }
  }
}
```

We chose to host this service within Internet Information Server (IIS). Listing 13.8 shows the GameReviewService.svc used to host the service.

LISTING 13.8 GameReviewService.svc

```
<%@ ServiceHost Language="C#" Debug="true"
➥Service="EssentialWCF.GameReviewService"
➥CodeBehind="~/App_Code/GameReviewService.cs" %>
```

Listing 13.9 shows the configuration information used to host the GameReviewService. The most important aspect of this configuration information is the use of the webHttpBinding binding and the enableWebScript endpoint behavior. This enables the use of JSON and generates the necessary client-side proxy code for the GameReviewService with ASP.NET.

LISTING 13.9 web.config

```
<system.serviceModel>
    <serviceHostingEnvironment
        aspNetCompatibilityEnabled="true"/>
    <services>
        <service name="EssentialWCF.GameReviewService"
    behaviorConfiguration="MetadataBehavior">
            <endpoint address=""
                    behaviorConfiguration="AjaxBehavior"
                    binding="webHttpBinding"
                    contract="EssentialWCF.GameReviewService"/>
            <endpoint address="mex"
                  binding="mexHttpBinding"
```

LISTING 13.9 continued

```
                            contract="IMetadataExchange"/>
            </service>
        </services>
        <behaviors>
            <endpointBehaviors>
                <behavior name="AjaxBehavior">
                    <enableWebScript/>
                </behavior>
            </endpointBehaviors>
            <serviceBehaviors>
                <behavior name="MetadataBehavior">
                    <serviceMetadata httpGetEnabled="true"
                                     httpGetUrl=""/>
                </behavior>
            </serviceBehaviors>
        </behaviors>
    </system.serviceModel>
```

You configure the GameReviewService to be used with ASP.NET by adding a reference to the service using the ASP.NET ScriptManager. Listing 13.10 shows the markup used to reference the GameReviewService. Behind the scenes this is generating client-side script that references a JavaScript file with the client-side proxy. For our example, the URI to the client-side JavaScript is http://localhost/GameReviewService/GameReviewService.svc/js.

LISTING 13.10 Referencing Services Using ASP.NET ScriptManager

```
<asp:ScriptManager ID="ScriptManager1" runat="server">
    <Services>
        <asp:ServiceReference Path="GameReviewService.svc" />
    </Services>
</asp:ScriptManager>
```

We have included the ASP.NET Web form used to build the XBOX 360 Game Review Web application. This shows how the services are called from client-side script and how the results are used to dynamically populate controls.

LISTING 13.11 Making Client-Side Proxy Calls

```
<%@ Page Language="C#" AutoEventWireup="true"
➥CodeFile="Default.aspx.cs" Inherits="_Default" %>

<%@ Register Assembly="AjaxControlToolkit"
➥Namespace="AjaxControlToolkit" TagPrefix="cc1" %>
<!DOCTYPE html PUBLIC "-//W3C//DTD XHTML 1.0 Transitional//EN"
"http://www.w3.org/TR/xhtml1/DTD/xhtml1-transitional.dtd">
<html xmlns="http://www.w3.org/1999/xhtml">
<head id="Head1" runat="server">
    <title>XBOX 360 Game Reviews</title>

    <script type="text/javascript">

      function pageLoad() {
      }

    </script>

</head>
<body>
    <form id="form1" runat="server">
    <div>
        <asp:ScriptManager ID="ScriptManager1" runat="server">
            <Services>
                <asp:ServiceReference Path="GameReviewService.svc" />
            </Services>
        </asp:ScriptManager>

        <script type="text/javascript">
        EssentialWCF.GameReviewService.set_defaultFailedCallback(OnError);
        function ListGames()
        {
          EssentialWCF.GameReviewService.Games(OnListGamesComplete);
        }
        function ListReviews()
        {
            var gameListBox = document.getElementById("GameListBox");
            EssentialWCF.GameReviewService.Reviews(gameListBox.value,
                OnListReviewsComplete);
        }
        function AddReview()
        {
            var gameListBox = document.getElementById("GameListBox");
            var reviewTextBox =
                document.getElementById("ReviewTextBox");
            EssentialWCF.GameReviewService.AddReview(gameListBox.value,
                reviewTextBox.value, OnUpdateReviews);
        }
```

LISTING 13.11 continued

```
function ClearReviews()
{
    var gameListBox = document.getElementById("GameListBox");
    EssentialWCF.GameReviewService.ClearReviews(gameListBox.value,
        OnUpdateReviews);
}
function OnListGamesComplete(result)
{
  var gameListBox = document.getElementById("GameListBox");
  ClearAndSetListBoxItems(gameListBox, result);
}
function OnListReviewsComplete(result)
{
  var reviewListBox = document.getElementById("ReviewListBox");
  ClearAndSetListBoxItems(reviewListBox, result);
}
function OnUpdateReviews(result)
{
  ListReviews();
}
function ClearAndSetListBoxItems(listBox, games)
{
    for (var i = listBox.options.length-1; i >-1; i--)
    {
        listBox.options[i] = null;
    }

    var textValue;
    var optionItem;
    for (var j = 0; j < games.length; j++)
    {

            textValue = games[j];
        optionItem = new Option( textValue, textValue,
        false, false);
        listBox.options[listBox.length] = optionItem;
    }
}
function OnError(result)
{
  alert("Error: " + result.get_message());
}
function OnLoad()
{
  ListGames();

  var gameListBox = document.getElementById("GameListBox");
  if (gameListBox.attachEvent) {
```

```
        gameListBox.attachEvent("onchange", ListReviews);
      }
      else {
        gameListBox.addEventListener("change", ListReviews, false);
      }
    }
    Sys.Application.add_load(OnLoad);
    </script>

    <h1>XBOX 360 Game Review</h1>
    <table>
    <tr style="height:250px;vertical-align:top;"><td
        style="width:240px">Select a game:<br /><asp:ListBox
        ID="GameListBox" runat="server"
        Width="100%"></asp:ListBox></td>
        <td style="width:400px">Comments:<br /><asp:ListBox
        ID="ReviewListBox" runat="server" Width="100%"
        Height="100%"></asp:ListBox></td></tr>
    <tr style="vertical-align:top;"><td colspan="2">
        Enter a comment:<br />
        <asp:TextBox ID="ReviewTextBox" runat="server"
        width="400px"></asp:TextBox>
        <input id="AddReviewButton" type="button" value="Add"
            onclick="AddReview();" />
        <input id="ClearReviewButton" type="button" value="Clear"
            onclick="ClearReviews();" />
        </td></tr>
        </table>
    </div>
    </form>
</body>
</html>
```

Using the WebOperationContext

One common thing to do when hosting services using the WebHttpBinding binding is to read or write to the HTTP context. This can be done using the WebOperationContext class. There are a variety of reasons to access the HTTP context. You might want to read custom authentication or authorization headers, control caching, or set the content type, for example.

Figure 13.3 shows a Web application that displays wallpaper images on the current machine. The entire application is built using a WCF service and is accessible using any Web browser.

FIGURE 13.3 Wallpaper Web application

Listing 13.12 shows code for the WallpaperService service. There is an Images operation that displays an HTML page of all images. This operation sets the ContentType header so that the browser interprets the output as HTML. It also sets the Cache-Control header so that additional images can be added to the application without the browser caching the display. Finally, there is an Image operation that returns an image to the browser. This operation sets both the ContentType and ETag header.

■ NOTE   **Taking the .svc Out of REST**

WCF Services hosted in IIS use the .svc extension. This does not follow common REST URI naming practices. For example, the service in Listing 13.12 is accessed using the following URI:

http://localhost/Wallpaper/WallpaperService.svc/images

You can remove the .svc extension by using an ASP.NET HttpModule (with IIS 7.0 only) to call HttpContext.RewritePath to modify the URI. This would allow the URI to take the following form:

http://localhost/Wallpaper/WallpaperService/images

LISTING 13.12 Wallpaper Image Service

```
using System;
using System.Collections;
using System.Collections.Generic;
using System.IO;
using System.Runtime.Serialization;
using System.Text;
using System.Web.UI;
using System.Web.UI.WebControls;
using System.ServiceModel;
using System.ServiceModel.Activation;
using System.ServiceModel.Web;

namespace EssentialWCF
{
    [DataContract]
    public class Image
    {
        string name;
        string uri;

        public Image()
        {
        }

        public Image(string name, string uri)
        {
            this.name = name;
            this.uri = uri;
        }

        public Image(string name, Uri uri)
        {
            this.name = name;
            this.uri = uri.ToString();
        }

        [DataMember]
        public string Name
        {
            get { return this.name; }
            set { this.Name = value; }
        }

        [DataMember]
        public string Uri
        {
            get { return this.uri; }
            set { this.uri = value; }
        }
```

LISTING 13.12 continued

```
        }
    }

    [ServiceContract]
    [AspNetCompatibilityRequirements(RequirementsMode =
        AspNetCompatibilityRequirementsMode.Required)]
    public class WallpaperService
    {
        private static UriTemplate ImageUriTemplate =
            new UriTemplate("/image/{name}");

        private string ImagePath
        {
            get
            {
                return @"C:\Windows\Web\Wallpaper";
            }
        }

        private Image GetImage(string name, Uri baseUri)
        {
            return new Image(name,
                ImageUriTemplate.BindByPosition(baseUri,
                new string[] { name }));
        }

        private void PopulateListOfImages(List<Image> list,
                                          Uri baseUri)
        {
            System.Web.HttpContext ctx =
                System.Web.HttpContext.Current;
            DirectoryInfo d = new DirectoryInfo(ImagePath);
            FileInfo[] files = d.GetFiles("*.jpg");

            foreach (FileInfo f in files)
            {
                string fileName = f.Name.Split(new char[] { '.' })[0];
                string etag = fileName + "_" +
                    f.LastWriteTime.ToString();
                list.Add(GetImage(fileName, baseUri));
            }
        }

        [OperationContract]
        [WebGet(UriTemplate="/images")]
        public void Images()
        {
            WebOperationContext wctx = WebOperationContext.Current;
```

```csharp
wctx.OutgoingResponse.ContentType = "text/html";
wctx.OutgoingResponse.Headers.Add("Cache-Control",
    "no-cache");

Uri baseUri =
    wctx.IncomingRequest.UriTemplateMatch.BaseUri;
List<Image> listOfImages = new List<Image>();
PopulateListOfImages(listOfImages, baseUri);

TextWriter sw = new StringWriter();
Html32TextWriter htmlWriter = new Html32TextWriter(sw);

htmlWriter.WriteFullBeginTag("HTML");
htmlWriter.WriteFullBeginTag("BODY");
htmlWriter.WriteFullBeginTag("H1");
htmlWriter.Write("Wallpaper");
htmlWriter.WriteEndTag("H1");
htmlWriter.WriteFullBeginTag("TABLE");
htmlWriter.WriteFullBeginTag("TR");

int i = 0;

Image image;
while (i < listOfImages.Count)
{
    image = listOfImages[i];

    htmlWriter.WriteFullBeginTag("TD");
    htmlWriter.Write(image.Name);
    htmlWriter.WriteBreak();
    htmlWriter.WriteBeginTag("IMG");
    htmlWriter.WriteAttribute("SRC", image.Uri);
    htmlWriter.WriteAttribute("STYLE",
        "width:150px;height:150px");
    htmlWriter.WriteEndTag("IMG");
    htmlWriter.WriteEndTag("TD");

    if (((i+1) % 5) == 0)
    {
        htmlWriter.WriteEndTag("TR");
        htmlWriter.WriteFullBeginTag("TR");
    }
    i++;
}
htmlWriter.WriteEndTag("TR");
htmlWriter.WriteEndTag("TABLE");
htmlWriter.WriteEndTag("BODY");
htmlWriter.WriteEndTag("HTML");

System.Web.HttpContext ctx =
```

LISTING 13.12 continued

```
                    System.Web.HttpContext.Current;
            ctx.Response.Write(sw.ToString());
        }


        [OperationContract]
        [WebGet(UriTemplate = "/image/{name}")]
        public void GetImage(string name)
        {
            WebOperationContext wctx = WebOperationContext.Current;
            wctx.OutgoingResponse.ContentType = "image/jpeg";

            System.Web.HttpContext ctx =
                System.Web.HttpContext.Current;

            string fileName = null;
            byte[] fileBytes = null;
            try
            {
                fileName = string.Format(@"{0}\{1}.jpg",
                                        ImagePath,
                                        name);
                if (File.Exists(fileName))
                {
                    using (FileStream f = File.OpenRead(fileName))
                    {
                        fileBytes = new byte[f.Length];
                        f.Read(fileBytes, 0,
Convert.ToInt32(f.Length));
                    }
                }
                else
                    wctx.OutgoingResponse.StatusCode =
System.Net.HttpStatusCode.NotFound;
            }
            catch
            {
                wctx.OutgoingResponse.StatusCode =
System.Net.HttpStatusCode.NotFound;
            }

            FileInfo fi = new FileInfo(fileName);
            wctx.OutgoingResponse.ETag = fileName + "_" +
fi.LastWriteTime.ToString();
            ctx.Response.OutputStream.Write(fileBytes, 0,
fileBytes.Length);
        }
    }
}
```

The following configuration in Listing 13.13 is used to host the WallpaperService service. The service is hosted using the WebHttpBinding binding and the WebHttpBehavior endpoint behavior.

LISTING 13.13 Wallpaper Image Service Configuration

```
<system.serviceModel>
  <serviceHostingEnvironment aspNetCompatibilityEnabled="true"/>
  <services>
    <service name="EssentialWCF.WallpaperService"
             behaviorConfiguration="MetadataBehavior">
      <endpoint address="" behaviorConfiguration="WebBehavior"
                binding="webHttpBinding"
                contract="EssentialWCF.WallpaperService"/>
      <endpoint address="mex"
                binding="mexHttpBinding"
                contract="IMetadataExchange"/>
    </service>
  </services>
  <behaviors>
    <endpointBehaviors>
      <behavior name="WebBehavior">
        <webHttp />
      </behavior>
    </endpointBehaviors>
    <serviceBehaviors>
      <behavior name="MetadataBehavior">
        <serviceMetadata httpGetEnabled="true" httpGetUrl="" />
      </behavior>
    </serviceBehaviors>
  </behaviors>
</system.serviceModel>
```

Listing 13.14 shows the .svc file used to host the WallpaperService in IIS.

LISTING 13.14 WallpaperService.svc

```
<%@ ServiceHost Language="C#" Debug="true"
Service="EssentialWCF.WallpaperService"
➥CodeBehind="~/App_Code/WallpaperService.cs" %>
```

Hosting for the Web

Arguably one of the best improvements in WCF is the feature for hosting services on the Web. Prior to .NET Framework 3.5, you had to provide configuration or write code to host services. This was true even if you hosted your services within IIS. This became tedious for those hosting services on the Web. There are many capabilities offered by WCF to host services, but only a limited configuration was used by Web developers building services. For example, you would not expect an AJAX-based application to support multiple bindings, use message-level security, or require transactions. To simplify hosting of services, WCF introduced a feature called Configuration Free Hosting. This allows developers to host services without providing configuration or writing any code. The infrastructure for this feature was always a part of the hosting model within WCF. We will examine two ways to use this feature.

WebScriptServiceHost

There is a new class available in the System.ServiceModel.Web namespace called the WebScriptServiceHost class. This class allows for self-hosting of services using the WebHttpBinding binding and the WebScriptEnablingBehavior endpoint behavior. The advantage to using this class over the ServiceHost class is that you do not have to provide any binding or behaviors to host a service.

WebScriptServiceHostFactory

Another class in the System.ServiceModel.Activation namespace, called the WebScriptServiceHostFactory class, is meant to be used with IIS hosting and .svc files. It allows for hosting of services in IIS using the WebHttpBinding binding and the WebScriptEnablingBehavior endpoint behavior without the need for configuration. Listing 13.15 shows an example of an .svc file that uses the WebScriptServiceHostFactory class. This is the same .svc file used to host the WallpaperService service shown in Listing 13.12. The advantage of this approach is that the configuration information shown in Listing 13.13 is no longer required to host the service.

> **■ NOTE**   **Configuration-Free Hosting for WebHttp**
>
> Two additional classes, called `WebServiceHost` and
> `WebServiceHostFactory`, host services using the `WebHttpBinding`
> binding and the `WebHttpBehavior` endpoint behavior. They
> offer the same configuration-free hosting capabilities as the
> `WebScriptServiceHost` and `WebScriptServiceHostFactory` classes.

LISTING 13.15 `WallpaperService.svc` (Configuration Free)

```
<%@ ServiceHost Factory=
➥"System.ServiceModel.Activation.WebScriptServiceHostFactory"
➥Language="C#" Debug="true" Service="EssentialWCF.WallpaperService"
CodeBehind="~/App_Code/WallpaperService.cs" %>
```

Content Syndication with RSS and ATOM

RSS and ATOM are content syndication formats for the Web. These formats
are used for all types of content syndication, such as news, video, and
blogs. By far the widest use for these formats is for blogging. Since its initial
popularity, RSS and ATOM have been used by every major Web site. WCF
provides several mechanisms for working with RSS and ATOM syndication
feeds. A new namespace, called `System.ServiceModel.Syndication`, contains classes for creating, consuming, and formatting syndication feeds
based on RSS and ATOM. The core class for creating and consuming content syndication feeds is the `SyndicationFeed` class. Listing 13.16 shows an
example application using this class to expose an RSS and ATOM. This
application enumerates over a music collection and exposes the information using a syndication feed.

LISTING 13.16 Zune Music Syndication

```
using System;
using System.IO;
using System.Collections.Generic;
using System.ServiceModel;
using System.ServiceModel.Syndication;
using System.ServiceModel.Web;
```

LISTING 13.16 continued

```csharp
[ServiceContract]
public class ZuneFeedService
{
    private static Uri LiveSearchBaseURI =
        new Uri("http://search.live.com");
    private static UriTemplate LiveSearchTemplate =
        new UriTemplate(@"/results.aspx?q={terms}");

    private string MusicPath
    {
        get
        {
            return @"C:\Users\ricrane\Music\Zune";
        }
    }

    private SyndicationFeed ZuneFeed
    {
        get
        {
            SyndicationFeed feed = new SyndicationFeed()
            {
                Title =
                new TextSyndicationContent("My Zune Music Library"),
                Description =
                new TextSyndicationContent("My Zune Music Library")
            };

            DirectoryInfo di = new DirectoryInfo(MusicPath);
            DirectoryInfo[] artists = di.GetDirectories();

            List<SyndicationItem> items = new List<SyndicationItem>();

            foreach (DirectoryInfo artist in artists)
            {
                SyndicationItem item = new SyndicationItem()
                {
                    Title =
    new TextSyndicationContent(string.Format("Artist: {0}", artist.Name)),
                    Summary =
                        new TextSyndicationContent(artist.FullName),
                    PublishDate = DateTime.Now,
                    LastUpdatedTime = artist.LastAccessTime,
                    Copyright =
                        new TextSyndicationContent(@"Zune Library (c)")
                };
```

```
                Uri searchUri =
➥LiveSearchTemplate.BindByPosition(LiveSearchBaseURI, artist.Name);
                item.Links.Add(new SyndicationLink(searchUri));
                items.Add(item);
            }

            feed.Items = items;

            return feed;
        }
    }


    [OperationContract]
    [WebGet]
    [ServiceKnownType(typeof(Atom10FeedFormatter))]
    [ServiceKnownType(typeof(Rss20FeedFormatter))]
    public SyndicationFeedFormatter<SyndicationFeed>
            GetMusic(string format)
    {
        SyndicationFeedFormatter<SyndicationFeed> output;

        if (format == "rss")
            output = new Rss20FeedFormatter(ZuneFeed);
        else
            output = new Atom10FeedFormatter(ZuneFeed);

        return output;
    }
}
```

Listing 13.17 shows the code to host the syndication service. The application self-hosts the service using the `WebServiceHost` class. It then consumes the service and outputs the feed to the display.

LISTING 13.17 Zune Music Feed Console Application

```
using System;
using System.Collections.Generic;
using System.Diagnostics;
using System.ServiceModel;
using System.ServiceModel.Description;
using System.ServiceModel.Syndication;
using System.ServiceModel.Web;

namespace ZuneFeed
{
```

LISTING 13.17 continued

```
class Program
{
    static void Main(string[] args)
    {
        ServiceHost host = new ServiceHost(typeof(ZuneFeedService),
            new Uri("http://localhost:8000/zune"));

        ServiceEndpoint atomEndpoint =
            host.AddServiceEndpoint(typeof(ZuneFeedService),
        new WebHttpBinding(), "feed");
        atomEndpoint.Behaviors.Add(new WebHttpBehavior());

        host.Open();

        Console.WriteLine("Service host open");

        SyndicationFeed feed =
           SyndicationFeed.Load(
           new Uri("http://localhost:8000/zune/feed/?format=rss"));

        foreach (SyndicationItem item in feed.Items)
        {
            Console.WriteLine("Artist: " + item.Title.Text);
            Console.WriteLine("Summary: " + item.Summary.Text);
        }

        Console.WriteLine("Press [Enter] to exit.]");
        Console.ReadLine();
    }
  }
 }
```

SUMMARY

The new Web programming capabilities in WCF simplify the building of services for use on the Web. They help Web developers get stuff done quickly in the manner that they wish to build and consume services for the Web. This means providing features that allow developers to work with the Web. The following summarizes those capabilities of WCF for the Web:

- The .NET Framework 3.5 provides a new `UriTemplate` class that allows for the efficient parsing of URIs based on their path and a query component. The `UriTemplate` class is used by WCF in its Web programming model calls to services.

- Information can be exposed with WCF using a variety of serialization formats including SOAP and POX. .NET Framework 3.5 adds support for JSON as a serialization format.

- An additional binding provided by WCF, called the `webHttpBinding` binding, exposes services using WCF's Web programming model.

- The `webHttpBinding` binding is used with either the `WebHttpBehavior` or `WebScriptEnablingBehavior` endpoint behaviors. The `WebHttpBehavior` endpoint behavior is used to expose services using POX or JSON. The `WebScriptEnablingBehavior` endpoint behavior is using JSON with additional support for generating ASP.NET AJAX client proxies.

- WCF provides a new hosting feature called configuration-free hosting. This feature allows services to be hosted in IIS without the need for configuration. Out of the box, WCF provides two classes that support configuration-free hosting: `WebServiceHostFactory` and `WebScriptServiceHostFactory`. The `WebServiceHostFactory` supports configuration-free hosting using the `webHttpBinding` binding and the `WebHttpBehavior` endpoint behavior. The `WebScriptServiceHostFactory` supports configuration-free hosting using the `webHttpBinding` binding and the `WebScriptEnablingBehavior` endpoint behavior.

- WCF in .NET Framework 3.5 provides a rich extensible programming model for content syndication found in the `System.ServiceModel.Syndication` namespace. Support for both RSS and ATOM syndication feeds is included, using the `Atom10FeedFormatter` and `Rss20FeedFormatter` classes.

◾ APPENDIX ◾
Advanced Topics

THERE ARE MANY things to know to develop applications with Windows Communication Foundation (WCF). Although this book has tried to incorporate everything the average developer needs to know about WCF, some things did not get discussed. The purpose of this appendix is to fill some of those gaps.

Publishing Metadata Endpoints

We have already discussed metadata in Chapter 1, "Basics." This discussion gave an introduction to exposing the configuration of services using metadata. However, it did not go into details on how the metadata is exposed. Later on we introduced the concept of bindings in Chapter 4, "Bindings," but limited the discussion to those bindings meant to expose services; we did not focus on metadata bindings. WCF provides four additional bindings: `mexHttpBinding`, `mexHttpsBinding`, `mexTcpBinding`, and the `mexNamedPipeBinding` binding. These bindings expose the configuration of services using metadata over different transport protocols.

> ## ■ TIP   Bindings That Start with "mex" Expose Service Metadata
>
> Windows Communication Foundation prefixes all bindings that are meant to expose metadata with the "mex" prefix.

mexHttpBinding

The mexHttpBinding binding exists so that metadata can be exposed over the HTTP transport protocol. This is the appropriate metadata binding to use if exposing services over the basicHttpBinding, wsHttpBinding, ws2007HttpBinding bindings, or any custom binding that contains the HttpTransportBindingElement binding element. For most situations the mexHttpBinding binding is what you will want to use because it offers the broadest access to your metadata. This means that the metadata is directly accessible through client tools such as svcutil.exe and Visual Studio 2005 through Add Service Reference. It also means that this metadata can be accessed using other HTTP clients. This includes web browsers such as Internet Explorer, Firefox, and Opera. Depending on your security requirement, this may not be desirable. For example, if you are exposing services locally for on-machine communication using the netNamedPipeBinding binding, you probably do not want to use this binding.

mexNamedPipeBinding

The mexNamedPipeBinding binding exists so that metadata can be exposed over the Named Pipes transport protocol. This binding exists to expose metadata for services that use the netNamedPipeBinding binding or any custom binding that contains the NamedPipeTransportBindingElement binding element. The mexNamedPipeBinding binding does not expose metadata to the network and guarantees that it is accessible only from the local machine. WCF specifically limits the use of named pipes to local machine communication. This was discussed in the "Local Machine Communication Between .NET Applications" section of Chapter 4.

mexTcpBinding

The mexTcpBinding binding exists so that metadata can be exposed over the TCP transport protocol. This binding exists to expose metadata for services that use either the netTcpBinding or netPeerTcpBinding bindings or any custom bindings based on the TcpTransportBindingElement binding element. There is one issue to consider when using the mexTcpBinding binding with port sharing. The underlying TcpTransportBindingElement binding element used by the mexTcpBinding binding has port sharing disabled. If port sharing is needed, a custom binding based on the mexTcpBinding binding can be created to set the PortSharingEnabled property to true on the transport. For more information, see "Sharing Ports Between Services" later on in this appendix.

mexHttpsBinding

The mexHttpsBinding binding exists so that metadata can be exposed over the HTTP transport protocol using SSL/TLS transport encryption (HTTPS). Like the mexHttpBinding binding, the mexHttpsBinding is intended to be used with the basicHttpBinding, wsHttpBinding, or ws2007HttpBinding bindings or any custom binding based on the HttpTransportBindingElement binding element. Using the mexHttpsBinding binding allows for transport-level encryption, which prevents metadata from being exposed on the network.

Creating Clients from Metadata

The MetadataResolver class allows for binding information to be retrieved programmatically rather than using configuration. This means that clients can be created dynamically without the need for specifying a configuration file. This is useful if you want to deploy clients and then later change the configuration of the service. Listing A.1 shows an example of how to use the MetadataResolver class to point to a known metadata endpoint. The Resolve method on the MetadataResolver class is used to build the binding information. The binding information is contained within one or more ServiceEndpoint instances. There is one instance of a ServiceEndpoint class for every available endpoint. The ServiceEndpoint instance is then used to create a client.

LISTING A.1 Using the MetadataResolver class

```
using System;
using System.Collections.Generic;
using System.ServiceModel;
using System.ServiceModel.Description;
using System.Text;
using System.Windows;
using System.Windows.Controls;
using System.Windows.Data;
using System.Windows.Documents;
using System.Windows.Input;
using System.Windows.Media;
using System.Windows.Media.Imaging;
using System.Windows.Shapes;

namespace EssentialWCF
{
    /// <summary>
    /// Interaction logic for MainWindow.xaml
    /// </summary>

    public partial class MainWindow : System.Windows.Window
    {

        public MainWindow()
        {
            InitializeComponent();
        }

        void GetPriceButton_Click(object sender, RoutedEventArgs e)
        {
            Type typeOf = typeof(ISimpleStockService);
            Uri metadataUri =
    new Uri("http://localhost/SimpleStockService/Service.svc/mex");
            EndpointAddress metadataAddress =
                    new EndpointAddress(metadataUri);
            ServiceEndpointCollection endpoints =
                    MetadataResolver.Resolve(typeOf, metadataAddress);
            string symbol = SymbolTextBox.Text;
            decimal price;

            foreach (ServiceEndpoint point in endpoints)
            {
                if (point != null)
                {
                    using (ChannelFactory<ISimpleStockService> cf =
    ➡new ChannelFactory<EssentialWCF.ISimpleStockService>(point))
                    {
                        ISimpleStockService client =
```

```
                    cf.CreateChannel();
                price = client.GetQuote(symbol);

                SymbolPricesListBox.Items.Insert(0,
                    symbol + "=" + price.ToString());
            }
        }
    }
}

    }
}
```

Creating Silverlight Clients from Metadata

Silverlight is Microsoft's technology for delivering next-generation media experiences and rich interactive applications for the Web. It allows developers to build compelling user interfaces for the Web with interactivity, animation, video, and graphics. One major advantage to Silverlight is that it is a cross-platform, cross-browser technology that runs on multiple operating systems such as Windows, Mac OS, and Linux, and multiple browsers such as Internet Explorer, Firefox, and Safari. There are two versions of Silverlight available, v1.0 and v1.1.

Silverlight 1.0 is the first release, which focuses on rich media experiences including interactivity, animation, video, and graphics. This version supports JavaScript code-behind. This means that JavaScript hosted in the browser is used to interact with the user interface that is developed in Silverlight. WCF allows for Silverlight applications using JavaScript to consume services based on REST/POX style endpoints using AJAX. This approach is described in detail in Chapter 13, "Programmable Web."

Silverlight 1.1 (a.k.a. SL 1.1 alpha) is currently in an alpha release and is subject to change, but it is important enough to understand how it works with WCF. SL 1.1 alpha includes a mini version of the .NET Common Language Runtime. This allows for Silverlight applications to be developed with .NET code-behind. Although using JavaScript is still possible, many .NET developers will want to use .NET code-behind because this is familiar to them. This also means that we can generate WCF client proxies that are based on .NET code and reference them in code. Client proxies are generated using a new utility called `slwsdl.exe`. This utility is an update to the `wsdl.exe` utility available with the .NET Framework. This utility allows developers to generate client code for calling into Web services from Silverlight. An example of using the `slwsdl.exe` to generate a client proxy is shown next:

```
slwsdl.exe /silverlightClient http://localhost/Service.svc
```

The generate proxy is a .NET class based on base classes found in the Silverlight version of the .NET Framework. This is similar to how a developer generates a client proxy using `svcutil.exe` for WCF-enabled desktop applications. The eventual goal is for developers to have a similar experience when developing WCF-enabled Silverlight applications as they do when they develop WCF-enabled desktop applications.

For more information about Silverlight, visit the Microsoft Silverlight Web site at www.silverlight.net. Additional information can be found at the Moonlight project page at www.mono-project.com/Moonlight. Moonlight is the open source implementation of Silverlight on Linux.

Sharing Ports Between Services

Internet Information Services 6.0 (IIS) and later provides a way to share ports across multiple processes. The actually mechanism that is responsible for sharing ports is the new HTTP service (`http.sys`). This is a kernel-mode service that does connection management for both IIS and self-hosted WCF services. This approach works well for services that use the HTTP transport protocol and is transparent across hosting environments. WCF provides the Net.Tcp Port Sharing Service Windows Service to facilitate port sharing for TCP connections. By default this service is disabled. Figure A.1 shows how to start the Net.Tcp Port Sharing Service from the command line.

FIGURE A.1 Starting Net.Tcp Port Sharing Service from command line

Port sharing can be enabled on a binding after the port sharing service is started. Listing A.2 shows how to enable port sharing using configuration.

LISTING A.2 Enabling Port Sharing in Configuration

```
<system.serviceModel>
  <bindings>
    <netTcpBinding>
      <binding name="NetTcpWithPortSharing"
               portSharingEnabled="true" />
    </netTcpBinding>
  </bindings>
</system.serviceModel>
```

Listing A.3 shows how to enable port sharing using code.

LISTING A.3 Enabling Port Sharing in Code

```
public void EnablePortSharing()
{
    NetTcpBinding b = new NetTcpBinding();
    b.PortSharingEnabled = true;
}
```

Configuring Service Quota Settings

Microsoft products ship with a "secure by default" approach. This includes WCF, which means that various settings within WCF are set to prevent attacks such as denial-of-service attacks. Microsoft chose the default values for many of these settings based on a single machine development environment. This means that some of the default settings may need to be changed for use in a production environment.

One set of default settings that may need changing are those set by the ServiceThrottlingBehavior behavior. This behavior limits the amount of resources consumed by placing quota limits on services. This behavior has three settings: MaxConcurrentCalls, MaxConcurrentInstances, and MaxConcurrentSessions. Table A.1 lists the properties of the ServiceThrottlingBehavior behavior along with their default values.

TABLE A.1 ServiceThrottlingBehavior Properties

Setting	Description	Default Value
MaxConcurrentCalls	Limits the total number of simultaneous calls that will be processed.	16
MaxConcurrentSessions	Limits the maximum number of concurrent sessionful channel connections to a service.	10
MaxConcurrentInstances	Limits the maximum number of concurrent instances to a service.	Int32.MaxValue

Both the MaxConcurrentCalls and the MaxConcurrentSessions have default values that can potentially limit the throughput in a production environment. You will want to adjust these settings if your services need to accept more throughput and your servers have resources available to handle the additional load. Just be aware of the potential impact these settings have on denial-of-service attacks. Listing A.4 shows how to adjust these settings using configuration.

LISTING A.4 Adjusting ServiceThrottling in Configuration

```
<system.serviceModel>
  <behaviors>
    <serviceBehaviors>
      <behavior name="ServiceThrottlingBehavior">
        <serviceThrottling maxConcurrentCalls="1000"
```

```
                        maxConcurrentInstances="1000"
                        maxConcurrentSessions="1000" />
        </behavior>
      </serviceBehaviors>
    </behaviors>
</system.serviceModel>
```

Listing A.5 shows how to adjust the settings using code.

LISTING A.5 Adjusting ServiceThrottling in Code

```
public void IncreaseThrottle(ServiceHost serviceHost)
{
    ServiceThrottlingBehavior throttleBehavior =
➥serviceHost.Description.Behaviors.Find<ServiceThrottlingBehavior>();

    if (throttleBehavior == null)
    {
        throttleBehavior = new ServiceThrottlingBehavior();
        serviceHost.Description.Behaviors.Add(throttleBehavior);
    }

    throttleBehavior.MaxConcurrentCalls = 4000;
    throttleBehavior.MaxConcurrentInstances = 4000;
    throttleBehavior.MaxConcurrentSessions = 4000;
}
```

Configuring HTTP Connections

The HTTP 1.1 specification includes a feature called HTTP Keep-Alives. HTTP Keep-Alives allow for HTTP connections to be persisted connections between clients and servers. This allows clients to keep connections open so that they can be reused for subsequent requests. To limit the resources used by a single client, the HTTP 1.1 specification specifies a maximum of two connections per server from an application. By default, HTTP clients in the .NET Framework use HTTP 1.1 Keep-Alives including WCF.

The HttpTransportBindingElement binding element leverages classes found in the System.Net namespace for managing and making HTTP requests. The HttpTransportBindingElement binding element uses the HttpWebRequest class to make HTTP requests. The HttpWebRequest class uses other classes, ServicePointManager and ServicePoint, to manage HTTP connections. These classes help manage HTTP connections including connection lifetime. This section looks at how to manage HTTP connections to get the best performance and scalability for WCF services.

Recycling Idle Connections

The MaxIdleTime property on the ServicePoint class specifies the time that connections can remain idle before they are closed. Each new ServicePoint instance has a default value of 100 seconds. This is based on the MaxServicePointIdleTime property of the ServicePointManager class. Adjusting this property is especially useful when load balancing services across a farm of servers. Setting this value lower increases the likelihood that idle connections will be recycled. This allows for clients to establish new connections to other servers within the load-balanced server farm. Listing A.6 shows how to adjust the MaxIdleTime property on the ServicePoint class.

LISTING A.6 Setting MaxIdleTime for HTTP Using Code

```
public void SetConnections()
{
    Uri myUri = new Uri("http://www.somewhere.com/");
    System.Net.ServicePoint sp =
        ServicePointManager.FindServicePoint(myUri);
    sp.MaxIdleTime = 30000;
}
```

Adjusting Connection Lifetime

The ConnectionLeaseTimeout property on the ServicePoint class specifies the maximum time a connection can remain active before it is eligible for recycling. Each new ServicePoint instance has a default value of –1. A value of –1 means that connections can remain open indefinitely. This may not be desirable in load-balanced server farms because clients stay connected to the same server. Connections can be recycled after a period of time by setting the ConnectionLeaseTimeout to a value greater than 0. For each new request, the ConnectionLeaseTimeout is checked. If the connection lifetime has elapsed, the active connection closes and a new connection is created. Connections can be forced to be closed after each request by setting the ConnectionLeaseTimeout to 0. Listing A.7 shows how to adjust the ConnectionLeaseTimeout on the ServicePoint class.

```
public void SetConnections()
{
    Uri myUri = new Uri("http://www.somewhere.com/");
    System.Net.ServicePoint sp =
        ServicePointManager.FindServicePoint(myUri);
    sp.ConnectionLeaseTimeout = new TimeSpan(0,0,30);
}
```

Disabling HTTP Keep-Alives

Adjusting the `MaxIdleTime` and `ConnectionLeaseTimeout` properties of the `ServicePoint` class helps manage connection lifetime. This is especially useful when working with load-balanced server farms. Unfortunately, not all load-balanced scenarios support HTTP Keep-Alives. Sometimes the only way to achieve an even load balance is to turn off the use of HTTP Keep-Alives. This can be achieved a number of ways.

Many places affect whether HTTP Keep-Alives is used. For example, HTTP Keep-Alives can be set by Internet Information Services (IIS). Figure A.2 shows the HTTP Response Headers feature available in IIS 7.0 on Windows Server 2008 and Windows Vista with Service Pack 1.

The IIS 7.0 setting for HTTP Keep-Alives can also be set using the command line. The following command shows how to disable HTTP Keep-Alives for IIS 7.0 using the command line. This was the only way to disable HTTP Keep-Alives in IIS 7.0 on Window Vista prior to SP1.

```
appcmd set config /section:httpProtocol /allowKeepAlive:false
```

HTTP Keep-Alives can also be enabled or disabled using the `KeepAliveEnabled` property of the `HttpTransportBindingElement` binding element. Listing A.8 shows how to disable HTTP Keep-Alives on the `HttpTransportBindingElement` binding element.

```
public void SetHttpKeepAlives()
{
    HttpTransportBindingElement be = new HttpTransportBindingElement();
    be.KeepAliveEnabled = false;
}
```

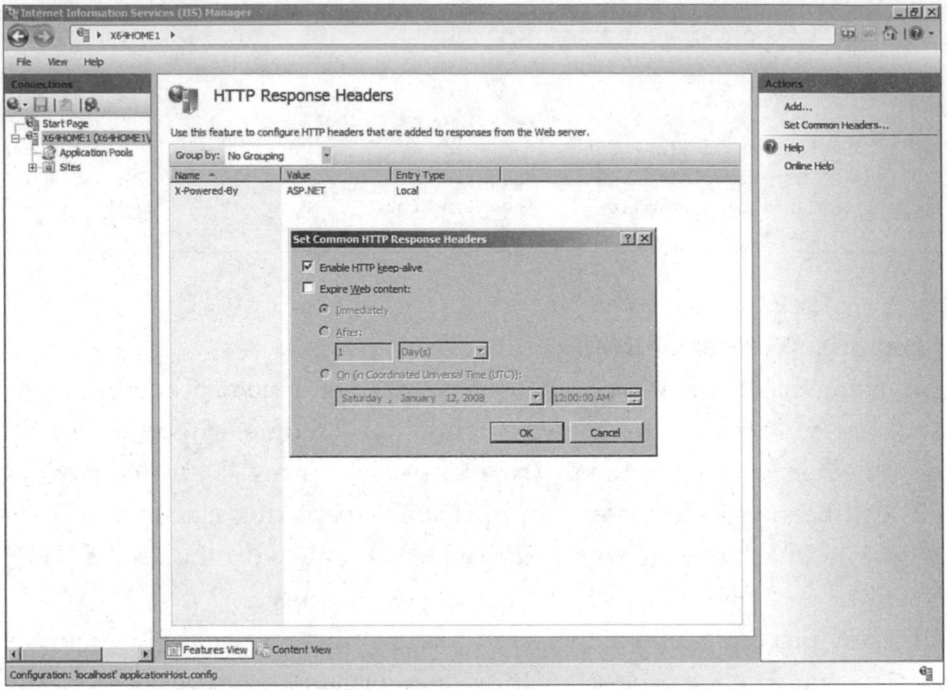

FIGURE A.2 IIS 7.0 settings for HTTP Keep-Alives

HTTP Keep-Alives can also be disabled in configuration using a custom binding based on the `HttpTransportBindingElement` binding element. Listing A.9 shows how to disable HTTP Keep-Alives using a custom binding in configuration.

LISTING A.9 Setting `keepAliveEnabled` Using `httpTransport` Element

```
<system.serviceModel>
  <bindings>
    <customBinding>
      <binding name="CustomBindingWithoutKeepAlives">
        <httpTransport keepAliveEnabled="false" />
      </binding>
    </customBinding>
  </bindings>
</system.serviceModel>
```

The last approach, which was mentioned previously, is to set the `ConnectionLeaseTimeout` on the `ServicePoint` class. Setting the value to 0 means that connections will be closed after each request. This forces each new request to obtain a new connection. This has the same effect as disabling HTTP Keep-Alives.

Increasing Number of Connections

The `ConnectionLimit` property on the `ServicePoint` class specifies the maximum number of connections the `ServicePoint` instance can open. The default value is set based on the host environment. The value is set to 2 connections per `ServicePoint` instance in client and 10 connections per `ServicePoint` instance in ASP.NET server environments. This is based on the `DefaultConnectionLimit` property of the `ServicePointManager` class. Increasing the `ConnectionLimit` property may increase throughput in server-to-server communication or multithreaded client scenarios. Listing A.10 shows how to set the maximum number of connections using configuration.

LISTING A.10 Setting MaxConnection for HTTP Using Configuration

```
<system.net>
  <connectionManagement>
    <add address="http://www.somewhere.com/" maxconnection ="1000" />
  </connectionManagement>
</system.net>
```

Configuring TCP Connections

Unlike HTTP connections, WCF does not leverage classes in the .NET Framework to manage TCP connection lifetime. Instead, WCF uses a connection pool to cache connections. The connection pool can be managed using the `ConnectionPoolSettings` property of the `TcpTransportBindingElement` binding element. The `ConnectionPoolSettings` property returns an instance of the `TcpConnectionPoolSettings` class. This class has three properties that help manage connections in the connection pool: `IdleTimeout`, `LeaseTimeout`, and `MaxOutboundConnectionsPerEndpoint`.

Recycling Idle Connections

The `IdleTimeout` property specifies how low a connection can remain idle in the connection pool before it is closed and removed from the connection pool. The default value is set to two minutes. Setting this value lower can be useful in load-balancing scenarios by increasing the likelihood that idle connections will be recycled.

Adjusting Connection Lifetime

The `LeaseTimeout` property specifies how long a connection can be active before it is eligible for recycling. After the lifetime is elapsed, idle connections can be closed and removed from the connection pool. The default value is set to five minutes. Setting this value lower can be useful in load balancing scenarios by decreasing the time before connections can be rebalanced across a server farm.

Increasing Number of Connections

The `MaxOutboundConnectionsPerEndpoint` property specifies the maximum number of connections that can be cached in the connection pool. By default the value is set to 10 connections. Increasing this value may improve performance and scalability in server-to-server or multithreaded client communication scenarios.

Using LINQ with WCF

Language Integrated Query (LINQ) is one of the new technologies available in .NET Framework 3.5 that allows for data to be queried using C# or Visual Basic .NET. Traditionally, data is queried by an application using a string expression, such as SQL or XPath query expressions, without the benefits of compile time checking or IntelliSense support. LINQ enables these capabilities by making a query a first-class language construct. LINQ supports several data sources including SQL Server databases, XML documents, ADO.NET DataSets, and .NET objects. LINQ provides a single mechanism for querying data across these different data sources. Using LINQ can help bridge the world of data and the world of objects.

Exposing LINQ-to-SQL Entities

LINQ-to-SQL refers to the features in LINQ that expose relational data stored in SQL Server as objects. This is great for mapping entities stored within tables in the database to objects within an application. This is often referred to as *object-relational mapping (ORM)*. To help facilitate the mapping process, Visual Studio 2008 provides the Object Relational Designer. This provides a visual designer for creating LINQ-to-SQL entities. Figure A.3 shows the Object Relational Designer for LINQ-SQL entities.

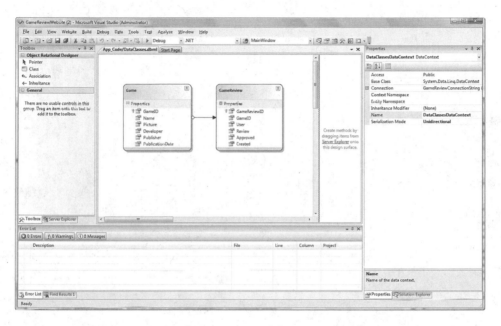

FIGURE A.3 LINQ-to-SQL Object Relational Designer

One thing to know is that the designer does not expose LINQ-to-SQL entities using the DataContractSerializer by default. This means that LINQ-to-SQL entities cannot be exposed over WCF services. The capability to expose entities stored in a database using a service is important to developers building service-oriented applications. Fortunately, Microsoft provided a property called Serialization Mode, which is available on the LINQ-to-SQL design surface. Setting this property to UniDirectional allows LINQ-to-SQL entities to be attributed with the [DataContract] and [DataMember] attributes. This exposes LINQ-to-SQL entities as a data contract that can be serialized by WCF. This setting is also available using the SqlMetal.exe command-line utility. This utility can be used to generate code for LINQ-to-SQL entities from a SQL Server database. Passing the /serialization:Unidirectional parameter on the command line instructs SqlMetal.exe to generate types that can be serialized using WCF.

Index

Microsoft .NET Development Series

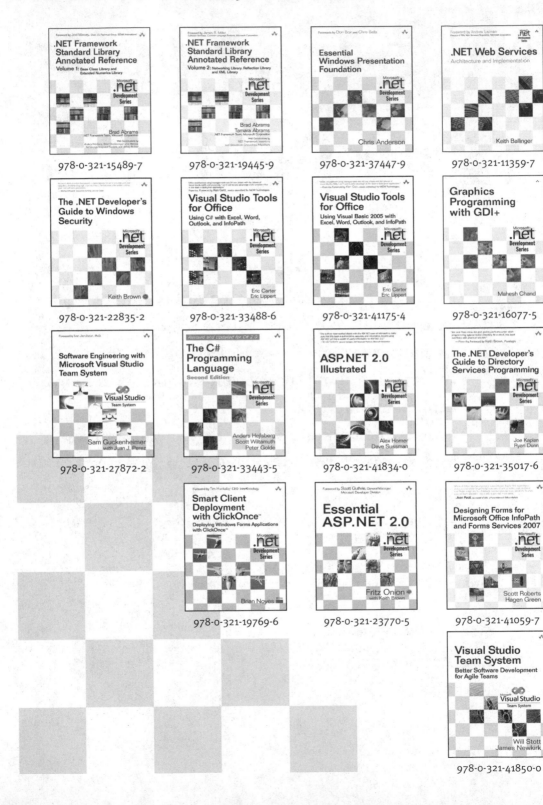

.NET Framework Standard Library Annotated Reference, Volume 1: Base Class Library and Extended Numerics Library — Brad Abrams — 978-0-321-15489-7

.NET Framework Standard Library Annotated Reference, Volume 2: Networking Library, Reflection Library and XML Library — Brad Abrams, Tamara Abrams — 978-0-321-19445-9

Essential Windows Presentation Foundation — Chris Anderson — 978-0-321-37447-9

.NET Web Services: Architecture and Implementation — Keith Ballinger — 978-0-321-11359-7

The .NET Developer's Guide to Windows Security — Keith Brown — 978-0-321-22835-2

Visual Studio Tools for Office: Using C# with Excel, Word, Outlook, and InfoPath — Eric Carter, Eric Lippert — 978-0-321-33488-6

Visual Studio Tools for Office: Using Visual Basic 2005 with Excel, Word, Outlook, and InfoPath — Eric Carter, Eric Lippert — 978-0-321-41175-4

Graphics Programming with GDI+ — Mahesh Chand — 978-0-321-16077-5

Software Engineering with Microsoft Visual Studio Team System — Sam Guckenheimer with Juan J. Perez — 978-0-321-27872-2

The C# Programming Language, Second Edition — Anders Hejlsberg, Scott Wiltamuth, Peter Golde — 978-0-321-33443-5

ASP.NET 2.0 Illustrated — Alex Homer, Dave Sussman — 978-0-321-41834-0

The .NET Developer's Guide to Directory Services Programming — Joe Kaplan, Ryan Dunn — 978-0-321-35017-6

Smart Client Deployment with ClickOnce: Deploying Windows Forms Applications with ClickOnce — Brian Noyes — 978-0-321-19769-6

Essential ASP.NET 2.0 — Fritz Onion with Keith Brown — 978-0-321-23770-5

Designing Forms for Microsoft Office InfoPath and Forms Services 2007 — Scott Roberts, Hagen Green — 978-0-321-41059-7

Visual Studio Team System: Better Software Development for Agile Teams — Will Stott, James Newkirk — 978-0-321-41850-0

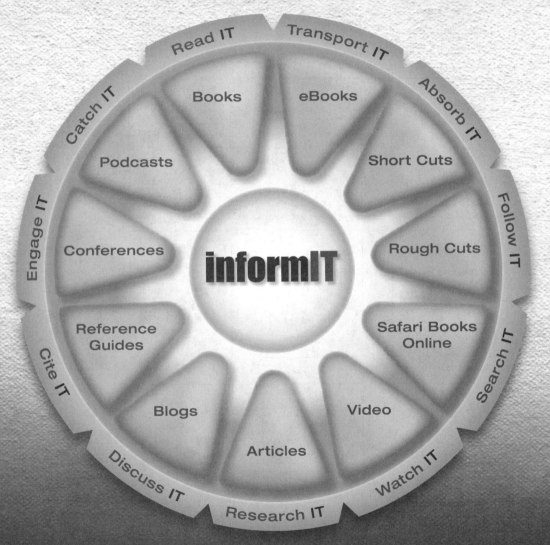

LearnIT at InformIT

Go Beyond the Book

informIT

Read IT — Books
Transport IT — eBooks
Catch IT — Podcasts
Absorb IT — Short Cuts
Engage IT — Conferences
Follow IT — Rough Cuts
Cite IT — Reference Guides
Search IT — Safari Books Online
Discuss IT — Blogs
Watch IT — Video
Research IT — Articles

11 WAYS TO LEARN IT at **www.informIT.com/learn**

The online portal of the information technology
publishing imprints of Pearson Education

Safari Library
Subscribe Now!
http://safari.informit.com/library

Safari's entire technology collection is now available with no restrictions. Imagine the value of being able to search and access thousands of books, videos and articles from leading technology authors whenever you wish.

EXPLORE TOPICS MORE FULLY

Gain a more robust understanding of related issues by using Safari as your research tool. With Safari Library you can leverage the knowledge of the world's technology gurus. For one flat monthly fee, you'll have unrestricted access to a reference collection offered nowhere else in the world -- all at your fingertips.

With a Safari Library subscription you'll get the following premium services:

- **Immediate access to the newest, cutting-edge books** - Approximately 80 new titles are added per month in conjunction with, or in advance of, their print publication.

- **Chapter downloads** - Download five chapters per month so you can work offline when you need to.

- **Rough Cuts** - A service that provides online access to pre-published information on advanced technologies updated as the author writes the book. You can also download Rough Cuts for offline reference.

- **Videos** - Premier design and development videos from training and e-learning expert lynda.com and other publishers you trust.

- **Cut and paste code** - Cut and paste code directly from Safari. Save time. Eliminate errors.

- **Save up to 35% on print books** - Safari Subscribers receive a discount of up to 35% on publishers' print books.

THIS BOOK IS SAFARI ENABLED

INCLUDES FREE 45-DAY ACCESS TO THE ONLINE EDITION

The Safari® Enabled icon on the cover of your favorite technology book means the book is available through Safari Bookshelf. When you buy this book, you get free access to the online edition for 45 days.

Safari Bookshelf is an electronic reference library that lets you easily search thousands of technical books, find code samples, download chapters, and access technical information whenever and wherever you need it.

TO GAIN 45-DAY SAFARI ENABLED ACCESS TO THIS BOOK:

- Go to **informit.com/safarienabled**

- Complete the brief registration form

- Enter the coupon code found in the front of this book on the "Copyright" page

If you have difficulty registering on Safari Bookshelf or accessing the online edition, please e-mail customer-service@safaribooksonline.com.